BIBLICAL IDEAS OF NATIONALITY
ANCIENT AND MODERN

Biblical Ideas of Nationality
Ancient and Modern

Steven Grosby

Winona Lake, Indiana
EISENBRAUNS
2002

Cataloging-in-Publication Data

Grosby, Steven Elliott, 1951-
    Biblical ideas of nationality : ancient and modern / Steven Grosby.
        p.   cm.
    Includes bibliographical references and index.
    ISBN 1-57506-065-5
    1. Nationalism—Biblical teaching.   2. Nationalism—Religious
aspects.   3. Nationalism—Middle East.   4. Religion and state.
5. Jewish nationalism.   I. Title.
    BS1199.N3 G76 2002
    220.8′32054—dc21
                                                          2002009253

For Naomi and Samuel

Contents

Acknowledgments

Grateful acknowledgment for permission to republish articles that first appeared elsewhere is hereby noted:

Chapter 1: "Religion and Nationality in Antiquity: The Worship of Yahweh and Ancient Israel," was previously published in *European Journal of Sociology* 32 (1991): 229-65, and is reprinted here with permission.

Chapter 2: "Kinship, Territory and the Nation in the Historiography of Ancient Israel," was previously published in *Zeitschrift für die alttestamentliche Wissenschaft* 105 (1993): 3-18, and is reprinted here with permission.

Chapter 3: "Sociological Implications of the Distinction between 'Locality' and 'Extended Territory' with Particular Reference to the Old Testament" was previously published in *Social Compass* 40/2 (1993): 179-98, and is reprinted here with permission.

Chapter 4: "The Chosen People of Ancient Israel and the Occident: Why Does Nationality Exist and Survive?" was previously published in *Nations and Nationalism* 5/3 (1999): 357-80, and is reprinted here with the permission of the editors of *Nations and Nationalism*, Journal of the Association for the Study of Ethnicity and Nationalism (London School of Economics).

Chapter 5: "Borders, Territory, and Nationality in the Ancient Near East and Armenia," was previously published in *Journal of the Economic and Social History of the Orient* 40/1 (1997): 1-29, and is reprinted here with permission.

Chapter 6: "'Aram Kulloh and the Worship of Hadad: A Nation of Aram?" was previously published in *ARAM* 7 (1995): 337-52, and is reprinted here with permission.

Chapter 7: "The Category of the Primordial in the Study of Early Christianity and Second-Century Judaism," was previously published in *History of Religions* 36/2 (1996): 140-63; © 1996 by the University of Chicago; and is reprinted here with permission.

Chapter 8: "Territoriality," was previously published in *Nations and Nationalism* 1/2 (1995): 143-62, and is reprinted here with the permission of the editors of *Nations and Nationalism*, Journal of the Association for the Study of Ethnicity and Nationalism (London School of Economics).

Chapter 9: "The Nation of the United States and the Vision of Ancient Israel," was previously published in R. Michener, ed., *Nationality, Patriotism, and Nationalism* (St. Paul: Paragon, 1993), 49-79, and is reprinted here with permission.

Chapter 10: "Nationality and Religion," was previously published in M. Guibernau and J. Hutchinson, eds., *Understanding Nationalism* (Oxford: Blackwell, 2001), 97-199, and appears here with permission.

Introduction

The determination of biblical ideas of nationality, the attendant phenomena of bounded territoriality and kinship, and the setting of these
ideas in the life of the worshipers of Yahweh requires a critical evaluation
of the Hebrew Bible. This is certainly so, as is evident from many older
works that dealt with various forms of kinship in the history of ancient Israel and the ancient Near East, such as Martin Noth's *Das System der Zwölf
Stämme Israels* and his comments on the use of the concept *Volk* in the introduction to his *Geschichte Israels*, and from recent works such as Harry
Orlinsky's "Nationalism-Universalism and Internationalism in Ancient
Israel," Mario Liverani's "Nationality and Political Identity," and Kenton
Sparks's *Ethnicity and Identity in Ancient Israel*.[1] Moreover, any investigation into biblical ideas of nationality has theological and moral implications, as has always been clear and as is evident from many older works,
such as Abraham Kuenen's *National Religions and Universal Religions*, and
from recent works such as V. Nikiprowetzky's "Ethical Monotheism,"
W. D. Davies' *The Territorial Dimension of Judaism*, and Robert Goldenberg's *The Nations That Know Thee Not: Ancient Jewish Attitudes toward
Other Religions*.[2] Nevertheless, the concerns of this book are explicitly

---

1. Martin Noth, *Das System der Zwölf Stämme Israels* (BWANT 4/1; Stuttgart: Kohlhammer, 1930); *Geschichte Israels* (Göttingen: Vandenhoeck & Ruprecht, 1950), re-
vised English translation, *The History of Israel* (London: Adam and Charles Black,
1960); H. M. Orlinsky, "Nationalism-Universalism and Internationalism in Ancient
Israel" in *Essays in Biblical Culture and Bible Translation* (New York: KTAV, 1974);
M. Liverani, "Nationality and Political Identity" in D. N. Freedman (ed.), *Anchor Bible
Dictionary* (New York: Doubleday, 1992); Kenton L. Sparks, *Ethnicity and Identity in
Ancient Israel* (Winona Lake, Ind.: Eisenbrauns, 1998). Any analysis of the biblical
conception of nationality must also take into account L. Rost, "Die Bezeichnungen für
Land und Volk im Alten Testament," in *Festschrift Otto Procksch* (Leipzig: J. C. Hin-
richs, 1934); E. A. Speiser, "People and Nation of Israel," *JBL* 79 (1960): 157-63; and
A. Cody, "When Is the Chosen People Called a Goy?" *VT* 14 (1964): 1-6.

2. Abraham Kuenen, *National Religions and Universal Religions* (New York: Charles
Scribner's Sons, 1882); V. Nikiprowetzky, "Ethical Monotheism," *Daedalus* 104/2
(1975): 69-89; W. D. Davies, *The Territorial Dimension of Judaism* (Berkeley: University of California Press, 1982); Robert Goldenberg, *The Nations That Know Thee Not:
Ancient Jewish Attitudes Toward Other Religions* (New York: New York University Press,
1998).

neither textual criticism, traditiohistorical or otherwise, nor theological reflection. Even though many of the following studies acknowledge these requirements and implications, they do so often only in passing. This is because the primary motivation for these studies was the desire to take up what I perceive to be ongoing problems of the *Geisteswissenschaften*: the limits of historicism, or, formulated positively, the merit of philosophical anthropology. While this motivation is obvious in the chapters "The Chosen People of Ancient Israel and the Occident: Why Does Nationality Exist and Survive?," "The Category of the Primordial in the Study of Early Christianity and Second-Century Judaism," "Territoriality," and "Sociological Implications of the Distinction between 'Locality' and Extended 'Territory' with Particular Reference to the Old Testament," it is nevertheless the point of departure for all of the studies of this volume.

How could it be otherwise for a student of religion and its history? To be interested in religion is to be interested in what it means to be human, not only in its diversity but also in its commonality: humanity's perennial preoccupations with vitality, its transmission, and its organization[3]; and with a meaning attributed to life that transcends that of vitality.[4] The fact that ancient documents of another millennium—the Hebrew Bible, the New Testament, the Qur'ân—are not merely objects of historical research but, insofar as they continue to have a bearing on the beliefs and actions of individuals and collectivites of individuals, "live" today is reason enough for this point of departure. Even though the cultural and historical distance separating, for example, the Deuteronomistic historian, the prophet Jeremiah, or the author(s) of the Book of Job, on the one hand, and us today, on the other, is great, when we read these works and when we attempt, with varying degrees of success, to understand them, including the contexts in which they were written, it is still one human mind speaking across time and space to another. If, in fact, human nature were entirely Protean, adapting itself, each time in a completely unique way, to varying circumstances,[5] then any understanding of alien cultures, indeed history itself, would not be possible. The formation of the categories by

---

3. See S. Grosby, "The Verdict of History: The Inexpungeable Tie of Primordiality," *Ethnic and Racial Studies* 17/1 (1994): 164-71, reprinted in John Hutchinson and Anthony D. Smith, *Ethnicity* (Oxford: Oxford University Press, 1996).

4. See Martin Nilsson, "Religion as Man's Protest against the Meaninglessness of Events," in *Opuscula Selecta*, Vol. III (Lund: CWK Gleerup, 1960); and the concluding chapter of this book, "Nationality and Religion."

5. So Johann Gottfried von Herder's work of 1774, *Auch eine Philosophie der Geschichte zur Bildung der Menscheit*, Vol. 5, *Herders Sämmtliche Werke* (Berlin: Weidmannische Buchhandlung, 1877-1913), p. 509.

which we analyze these cultures presupposes this common humanity; and it is a tribute to it. It is this methodological presupposition which adds gravity to historical works such as William Hallo's *Origins: The Ancient Near Eastern Background of Some Modern Western Institutions;*[6] and the findings of these works confirm the presupposition.

Such is the methodological assumption and procedure of the following investigations into the existence of boundaries, territoriality, and nationality in the ancient Near East. The point of departure for these studies was that it was not *a priori* illegitimate to apply the category of nationality and the bounded territory and extensive kinship structure that the category implies to various societies of antiquity. Of course, the historicists would and still do claim otherwise, insisting that nationality and relatively extensive, bounded territories are exclusively modern phenomena.[7] They wrongly assert that, in antiquity, there are only imprecise frontiers and that demarcated boundaries are to be found only in the current historical period of what they call "modernity." In contrast, the results of the following studies, for example, "Borders, Territory, and Nationality in the Ancient Near East and Armenia," confirm their point of departure—results that have, in turn, confirmed earlier studies and that find further confirmation in subsequent work.[8]

This is not to deny the existence of differences between societies of the past and those of today brought about by the development of modern means of communication and transportation, a market-place for industrial goods, an increasingly pervasive *lex terrae*, and modern conceptions of citizenship—developments that have facilitated the emergence and consolidation of extensive, yet bounded territories and their respective structures of kinship. Nor is it my claim that nationality was, in antiquity, the only or even the primary way in which human beings organized

6. William W. Hallo, *Origins: The Ancient Near Eastern Background of Some Modern Western Institutions* (Leiden: E. J. Brill, 1996).

7. Perhaps the most articulate representative of the historicist position is E. Gellner, *Nations and Nationalism* (Ithaca: Cornell University Press, 1983). See also, the cruder work of E. J. Hobsbawm, *Nations and Nationalism since 1780* (Cambridge: Cambridge University Press, 1990). For an overview of the problem, see Anthony D. Smith, *Nationalism and Modernism* (London: Routledge, 1998).

8. See, for example, the discussion of territory and boundaries in Mario Liverani, *Prestige and Interest: International Relations in the Near East ca. 1600-1100 B.C.* (Padova: Sargon, 1990); Peter Machinist, "Assyrians on Assyria in the First Millennium B.C.," in Kurt Raaflaub (ed.), *Anfänge politischen Denkens in der Antike: Die nahöstlichen Kulturen und die Griechen* (Munich: R. Oldenbourg, 1993); and, for Judaism, Isaiah M. Gafni, *Land, Center and Diaspora: Jewish Constructs in Late Antiquity* (Sheffield: Sheffield Academic Press, 1997).

themselves.[9] The chapter on *ʾAram Kulloh*—an examination of the likely sociological significance of the Aramaic use of כלה 'all', as in "all Aram" in the Sefire Stele, perhaps similar to the Greek use of παν, as in πανελληνας 'all the Hellenes'[10]—indicates a few of the difficulties in applying the category of nationality to various societies of antiquity. Moreover, I am well aware of the "moving, expanding borders" of, for example, the Assyrian empire, especially during the reign of Tiglath-pileser III.[11] Nevertheless, one finds in the inscriptions of Tiglath-pileser III unambiguous evidence for the existence of clearly demarcated Assyrian provinces. Still, the geographical and sociological situation was fluid. Yet, is it not so also today in Africa, the Indian sub-continent, the Russian empire, and even in the United Kingdom? Moreover, if we learn anything from the experience of the bellicose twentieth century, it is that we, in fact, live primarily in monolatrous societies; that modern man attributes a common kinship to those who, like himself, are born in the territory in which he was born and inhabits—to those who are "native of the land" (a formulation that one also finds in the Hebrew Bible, for example, at Exod 12:19, 48[12]); and that the god of the land and lineage, and its representatives in the "center," continue to receive our deference, albeit in an age of monotheism, reformulated as patriotism or, when taken to ideological extremes, nationalism. These historical similarities, however approximate, spanning a period of three thousand years, and those perennial problems of life that the very existence of the similarities imply, deserve far greater attention from scholars than they now receive.

Many of humanity's attempts to grapple with the perennial problems of life find expression in the Hebrew Bible; this is, from the perspective of the historian and social scientist, what makes it so remarkable. Is there any meaning to our existence? Such is the clear implication of the anguished question of Abraham at Gen 18:25. Or is it the case that even if there is such a meaning, it will always elude our grasp (2 Ezra 4:10-11);

---

9. For the problem of nationality in the history of ancient Greece and Rome, still valuable are Frank Walbank, "The Problem of Greek Nationality," and "Nationality as a Factor in Roman History," in *Selected Papers* (Cambridge: Cambridge University Press, 1985).

10. *Iliad* II.530. Irrespective of whether or not this line is an interpolation, the very existence of the term is significant.

11. See H. Tadmor, *The Inscriptions of Tiglath-pileser III, King of Assyria* (Jerusalem: The Israel Academy of Sciences and Humanities, 1994).

12. One is understandably tempted to translate אזרח הארץ 'native of the land' as 'citizen of the country'. Our problem is to ascertain just how anachronistic such a translation is, or is not.

but that we should nonetheless shun evil, as appears to be implied by Job 28:28, 35:2-8? And if there is meaning to our existence, what is its relation to the primordial beliefs that attribute a meaning to the origin and transmission of life itself? Does the meaning of our existence revolve around those primordial beliefs about the significance of the objects of that origin and transmission—descendants and land—conveyed unambiguously by the so-called unconditional covenant in Gen 17:7, 28:15, and especially 2 Samuel 7; or are such beliefs and the existence of the collectivities that bear them—the family and that bounded territorial collectivity of nativity, the nation—subordinate to a meaning of righteousness that transcends, hence conditions, vitality and its transmission as stated in Deuteronomy 30? The matter is even more complicated; for once one recognizes the hold of primordial attachments to various forms of kinship on the human imagination, as the Hebrew Bible clearly does with the concepts of a chosen people and a promised land, then what is the relation between that chosen people and humanity? The problem of what it means to be chosen within the context of recognizing one God of all of humanity, monotheism—or as Jacob Talmon formulated the tension-filled relation, "the unique and the universal"[13]—is, perhaps, the problem *par excellence* of the Hebrew Bible. Certainly the rabbinic commentators of the Hebrew Bible were troubled by how to justify Israel's uniqueness as being the chosen people of the one and only God as can be seen in the *Babylonian Talmud's 'Abodah Zarah* 2b, where it is explained that God offered the Torah to every nation, but none accepted it until he came to Israel, who received it.

Such problems and others within the Hebrew Bible resonate within us today, reminding one of Adolf Harnack's observation that the history of the religion of the Old Testament offers the keys to understanding many of the universal problems of the history of religion, without which those problems would remain unsolved.[14] However, we must not remain content with Harnack's insight; rather, we must press ahead by asking ourselves a question with philosophical implications. What is the significance of this resonance? Is it the case that the ability of the various and at times seemingly conflicting meanings of the Hebrew Bible to resonate within us, and the extent to which the Hebrew Bible has become a constitutive element of the Occidental tradition, are consequences of the Bible having incorporated within itself many of the

---

13. J. L. Talmon, *The Unique and the Universal* (New York: George Braziller, 1965).

14. Adolf Harnack, "Die Aufgabe der theologischen Fakultaten und die allgemeine Religionsgeschichte," *Reden und Aufsätze* (Giessen: J. Ricker, 1904).

problems of life that confront us today? To be sure, considerations of any number of social factors and constellations of power are necessary to historical analyses. Nevertheless, this incorporation of many of the problems of life is confirmed by the persistence of the image of a chosen people and promised land throughout subsequent European history. It is not true that we, today, are all Marcionites. Although at times it seems that such a provocative characterization may apply to many members of the faculties of theology and religion, it most certainly does not apply to the history of the Occident. The persistence of the image of the chosen people and the promised land in settings outside ancient Israel is the object of the penultimate chapter of this book.[15]

Objections, emphasizing historical discontinuities, to this point of departure will be raised: What about the "secularization" of the Occident beginning in the sixteenth century? What about the fragmentation of the public sphere that is putatively characteristic of modern life? What about the distinction of Max Weber, and following Weber that of Karl Jaspers and S. N. Eisenstadt, between, on the one hand, the ethical world religions of the book—the religions of the axial age—that assert a fundamental rupture between a mundane order and a transcendent, supra-mundane order and, on the other, those primordial religions that do not?[16]

Clearly, each national culture and civilization addresses the perennial problems of life in its own way. One cannot, for example, help but be struck by the contrast between, on the one hand, the emergence of nations and their distinctive territories in Europe in late antiquity and very early in the Middle Ages[17] and, on the other, the relative lack of such a development in Islamic civilization, notwithstanding the national consoli-

---

15. See also Anthony D. Smith, "Ethnic Election and National Destiny: Some Religious Origins of Nationalist Ideals," *Nations and Nationalism* 5/3 (1999): 331-55.

16. Max Weber, "The Sociology of Religion" in *Economy and Society* (Berkeley: University of California Press, 1978); Karl Jaspers, *The Origin and Goal of History* (New Haven: Yale University Press, 1953); S. N. Eisenstadt, *The Origins and Diversity of the Axial Age Civilizations* (Albany: State University of New York Press, 1986).

17. See Adrian Hastings, *The Construction of Nationhood: Ethnicity, Religion, and Nationalism* (Cambridge: Cambridge University Press, 1997); Thomas Eichenberger, *Patria-Studien zur Bedeutung des Wortes in Mittelalter (6.-12. Jahrhundert)* (Sigmaringen: Jan Thorbecke, 1991); Bernd Schneidmüller, *Nomen Patriae: Die Entstehung Frankreichs in die politisch-geographischen Terminologie (10.-13. Jahrhundert)* (Sigmaringen: Jan Thorbecke, 1987); Susan Reynolds, *Kingdoms and Communities in Western Europe 900-1300* (Oxford: Oxford University Press, 1984); and earlier works such as G. Post, "Two Notes on Nationalism in the Middle Ages," *Traditio* 9: 281-329, and E. Kantorowicz, "Pro patria mori" in *The King's Two Bodies* (Princeton: Princeton University Press, 1957).

dation of Shi'ite Safavid Iran in opposition to the Sunni Ottomans. It is likely that one factor contributing to this difference is that Christianity has doctrinally recognized the legitimacy of the "city of man," thereby facilitating the existence of a considerable degree of latitude for the emergence and consolidation of territorial attachments; while Islam, in contrast, enjoins an other-worldly transformation of this world through actions in this world, the consequence of which was, at least in principle, the ascendancy of the world-wide *Ummah*, the community of the faithful, at the expense of ethnic and national traditions. Nonetheless, what appear to me to be overly facile, dichotomous categories such as "secularization" and "modernity" often obscure more than they clarify.

Secularization originally meant the expropriation of the property of the Church by the State. Albrecht Alt, followed by Martin Buber, applied with justification this meaning of secularization to Josiah's policy of destroying all the local sanctuaries throughout the land of Israel in favor of a place (Jerusalem and its temple) at which all operations of the cult of Yahweh were bound and should remain bound.[18] Such is the description of Josiah's actions in 2 Kings 22–23, presumably in accordance, as most scholars since W. M. L. de Wette in 1805 have argued, with much of Deuteronomy, that is, the newly discovered Book of Law.[19] Alt thought that the result of these policies was a complete secularization of life throughout the land outside of Jerusalem. However, pointing, paradoxically, to how such seductively simplistic analytical categories like secularization obfuscate a more complicated situation was Alt's recognition that Deuteronomy demanded an order of life and an order of law which should be in force all the time throughout the land.[20] Is not the consequence of such a demand a sanctification of life throughout the entire territory and the territory itself? Is this expectation of a consistency of life throughout the land not also one consequence of the Protestant Reformation and the Augsburg principle of *cuius regio, eius religio*? Today, the term secularization is often understood as a decline of religiosity resulting from a principle of the religious indifference of the state. However, in actuality, the

---

18. A. Alt, "Die Heimat des Deuteronomiums," *Kleine Schriften II* (Munich: C. H. Beck, 1953), p. 254; M. Buber, *The Prophetic Faith* (New York: MacMillan, 1977), p. 169.

19. The possibility that the lost book discovered during the reign of Josiah was much of Deuteronomy was also raised in antiquity; see Saint Chrysostom's Homily IX on Matthew, and Saint Hieronymus's commentary on Ezek 1:1.

20. Alt, "Die Heimat," p. 252.

principle is utopian because it could only represent a relative goal. This is because the state must of necessity be concerned with serious things.

Secularization, and the attendant fragmentation of public life that the term has come to imply, is thought to be characteristic of the declining significance of religion in modern life. However, that fragmentation achieved its most thoughtful formulation not with Hobbes' *Leviathan*, the longest section of which is nonetheless the often ignored "Of a Christian Commonwealth," but with Augustine's *City of God*. I mention this both as a cautionary note against the neat and tidy periodizations that are so popular in many historical analyses and as an indication that the so-called distinction between the ancients and the moderns is overwrought, justifying further the assumption of these studies. The fact, for example, that in his *Discourse on the Origin of Inequality*, Jean-Jacques Rousseau said little that was not said much better by Pelagius in his controversy with Augustine over the doctrine of original sin is yet another indication, among many others, for introducing the perspective of the perennial problems of life into the subject matter of these studies.

Although the conceptual turn by the Israelite prophets to a purpose or meaning to the events of this world that transcend those actual events may have accounted for national defeat while maintaining a belief in the nation and its god (Amos 3:2; Isa 10:5-6), it necessarily opened the door to a history that was understood as being the theater of one God (Amos 9:7) whose existence and standards, insofar as they can be grasped, necessarily transcend the empirical reality of this world. While believed to be other-worldly in origin, such standards are appealed to so as to order the actions of individuals in this world through the expectation that they be conformed to. The classic, symbolic expression of the other-worldly origin of such standards are the Ten Commandments portrayed as being given to Moses *from* God above. The world religions that assert a fundamental distinction between two realms—the events of "this world," on the one hand, and the deity and its standards of the "other-world," on the other—are what Max Weber called the world religions of the book and what Karl Jaspers and S. N. Eisenstadt have referred to as the *geistige* developments of the axial age.

The distinction between these world religions of the axial age and the primordial religions of locality and lineage that emphasize vitality and its transmission appears, at least theoretically, to be a valid one. The distinction is a variation of Max Weber's observation that the great achievement of ethical religions was to shatter the fetters of the sib by establishing the superior community of faith and a common ethical way of life in opposition to the community of blood.[21] The tension between such a superior community of faith, a kingdom of priests (Exod 19:6), and the significance of vitality per se, the promise of land and descendants, is evident in Exodus 32 where the possibility of the destruction of the community is posed on account of the violations of the commands of an ethical way of life. Of course, the worship of Yahweh and subsequently Judaism represent a complication of this distinction between universal and primordial religions, because they explicitly and simultaneously maintain two concerns of life: not only righteousness, but also vitality. The question for us now becomes the extent to which this tension-filled complication is paradigmatic; that is, the extent to which any of the world religions, either doctrinally or more often historically, can ignore altogether the orientation to vitality that is so manifest in ethnicity and nationality. Is it in fact the case, as Weber observed, that all the great monotheistic religions inevitably make concessions to polytheism?[22] If so, is that yet one further justification for the assumption of these studies, in particular, the concluding chapter, "Nationality and Religion"?

Such a possibility does not undermine entirely the merit of Weber's, Jaspers', and Eisenstadt's distinction between pre-axial, primordial religions of locality and lineage that have a high degree of magic, on the one hand, and doctrinal world religions that recognize a chasm between this-worldly and other-worldly realms. However, the evident persistence of the primordial attachments of vitality, expressed through kinship and territory, within the axial age civilizations certainly calls into question the depth and breadth of that chasm.

It used to be thought, under the influence of such works as Henry Sumner Maine's *Ancient Law*,[23] that in antiquity structures of kinship were constituted only through recognition of direct biological ancestors, that is, using the old idiom, through blood.[24] It was further thought by Maine that modern societies were exclusively contractual in their constitution. Ferdinand Tönnies developed further this perspective with his influential distinction between *Gemeinschaft* and *Gesellschaft*.[25] Despite the

---

21. Max Weber, *The Religions of China: Confucianism and Taoism* (New York: The Free Press, 1951), p. 237.

22. Weber, *Economy and Society*, p. 1173.

23. H. S. Maine, *Ancient Law* (Gloucester: Peter Smith, 1970), first published in 1861.

24. So G. Buccellati, *Cities and Nations of Ancient Syria* (Rome: Instituto di Studi del Vicino Oriente, 1967).

25. F. Tönnies, *Gemeinschaft und Gesellschaft* (New York: American Books, 1940), first published in 1887.

obvious heuristic utility of Tönnies' categories, as a historical schema of an earlier *Gemeinschaft* and a latter *Gesellschaft*, the distinction is theoretically antiquated and should be put aside. It is more accurate to recognize that, as expressions of patterns of conduct and human organization, *Gemeinschaft* and *Gesellschaft* overlap one another in various ways throughout history. Already in 1927, the anthropologist Robert Lowie in *The State* rightly took issue with Maine by noting that in ancient and tribal societies there were indeed territorial collectivities to which kinship was attributed to those who dwelled within the territory.[26] Martin Noth, in his *Geschichte Israels*, shared this recognition by noting that several of the ancient Israelite tribes, for example Ephraim and Benjamin, seemed to be constituted on the basis of geographical reference;[27] but he did not generalize upon this recognition. The likely geographical element in the constitution of ancient Near Eastern tribes deserves reconsideration; and, in this regard, the earlier, more geographical work of Albrecht Alt and the recent work of Zecharia Kallai merit greater attention.[28] Most important were M. B. Rowton's many fine studies on enclosed nomadism in the ancient Near East that further undermined Maine's dichotomy between a historically early kinship through blood and a historically later territorial organization of society.[29] The inability to recognize that locational contiguity may be a referent in the relation of kinship has created many problems in the analysis of both ancient Israel in particular and nationality in general. This problem of the attribution of kinship in the constitution of territorial collectivities is taken up in several of the following studies, but in particular in "Religion and Nationality in Antiquity" and especially in "Kinship, Territory, and the Nation in the Historiography of Ancient Israel" and "Territoriality." The approach employed in these studies may offer the key to the problem posed a number of years ago by J. N. Postgate about how to understand the category of the *bīt PN* and its

---

26. Robert Lowie, *The State* (New York: Harcourt, Brace and Co., 1927).
27. *Geschichte Israels*, 60-62.
28. For example, Albrecht Alt, "Die syrische Stattenwelt vor dem Einbruch der Assyrer," *Zeitschrift der deutschen morgenländischen Gesellschaft* 88 (1934): 233-58; Z. Kallai, *Biblical Historiography and Historical Geography* (Frankfurt am Main: Peter Lang, 1998).
29. For example, M. B. Rowton, "Autonomy and Nomadism in Western Asia," *Orientalia* N.S. 42 (1973): 247-58; "Urban Autonomy in a Nomadic Environment," *Journal of Near Eastern Studies* 32 (1973): 201-15; "Enclosed Nomadism," *Journal of the Economic and Social History of the Orient* 17 (1974): 1-30. Relevant here is the discussion of such "ethno-geographic terms" as *gayum* in A. Malamat, *Mari and the Early Israelite Experience* (Oxford: Oxford University Press, 1989).

Assyrian equivalent *bītu PN*,[30] a problem discussed in passing at the end of the study of *'Aram Kulloh*.

Already many years have passed since I had the good fortune to come under the influence of primarily Professor Edward Shils and to a much lesser extent Professor Arnaldo Momigliano at The University of Chicago. It will be obvious to those who know Shils's work how much these studies owe to him. Momigliano put before me the problem of history; and there was no one better to have done so. Also at Chicago, Professor Gösta Ahlström was unfailingly generous with his time devoted to many discussions about the history of ancient Israel and the Near East. In more recent years I have been influenced especially by the work of Professors Ernest Nicholson, Peter Machinist, Anthony Smith, and the humanistic geographer Yi-Fu Tuan. This influence has been the result of my deep appreciation more for the orientation of their work than for any particular argument. I take this opportunity to express my gratitude to them for what I have learned from them and continue to learn from them. I also thank Professor S. N. Eisenstadt for the interest he has shown in my work over the years. Professor Eisenstadt's work on the civilizations of the axial age has given me much to ponder, as is evident from this introduction and the concluding chapter.

Approximately seventy-five years ago, the sociologist Max Weber's *Ancient Judaism* rightly drew the attention of Albrecht Alt and Martin Noth, even if the most noteworthy influence of that work on their thought was the ill-fated hypothesis of the twelve-tribe amphictyony.[31] Today, Weber's *Ancient Judaism* still rightly receives the attention of biblical scholars, as may be seen, for example, in E. W. Nicholson's *God and his People*.[32] Historians of ancient Israel, its religion, and the ancient Near East have much to contribute to the discussions of social scientists and historians of other periods on the nature of boundaries, territory, and nationality. By doing so, they will acknowledge their obligation to the contribution made by Max Weber to the study of ancient Israel and its religion.

---

30. J. N. Postgate, "Some Remarks on Conditions in the Assyrian Countryside," *Journal of the Economic and Social History of the Orient* 17/3 (1974): 225–43.

31. M. Weber, *Ancient Judaism* (New York: The Free Press, 1967), originally published in 1921.

32. E. W. Nicholson, *God and His People: Covenant and Theology in the Old Testament* (Oxford: Clarendon Press, 1986).

Chapter 1

Religion and Nationality in Antiquity

The Worship of Yahweh and Ancient Israel

There is a particularly interesting, important, and, I think, generally unacknowledged cleavage within the study of the *Geist*, cultural history, *Geisteswissenschaften*, the human sciences, sociology or whatever term you employ. This deserves our consideration.

On the one hand, for more than two hundred years now (Herder 1782), scholars of the Old Testament have referred to ancient Israel as a nation. Different positions have been held by various scholars of the Old Testament as to when ancient Israel became a nation;[1] or—if you prefer a less contentious formulation—when ancient Israel became "Israel." What I mean by "Israel" is that collectivity which is referred to in the Old Testament as 'all Israel', *kol yiśrā'ēl* (Deut 13:11; 21:21; Josh 7:25; 1 Sam 3:20; 2 Sam 3:12; 17:11; 1 Kgs 1:20)—the people of Israel, the united twelve tribes, the putative descendants of Abraham-Isaac-and-Jacob (Deut 1:8; 6:10; 9:5; 9:27; 29:13; 30:20), who obeyed the law (Deut 27:9), and to whom Yahweh was believed to have promised the land of Israel "from Dan to Beersheba" (2 Sam 3:10; 17:11; 24:2).

In contrast with this usage among scholars of the Old Testament, it appears that in the period of the last twenty-five years the majority within the disciplines of the social sciences believe that nationality is exclusively a modern phenomenon.[2] We must leave for another time the interesting question of the reasons why this belief has become so dominant within the social sciences today.

The importance of this cleavage is surely not simply that there is a disagreement between scholars of the Old Testament and the historians of ancient Israel and Syro-Palestine on the one hand, and many—but not all

---

1. For the formation of the nation of ancient Israel before the "conquest of Palestine," see Wellhausen (1881: 429, 432); however, see also Wellhausen (1883: 413). For the existence of the nation as a pre-Davidic, tribal unity, see Alt (1925: 161-63); Noth (1930). For the existence of the nation beginning with the reign of David, see Weber (1921: 45).

2. For just one among many examples, Ernest Gellner (1983).

(Hertz 1944; Chadwick 1945; Armstrong 1982)—of those within the social sciences on the other. If it was simply a matter of a disagreement between different departments within the university, we should be inclined
to give the benefit of the doubt to the scholars within the Divinity Schools
and the departments of the history of the ancient Near East. I say this not
because I want to denigrate sociology; the tradition of sociology is deserving of serious consideration and, within that tradition, the work of
such writers as Max Weber, Émile Durkheim, Marcel Mauss, W. I. Thomas and Robert Park should be pondered on and followed up. Nevertheless, for much of the last two thousand years many of the best minds of
our civilization have been devoted to the study of the Old Testament.
This fact alone requires that we treat seriously the conclusion drawn by
scholars of the Old Testament that ancient Israel was a collectivity which
was different from either a clan, a tribe, or an empire.

In order to clarify this problem we need a better understanding of the
nature and development of the worship of Yahweh as a factor in the history of ancient Israel; we need a better understanding of the nature of nationality in antiquity—here, we want to develop the criteria to enable us
to distinguish from one another such patently different collectivities as
empire, nation, tribal confederacy, and city-kingdom; and we also need a
better understanding of modern nationality, which is perhaps the most
important social phenomenon of the last several centuries. Our understanding of modern nationality will be furthered greatly by considering
in what ways it is similar to and in what ways it is different from nationality in antiquity.

I am going to discuss primarily the first matter; namely, the history of
ancient Israel as the history of a nation, and in what ways the belief in the
worship of Yahweh contributed to the formation of ancient Israel as a nation. I will also keep the other two matters before us, for they must also
be pursued.

I. *The Belief in Ancient Israel as a Nation*

I wish to establish first the existence of those beliefs held by the ancient Israelites which would indicate that ancient Israel was a nation. In
order to do this, we must examine the beliefs of the ancient Israelites as
we have them before us in the Old Testament, the primary evidence of
those beliefs. This examination, however, is not a straightforward task;
for the Old Testament has its own history of development, having under-
gone a significant revision—possibly even composition—relatively late in
the history of ancient Israel, probably after the fall of Jerusalem in the

sixth century B.C.[3] Nevertheless, I shall, for the time being, put aside considerations of the historical development both of the beliefs of the Old Testament and of the society of ancient Israel. In so doing, it is in no way my intention to deny that a historical analysis of the development of ancient Israel and its religion is necessary if one wants to understand both properly. I acknowledge this necessity, especially if one wants to appreciate, to use the apt phrase of Abraham Kuenen (1880), the great Leiden Biblical scholar, "the workshop of the spirit." Nevertheless, it is reasonable to assume that the very existence of the Pentateuch and the Deuteronomistic History (Noth 1943), that is, the books of Joshua, Judges, 1 and 2 Samuel, and 1 and 2 Kings, are evidence of the existence of a community of belief for which these historical books and their—so it would seem—indeterminate predecessors were canonical. To repeat, I will for the moment put aside the question as to when the beliefs described in the Old Testament became so prevalent among the ancient Israelites. For the time being, it is sufficient to say that at some point in the history of ancient Israel those beliefs were prevalent among, at least, the leading strata of Israelite society.

At some point in their history, the ancient Israelites evidently understood themselves to have been an *'am* and a *gôy*. The Hebrew terms *'am* and *gôy* which appear repeatedly throughout the Old Testament have been translated respectively as "people" and "nation" (Speiser 1960; Cody 1964). It should be noted that E. A. Speiser concluded that what distinguished a *gôy* from an *'am* for the ancient Israelites was that a *gôy*— a nation—was understood to be an *'am*—a people—with its own land. Whether or not Speiser was correct, it is sufficient, for our purposes, to note that both *'am* and *gôy* were used in such a way that they were indisputably understood by the Israelites to indicate the existence of a collectivity which embraced within itself the smaller collectivities of the *šēbeṭ*, usually translated as 'tribe', the *mišpāḥā*, usually translated as 'clan' or 'sib', and the *bêt 'āb*, the 'house of the father' or the 'family' (de Geus 1976; Lemche 1985; de Vaux 1958).

This trans-clan, trans-tribal collective entity described as the *'am* or *gôy* of 'all Israel' is depicted in Joshua 3 and 4. According to these passages, the crossing of the Jordan River was understood by later generations not to have been undertaken by a single clan or tribe or several

---

3. For a recent treatment of the much discussed question of the dating of the composition of the Pentateuch, see Freedman (1987: 29–37). The entire issue of the *Journal for the Study of the Old Testament* 3 (1977) was devoted to this problem. See also Noth (1943, 1948).

clans or tribes, but by the entity 'all Israel' which encompassed the twelve tribes.[4]

> Early in the morning, Joshua struck camp and set out from Shittim *with all the Israelites* [*wĕkol-bĕnê yiśrā'ēl*]. They reached the Jordan and camped there before they crossed. [. . .]
>
> Yahweh said to Yoshua, "This very day I will begin to make you a great man in the eyes of *all Israel* [*kol-yiśrā'ēl*] [. . .]."
>
> Then Joshua said to the Israelites, "[. . .] choose twelve men at once *from the tribes of Israel* [*miššibṭê yiśrā'ēl*] one man from each tribe. As soon as the priests with the ark of Yahweh, the Lord of the whole earth, have set their feet in the waters of the Jordan, the upper waters of the Jordan flowing down will be stopped in their course and stand still in one mass [. . .]."
>
> *The people* [*hā'ām*] crossed opposite Jericho. The priests who carried the ark of the covenant of Yahweh stood still on dry ground in mid-Jordan, *and all Israel* [*wĕkol-yiśrā'ēl*] continued to cross dry-shod till *the whole nation* [*kol-haggôy*] had finished crossing of the river. [. . .]
>
> When *the whole nation* [*kol-haggôy*] had finished crossing the Jordan, Yahweh spoke to Joshua, "Choose out twelve men *from the people* [*min hā'ām*], one man *from each tribe* [*miššābeṭ*] [. . .].

In fact, the term "all Israel," signifying an entity comprising the entire twelve tribes, appears repeatedly throughout the book of Joshua. The question of the historical accuracy of this account of "all Israel" crossing the Jordan River and occupying the entire land need not concern us at this point. What can be observed from such passages as Joshua 3 and 4, and what is particularly important for the consideration of ancient Israel as a nation is the existence at some point during the history of ancient Israel of a belief that there existed a people, called "Israel," which transcended the boundaries of clan and tribe.

More can be observed from the evidence provided by the Old Testament and specifically the book of Joshua as to the subsidiary collectivities encompassed by "all Israel." Josh 7:14–18 clearly indicates a hierarchy of collectivities where the 'house of the father', *bêt 'āb*, is a subdivision of the 'clan', *mišpāḥâ*, and the 'clan', in turn, is a subdivision of the 'tribe', *šēbeṭ*.

> In the morning therefore you [Israel] will come forward *tribe by tribe* [*lĕšibṭēkem*][5] and *the tribe* [*haššēbeṭ*] that Yahweh marks out by lot will come

---

4. Unless indicated otherwise, the English translation of the passages of the Old Testament is from the Jerusalem Bible edition. For Hebrew citations, I have used the *Biblia Hebraica Stuttgartensia* edition (1966/77) of the Masoretic Text.

5. Literally, 'by your tribes'. The possessive suffix -*kem* unfortunately does not appear in the translation of the Jerusalem Bible edition. The possessive suffix emphasizes that the tribes were understood to be a part of Israel.

forward *clan by clan [lammišpāḥōt]*[6] *and the clan [wĕhammišpāḥâ]* that Yahweh marks out by lot will come forward *family by family [labātîm],*[7] *and the family [wĕhabbayit]* that Yahweh marks out by lot will come forward man by man. And then the man taken with the thing that is banned is to be delivered over to the fire, he and all that belongs to him, because he has violated the covenant with Yahweh and committed an infamy *in Israel [bĕyiśrā'ēl]*.

Joshua rose early, he made *Israel ['et-yiśrā'ēl]* come forward tribe by tribe, and the lot marked out the *tribe of Judah [šēbeṭ yĕhûdāh]*. He called up to him the *clan of Judah [mišpaḥat yĕhûdâ]*, and the lot marked out the *clan of Zerah [mišpaḥat hazzarḥî]*. He called up the clan of Zerah, family by family, and Zabdi was marked out. Then Joshua called up *the family ['et-bêtô]*[8] of Zabdi; and it was Achan son of Carmi, son of Zabdi, son of Zerah, of the tribe of Judah, who was chosen by lot.

From such passages it is clear that the term "Israel" was understood by the Israelites to designate not only a trans-tribal collectivity, but also to encompass within itself numerous clans which, in turn, included numerous families.

Although these two passages indicate with evident clarity the beliefs in the existence of a trans-tribal collectivity of the *gôy* of Israel, one observes within the Old Testament an inconsistent usage of the terms *'am, gôy, šēbeṭ, mišpāḥâ,* and *bêt* (de Vaux 1958: 8). For example, in the first passage cited, a 'people' is sometimes called a *gôy* and sometimes an *'am*. In other passages in the Old Testament, sometimes the term *šēbeṭ* (tribe) and quite often the term *mišpāḥâ* (clan) seem to refer to a 'people', and even the term *bêt* (house) is used to refer to a 'people'.[9] For example, in the second passage, Judah is referred to as a tribe and as a clan.[10] How are we to understand this apparent inconsistency and what does it tell us about the nature of nationality?

Before we begin an analysis of the significance of this apparently inconsistent usage for our understanding of nationality, let us deal briefly with one possible explanation for this inconsistency, namely, scribal error in the copying and transmission of the text. Our source for information on the nature of ancient Israelite society, the Old Testament, has its own history of development, revision, and transcription. Consequently, one always faces when examining passages of the Old Testament the possibility that they have become textually corrupt as a result of revision

---

6. Literally, 'by clans'.

7. Literally, 'by houses'. Of course, 'house' is translated as 'family'.

8. Literally, 'his house'.

9. For examples, see below, p. 20.

10. The Septuagint avoids this problem by reading in this second instance "clans" of Judah instead of "clan" of Judah.

upon revision of earlier material and repeated transcriptions. Nonetheless, a reflective treatment of such inconsistencies should prevent reaching too quickly the conclusion that such textual inconsistencies indicate that the distinction between these different collectivities did not exist within the society of ancient Israel. It would be an error to conclude that such apparent terminological imprecision indicates that the distinctions of relations to ancestry and the 'people of Israel' (*ʿam, gôy, kol-yiśrā'ēl*), and the hierarchy of 'tribe', 'clan', 'house of the father' are nothing more than a careless usage without any correspondence to what really existed—whether that be at the time which such a description purports to describe, or the beliefs of the time it was written.

Other passages such as 1 Sam 10:19–24 also reveal the existence of a family-clan-tribe distinction and ascending hierarchy within the "people" of ancient Israel. In any event, the more probable explanation for such instability of usage is that the boundaries between these different categories were "fluid" (Pedersen 1920: 46–48; Robinson 1936: 50; Noth 1950: 106–7; Lemche 1985: 268). Let us examine more closely this phenomenon of the fluidity between the boundaries of different collectivities and its significance for our understanding of nationality and in particular ancient Israel as a nation.

There could be several reasons why such distinctions were "fluid." The material of the Old Testament was handed down, compiled, and edited over a very long period of time and purports to be a description of an even longer period of time. If we take the period beginning with the reign of Ramses II (thirteenth century B.C.) and ending with the presence of Ezra in Jerusalem (fifth century B.C.), we have a span of approximately eight hundred years which witnessed some immigration into Palestine, the decline of the Canaanite city-states, the military victories of the Israelitish tribes as they consolidated their power beyond the hill country, the rise and fall of the united kingdom, the destruction of the kingdom of Northern Israel by the Assyrians, and finally the Babylonian exile of the leading sections of the Judaean population. Obviously, the actual condition in Palestine during this tumultuous period would have provided opportunity for no small amount of "fluidity" in social organization. For example, one may assume that during this period and especially during the instability of the Late Bronze II Age and Early Iron I Age there were numerous instances of detribalization and retribalization (Rowton 1977: 185–87).[11] Concomitant with such changing conditions and instability,

---

11. Regarding detribalization, consider the apparent dispersion of the tribes Simeon and Reuben. For retribalization, recall the description of Benjamin's birth in

the criteria which distinguished a (very large) clan from a tribe might not have been so unambiguous. [12] For example, it is quite possible that Judah was originally a clan which subsequently became a tribe and then later a kingdom. This fluidity of the boundaries which resulted in variations of classification does not invalidate the argument that various units were sorted out into a hierarchy of categories at any particular time and as an image of the past bearing on the present. [13]

I have referred to two factors which I believe to have been integral to this terminological inconsistency: one, the tumultuous history of the area; and two, and more decisive, the ambiguous criteria of classification. One should resist adopting a facile explanation that such apparent terminological inconsistency and ambiguous criteria of classification are consequences of a "primitive mentality." Consider the imprecise terminology in the classification of the family commonly found in recent sociological literature: "nuclear" family, "extended" family, "blended" family.

An excellent example as to the changing criteria involved in the establishment of the boundaries of different collectivities can be observed in

---

Canaan (Gen 35:18) and the description of Judah as younger than Israel (2 Sam 19:44).

I note here in passing that the phenomena of detribalization and retribalization, and the seasonal migration of sheepbreeders within a relatively limited area would have facilitated the spread of the local traditions of a clan to other clans and tribes. This is especially so given that the "enclosed nomadism" of the area is characterized by a close relation between semi-nomadic and sedentary populations—sometimes both part of the same tribe (Rowton 1974; Lemche 1985: 152–63; Finkelstein 1988: 324–56). For a modern parallel of the phenomenon, see Barth (1981: 196), "Looking at the southern chain of peoples [. . .] it is apparent that in many regions we find a fusion of pure pastoralists and mixed farmers in part-nomadic tribal units."

12. Weber (1921: 11–12), "The difference between a weak tribe and strong sib is fluid." In Judg 13:2, the "tribe" Dan is referred to as a 'clan', *mišpāḥâ*.

13. Whether the tribe should be understood as either one level of organization in an evolutionary development of society or as an evolutionary *cul de sac* need not be pursued here in detail. Because de Geus (1976) argued that the history of the society of ancient Israel was one of the development from the town to the state rather than from the tribe to the state, he insisted that the tribe was an evolutionary *cul de sac*. In so doing, de Geus followed the conclusion of M. H. Fried (1965: 539). However, the counterposition between the tribe and town is unnecessary, as Rowton (1973, 1974) has convincingly argued.

Our concern here is to establish the existence of the belief in an "all Israel" which encompassed the *šēbeṭ*. The grounds for believing in the existence of the *šēbeṭ* during the pre-history and history of ancient Israel do not rest with only the traditions found in the Old Testament; for certainly, the material from, for example, Mari (the description of the Haneans and Benjamites) may be appealed to for support. Of course, the historical accuracy of the depiction of a united twelve-tribe alliance is an altogether different matter which will be discussed subsequently.

the determination of who was an Israelite and a Jew (Daube 1981: 1-32). According to the Pentateuch, in order to be an Israelite, a male must have been circumcised. A female was an Israelite if she married an Israelite (a circumcised male) or her father or husband converted (and hence, underwent circumcision). During the period of the second temple, the practice of baptism permitted a female to become an Israelite without marriage to an Israelite. It was not until the period of the second century A.D. onwards, and finally established as law only around A.D. 400, that the child of a Jewess and a Gentile was considered a Jew.

There is a third factor in our analysis of this terminological inconsistency which is the most significant for our understanding of the formation of ancient Israel as a nation: the attribution of being related by blood to collectivities larger than the family, the *bêt 'āb*. This extension of the conception of relationships by blood-ties to collectivities also constituted by territorial reference, i.e., possibly the clan (de Geus 1976: 138-39; Gottwald 1979: 257, 316; Lemche 1985: 269) and probably the tribe,[14] necessarily entails imprecision. It is an imprecision similar to what occurs in the multiple uses of "house." For example, we have seen from Josh 7:14, 17 that "house" was used for "family." However, "house" was also used in other ways, such as: the "House of God" in reference to a sanctuary (Josh 6:24; Judg 18:31) or the Jerusalem temple (Hos 9:4; 1 Kgs 8:16-21; 2 Kgs 12:4, 9, 10, 13; 14:14; 18:16), the "House of David" (1 Kgs 12:19, 20; 13:2; 2 Kgs 17:21; Jer 21:12)[15] in reference to the dynastic lineage of the Judaean kings, and the "House of Israel" in reference to the entire Israelite people (Num 20:29; 1 Sam 7:2; 2 Sam 12:8; 1 Kgs 12:21; Amos 6:1, 14). A similiar imprecision can be noted by the use of *mišpāḥâ*, where, while often indicating a "clan" as in the passages cited above, it may also refer to an entire people (Jer 10:25; Amos 3:1) or to both the "House of Israel" and the "House of Judah" (Jer 33:24). This imprecision is a consequence of the application of the image of being related by blood to collectivities where factually this is not the case.

Once again, this interpretation of larger collectivities in terms of smaller, which have different constitutive features or criteria, cannot be dismissed as a consequence of a "Semitic way of thinking" or of a "primitive mentality." Modern man continues to attribute ties of kinship to col-

---

14. Whether or not the tribes, as a system, were derived from the territorial administrative districts of the kingdom of Solomon, the tribal names Judah, Ephraim, Benjamin, and Naphtali indicate that they refer to territorial location (Noth 1950: 56-67; Lemche 1985: 282).

15. It should also be noted that the original meaning of Pharaoh, *Per-ʿo*, meant "Great House" (Gardiner 1961: 52).

lectivities larger than the family. For example, consider our attribution of kinship to the "people" of the nation (Schneider 1969), or our use of such terms as "fatherland," "motherland," and "homeland." This terminological imprecision which we have observed is a consequence of the characterization of collectivities larger than the family, especially nationalities, both ancient and modern, as being constituted of ties of kinship. It is probable that one element of our difficulty in better understanding modern nationality is the imprecision involved in the attenuation of the primordial tie (Shils 1957) from that of the family to that of the "people" of the nation.

This attribution of relation of kinship to collectivities larger than the family probably indicates the inexpungeability of the primordial. Here, I draw attention to an important error often made under the rubric of the distinction between the tie of kinship in contrast to the tie of territorial co-residence; the former is often asserted (Maine 1861: 124-26) to be characteristic of only small, primitive societies, while the latter is often asserted to be characteristic of only large, modern societies. Sometimes this error is made under the rubric of the distinction between *Gemeinschaft* and *Gesellschaft*. For a conception to have become attenuated does not mean that it has become residual or vestigial, and that it is bound to pass away. The existence of a "people," an example of the attenuation of the primordial blood-tie, is often a relatively late development in the history of the formation of a nation. This existence of a "people" as a relatively late development in the formation of a nation indicates that an image of a relatively large, designated territory and co-residence in that territory are factors in the formation of the "people" of the nation. In other words, kinship has been attributed to members of a territorially extensive society; hence, the term *mišpāḥâ* to refer to the inhabitants of the land of Israel from "Dan to Beersheba," or the term, "the American family" to refer to the inhabitants of the territory of the United States. In point of fact, relations engendered to blood-tie and relation engendered to territorial co-residence are, it seems to me, difficult to separate empirically when we deal with collectivities larger than the family (Lowie 1927: 51-73).

One obstacle in the historiography of ancient societies—above all in the history of ancient Israel—to understanding the development of these societies and especially ancient nations has been the inability to realize that the "people," the shared belief in the existence of a people as a people, arose over time in the land which that people occupied. (The same is often true of the *šēbeṭ*, the tribe, an even the *mišpāḥâ*, the clan.) I, of course, acknowledge that the existence of a "people" is predicated upon previous events such as migrations and invasions. However, we are interested in a "stability," that is, a steady recurrence over generations, in the belief in the existence of a "people" implied by the very existence of a nation. In the history of ancient Greece, one can observe the image of the people of the nation *beginning* to take shape through the attribution of a common biological kinship in *The History* of Herodotus, Book 8, Chapter 144 where the Athenians speaking to the Spartans refer to "our common Greekness: we are one in blood and one in language." Note that the consolidation of this awareness of a "common Greekness" apparently occurred relatively late in the history of the components, e.g., Sparta and Athens, to which the term refers (Finley 1954; Schaefer 1963). Turning to another example, one wonders if the phrase "all Aram" which appears in the Sefire Stele, approximately 740 B.C. (Mazar 1962; Fitzmyer 1967; Malamat 1973; Gibson 1975), and the term "Aram" common to the designations of the city-kingdoms of Aram-Naharaim, Aram-Zobah, Aram Beth-Rehob, and Aram-Damascus (2 Sam 10:6) might also indicate the early stages in the formation of an Aramean "people," a "*volklichen Zusammengehörigkeit*" (Noth 1962: 220) rather late in the history of the Aramean city-kingdoms.

Let us return to ancient Israel and draw our first conclusion about its existence as a nation. What is important and what is clearly revealed in such passages as Joshua 3, Joshua 4 and Joshua 7 is the existence of a rising hierarchy of inclusiveness of collectivities from the *bêt 'āb* to the *mišpāḥâ* to the *šēbeṭ* and finally to the *ʿam* or *gôy* of *kol yiśrāʾēl*, 'all Israel'. Furthermore, we need hardly be reminded that at some point in the history of ancient Israel, there came into existence the belief in "all Israel," the "sons of Israel," as the putative descendant of Abraham-Isaac-and-Jacob. Here again we may note the primordial attribution of a biological kinship, in this case of a putative lineage of Abraham-Isaac-and-Jacob, to a collectivity, "all Israel" which was more extensive than a clan or a tribe. We should also note that this amalgamation of previously local ancestors into a genealogy common to "all Israel" was probably firmly established as a common Israelite tradition during a period relatively late in Israelite history, quite possibly no earlier than the seventh century B.C. (Lemche 1985: 314). Here is one, although by itself not decisive, element of nationality, the existence of a belief that its members were a "people," "all Israel."

I have, up to this point, separated the belief in the existence of this people, Israel, from the historical factors which contributed to its formation. By doing so, I have not only suspended consideration of those factors, but I have also, for the sake of argument, deliberately separated out those referents in the collective consciousness of the Israelites which made possible the belief in the existence of the people of Israel as Israel, specifically the land of Israel and the religion of Israel. Let us turn to these considerations.

In order for a nation to exist, in addition to the belief in the existence of a "people," there must also be a belief in the existence of a specific territory which is believed to be in some way "appropriate for," "having a special affinity with," or "belonging to" only that people (Hertz 1945: 146–51; Dumont 1970: 108; Shils 1983: ix–xvi). In other words, and in contrast to an empire, one necessary characteristic of nationality is that its territory is delimited, *in principle*. On the other hand, in contrast to a patchwork of territorially distinct and smaller city-kingdoms, the existence of a nation presupposes a conception of a larger territory that is not only bounded, but is also perceived to be contiguous within those boundaries. Note here that I have begun to introduce elementary criteria to distinguish empire, nation and city-kingdom from one another.

Did the ancient Israelites at some point in their history have a conception of "all Israel" as being constituted by a bounded territory? We read in Numbers 34:

> Yahweh spoke to Moses and said, "When you go into the land, this is the territory that will be your inheritance. This is the land of Canaan defined by its boundaries.
>
> The southern part of your country will stretch from the wilderness of Zin, on the borders of Edom. Your southern boundary will start on the east at the end of the Salt Sea. It will then turn south toward the Ascent of the Scorpions and go by Zin to end in the south at Kadesh-barnea. Then it will go toward Hazar-addar and pass through Azmon. From Azmon the boundary will turn toward the wadi of Egypt and end at the Sea.
>
> Your seaboard will be the Great Sea; this will be your western boundary.
>
> This will be your northern boundary. You will draw a line from the Great Sea to Mount Hor, then from Mount Hor you will draw a line to the Pass of Hamath, and the boundary will end at Zedad. From there it will go on to Ziphron and end at Hazar-enan. This will be your northern boundary.
>
> You will then draw your eastern boundary from Hazar-enan to Shepham. The boundary will go down from Shepham toward Riblah on the east side of Ain. Further down it will keep to the eastern shore of the Sea of Chinnereath. The frontier will then follow the Jordan and end at the Salt Sea.
>
> This will be your land with the boundaries surrounding it."

All that such a description of the territory of ancient Israel lacks is the degrees of latitude and longitude—a not insignificant point, viz., the importance of modern land-surveying techniques for designating the territory of the modern nation-state. (In this regard, recall the slogan of the 1840s in the United States, "54,40 and fight.") Nonetheless, what is decisive for our consideration of ancient Israel as a nation is the existence of an image of a bounded territory which was understood to be, at least in part, constitutive of Israel.

At this point we can with confidence conclude that at a certain point in the history of ancient Israel: (1) there was a belief in the existence of a trans-clan/tribal people, namely, Israel; and (2) there was a belief in the existence of a trans-local territory, Israel. Note that the term "Israel" applies both to the "people" and to the "land." This terminological "conflation" represents a "conjoining" of a people to a land. This conjoining is a characteristic referent in the shared beliefs constitutive of nationality, ancient and modern: a people has its land and a land has its people. Indicative of this conjoining are two consecutive passages (Ezek 7:2–7) where Yahweh is described as not only having addressed both the land and the people, but having referred to both as "you":

> The Lord Yahweh says this to the land of Israel: "Finished! The end is coming for the four quarters of the land. Now all is over with you [. . .]."

> The Lord Yahweh says this: "Now disaster is going to follow on disaster. The end is coming, the end is coming for you; it is coming now. Now it is your turn, you will live in this country."

Note also the conjoining of a land and a people implied in such passages as Lev 18:25–28:

> The land became unclean: I [Yahweh] exacted the penalty for its fault and the land had to vomit out its inhabitants. [. . .] If you [Israel] make it [the land] unclean, will it [the land] not vomit you out as it vomited the nation [gôy] that was here before you?[16]

Lucien Lévy-Bruhl (1910: 40) thought such a conjoining or union between the animate (the people) and the inanimate (the land) was indicative of a "primitive mentality." However this conjoining is by no means exclusively characteristic of a "primitive mentality"; it is also characteristic of modern nationality as well.

The existence of the images of a territory and of a people must not be taken for granted; their existence must be accounted for. What constellation of beliefs is necessary for the emergence, stability, and wide acceptance of the beliefs in a bounded, contiguous territory conjoined with a "people"? What conceptual prerequisite is required for the beliefs in a "land" and in a "people" to have become constitutive referents in the col-

---

16. See also Deut 29:24–28.

lective consciousness of a nation? Is it not that there has been a unifying sacrality attributed to a relatively large area of land—the boundaries of which, as for all nations, were not to be violated—and to a people, now recognized as such—that is "related"—who inhabit that land? The territory of ancient Israel was understood to have been delimited as sacred territory; its boundaries were sacred (see, for example, Joshua 22 and 24). The Israelites believed that Yahweh lived in the land of Israel—his land (Josh 22:19; Hos 9:3; Isa 14:2; Jer 2:7)—making the land sacred. They also believed that Yahweh, having entered into covenant with the Israelites, lived among the sons of Israel, thereby making the people of Israel holy (Lev 26:11-13; Deut 7:6; 14:2). The, for the lack of a better term, "homogenization" or "unification" both of the various areas of land into the bounded, contiguous territory of Israel and of the distinct peoples, the various *mišpāḥôt* or *šibṭîm*, inhabiting that land, into the people of Israel, so that a land has its people and a people has its land, was facilitated by the beliefs that the land of Israel was the land of Yahweh and that the people of Israel, the putative descendants of Abraham-Isaac-and-Jacob, were chosen by Yahweh to inhabit that land. In other words, the emergence of ancient Israel as a nation was facilitated by the monolatrous development (Wellhausen 1883: 231-32; W. Robertson Smith 1881: 282; Driver 1902: xxviii; Weber 1921: 133, 138, 157, 340; Meek 1936: 206-16; von Rad 1957: 211; Ringgren 1963: 67; V. Nikiprowetzky 1975: 68-69) of the worship of Yahweh, in particular the specific expression of that development: the theology of the covenant (Eichrodt 1933; Perlitt 1969; Nicholson 1986), the *běrît* (see Deuteronomy, Joshua 24 and 2 Kings 23).

One element of that development was that the Deuteronomic code was conceived to be a *lex terrae*. The Deuteronomic code begins (Deut 12:1):

> Now these are the laws and customs that you must keep and observe, *in the land* that Yahweh the God of your fathers has granted you to possess, for as long as you live *in that land*[17] [my emphasis].

As such, it was to have been the only law to be obeyed in the land (Deut 11:12-17, 26-28; 12:29-31; 13).[18] As the only law of the land, it unified

---

17. Note also such introductory phrases as "In the land Yahweh is giving you as your possession . . . ," Deut 21:1.

18. The Israelites believed that Yahweh dwelled in the land of Israel and amongst the people of Israel only insofar as the law of Yahweh was the only law obeyed by the Israelites. See, for example, Deut 26:17-19; 28:9; 29:15-20.

both the inhabitants of the land into the people of Israel and the land itself into the land of Israel. Thus, one of the consequences of the Deuteronomic legal code was the ascendancy of the collectivity of "all Israel" and the attendant ascendancy of an "all Israel" perspective over the smaller law-communities, the *Rechtsgemeinschaften*, the *mišpāḥôt*. An example of this ascendancy can be seen in the existence of such Deuteronomic terminology as "an infamy/crime committed in Israel" instead of a wrong done to a clan. Another example can be observed in Deut 24:16 which acknowledges that the responsibility for a crime rests with the individual Israelite who is discovered to be guilty of having committed that crime in contrast to the more primordial attribution of "blood guilt" to the entire family and to the future generations of the perpetrator.

Finally, the procedure for the administration of the law also indicates an "all Israel" jurisdiction of the law (Deut 16:18).

> You are to appoint judges and scribes in each of the towns that Yahweh is giving you, for all your tribes; these must administer an impartial judgment to the people.

If the case was too difficult to decide at the local level, then an appeal could be made to the "levitical priests and the judge then in office" at "the place Yahweh your God chooses" (Deut 17:8-9), presumably Jerusalem.

It was precisely these factors—the constitutive prominence of the "land" and the "people" in the worship of Yahweh, and a law the jurisdiction of which was conceived to be both that land and that people—which were absent in the histories of the ancient Greeks and the Aramean city-kingdoms. Equally important in the formation of ancient Israel as a nation was that ancient Israel had a center, Jerusalem, to which "all Israel" could and did look. No such center existed in ancient Greece. In the case of "all Aram," Damascus was prevented by the Assyrians from developing into its center.

The ancient Israelites at some point during their history became a nation when they believed that the territory of Israel in its entirety belonged to them, as *kol yiśrā'ēl*, and only to them because Yahweh, their God and the only God to be worshiped in the land (and thus, whose law was the only law to be obeyed in the land), had promised it to them. They became a nation when they believed that, as a nation, they did not and could not exist without the land because the land was essential for their existence as Israel (Hos 9:17).

In order for a nation to live, to realize itself, it must have its land. For Israel to live, it, too, must have its land. Without the land promised to them by Yahweh, the chosen people of Israel were "incomplete" (Deut 30:19-20):

Choose life, then, so that you and your descendants may live, in the love of Yahweh your God, obeying his voice, clinging to him; for in this your life consists, and on this depends your long stay in the land which Yahweh swore to your fathers Abraham, Isaac, and Jacob he would give them.

Without its land, Israel would be nothing more than a "byword among all the nations." Thus, in 1 Kgs 9:6–7, Yahweh says to Solomon,

But if you turn away from me, you or your sons, and do not keep the commandments and laws I have set before you, and go and serve other gods and worship them, then I will cut Israel off from the land I have given them, and I will cast out from my presence this temple that I have consecrated for my name, and Israel will become a proverb and a byword among all nations.

The existence of the nation, whether ancient Israel or the modern nation-state, is predicated upon the existence of a collective consciousness constituted by a belief that there exists a territory which belongs to only one people, and that there is a people which belongs to only one territory. The collective existence, self-preservation, and future of the nation depend upon its connection with its land. As the possession of the land is essential to the life of the nation, the "life-force" of the nation, the spirit of the people, the traditions of the people, permeate that land thereby transforming it into a national territory. Separated from its land, the nation will die (Deut 29:27–28; Jer 9:18–19; Lev 26:27–42). That is why the territory of the nation is held sacred to the nation.

II. Ancient and Modern Nationality

From even this brief examination of some of the beliefs of the ancient Israelites as we have them before us in the Old Testament, we may conclude that an image of a relatively extensive area of land was a referent in the collective consciousness of Israelite society; and that a belief in common kinship or in a common biological tie was a referent in the collective consciousness of that territorially extensive society. Herein lies a fundamental similarity between ancient and modern nationalities: both are predicated upon the existence of an image of a relatively extensive area of land—an image which is shared by the inhabitants of that land, and to whom is attributed, by virtue of that co-residence, a kinship. To be sure, there are a number of differences between ancient and modern nationalities. Let us attempt to enumerate them in a preliminary manner.

One, it would appear that the phenomenon of nationality is more prevalent today than in antiquity. However, we ought not to take this apparent prevalence for granted. For example, the Soviet Union is probably best described as an empire, the nation of India is most problematic, and the very existence of nationalities in Islamic lands (e.g., Pakistan) and in Africa is certainly open to doubt. Furthermore, it was not very long ago when the *millet* system of the Ottomans dominated the Middle East. In other words, the characterization of our times as an "age of the nation-state" may be rather superficial as it may not apply to a majority of the population of the world. It may also be a result of an over-exaggeration of the significance of a relatively brief period in European history—a period which, it should be noted, has been and continues to be unstable in its recognition of different "peoples" (e.g., Northern Ireland, Scotland, the Bretons, Yugoslavia, Quebec, etc.).

In any event, with this cautionary note let us acknowledge the greater prevalence of the phenomenon of nationality today. We need not discuss in detail here such factors as the techniques of modern communication, modern transportation, and the market for industrial goods which appear to have been contributing factors to this greater prevalence.[19] To be sure, for the integration necessary for a "people" to exist, for a stable, recurrent, territorially extensive circumscribed pattern of action to exist, for the shared recognition that some significant properties are common to a multitude of individuals to exist, technological advancement is a prerequisite (Lowie 1948: 319). It is necessary simply for the administration of this relatively extensive territory of the nation. These technological advancements permit a relatively large area of land to be managed, organized, and unified by its respective center.

Nevertheless, in antiquity there were important advancements which contributed to the manageability of a territory and hence its unification. There was the construction and maintenance of such roads as, in ancient Israel, the *Via Maris* along the Mediterranean coastline and "The Kings Highway" (Num 20:17; 21:22) along the Transjordan range (Aharoni 1962: 43–63). There was the implementation of large-scale irrigation, for example, of the Nile in Egypt. However, the scope of these advances in antiquity and their ability to contribute to the incorporation of the hinterland were meager when compared to the modern techniques of communication, the newspaper, radio, television, movies; and of transportation, the railroad, automobiles, and airplanes. Consequently, ancient nationalities tended to be territorially smaller than modern, for example, Israel, Moab, and Edom (although note the probable exception of Egypt).

---

19. As has been pointed out in many recent works. For a relatively early treatment, see Deutsch (1953).

Two, modern nationality has more clearly defined boundaries than an-cient. However, as the example of ancient Israel has shown, this does not mean that the image of a trans-local, bounded territory was not a consti-tutive factor of a collectivity in antiquity. Too often it is incorrectly as-serted that there was no conception of a bounded territory in antiquity (Giddens 1985: 50-51).

I have already briefly introduced criteria to distinguish a nation from a city-kingdom and from an empire. The existence of a nation is predicated upon a shared conception of a specific, relatively extensive designated area of land which is believed to be "appropriate for" a particular people. A city-kingdom is usually a smaller area of land, obviously around a ma-jor city,[20] which may contain many "peoples."[21] An empire, by its very na-ture, contains many peoples; insofar as it has established boundaries, it is as a consequence of more or less momentary relations of power. In or-der to continue with this differentiation as well as the differences be-tween ancient and modern nationality, we must consider, once again, one further and most important point, namely in what way a land may be "unified."

For the modern nation, the developments of both the people and the territory of the nation have been facilitated by the existence of a *lex terrae* and, in particular, the conception of citizenship. In antiquity, the corre-sponding element in the constitution of nationality was the saliency of the belief in the "god of the land" relative to the other deities worshiped by the people (and other "peoples") who dwelt in the land. If the "god of the land" was simply one among a number of other equally important or more important deities respected and worshiped in that territory, then the society was probably polytheistic, or essentially primordial—whether empire or city-kingdom—consisting of many different peoples and many

---

20. For example, Hazor, Ugarit, Mari, Alalakh, Nuzi. Of course, villages in the vi-cinity of the city-kingdom would also be within its jurisdiction. For example, the Su-merian city-state of Lagash included the village communities of Gir-su[ki], Lagaša[ki], Siraran[ki], Ki-nu-nir[ki], E-nin-mar[ki], Gú-ab-(b)a[ki] (Diakonoff 1974: 15, n. 16). See also Judg 1:27, ". . . Beth-shean and its outlying villages, or Tannach and its villages. He did not drive out the inhabitants of Dor and its outlying villages, or of Ibleam and its vil-lages, or of Megiddo and its villages," and Judg 11:26, ". . . Heshbon and its outlying villages, or in Jazer and its villages. . . ." Note that the Hebrew is literally not "villages"; but rather, the plural "daughters" (*běnôt*, irregular noun) is used to describe the outly-ing, dependent villages.

21. For example, Brinkman (1984: 16 and n. 62), "The king of Babylon presided over this heterogeneous population. . . . It is surely significant that in this period—and indeed from the time of the Kassite dynasty down through the reign of Nabonidus—there was no single native term to express 'Babylon' as a unit."

different legal communities under the authority of a patrimonial ruler. However, if the god of the land was either clearly the primary deity within a pantheon or the only deity—the latter being monolatry—whose law was obligatory for all who dwelt in his land, then perhaps we may speak of the existence of a nation. Let us note, in passing, the existence of numerous written legal codes in antiquity (for example, Israelite, Hittite, Babylonian) the respective existence of which and obedience to which would have facilitated a common way of life among those who were within its jurisdiction. Such codes were enforced by royal and temple officials who were dispersed throughout the territory of the royal house (and of the god!), especially at its borders.[22]

We may point to several examples of this ascendancy of the "god of the land" relative to other deities which would indicate the existence of nationality. First and most obvious is ancient Israel. Perhaps this phenomenon may be observed in Moab, the land of Chemosh (Pritchard 1955: 320), and Edom, the land of Qaus,[23] as well. Note also the most interesting description of the Caunians in *The History* of Herodotus (1.172),

> There were foreign rites established among them, but later they turned against them and resolved to follow none but their own gods; and so all the Caunians, putting on their armor—all, that is, of military age—advanced to the boundaries of their country, beating the air with their spears and saying that they were driving out the gods of the foreigners.

In ancient Egypt (Steindorf and Seele 1942; Frankfort et al. 1946; Wilson 1951; Gardiner 1961; Trigger et al. 1983),[24] the evident persistence and prominence of the territorial designation of the "throne (or god, or pharaoh) of the two lands"[25] throughout the long history of ancient

---

22. See, for example, for Egypt, "The Instruction for King Merikare" (Pritchard 1955: 415-17); for the "land of Hatti," see "From the Instructions for the Commander of the Border Guards" (Pritchard 1955: 210-11); for ancient Israel, see Deuteronomy 16-17. Were the Levites also royal officials (Ahlström 1982, especially chaps. 2 and 4)?

23. Was Edom the land of Qaus? T. C. Vriezen (1965) argued that Qaus was the warrior-god of the Edomites.

24. For dating, I have used Wilson (1951).

25. Over a period of a thousand years, the location of the southern border shifted from approximately the first cataract of the Nile (Elephantine) to the second cataract (Semma) to possibly even past the fourth cataract (el-Kenisa). That Elephantine was initially the southern border may be concluded from an inscription from the tomb of Weny, "during the time of Pepy I" (ca. 2325 B.C.), "When His Majesty inflicted punishment upon the Asiatics and Sand-dwellers, His Majesty made an army of many tens of thousands from the entire [land of] Upper Egypt, from Elephantine in the south to Medjneye in the north, from Lower Egypt . . . " (Gardiner 1961: 95). Note also, for example, from "The Instruction of King Amenemhet I" (who reigned ca. 1991-1961

Egypt[26] was certainly an important ingredient in its probable existence as a nation. We also observe the ascendancy of a god within the Egyptian pantheon, an ascendancy which was apparently often associated with a syncretism of some geographical significance as well, for example, Horus (Lower Egypt)-Seth (Upper Egypt)[27] and later Amen (Theban)-Re.

Furthermore, the belief that the land of Egypt belonged to only the Egyptians may be seen in the depiction of the debate between the pharaoh Kamose and his council concerning how to wage war against the Hyksos (Grayson and Redford 1973: 22; Wilson 1951: 164).

> I should like to know for what purpose is my strength. One prince sits in Avaris [the stronghold of the Hyksos in the eastern delta] and another in Nubia, and here [Thebes] sit I together with an Asiatic[28] and a Nubian, each one having his slice of Egypt. . . . I will grapple with him, and rip open his belly. My desire is to save Egypt which the Asiatics have smitten. . . . Your counsel is wrong and I will fight with the Asiatics. . . . Men shall say of me in Thebes: Kamose, the protector of Egypt.

B.C.), "I trod as far as Elephantine, I attained to the marshes of the Delta; I stood upon the boundaries of the land and saw its enclosure; I reached the limits of the armed territory . . ." (Pritchard 1955: 418). Perhaps the "Wall of the Ruler" marked the northeastern boundary; see, for example, "The Prophecies of Neferti" (Pritchard 1955: 446). For the northeastern boundary known as the "Ways-of-Horus," see "The Instruction for King Merikare" (Pritchard 1955: 416), and, "An Egyptian Letter" (Pritchard 1955: 478).

That Semma was the southern border during the reign of Senusret III (ca. 1878–1840) may be concluded from two inscriptions from Semma, ". . . His Majesty made the southern boundary. . . . As for any son of mine who shall maintain this boundary which My Majesty had made, he is a son of mine who was born to My Majesty. . . . But as for whoever shall abandon it, and who will not fight for it, he is no son of mine, and was not born to me . . ." and "the southern boundary which was created . . . to prevent any Nubian from passing it when faring northwards . . ." (Kemp 1989: 172–76).

As for the last, during the reign of Tuthmosis III (ca. 1490–1436), the following inscription was written, "As for any Nubian who shall disregard this notice, my father Amun hath granted for me that . . . Amen-Re and Atum . . . his cattle. He shall have no heirs(?) . . . (Arkell 1950: 36).

Note (1) the use of the terms "Asiatics," "Sand-dwellers" and "Nubians" to distinguish various peoples from Egyptians, and (2) the respective designation of boundaries.

26. With the exceptions of (1) the period of anarchy from the seventh through the tenth dynasties, after which Egypt was reunified under Mentuhotep I; and (2) the reign of the Hyksos, brought to an end by Kamose and Ahmose I.

27. See the throne base of Senusret I (ca. 1971–1928 B.C.), a picture of which appears in Kemp (1989: 28), and the "Memphite theology."

28. Note that the Turin King-list distinguished the Hyksos pharaohs by writing their names without a cartouche and with a hieroglyphic sign added which designates them as foreign, and by using the term "foreign kings" to describe them, Trigger et al. (1983: 156).

Surely, it is significant that Kamose is portrayed as considering himself responsible for not only Thebes or "Upper Egypt," but for Egypt.

Consider also the attachment to the land which was believed to be one's own and the image of that land as expressed in the popular "Song of Sinuhe." Sinuhe, having previously fled Egypt, and having become prosperous and much esteemed in "Upper Retenu" (Palestine), nevertheless states (Erman 1927),

> I am even so a foreigner whom none loveth, any more than a Bedouin would be loved in the Delta.... What is a greater matter than that my corpse should be buried in the land wherein I was born? Come to my aid! May good befall, may God show me mercy ... in order to make good the end of him whom he hath afflicted, his heart being compassionate on him whom he hath compelled to live abroad.

In contrast to these evident examples of nationality in antiquity, it would appear that in Greece, Aram, and generally throughout Mesopotamian history—Sumerian, Babylonian, and Assyrian—the belief in the god of the land, while present, was not as salient. I have already referred to Greece and Aram. Both would appear to exhibit elements of nationality, however their respective developments into nations were arrested.

As we have already observed from Herodotus' account of the Athenian's speech in Book 8, chapter 144, there would appear to have been some notion of a trans-city-state Greek territory; after all, Leonidas died defending this "common Greekness" far to the north of his Spartan home. Nevertheless, the polis was too firmly established in ancient Greece as the object of the political loyalty of its members. This loyalty represented an obstacle to the development of both a political loyalty to a trans-polis Greek territory and the emergence of an ascendant center. Surely, another reason for Greece not developing further into a nation was that the Greek religion was much more particularistic than the worship of Yahweh of the seventh century B.C. The Greek religion had no developed theology, no theological ethics, nor any sacred books such as the one "found" in the Jerusalem temple during the reign of Josiah.

In Sumerian history, it would appear that loyalty to the city-state came first and was never altogether superseded by a loyalty to Sumer[29] as a whole (Kramer 1963: 260).[30] The inhabitants of a city were known as its "sons" and were considered a closely related, integrated unit (Kramer 1963: 260). Indeed, slaves could be from a neighboring city defeated in

---

29. For the term "Sumer" as a territorial designation, see Jacobsen (1939: 417–18, n. 11).

30. The most obvious example is the border conflict between Lagash and Umma.

battle (Kramer 1963: 78). Thus, in contrast to the national "god of the land," a national "people," and a national territory,[31] each Sumerian city-state was under the protection of its own god who ideally owned the city-state (Roux 1980: 127; Nissen 1988: 142, 147–48; Landsberger 1945; Jacobsen 1961, 1963).[32] The city Lagash, for example, belonged to the god Ningirsu and its rival Umma to the god Shara and Ur to the moon-god Nanna (Roux 1980: 127). This depiction corresponds to our understanding of an aggregate of city-states in contrast to the nation.

However, even within this aggregate of Sumerian city-states there are elements of nationality to be observed. For example, the "Sumerians" appeared to have worshiped in common the god Enlil (Frankfort 1984: 216–17, 258–59), the ruler of the gods (Oppenheim 1964: 195) and also the god of the city Nippur. (Note, however, that Nippur never became a political center, which, as such, would have united the worshipers of Enlil into a people as Jerusalem united the worshipers of Yahweh into "all Israel.") Consider such phrases, indicating a degree of "relatedness" characteristic of an element of nationality,[33] found in a number of Sumerian inscriptions: "the kingship of Sumer" (Utuhegal tablet, Kramer 1963: 325); "the chieftains of Sumer" (Lugalzaggesi vase, Kramer 1963: 323); "kingship of the land" (Lugalzaggesi vase);[34] "the *en* of Sumer, the king of the land" (Enshakushanna, Kramer 1963: 308). Note also in the poem "Enki and the World Order" (Kramer 1963: 174–83) the description of the deity Nidaba who

> Has taken for herself the measuring rod . . .
> Fixes the borders, marks off the boundaries—
> Has become the scribe of the land. . . .

Nor is such a reference to "the borders" unique; for example, in a letter from Aradmu to Shulgi we find (Kramer 1963: 331),

> To my king speak; thus says your servant Aradmu: you have commissioned me to keep in good condition the expedition roads to the land of Subir, to

---

31. The destruction of arable soil as a result of gradual salting may have been one factor in retarding the emergence of an image of a national territory in Sumerian history, see Jacobsen and Adams (1958).

32. Nissen (1988) refers to "the pronounced particularism of the Babylonian cities," and Landsberger (1945) emphasized the polytheism and polymorphism of Sumerian religion. For the Old Assyrian city-kingdom Assur, see Mogens Trolle Larsen (1976: 116–17).

33. Consider also, for example, Kramer (1963: 53–55), where Misilim, king of Kush, is evidently acknowledged as having the authority to arbitrate the border dispute between the cities of Lagash and Umma.

34. Where "the land" refers to southern Babylonia, see n. 29.

stabilize the boundaries of your country, to make known the ways of your country. . . .

Nonetheless, such references indicate primarily the episodic ascendancy of one city-kingdom over its neighbors.[35]

This element of "relatedness" between different city-states, which we also observed in ancient Greece and Aram, is a most difficult and most important phenomenon to understand as to both its origin and nature. The very existence of a term which indicates a trans-city-state "relatedness," for example, "Sumer" or "Sumer and Akkad" or "Elam"[36] or "Hellenes,"[37] emphasizes this phenomenon. The history of any particular society already presupposes and arises out of this "relatedness"; hence, its origin is shrouded in obscurity.[38] As to the nature of this "relatedness," perhaps one can say that it indicates the existence of a "linguistic group" or a "civilization." These are not altogether satisfactory alternatives as an expression of the significance of, or an explanation of the origin of, for example, the evolution of an orderly pantheon. One may turn to Meinecke's (1928) distinction between *Kulturnation* and *Staatsnation* in order to account for this trans-city-state image of relatedness paralleling the particularistic loyalty to the respective city-state. However, the category of *Kulturnation* obscures the evident necessity and merit of distinguishing city-kingdom, empire, and nation from one another.

Let us now briefly turn to an examination of the Akkadian, Assyrian, and Babylonian evidence. Here, too, we must be content with a few overly general observations which attempt to summarize an approximate period of 1,500 years. Oppenheim (1964: 58; Nissen 1988: 165) suggestively and sweepingly contrasted the society of the Sumerians, on the one hand, and that of the "Akkadians" and (Middle- and Neo-) Assyrians, on the

---

35. For example, Eannatum of Lagash (twenty-fifth century B.C.), where the relevant inscription reads, "To Eannatum, the *ensi* of Lagash, whom Ningirsu had conceived of (in his mind); Inanna, because she loved him, gave him the kingship of Kish in addition to the *ensi*-ship of Lagash," Kramer (1963: 310); and Lugalzaggesi of Umma, as indicated above.

36. Specifically, for example, the title "King of Shimashki and Elam," see Carter and Stolper (1984).

37. For example, in *The Persians*, lines 401–2, Aeschylus writes, "A great concerted cry we heard, 'O sons of the Hellenes, advance! Free your fathers' land . . . ,'" Grene and Lattimore (1959).

38. For example, in Sumerian history, the apparent "all-Sumerian" position of Nippur and Enlil, see Jacobsen (1957); or, in the history of ancient Egypt, the nature of pre-dynastic Egypt such that it led to the dual designation of "Upper and Lower Egypt," see Trigger et al. (1983: 44–61), for a brief overview of the problems involved; or, in ancient Israel, a putative Sinai revelation or a northern tribal confederacy centered at Shechem.

other, as a "shift from a city-state concept (including dominion over other cities and leagues of cities) to the concept of a territorial state." This shift was marked by the reign of Sargon I (2334 B.C.) as indicated by the following inscription (Kramer 1963: 324).

> To Sargon, the king of the Land, Enlil gave no rival; (indeed) Enlil gave him the entire territory from the sea above to the sea below. Akkadians (literally, "sons of Akkad") held the *ensi*-ships (everywhere), from the lower sea and above; the men of Mari (and) the men of Elam served Sargon, the king of the land (as their master).

Oppenheim (1964: 52) further remarked,

> We will never know what specific economic, social, or ideological changes caused this shift in political outlook. The successes of these kings henceforth had a dominant influence on the political concepts and claims of Mesopotamian rulers. Not only did the Sumerian dynasty of Ur (called Ur III) follow Sargon's example [of forming a "territorial state"], but the Assyrian kings of the next millennium or more took him as their prototype and the image on which to model their political aspirations.

This summary and, in particular, the contrast between city-state and "territorial state" have been generally accepted by many of the scholars of the ancient Near East. I also accept it, however, with one important reservation, the use of the term "territorial state." What are the problems with the use of this term in describing the different societies of the ancient Near East?

What I believe Oppenheim had in mind by "territorial state" was a primordial, polytheistic empire under patrimonial rule[39] which, by its very nature, contained many different peoples and whose boundaries varied according to military exigencies. Thus, characteristic of these societies is the relative lack of significance of the "god of the land." In this regard, city-kingdom and empire are essentially similar in contrast to nationality; both are pluralistic, in contrast to the stable existence of a trans-local, trans-tribal "people." The term "territorial state" obscures this fundamental similarity between city-kingdom and empire.[40]

Indicative of the relative insignificance of the "god of the land" and characteristic of polytheistic empires are such passages as from the Chronicle of Nabonidus, ca. 539 B.C.[41] (Pritchard 1955: 306):

---

39. Note that according to Roux (1980: 320) all Assyrians and foreign subjects were considered to be slaves, *ardê*, of the king.

40. This fundamental similarity may be observed in the transition from city-kingdom to empire, for example, Babylon under Hammurapi.

41. For dating, I have used J. A. Brinkman's "Mesopotamian Chronology" in Oppenheim (1964: 335–48).

In the month of [. . .] the gods of the city Marad, Ilbaba and the gods of Kish, Ninlil, [. . .] from Hursag-Kalamma entered Babylon. Until the end of the month the gods of Akkad [. . .] those from every direction entered Babylon [. . .] From the month of Kislev to the month of Adar, the Babylonian gods which Nabonidus had made to come into Babylon [. . .] returned to their sacred cities.

An empire ecompasses within its territory many different peoples with their respective deities. This situation is to be contrasted with the belief constitutive of a nation that a people has its land and a land has its people.

The absence of a salient belief in a national territory and a national people may be observed in the alignment of forces in the civil war between Ashurbanipal and his brother Shamash-shum-ukin, king of Babylon (652–648 B.C.). Even though the cities Uruk, Ur, and Eridu, all situated to the south of Babylon, could be considered within the sphere of influence of Babylon, they nonetheless declared their loyalty to Ashurbanipal (Brinkman 1984: 97). To be sure, other factors such as the presence of the Chaldeans may have influenced the alignment; but these factors only further underscore the imperial, particularistic, and polytheistic nature of these socities.

One may clearly observe this imperial incorporation from the annals of Adad-Nirari II (911–891 B.C.; Luckenbill 1926: 110–11):

Mighty hero, who marched with the help of Assur, his lord, from the other side of the Lower Zab, (by) the borders of the Lulume-land, of Kirhi, and of Zamua, as far as the passes of the land of Namri, and brought in submission to his feet the widespread Kumane, as far as the lands of Mehri, Salua and Uradri (Armenia); who brought under his sway Kutmuhi in its entirety and added (lit., turned) it to the border of his land. Conqueror of Karduniash (Babylonia) in its entirety, who established the overthrow of Shamash-mudammik, king of Karduniash, from Ialman to the river of Durilani;–(the land) from Lahiru to the plain of Salum was added to the territory of Assyria. The land of Der I conquered in its entirety. Arrapha, Lubda, strongholds of Karduniash, I restored to the territory of Assyria.

However, note, even here, the phrases "the border of his land" and "restored to the territory of Assyria." Such phrases are not uncommon. For example, also from the annals of Adad-Nirari II we find (Luckenbill 1926: 111):

I am he who returned the cities of Hit, Idu, and Zakku, strongholds of Assyria, to the territory of his land.

We also find, for example, throughout the inscriptions of Sargon II (721–705 B.C.), such descriptions of the activity of the king as "enlarging the territory which belongs to the god Assur as regards its boundaries" (Luckenbill 1926: vol. 2). Many inscriptions from the reign of Sargon II indicate the existence of the conception of boundaries.[42] Of course, it is perfectly clear that these inscriptions refer to the expanding boundaries of the Assyrian empire and hence of the expanding territory of the Assyrian god, Assur. This conception of the expanding territorial jurisdiction of the god of the Assyrians is to be contrasted with the Israelite conception of the land of Israel, the land of Yahweh, which was delimited in principle.[43]

Considering briefly the history of the Hittites, clearly Suppiluliumas, Mursilis, and Muwatillis (1375–1282 B.C.) ruled empires (Gurney 1952).[44] However, we know there are repeated references throughout Hittite inscriptions to the phrase "Land of Hatti."[45] The question is whether or not this phrase and its repeated appearance indicate that there may have been a Hittite "core" to this empire. If there was such a "core," what was its nature? A similar question may be posed about respectively the existence of an "Israelite core" to the empires of David and Solomon or an "Assyrian core"[46] to the neo-Assyrian empires. One of our problems in the examination of ancient societies is whether such a "core" indicates the existence of a nation, a city-kingdom or some kind of confederation. (In modernity, consider the existence of a "national core" in a colonial empire.)

---

42. See also, for example, Grayson (1963). In this inscription (ca. 690 B.C.), observe the conception of an area of land and/or cities which were perceived to be "Assyrian." "I went to ELAM, surrounded in the course of my campaign . . . cities . . . which the king of ELAM had taken by force in the time of my father, captured them, carried off their booty, stationed in them archers and shield bearers, returned them to the *boundary of Assyria* [*a-na mi-ṣir* *kurAš-šurki*] and entrusted (them) to the frontiers commander."

The relevant terms which should be examined in this context of a differentiated typology of city-kingdom, nation, and empire are *ba'ulātum*, 'dominion', *māt*, 'land', *il mātim*, 'god of the land', and *miṣru/mi-ṣir*, the latter term translated in standard and neo-Babylonian as (1) border; (2) territory, region, land; (3) political border, frontier. See the *Assyrian Dictionary*.

43. Are we also justified in contrasting the imperial period of Egyptian history (approximately 1465–1165 B.C.) with that of the Assyrians by virtue of the fact that Syro-Palestine was not considered by the Egyptians to be within the borders of Egypt?

44. As early as the reign of Mursilis I (ca. 1600 B.C.), the Hittites had attacked Babylon.

45. See, for example, the *Annals of Hattusili I*, and the treaty between Hattusilis III and Ramses II (Pritchard 1955: 201–3).

46. Nicholas Postgate (1989: 6), while describing the imperial nature of the Neo-Assyrian kingdoms, speaks of a "traditional heartland of Assyria on the Tigris and Zab rivers."

Does this phrase, "Land of Hatti," indicate the existence of a Hittite nation consolidated before and during the period of the Old Kingdom (approximately from 1800 to 1460 B.C.) in the area of the Halys River basin?[47] During that period in the time of Hattusilis I, it would appear[48] that the city Hattusa had become the acknowledged center of the land of Hatti. Thus, we observe perhaps a stable territorial designation distinct from the area of the empires of the period of the New Kingdom. However, it must be acknowledged that the evidence may not warrant even this tentative conclusion.

The terms *panku* and *tuliya* ('assembly'), the first appearing in the *Testament of Hattusili I* and both appearing in the *Telipinu Proclamation*, may indicate a dispersion of the authority of the patrimonial king to the larger community of Hatti. The word *panku* is basically an adjective meaning 'entire' (Bryce 1982: 113; Gurney 1952: 68–69; Beckman 1982). In the *Testament of Hattusili I*, the relevant passage is:

> The Great King Tabarna spoke to the warriors of the *panku* and the dignitaries. . . . If you see that any one of them commits an offense, either before a god or by uttering any (sacrilegious) wo[rd], you must consult the *panku*, and any dispute must be referred to the *panku*.

In the *Telipinu Proclamation*, the power of the king to punish the murderer of a member of the royal family is limited by the proclamation which recognizes the jurisdiction of the *panku* in such cases. It is difficult to be more precise as to the nature of this dispersion in the Old Kingdom. Does the term *panku* refer to some vague conception of citizenship; and, if so, what were its boundaries? Perhaps the term refers to a military aristocracy, or the nobility of the land.

Finally, we know that the Hittites worshiped the storm-god, to whom "the whole territory of Hattusa belonged."[49] It does seem that the Hittite storm-god was both the primary deity of the Hittite pantheon[50] and also

---

47. See the *Anitta Inscription*, the *Annals of Hattusili I*, the *Testament of Hattusili I*, and the *Telipinu Proclamation*. All are conveniently collected in Trevor R. Bryce (1982).

48. The inscriptions describing early Hittite history are copies written several hundred years after the events which they purport to describe.

49. See A. Goetze (1947), ". . . the country belongs to the storm god; heaven and earth and the people belong to the storm god. Thus he made a labarna, the king his governor. He gave him the whole country of Hattusa. So let the labarna govern the whole country with his hand. . . ."

50. The treaty between Hattusilis III and Ramses II was also described as a treaty between the Sun-god (Re) and the Storm-god of Hatti land. Note also the apparent ascendancy of the storm-god within the Hittite pantheon from the "Instruction for the Commander of the Border Guards," Pritchard (1955: 210–11), "Furthermore, due reverence shall be shown to the gods, but to the Storm-god special reverence shall be shown."

the "lord of the Hatti land" (Pritchard 1955: 205, 394). Particularly interesting is the difference drawn between a Hittite and a foreigner in the "Instruction for Temple Officials" (Pritchard 1955: 208):

> But a member of the community . . . is allowed to enter the house of god. . . . But if it is a foreigner, if it is not a Hittite man, and he ap[proach]es the gods, he shall be killed.

Of course, we do not know precisely what was meant by the phrase, "member of the community," its relation to "Hatti land," and what was meant by "not a Hittite man."

These foregoing comments were overly general and brief; their intention was only to highlight, in a preliminary manner, the similarities and differences between ancient and modern nationality. Of course, with the dominance of the monotheistic religions of Christianity and Islam in the Occident, we cannot expect a belief in the "god of the land" and an overtly religious legal code of the "god of the land" to have been explicit elements in the constitution of modern nations. The deities of Christianity and Islam are universal, trans-national deities. Moreover, in contrast to antiquity, the Christian Occident early on viewed as legitimate the development of both a legal code and a state bureaucracy distinct from the immediate authority of the religious hierarchy. Nonetheless, here, too, we should proceed with caution as to the apparent differences between antiquity and modernity, and in particular, the differences between ancient and modern nationality. For example, we recall even early in the history of Christianity the existence of such "national churches" as the Coptic and the Armenian (Woodward 1916).[51] Moreover, it is not too much to say that the Protestant reformation and the Eastern churches have recognized, at least implicitly, the primordial belief in the "god of the land."

In the analysis of the different organizations of society (in antiquity, whether tribal confederacy, city-kingdom, nation, or empire; in modernity, whether the communalism of Lebanon or Sri Lanka, the nation-state, or the empire of the Soviet Union) one must also consider the correspondingly different communities of beliefs implied by their existence. We must understand these differences as more than simply the consequences of certain historical relations of military domination and geographical peculiarities. The different organizations of society are also differences respectively in the nature of the boundaries of the people, the nature of the boundaries of the land, and the jurisdiction of the law.

---

51. I acknowledge that A. H. M. Jones (1959) was correct in his criticism of Woodward as far as Donatism is concerned.

III. The History of Ancient Israel

In the now more than a century which has passed since the publication of Julius Wellhausen's *Prolegomena to the History of Ancient Israel*, we have rightly become accustomed to analyzing critically the beliefs in a "promised land" and a "chosen people"; specifically, apparently these beliefs became salient in both the worship of Yahweh and Israelite history when the existence of the "land" and the "people" were threatened, i.e., during a period roughly between the eighth and the sixth centuries B.C. However, what if the salience of the very conceptions of a particular bounded territory, Israel, and a specific people, Israel, irrespective of whether or not they were understood respectively as "promised" and "chosen," was also a relatively late development in the history of pre-exilic ancient Israel? If the latter is possible, then it is probable that the existence of ancient Israel as a nation is a phenomenon later than what has usually been assumed in the scholarship of the Old Testament and in the various histories of ancient Israel.

To put this possibility in a different way, if Wellhausen (1883; Zimmerli 1965) was generally correct that the law was subsequent to the prophets,[52] what about the jurisdiction of that law? If we take the liberty to amend slightly Wellhausen's understanding of the fundamental beliefs of "Yahwism" and of the collective consciousness of Israel (*Gemeinbewußtsein Israels*) from "Israel, the people of Yahweh" and "Yahweh, the God of Israel" (Wellhausen 1905: 28) to include also "Israel, the land of Yahweh" (Josh 22:19; Hos 9:3; Jer 2:7) then the framework for our understanding the religion of ancient Israel, the society of ancient Israel, and the history of both is changed drastically. From this different perspective we must find out when "all Israel," "from Dan to Beersheba," became the land of Yahweh, and thus, how "all Israel" developed in the land. Most certainly, given the importance of the land in "Yahwism" as we know it, this amendment is neither arbitrary nor of marginal importance.

Let us proceed with the briefest of outlines of the history of ancient Israel, paying particular attention to the development of the images of the territory "from Dan to Beersheba" and of the "people" of ancient Israel.

(1) A collectivity called "Israel" is mentioned in the Merneptah stele in the late thirteenth century B.C. (Pritchard 1955: 378). However, it would appear that from the late thirteenth to the eleventh century B.C. the

---

52. The dating of Deuteronomy to the time of Josiah was postulated already by Athanasius, Jerome, Chrysostom, and Procopius of Gaza (Nestle 1902: 171, 312; Nicholson 1967: 1, n. 2).

territory of this "Israel" never extended significantly beyond the tribal area of Ephraim and northern Benjamin. This possible extent of the territory of northern Israel before the time of Saul is based on 1 Sam 7:15-17 as interpreted by Ahlström (1986: 80). Occasionally, the apparently numerously intermittent, primarily local (Tola, Jair, Ibzan, Abdon) clan and tribal confederacies of unstable membership may, at times, have included clans from the areas to the north, Manasseh, Zebulun, and Naphtali (Judges 4-5). However, the book of Judges also provides evidence for the existence of intra-clan warfare (see Judg 8:13-21; 12:1-7, 20-21). The latter probably indicates the fragility and tenuous nature of this essentially Ephraimite "Israel" of this period. The population of this area during much of this time would appear to have been worshipers of Baal; so one may conclude from: (a) the names of two of the Judges, Jerubbaal, which means "Baal make you great" (Kuenen 1870: 406-7; Noth 1928: 206-7; Emerton 1976) and not as the Deuteronomistic historian would like us to believe, "Baal must plead against him" (Judg 6:30-32), and Shamgar son of Anath (Judg 3:31), who, as a warrior-chief, may have been named after the warrior-god Anat;[53] and (b) the worship of such deities as *Ba'al-berit* of Shechem (Judg 8:33; 9:4). One may perhaps see here vague anticipations of a *northern* "Israelite" nationality facilitated by a tradition of military *bĕrît* amongst the northern clans and the existence of the old Canaanite sacred sites of Shiloh and Shechem,[54] revered—one presumes—throughout the area of Ephraim. There is no relation between this "Israel" and Judah during this period. Furthermore, it is not clear to what extent this northern hill population should be considered distinct from the "Canaanites."[55]

(2) During this period Jerusalem is to be considered as "Jebusite" (see Josh 15:63; Judg 1:21; 19:11-12).

(3) The area of Judah during the eleventh century B.C. was inhabited by Calebites and other (probably) Edomite and Midianite clans.[56] There

---

53. In the Ugaritic texts from Ras Shamra, Anat is described as the sister of Baal. See Kapelrud (1963); Gibson (1977); (Pritchard 1955: 136B).

54. In this context, consider Gen 33:20.

55. For example, of the many wives of Gideon (Judg 8:30), one, the mother of Abimelech, was a Shechemite. Evidently, her family and her son were worshipers of Baal (Judg 9:4).

56. Josh 15:3 recounts that "Caleb son of Jephunneh was given a portion among the sons of Judah. . . ." We know from Josh 14:6, 14, and Num 32:12 that Caleb son of Jephunneh was a Kenizzite. The connection between the Kenizzites and Edom is derived from Gen 36:11, 15 where Kenaz is described as a descendant of Esau, i.e., Edom.

is no convincing reason to consider this area as part of "Israel" during the eleventh century. Judah was politically united probably for the first time under David (Wellhausen 1881: 442-43; de Vaux 1971: 547-49).[57] It may be that David was a Moabite (Ruth 4:18-22; 1 Sam 22:1-4); and, in any event, he apparently was a vassal of the Philistines (1 Sam 27:5-12).

(4) For reasons many of which remain obscure (although the opportunism and the military adventurism of David are surely two), the military confederacies of Israel under Saul and Judah under David joined forces to defeat the Philistines. The question may be raised as to why Israel and Judah should have joined forces. Does the fact that they did so indicate the existence of a nation—an interpretation somewhat similar to or a variation of the amphictyony thesis of Martin Noth (1930); or Max Weber's (1921: 45) and Rudolf Kittel's (1925: 134) assertion that here we have the emergence of the Israelite nation? I think not. The tradition depicts this alliance between Israel and Judah as being always unstable; this is shown by the conflict between Saul and David. Note that David, wary of Saul, placed his father and mother under the protection of the King of Moab (see 1 Sam 11:1-4). This conflict finally led to open war between the "House of Saul" and the "House of David" (see 2 Samuel 2). The latter was a "civil war" only from the subsequent perspective of the Deuteronomistic historian who believed that Israel was already a nation when the Houses of David and Saul were at war with each other.

(5) For no more than the brief period of 80 years (out of 620 years, from the approximate date of the Merneptah stele, 1208, to 587, the date of the fall of Jerusalem), northern Israel and southern Judah were "united" under David and Solomon into an imperial monarchy containing numerous peoples, each worshiping its own deities (2 Samuel 8). Albrecht Alt (1930), followed by Martin Noth, more or less correctly characterized the united monarchy of David and Solomon as a "personal union," a "territorial state," or an "empire"—characterizations which both Alt and Noth understood to indicate that the united monarchy lacked the "compactness" or the "feeling of solidarity" (their terms) of a nation.

Within this "empire" was there a central core of a northern Israel and southern Judah arising out of both the military alliance between Saul and David against the Philistines and the subsequent victory of the House of David over the House of Saul? The subsequent history of the worship of Yahweh would seem to indicate that there may have been, i.e., the promi-

---

57. Consider 1 Sam 30:26-31 in this context. Y. Aharoni (1967: 390) argued that, based on the archaeological evidence, the boundary villages of Judah, as described in Josh 15:21-32, could not have existed much earlier than the tenth century B.C.

nence of the "promised land" from "Dan to Beersheba." In any event, for most of their history, ancient Israel, northern Israel and southern Judah were territorially circumscribed from the south by Egypt, from the west by the Mediterranean Sea and the Philistines, from the east by Edom and Moab, and from the north by Aram-Damascus. The existence of these countries[58] and their geographical location would have facilitated the consolidation of this northern Israel/southern Judah axis once it was established under Saul/David/Solomon.

Two developments from this period were essential to the subsequent emergence of ancient Israel as a nation. The first was that there existed, for the first time, a society whose territory extended from Dan to Beersheba. The second was that the god of the victorious Judaean David, Yahweh, now became the god of the united monarchy and hence (now, perhaps for the first time?) of northern Israel.

Nonetheless, we may conclude from the subjection of northern Israel to forced labor, heavy taxes, and the census that the base of support for David and Solomon appears to have been Judah and not "all Israel" (see 2 Samuel 24; 1 Kgs 5:27; 11:28; 12:18). Opposition of the population, in this case northern Israel, to the "census" is common to patrimonial states (what Alt called a "personal union"), where the rule of the royal house is primarily based on loyalty to that house (Weber 1978: 1010-69). This opposition indicates that the rule of law, especially its consistent application throughout the land of Israel and to all the "sons of Israel," is not a feature by which we can characterize this period. It also indicates in this period the absence of the loyalty of the Israelites, as members of a nation, to Israel. After the split between northern Israel and southern Judah, northern Israel seems to have returned to Baal as the god of the land (see 1 Kings 12-13).

(6) It was under the threat of the military destruction of northern Israel in the eighth century B.C. that circles in the north, which may be the place of origin of Deuteronomy (Alt 1953; Nicholson 1967), began actively campaigning for a renewed political, and necessarily religious unity of "all Israel" under the warrior-god of the previously victorious united monarchy, the nature and history of which were reinterpreted (Noth 1943).

This new unity required the suppression of all that stood in the way of reestablishing this perceived past unity; unity required that especially the

---

58. "Edom" appears in a papyrus from approximately the same time as the Merneptah stele (Pritchard 1955: 259).

worship of Baal which was apparently earlier reembraced in the north as a means of opposition to Judah be placed under the ban. This period—the eighth and seventh century B.C.—is the time of the ascendancy of "exclusive Yahwism."[59]

It was the belief (apparently propagandized by the prophets as can be seen in, for example, Isa 11:13-14; Hos 3:2), in the necessity of a new unity, the ascendancy of the perspective of "all Israel," which indicates the emergence of ancient Israel as a nation. The ascendancy of these beliefs constitutive of the nation of ancient Israel was predicated upon two developments, one, political, and the other, religious. Paradoxically, the first was the destruction of the northern kingdom of Israel by the Assyrians. With the elimination of northern Israel as a competitor to southern Judah, an "all Israel" perspective could now emerge, albeit from a southern Judaean perspective, e.g., the description of the putative apostasy of Jeroboam (see 1 Kings 12-13). Presumably, both the presence of northern Israelite circles of worshipers of Yahweh in Judah after 721 B.C. and the subsequent collapse of Assyria during the seventh century abetted the political perspective of reestablishing the perceived past glory and boundaries of Israel, now understood as a nation which had existed as "all Israel" since before Moses, in the time of Jacob.

The religious factor was the so-called "Deuteronomic reformation." The new unity of "all Israel" necessary to save Israel from its enemies required (1) that only Yahweh be worshiped in the land of Israel; (2) that only the law of Yahweh be obeyed in the land of Israel and by the people of Israel; and (3) that Jerusalem be the religious center of the nation of "all Israel." With the kingdom of northern Israel having been destroyed by the Assyrians and then subsequently the collapse of Assyrian power, the Judaean Josiah was free to march under the banner of "all Israel" into the north and to destroy the sanctuary of Bethel (2 Kgs 23:15-20), thereby eliminating it as a competitor to Jerusalem. That these developments, indicating the emergence of the nation of Israel, were perceived *at that time* as a political and religious reformation (2 Kings 23) may be observed from the description of the sins of Solomon (1 Kings 11) and, above all, the anachronistic reference to Josiah in 1 Kgs 13:2. As with all reformations, these revolutionary transformations were also predicated

---

59. The possible existence of a consort of Yahweh does not invalidate the argument for the development of "exclusive Yahwism." The essential point for the development of the nation of ancient Israel was that the "House of Yahweh" be supreme within the territory from Dan to Beersheba. For the existence of a consort of Yahweh, see, for example, W. G. Dever (1984).

upon and referred to a perceived past glory; in this case, the reinterpreted past glory of a united "all Israel."

Given this understanding of the history of ancient Israel as presented in this brief outline, I do not see how there could have existed the conceptions of the land of the Israel "from Dan to Beersheba" and the people of the Israel "of the twelve tribes," "of the House of Jacob and the House of Judah," anytime before the united monarchy. As far as the united monarchy is concerned, it is here where we must acknowledge the existence of some of the ingredients or elements of nationality even though the Israelite nation did not yet exist: specifically, (a) Yahweh as the god of the "House of David," of "Israel," albeit an imperial Israel; and (b) the united monarchy providing the basis for the tradition of the past victorious unity of "all Israel."

IV. Conclusion

Two further points deserve some consideration. The first concerns the nature of tradition in the constitution of nationality. Tradition is not an unthinking reiteration; it must be accepted (Eliot 1950; Shils 1981). There are consequences to the action of the acceptance of tradition. One is that, through acceptance, traditions are consequently subject to constant change—this much is obvious from the history of ancient Israel, e.g., the reinterpretation of the previously local traditions of the different Judges within the framework of "all Israel," and the relatively late amalgamation of local ancestors into a common genealogy of "all Israel." However beliefs which make up traditions not only change, they also generate change; they actively transform the present, e.g., the development of the belief in a "people" of "all Israel" to whom and only to whom the law applies, or the messianic restoration of the Davidic kingdom.

How traditions transform the present can be seen in the development of the image of the bounded land of Israel as designated by the tribal boundaries of Israel in Joshua 13-19. While the description of these boundaries surely contains old materials, the image of the tribal territories of the land of Israel is to be dated probably from the time of Josiah in the last quarter of the seventh century B.C. (Lemche 1985: 285-88). The important point worth emphasizing here regarding the beliefs necessary for any nation to exist is that traditions which bear those beliefs develop, thereby actively influencing the present. They develop and influence the present as a consequence of becoming shared by those individuals who by so doing become members of the nation. They must be acquired (at least for a tradition beyond the narrow primordial setting of the family or the village). An important factor in these traditions becoming common to, and hence, constitutive of the nation of ancient Israel was the propagation of the worship of Yahweh by warrior-ascetics like the Rechabites (2 Kings 10; Jeremiah 35), the Levites and other officials of the cult, and, above all, the itinerant prophets (recall the Judaean Amos was in northern Israel) in the period before and especially after the fall of the northern kingdom in 721 B.C.

The second point deserving of consideration is my use of the phrase "ingredients (or elements) of nationality." We want to establish some rigor and consistency in our criteria for distinguishing nationality from city-kingdoms, tribal confederacies, and empires. I have sought the distinguishing characteristic of nationality in the belief in the existence of a designated trans-local territory which "belongs to" a specific trans-tribal/clan/city-kingdom people. Does my use of the phrase "ingredients of nationality" represent a departure from conceptual rigor? Perhaps. However, I think there are two reasons which justify the use of the phrase "ingredients of nationality." The first is that the actual expression of the phenomenon of nationality does not always precisely correspond to our conception of it. Once again, how should we characterize Pakistan today; or modern India; or the Soviet Union; or, for that matter, Cyprus or Sri Lanka?

The second reason for my use of the phrase "ingredients of nationality" is the historical aspect of the formation and constitution of nationality. Regarding this historical aspect, recall Ernest Renan's (1896) comments on "common memories of the past" as the essential ingredient of nationality. The formation of the nation of ancient Israel was possible because the (not necessarily historically truthful) memories of the past became "common" to, and hence also constitutive of "all Israel." The necessary but not definitive historical ingredients contributing to the creation of a common tradition of the nation of ancient Israel were the spread of the worship of Yahweh during the united monarchy, and the existence of the united monarchy, which helped this spread and which provided a focus for later beliefs in the earlier existence of the nation. A nation is a collectivity of *temporal depth*. It seems necessary and clarifying in a description of those temporal components constitutive of nationality to refer to them as ingredients or elements of nationality.

It might be that a part of our difficulty in achieving a better understanding of the nature of the "people" of ancient Israel, of the land of ancient Israel, and of the history of ancient Israel lies in the fact that our primary source for that history is the Old Testament, which spans the history of the transition of a society from polytheism to monolatry. Even so, it may also be possible that the Old Testament, within the context of a critical evaluation which recognizes a significant Deuteronomic redaction, is remarkable in its portrayal of the formation of a nation and the role of religion in that formation. In fact, it is the very existence of the Deuteronomic redaction with its "all Israel" perspective of a bounded promised land and a chosen people which is our evidence that the society of ancient Israel developed into a nation.

References

Aharoni, Y. 1962. *The Land of the Bible* (London: Burns & Oats).

_____. 1967. The Negev, pp. 385–403 in *Archaeology and the Old Testament*, ed. D. Winton Thomas (Oxford: Clarendon).

Ahlström, Gösta W. 1982. *Royal Administration and National Religion in Ancient Palestine* (Leiden: E. J. Brill).

_____. 1986. *Who Were the Israelites?* (Winona Lake, Ind.: Eisenbrauns).

Alt, Albrecht. (1925), 1966. The Settlement of the Israelites in Palestine, pp. 135–69 in *Essays on Old Testament History and Religion* (Oxford: Basil Blackwell).

_____. (1930), 1966. The Formation of the Israelite State in Palestine, pp. 171–237 in *Essays in Old Testament History and Religion* (Oxford: Basil Blackwell).

_____. 1953. *Die Heimant des Deuteronomiums*, pp. 250–75 in *Kleine Schriften*, II (München: C. H. Beck).

Arkell, A. J. 1950. Varia Sudanica, *Journal of Egyptian Archaeology*, 36: 36–39.

Armstrong, John A. 1982. *Nations Before Nationalism* (Chapel Hill: University of North Carolina Press).

Barth, Fredrik. 1981. A General Perspective on Nomad-Sedentary Relations in the Middle East, in *Process and Form in Social Life* (London: Routledge & Kegan Paul).

Beckman, G. 1982. The Hittite Assembly, *Journal of the American Oriental Society*, 102: 435–42.

Brinkman, John A. 1984. *Prelude to Empire–Babylonian Society and Politics, 747–626 B.C.* (Philadelphia: The Babylonian Fund).

Bryce, Trevor R. 1982. *The Major Historical Texts of Early Hittite History*. Asian Studies Monograph No. 1 (University of Queensland, Australia).

Carter, Elizabeth, and Stolper, Mathew W. 1984. *Elam, Near Eastern Studies* 25 (Berkeley: University of California Press).

Chadwick, H. Munro. 1945. *The Nationalities of Europe* (Cambridge: University of Cambridge Press).

Cody, Aelred. 1964. When is the Chosen People Called a Goy, *Vetus Testamentum*, 14: 1–6.

Daube, David. 1981. Conversion to Judaism in Early Christianity, pp. 1–32 in *Ancient Jewish Law* (Leiden: E. J. Brill).

Deutsch, Karl W. 1953. *Nationalism and Social Communication* (Cambridge: The M.I.T. Press).

Dever, W. G. 1984. Asherah, Consort of Yahweh? New Evidence from Kuntillet ʿAjrud, *Bulletin of the American Schools of Oriental Research*, 255: 21-37.

Diakonoff, I. M. 1974. Structure of Society and State in Early Dynastic Sumer. *Monographs of the Ancient Near East*, vol. 1, no. 3 (Malibu, Calif.: Undena Publications).

Driver, S. R. 1902. *Deuteronomy*[3] (Edinburgh: T & T Clark).

Dumont, Louis. 1970. *Religion, Politics and History in India* (Paris/The Hague: Mouton).

Eichrodt, Walther. (1933), 1961. *Theology of the Old Testament*[6] (Philadelphia: Westminster).

Eliot, T. S. (1919), 1950. Tradition and the Individual Talent, pp. 3-11 in *Selected Essays* (new ed.; New York: Harcourt, Brace & World, Inc.).

Emerton, J. A. 1976. Gideon and Jerubbaal, *Journal of Theological Studies*, 27: 289-312.

Erman, Adolf. (1927), 1971. *The Literature of the Ancient Egyptians* (New York: Benjamin Blom Inc.).

Finkelstein, Israel. 1988. *The Archaeology of the Israelite Settlement* (Jerusalem: Israel Exploration Society).

Finley, Moses I. 1954. The ancient Greeks and their nation: the sociological problem, *British Journal of Sociology*, 5: 253-64.

Fitzmyer, Joseph A., S.J. 1967. *The Aramaic Inscriptions of Sefire* (Rome: Pontifical Biblical Institute).

Frankfort, Henri. 1948. *Kingship and the Gods* (Chicago: University of Chicago Press).

Frankfort, Henri; Wilson, John A.; Jacobsen, Thorkild; and Irwin, William A. 1946. *The Intellectual Adventure of Ancient Man* (Chicago: University of Chicago Press).

Freedman, David Noel. 1987. The Earliest Bible, in *Backgrounds for the Bible*, ed. M. P. O'Connor and David Noel Freedman (Winona Lake: Eisenbrauns).

Fried, M. H. 1965. On the Concept of "Tribe" and "Tribal Society," *Transactions of the New York Academy of Sciences*, Series II, 28: 527-40.

Gardiner, Sir Alan. 1961. *Egypt of the Pharaohs* (Oxford: Clarendon).

Gellner, Ernest. 1983. *Nations and Nationalism* (Ithaca: Cornell University Press).

Geus, C. H. J. de. 1976. *The Tribes of Israel* (Amsterdam: Van Gorcum, Assen).

Gibson, John C. L. 1975. *Textbook of Syrian Semitic Inscriptions*, vol. II (Oxford: Clarendon).

_____. 1977. *Canaanite Myths and Legends* (Edinburgh: T & T Clark).

Giddens, Anthony. 1985. *The Nation-State and Violence* (Berkeley: University of California Press).

Goetze, A. 1947. Review of H. Bozkurt, M. Çiğ, H. G. Güterbock . . . , *Journal of Cuneiform Studies*, 1: 87-92.

Gottwald, Norman. 1979. *The Tribes of Yahweh* (Maryknoll: Orbis).

Grayson, A. Kirk. 1963. The Walters Art Gallery Sennacherib Inscription, *Archiv für Orientforschung*, 20: 83-96.

Grayson, A. Kirk, and Redford, Donald B. (eds.). 1973. *Papyrus and Tablet* (Englewood Cliffs, N.J.: Prentice-Hall).

Grene, David, and Lattimore, Richmond (eds.). 1959. *The Complete Greek Tragedies*, vol. 1 (Chicago: University of Chicago Press).

Gurney, O. R. 1952. *The Hittites* (Harmondsworth: Penguin).

Herder, Johann G. 1782. *The Spirit of Hebrew Poetry (Vom Geist ebraischer Poesie)*.

Herodotus. 1987. *The History*, translated by David Grene (Chicago: University of Chicago Press).

Hertz, Frederick. 1944. *Nationality in History and Politics* (London: Kegan Paul, Trench, Trubner & Co.).

Jacobsen, T., and Adams, R. 1958. Salt and Silt in Ancient Mesopotamian Agriculture, *Science*, 28: 1251-58.

Jacobsen, Thorkild. (1939), 1970. The Assumed Conflict Between the Sumerians and Semites in Early Mesopotamian History, pp. 187-92 in *Toward the Image of Tammuz and Other Essays in Mesopotamian History and Culture* (Cambridge: Harvard University Press).

_____. (1957), 1970. Early Political Development in Mesopotamia, pp. 132-56 in *Toward the Image of Tammuz and Other Essays in Mesopotamian History and Culture* (Cambridge: Harvard University Press).

_____. (1963), 1970. Mesopotamian Gods and Pantheons, pp. 16-38 in *Toward the Image of Tammuz and Other Essays in Mesopotamian History and Culture* (Cambridge: Harvard University Press).

Jones, A. H. M. 1959. Were ancient heresies national or social movements in disguise?, *Journal of Theological Studies*, 10: 280-98.

Kapelrud, Arvid S. 1963. *The Ras Shamra Discoveries and the Old Testament* (Norman: University of Oklahoma).

Kemp, Barry J. 1989. *Ancient Egypt* (London: Routledge).

Kittel, Rudolf. 1925. *Great Men and Movements in Israel* (London: Williams & Norgate).

Kramer, Samuel Noel. 1963. *The Sumerians* (Chicago: University of Chicago Press).

Kuenen, Abraham. (1870), 1882. *The Religion of Israel* (London: Williams & Norgate).

_____. 1880. Critical method, *The Modern Review*, 1.

Landsberger, Benno. (1945), 1974. The Intellectual Achievements of the Sumerians, pp. 13-18 in *Three Essays on the Sumerians. Monographs on the Ancient Near East*, vol. I, no. 2 (Malibu, Calif.: Undena Publications).

Larsen, Mogens Trolle. 1976. *The Old Assyrian City-State and its Colonies* (Copenhagen: Akademisk Forlag).

Lemche, Niels P. 1985. *Early Israel. Supplements to Vetus Testamentum*, vol. 37 (Leiden: E. J. Brill).

Lévy-Bruhl, Lucien. (1910), 1985. *How Natives Think* (Princeton: Princeton University Press).

Luckenbill, Daniel David. 1926. *Ancient Records of Assyria and Babylonia* (Chicago: University of Chicago Press).

Lowie, Robert. 1927. *The State* (New York: Harcourt, Brace and Co.).

_____. 1948. *Social Organization* (New York: Holt, Rinehart and Winston).

Maine, Henry Sumner. (1861), 1970. *Ancient Law* (reprint; Gloucester, Mass.: Peter Smith).

Malamat, Abraham. 1973. The Aramaeans, pp. 134-55 in *Peoples of Old Testament Times*, ed. D. J. Wiseman (London: Oxford University Press).

Mazar, B. 1962. The Aramean Empire and its relations with Israel. *The Biblical Archaeologist*, 25: 98-120.

Meek, T. J. (1936), 1973. *Hebrew Origins* (reprint; Gloucester, Mass.: Peter Smith).

Meinecke, Friedrich. (1928), 1970. *Cosmopolitanism and the National State* (Princeton: Princeton University Press).

Nestle, Eberhard. 1902. *Zeitschrift für alttestamentliche Wissenschaft*, 176: 312-13.

Nicholson, Ernest W. 1967. *Deuteronomy and Tradition* (Oxford: Basil Blackwell).

_____. 1986. *God and His People* (Oxford: Clarendon).

Nikiprowetzky, V. 1975. Ethical monotheism, *Daedalus*, 104: 68-69.

Nissen, Hans J. 1988. *The Early History of the Ancient Near East 9000 B.C.-2000 B.C.* (Chicago: University of Chicago Press).

Noth, Martin. 1928. *Die israelitischen Personennamen in Rahmen der gemeinsemitischen Namengebung. Beiträge Zur Wissenschaft vom Alten und Neuen Testament*, Dritte Folge Heft 10 (Stuttgart: W. Kohlhammer).

_____. 1930. *Das System der zwölf Stämme Israels. Beiträge zur Wissenschaft vom alten und neuen Testament*, Vierte Folge Heft 1 (Stuttgart: W. Kohlhammer).

_____. (1943), 1981. *The Deuteronomistic History* (Sheffield: JSOT).

_____. (1948), 1981. *A History of Pentateuchal Tradition* (Chico, Calif.: Scholars).

_____. (1950), 1960. *The History of Israel* (London: Adam & Charles Black).

_____. 1962. *Die Welt des alten Testaments* (Berlin: Alfred Töpelmann).

Oppenheim, A. Leo. 1964. *Ancient Mesopotamia* (Chicago: University of Chicago Press).

Pedersen, J. (1920), 1973. *Israel. Its Life and Culture* (London: Oxford University Press).

Perlitt, Lothar. 1969. *Bundestheologie im Alten Testament. Wissenschaftliche Monographien zum Alten und Neuen Testament* 36 (Neukirchen: Neukirchener Verlag).

Postgate, Nicholas. 1989. Ancient Assyria. A multi-racial state, *ARAM* 1: 6.

Pritchard, James B. 1955. *Ancient Near Eastern Texts* (Princeton: Princeton Unviersity Press).

Rad, Gerhard von. (1957), 1962. *Old Testament Theology* (New York: Harper and Row).

Renan, Ernest. (1882), 1896. What is a Nation, pp. 61-83 in *The Poetry of the Celtic Races and other Studies* (London: W. Scott).

Ringgren, Helmer. (1963), 1966. *Israelite Religion* (Philadelphia: Fortress).

Robinson, H. Wheeler. 1936. The Hebrew Conception of Corporate Personality, *Werden und Wesen des Alten Testaments. Beiheft zur Zeitschrift für die alttestamentliche Wissenschaft*, 66: 49-62.

Roux, George. 1980. *Ancient Iraq* (Harmondsworth: Penguin).

Rowton, M. B. 1973. Urban autonomy in a nomadic environment, *Journal of Near Eastern Studies*, 32: 201-15.

_____. 1974. Enclosed nomadism, *Journal of the Economic and Social History of the Orient*, 17: 1-30.

_____. 1977. Dimorphic structure and the parasocial element, *Journal of Near Eastern Studies* 36: 181-98.

Schaefer, Hans. (1955), 1963. Das Problem der griechischen Nationalität, pp. 269-306 in *Probleme der alten Geschichte* (Göttingen: Vandenhoeck & Ruprecht).

Schneider, David M. 1969. Kinship, Nationality, and Religion in American Culture: Toward a Definition of Kinship, in *Forms of Symbolic Acts*, ed. Victor Turner (Tunanea: American Ethnological Society).

Shils, Edward A. (1957), 1975. Primordial, Personal, Sacred, and Civil Ties, pp. 111-26 in *Center and Periphery. Essays in macrosociology* (Chicago: University of Chicago Press).

_____. 1981. *Tradition* (Chicago: University of Chicago Press).

_____. 1983. The Constitution of a Nationality. Foreword to *Jewish Identities in France* by Dominique Schnapper (Chicago: University of Chicago Press).

Smith, W. Robertson. (1881), 1892. *The Old Testament and the Jewish Church* (New York: D. Appleton & Co.).

Speiser, E. A. 1960. People and nation of Israel, *Journal of Biblical Literature*, 79: 157-63.

Steindorff, George, and Seele, Keith C. 1942. *When Egypt Ruled the East* (Chicago: University of Chicago Press).

Trigger, B. G.; Kemp, B. J.; O'Connor, D.; and Lloyd, A. B. 1983. *Ancient Egypt: A social history* (Cambridge: Cambridge University Press).

Vaux, Roland de. (1958), 1961. *Ancient Israel* (New York: McGraw Hill).

_____. (1971), 1978. *The Early History of Israel* (London: Darton, Longman & Todd).

Vriezen, T. C. 1965. The Edomite Deity Quas, *Oudtestamentische Studiën*, 14: 330-53.

Weber, Max. (1921), 1967. *Ancient Judaism* (New York: Free).

_____. (1922), 1978. *Economy and Society* (Berkeley: University of California Press).

Wellhausen, Julius. (1881), 1973. "Israel," reprinted as an appendix to *Prolegomena to the History of Ancient Israel* (reprint; Gloucester, Mass.: Peter Smith).

_____. (1883), 1973. *Prolegomena to the History of Ancient Israel* (reprint; Gloucester, Mass.: Peter Smith).

_____. (1905), 1958. *Israelitische und Jüdische Geschichte* (Berlin: Walter de Gruyter).

Wilson, John A. 1951. *The Burden of Egypt* (Chicago: University of Chicago Press).

Woodward, E. L. 1916. *Christianity and Nationalism in the Late Roman Empire* (London: Longmans Green).

Zimmerli, W. 1965. *The Law and the Prophets* (Oxford: Basil Blackwell).

Chapter 2

Kinship, Territory, and the Nation
in the
Historiography of Ancient Israel

Albrecht Alt argued that ancient Israel as a nation should be understood as the union of Israelite tribes before the founding of the united monarchy of David and Solomon. He thought that the territorial unification of the whole of Palestine under David and Solomon represented a change from a national to a territorial state of Israel.

> Schon unter David und in deutlichem Zusammenhang mit seiner ganz anders gerichteten Politik, die auf die Vereinigung von ganz Palästina in seiner Hand hinauslief, ist offenbar dieser unvermeidliche Schritt vom National- zum Territorialstaat Israel vollzogen worden. . . . Die Einverliebung großer Teile des alten Stadtstaatensystems bedeutet somit den wichtigsten Vorgang im Ausbau des ursprünglich auf beschränkterer Grundlage errichteten israelitischen Staatswesens; daß dieser Ausbau zugleich ein innerer Umbau war, ein Übergang vom rein national umgrenzten zum territorial abgerundeten und infolgedessen nicht mehr streng nationalen Staat, kann hier nur festgestellt . . . werden.[1]

Alt described the rule of David as a Personalunion[2] in contrast to the putatively national rule of Saul.

Putting aside, for the moment, the merit of this description of the rule of David and the period before it, we note that Alt employed two characterizations of ancient Israel which deserve careful analysis, namely "nationality" and "territorial state." To be sure, Alt was not the first scholar to employ the concept of nationality to periods of the history of ancient Israel. As early as 1782, Johann Gottfried Herder in *Vom Geist der Ebräischen Poesie* repeatedly referred to ancient Israel as a nation. Julius Wellhausen, particularly in his attempts in *Israelitische und Jüdische Geschichte*[3] to describe the Gemeinbewußtsein, Gemeinwesen, and Solidari-

---

1. A. Alt, "Die Landnahme der Israeliten in Palästina," *KS* I (1925) 117-18.
2. A. Alt, "Die Staatenbildung der Israeliten in Palästina," *KS* II (1930) 45-47.
3. J. Wellhausen, *Israelitische und Jüdische Geschichte* (1905).

52

tätsgefühl constitutive of Israel, understood ancient Israel to be a nation. Indeed, Martin Noth, in the Introduction to *The History of Israel*, explicitly took up the applicability of the concept of nationality (Volk) to the society of ancient Israel.[4] I wish to examine briefly the use of the concept of nationality and the factors implicit in that concept, namely kinship, territoriality and common traditions, in the historiography of ancient Israel. Let us begin by returning to Alt's description of the rule of David.

The United Kingdom

Alt's understanding of the united kingdom of David and Solomon as different than a nation was correct.[5] Northern Israel and southern Judah were "united" under David not into a nation but as part of an imperial kingdom, a "territorial state," containing numerous "peoples," each worshiping its own deities.[6] As such, each of these primordial collectivities obeyed its own laws; they were Rechtsgemeinschaften. In contrast to a nation, these numerous Rechtsgemeinschaften were not united in their obedience to a "law of the land" which, in turn, recognized them, as residents in the land and as subjects to the law, as "related"; rather, they were "united" through their subordination to the military might of the patrimonial authority of the former mercenary of the Philistines (1 Samuel 27), David.[7]

As to a putative national core of "Israel," by which we are to understand an "all Israel" of northern Israel/southern Judah, within this territorial state of the united kingdom, the circumstances surrounding the possible *bᵉrît* between the northern Israel and David (2 Sam 5:3) should be considered within the context of 2 Samuel 2–4. Northern Israel was militarily defeated by David, whose victory was apparently abetted by the

---

4. M. Noth, *The History of Ancient Israel* (1959); *Geschichte Israels* (1950) 4–5.

5. Contra M. Weber, *Ancient Judaism* (1967); *Das Antike Judentum, 3, Gesammelte Aufsätze zur Religionssoziologie* (1921) 45, "The North land joined David only after Saul's sib had been liquidated, and, indeed, by means of a special treaty (*bĕrît*) between David and the elders of the tribes. A contract or covenant here established for the first time the national unity . . . of Israel under a national king."

6. 2 Samuel 8; 12:26–31; following Noth, *History*, 195, "He [David] put the Ammonite crown on his own head . . . and made himself king of Ammon." According to Deuteronomy 2, David's occupation of Edomite, Moabite and Ammonite territory violated the commands of Yahweh, indicating that the image of Israel as a bounded land may be subsequent to the united kingdom.

7. According to tradition, whose protector was the King of Moab, 1 Sam 22:3–4. Was David a Moabite (Ruth 4:18–22)? For the nature of patrimonial rule, M. Weber, *Wirtschaft und Gesellschaft* (1922) 679–723.

treachery of Abner to Ishbaal, son of Saul. Furthermore, we may conclude from the tradition depicting the subjection of northern Israel to forced labor, heavy taxes and the census (2 Samuel 24; 1 Kgs 5:27; 11:28; 12:18) that the base of support for David and Solomon appears to have been Judah[8] and not the "all Israel" from "Dan to Beersheba." The subsequent schism (1 Kings 12) between southern Judah and northern Israel supports decisively this conclusion.

Opposition of the population, in this case northern Israel, to the "census" is common to what Max Weber described as the "patrimonial state," where the rule of the royal house is primarily based on loyalty to that house.[9] This opposition, and the repeated challenges to the authority of David and of Solomon (2 Samuel 15; 20; 1 Kings 2; 11) indicate that the rule of law, especially its consistent application throughout the land of Israel and to all the "sons of Israel" was not a factor by which we can characterize this period. It also indicates in this period the absence both of a Solidaritätsgefühl among the Israelites as "Israelites" and of a loyalty of the Israelites, as members of a nation, to Israel.

It is, thus, perhaps more illuminating to consider the brief existence of both the united kingdom and the united monarchy within the context of Weber's categories of respectively the "patrimonial state" and "patrimonial authority." The various "peoples" found within the "territorial state" of the united monarchy, "from Dan to Beersheba," were not unified through a shared Sitte, Brauch, and Recht. I believe this is much of what Alt meant by the term Personalunion.

While Alt may have been correct in his characterization of the united monarchy as a Personalunion, there were a number of mistaken assumptions to this argument. He thought the nation of ancient Israel existed

---

8. 2 Sam 20:1, where Sheba son of Bichri, a Benjaminite, cried, "we have no share in David, we have no inheritance in the son of Jesse. Every man to his tents, Israel." Also, 1 Kgs 12:16. The administrative division of northern Israel (1 Kgs 4:7-19) may indicate a different treatment (for taxation?) of northern Israel than that of Judah; A. Alt, "Israels Gaue unter Salomo," KS II (1913) 76-89; Noth, History, 212-13; Y. Aharoni, The Land of the Bible (1979) 309-17. Several recent works have argued that Solomon's administrative division antedated an image of a tribal division of Israel, hence, was a factor in the development of that image: N. P. Lemche, Early Israel, SVT 37 (1985) 285-88; G. W. Ahlström, Royal Administration and National Religion in Ancient Palestine (1982) 33; C. H. J. de Geus, The Tribes of Israel (1976).

9. Wellhausen's evaluation of the authority of David, "Seine Herrschaft hatte noch keine tiefen Wurzeln geschlagen; er stützte sie nicht, wie Saul, auf seinen Stamm, sondern auf "seine Knechte," eine aus seinem persönlichen Gefolge erwachsene Truppe," Geschichte, 61; Weber's description of David as a charismatic military leader, Ancient Judaism, 45-46; and David as a homo novus, Alt, "Die Staatenbildung," 38-43.

before the united monarchy. Alt, Noth, and certainly Wellhausen recognized that a Gemeinbewußtsein, the awareness of a shared and bounded Sitte, Brauch, and Recht, is a necessary precondition for the existence of any nation. The problem is the nature of the Gemeinbewußtsein of "Israel" in the period before the united monarchy. This has been a much discussed question in the scholarship of the Old Testament. I do not intend to replicate in any detail this discussion. I am interested in examining a particular assumption shared by Alt, Noth, and Wellhausen which influenced their consideration of the boundaries of the Gemeinbewußtsein of ancient Israel, thereby permitting them to posit the existence of ancient Israel as a nation before the united monarchy. That assumption, still widely held, may be summarized as a separation of kinship from territory, that is, a separation of an image of a "people" from an image of a bounded area of land, in the formation of a society, specifically the nation.[10] Given the importance of the "people" and the "land" in the worship of Yahweh, this separation in the historiography of ancient Israel deserves examination. A proper appreciation of the development of the belief in the existence of the people, "Israel," and the land, "Israel," and the relation between the two is essential to our understanding of ancient Israel as a nation.

Kinship, Territory, and the Nation

How and when did an image of the bounded "land," irrespective of whether or not it was understood to have been "promised," arise in ancient Israel? How and when did an image of the "people," irrespective of whether or not they were understood to have been "chosen," arise in ancient Israel? Most importantly, when was that particular territory believed to belong to that particular people? I accept the argument that the belief in a land promised by Yahweh to a people chosen by him may have been a relatively late development in the worship of Yahweh and of (pre-exilic and exilic) ancient Israel. However, we must not take for granted the existence of the very conceptions of the "land" and the "people," and the relation between the two. At issue here is the image of a bounded territory as a factor in the constitution of a nation, specifically the attribution of

---

10. This separation of kinship in blood and relation by local contiguity is clearly formulated in H. S. Maine, *Ancient Law* (1861; reprint 1970) 124. Contra Maine, see R. Lowie, *The Origin of the State*, 51–73. G. Buccellati, *Cities and Nations of Ancient Syria* (1967) 56, 95, has uncritically adopted Maine's separation.

relation by blood-tie to those who reside within that area of land which is believed to be their own.[11]

It is difficult to see how an image of a bounded trans-local land which was believed to "belong" to "Israel," of a national territory (Numbers 34; Deut 34:1-3), from "Dan to Beersheba" (2 Sam 3:10; 17:11; 24:2; 1 Kgs 4:25), could have existed amongst the territorially distinct northern Israelite and southern Judaean tribes in the period before the united monarchy, especially as they were separated by Jebusite (Josh 15:63; Judg 1:21), Philistine, and Hivite territory (Judg 3:3-6). Given the abandonment of the hypothesis of a twelve-tribe amphictyony,[12] it is also difficult to see how an image of the "people" as we are interested in the term, that is, as "all Israel," the descendants of Abraham-Isaac-Jacob, united in their worship of Yahweh and in their obedience to his law, could have existed before the united monarchy.

I do not deny the existence of northern and southern religious and military confederacies,[13] the memories of which, in turn, influenced the subsequent image of ancient Israel as a nation. Indeed, given the existence of northern Israel from at least 1208 B.C. (approximate date of the Merneptah stele) to the time of Saul, it is reasonable to assume that a certain amount of shared traditions, of a Gemeinbewußtsein, would have developed during this period within the area of northern Israel. This development is presumably the source of much of the material in the book of Judges. However, it is difficult to say when these evidently previously local traditions became common throughout the north. In any event, the existence of such common traditions (Judges 4-5), constitutive of a loyalty to northern Israel among the various northern mišpāḥôt, would have

---

11. A designated trans-local land was believed to belong to the "people." As such, the land was a "part of" the people; the ʿam was a gôy; the image of the land was a referent in the concomitant image of a "people." The otherwise enigmatic Josh 13:1-7 should be considered in this context; R. Smend, "Das uneroberte Land," in G. Strecker, ed., Das Land Israel in biblischer Zeit (1983) 98. The Israelites believed that separated from the land, they would become a "byword among all nations," 1 Kgs 9:6-7. Thus, the people were also a "part of" the land. For the terms ʿam and gôy, E. A. Speiser, "People and Nation of Israel," JBL 79 (1960) 157-63; A. Cody, "When is the Chosen People Called a Goy," VT 14 (1964) 1-6; L. Rost, "Die Bezeichnungen für Land und Volk im Alten Testament," FS O. Procksch (1934) 125-48.

12. H. M. Orlinsky, "The Tribal System of Israel and Related Groups in the Period of the Judges," OrAnt 1 (1962) 11-20; de Geus, The Tribes; R. de Vaux, Histoire ancienne d'Israël (1971); A. D. H. Mayes, Israel in the Period of the Judges, SBT 29 (1974); Lemche, Early Israel.

13. Here, Wellhausen, Geschichte, 24, "Das Kriegslager, die Wiege der Nation, war auch das älteste Heiligtum"; Weber, Ancient Judaism, 127, 130-31.

been facilitated by the territorial proximity of such ancient, sacred sites as Shechem and Shiloh (separated by a distance of probably no more than a one day ride by donkey) and the apparently numerous and inter-mittent northern military alliances. Such alliances perhaps depict an ad-umbration of nationality of northern Israel. Nevertheless, once one puts aside the amphictyony hypothesis, there is too much contrary evidence[14] to follow Alt and assume that "the monarchy presupposes the existence of an [all] Israelite consciousness on which it could build a structure which in itself did not constitute Israel."[15]

That northern Israel (re)embraced Baal (the golden calf, 1 Kgs 12:28–30) as god of the land after the death of Solomon should dominate our understanding of ancient Israel. One concludes from this act that there was little depth or stability to the "Israelite" consciousness, as we are in-terested in the term, in the north between the twelfth and tenth centuries B.C. Moreover, the brevity of the "unity" between northern Israel and Judah, the united monarchy, indicates a lack of saliency of the beliefs in the "people" and in the "land" "belonging" to them, in a nation.

Clearly, in his analysis as to how the united kingdom as a Personal-union differed from a nation, Alt correctly perceived the essential impor-tance of a unified people to the existence of a nation. However, herein lies the very difficulty of our problem: how to account for the very existence of the "people," that image of "relatedness," that "Israelite conscious-ness," and the law and religion which united the "Israelites" as a people? If there are reasons to doubt an "[all] Israelite consciousness" before or during the period of the united monarchy, then that consciousness, the precondition for the existence of the Pentateuch and Deuteronomistic history,[16] must have become salient afterwards. Thus, while Alt was cor-rect that the united kingdom was not a nation, is it possible that the sub-sequent emergence of ancient Israel as a nation, in particular that "[all] Israelite consciousness" the existence of which Alt attempted to account for, was dependent upon the previous existence, and, above all, the (to be

---

14. Summarizing some of this well known and much discussed evidence: the wor-ship of Baal-berith at Shechem; the names of Jerubbaal, Shamgar ben Anath, Ishbaal, Meribbaal; Judg 12:1–6; the "sins of Solomon"; Solomon's sale of land which was "Is-raelite," indicating the absence of a conception of national territory in the period; Ne-hustan in the Jerusalem temple, etc.

15. So A. D. H. Mayes, "Israel in the Pre-Monarchy Period," *VT* 23 (1973) 167.

16. So, M. Noth, "Ein israelitisches Gemeinbewußtsein ist also älter als die Ursprünge der Pentateuchüberlieferung und bildet deren Voraussetzung," *Überliefer-ungsgeschichte des Pentateuch* (1948) 274.

sure, changing) memories of the existence of the united kingdom?[17] Is it possible that the rule of David marked the first time Yahweh became the most important god of the territory from "Dan to Beersheba"? I do not see how to avoid concluding that the earliest possible period for the stability of the conception of the territory of "all Israel," "from Dan to Beersheba," was the united monarchy. This is most important if the existence of ancient Israel as a nation, in particular one of the constitutive referents in that "Israelite consciousness," the image of the "people," was dependent upon the image of an area of land which was believed to belong to Yahweh and to his worshipers, the "Israelites."[18]

Too often the very image of a Volk is taken for granted; that image has its own historical development. In fact, the consolidation and stability of the image of the Volk may occur relatively late in the development of the Volk. For example, the image of the Athenians, Spartans, Corinthians, etc., as "Hellenes" was only *beginning* to take shape in the period from the seventh to the fifth century B.C.[19] We need not discuss here in detail those factors (the absence of an authoritative center comparable to Jerusalem, a religion much more particularistic than the worship of Yahweh of the seventh century B.C.) which retarded the consolidation and stability of that image of the Hellenes. There are two points to observe here. The first is the development of that image of the Volk, the Hellenes, in the land which was vaguely but increasingly understood to belong to them as Hellenes; the very image of the Hellenes appears to have been dependent upon the image of a common territory.[20] The second is the image of the Volk, the Hellenes, began to achieve a stability relatively late in the history of its territorially more local components.

One factor in the emergence, consolidation, and stability of the image of a trans-tribal, trans-local "people" as a referent in the collective consciousness of nationality in antiquity would appear to have been the ascendancy of the "god of the land" at the expense of other deities. Such an ascendancy, and the obligatory worship of the god implied by it, would have facilitated a territorially extensive, yet circumscribed Recht,[21] Sitte,

---

17. Only in this regard, i.e., the importance of the united monarchy for the subsequent emergence of ancient Israel as a nation, may we agree with Weber, n. 5.

18. So, Ezek 36:20, "These are the people of Yahweh; they have been exiled from his land."

19. Herodotus 8.144; Aeschylus, *The Persians*, 401-2.

20. *The Persians*, 401-2, "Advance, O sons of the Hellenes, Free your fathers' land."

21. Assuming some historical reliability to 2 Chr 17:7-10; 19:5-7, note the *beginning* of a "formal rationalization" of the law, i.e., a consistent application of fixed laws,

and Brauch.[22] The lack of the ascendancy of the "god of the land" was an important factor in the retardation of the development of the ancient Greek city-states into a nation. Within the worship of Yahweh, one observes this ascendancy of the "god of the land," and his concomitant relationship to the land, the people and the law in Num 35:34.

> You must not defile the land you inhabit, the land in which I live; for I, Yahweh, live among the sons of Israel.

Now, it should be noted that this passage comes after a description of the boundaries of the land—the jurisdiction of the law to be obeyed by the *běnê yiśrā'ēl* (1 Sam 26:19). If one is correct to recognize the constitutive significance of the ascendancy of the "god of the land" in ancient nationality, in particular, in the constitution of the "people" of "all Israel," then it may be that it is appropriate to speak of the nation of ancient Israel, that "Israelite consciousness," only in conjunction with the so-called Deuteronomic reformation. We shall return to this tentative conclusion shortly.

Alt, Noth, and reine Stammegötter

Let me reiterate my intentions. My concern is neither the amphictyony hypothesis nor an assertion of a general (sudden or gradual) occupation of the land by either Israelitish or Kenite/Calebite clans, although one often observes an assumption of a separation of kinship and territoriality in both. Certainly, the scholarship of the last twenty-five years renders unnecessary a refutation of the existence of either the nation of Israel at Kadesh or a pre-Davidic, twelve-tribe amphictyony. I am concerned with the nature and development of the very conceptions of a "people" and a "land," the former possibly dependent upon the latter, both in the history of ancient Israel and necessarily in its religion such that we are justified to consider ancient Israel, at some point in its history, a nation.

Perhaps one element underlying Alt's lack of appreciation of the image of a territory in the formation of a people was an adherence to a separation of lineage from territoriality in the formation of polities, especially of

---

in the reforms of Jehoshaphat. Note this conception of a consistent law throughout the land in Deut 17:4–13, 18–20.

22. W. D. Davies, *The Territorial Dimension of Judaism* (1982) 17–19, "This notion, that The Land belongs to Yahweh himself . . . expressed itself in the conviction that the soil of Israel was not tribal property. . . . The relationship of The Land to Yahweh also governed the relationship of the Law to The Land."

the nation. At times it appears that Alt adopted an historical sequence of first, relation by blood-tie, and then, relation attributed to co-residence in a territory. Was there implicit in Alt's belief in a pre-Davidic nation of Israel an assumption that it was there where a more "real" unity existed as a result of a "true" kinship through blood?

In his essay "Der Gott der Väter"[23] Alt seems to have assumed a sequence of first the promise of progeny made to the tribe represented by the Patriarch, and then, the later promise of the land to the settlers. He did so despite recognizing that the "God(s) of the Fathers" in the patriarchal sagas were associated with deities of locality,[24] e.g., ʾĒl Bêtʾēl of Bethel (Gen 31:33; 35:7), possibly ʾĒl ʿŌlām of Beersheba (Gen 21:33),[25] and ʾĒl Rōʾî of Beer-lahai-roi between Kadesh and Bered (Gen 16:14). Martin Noth seems to have followed Alt in this separation and sequence in his own discussion of the "God(s) of the Fathers." Noth assumed these local El deities were combined with, or had taken the place of the original "Stammesgötter" of the "(vor)israelitischen Stämme der protoaramäischen Schicht . . . Freilich sind sie nicht mehr reine [?!] Stammesgötter, sondern lokal gebunden."[26]

Alt also apparently adopted this separation and sequence in his article "Die Ursprünge des israelitischen Rechts."[27] He argued here that the casuistic laws found in the Pentateuch were essentially Canaanite in origin having been adopted by the Israelites when they settled in the land; while the apodeictic laws, responsible for the religious and national unification of the tribes, were originally and essentially Israelite having arisen from life in the desert. It would appear implicit in this separation of and sequence between lineage and territoriality was the belief that the tribes or clans had no constitutive territorial reference.

Noth continued this line of thought of Alt by arguing that the national character of ancient Israel was to be found in a pre-Davidic, putative tribal amphictyony. Consequently, he also counterposed the supposed national solidarity of the tribal amphictyony to the united monarchy and the territorial kingdoms. Indeed, reminiscent of Alt's contrast between the apodeictic and the casuistic law, Noth insisted upon interpreting the

23. A. Alt, "Der Gott der Väter," KS I (1929) 1-78.
24. The God of Jacob is associated with the area of Ephraim; paḥad Isaac with Beersheba and its neighborhood; and Abraham with Mamre and Hebron.
25. Contra, E. A. Speiser, *Genesis*, 159.
26. M. Noth, *Die israelitischen Personennamen im Rahmen der gemeinsemitischen Namengebung*, BWANT III, 10 (1928) 99-100.
27. A. Alt, "Die Ursprünge des israelitischen Rechts," KS I (1934) 278-332.

Deuteronomic code as a tribal, extra-territorial and anti-state law.[28] He thought that this assumed tradition of the Rechtsgemeinschaft of the putative tribal amphictyony continued throughout the history of pre-exilic ancient Israel in spite of and in contrast to the territorial states of the united monarchy, northern Israel, southern Judah and their respective laws.[29] The acceptance of this counterposition forced Noth into interpreting sections of the Deuteronomic code, especially Deuteronomy 17 as antimonarchical.[30] Such an interpretation is incorrect. Deuteronomy 17 recognizes the monarchy, although it also assumes the king was subject to the law of Yahweh.[31]

Moreover, it surely is a misinterpretation of the Deuteronomic code to ignore its evident territorial jurisdiction. Here, it will suffice to refer to only one passage. Deut 12:1 states,

> Now these are the laws and customs that you must keep and observe *in the land* that Yahweh the God of your fathers has granted you to possess, for as long as you live *in that land.*

As Yahweh was to be the only God of Israel, the only God to be found among the people and the only God to be found in the land (Deut 12:29–31), "their land" (Isa 14:1; Ezek 34:13) and "his land" (Deut 11:11-12), the law of Yahweh was to be the only law in the land—it was conceived to be a *lex terrae.*[32] The Deuteronomic code was not only the law of the "status community" of the worshipers of Yahweh—it was a law to be applied throughout the territory of the promised land of Israel. It was a law to be obeyed by all those who dwelled within the land; thereby unifying the inhabitants of the land, as subjects of the law, into the "people" of Israel,

---

28. M. Noth, "The Laws in the Pentateuch: Their Assumptions and Meaning," (1940) in: *The Laws in the Pentateuch and Other Studies* (1984) 7, 18-20, 27, 36.

29. Ibid., 29, 32, 36.

30. Ibid., 18, 36. Noth's interpretation of Deuteronomy 17 is widely held; F. M. Cross, *Canaanite Myth and Hebrew Epic* (1973) 221, 240; J. Bright, *A History of Israel* (1972) 224.

31. While guarding against the danger of historical comparison, F. Kern, *Gottesgnadentum und Widerstandsrecht im Früheren Mittelalter* (1914) may be studied with profit, particularly consensus fidelium and "fealty to the law."

32. Supporting this conclusion, note: Deut 16:4, *běkol gěbulkā,* "throughout your territory"; Deut 17:4, 14, 20; 19:1, 7-9:13; 21:1; characteristically Deuteronomic formulations as "you must not bring guilt *on the land* that Yahweh your God gives for your inheritance." See G. von Rad, "Verheißenes Land und Jahwes Land im Hexateuch" (1943), in *Gesammelte Studien zum Alten Testament* (1965) 87-100. The phrase "in Israel" may be understood as often referring to both the "people," "Israel," and the land, "Israel."

and unifying the land, the extent of the jurisdiction of the law, into the territory of Israel.

The misleading consequences of the separation of kinship from territoriality in the history of ancient Israel and the worship of Yahweh are immediately obvious if the belief in the people of "all Israel," understood as encompassing the twelve tribes, was predicated upon (or cannot be disassociated from) an image of the bounded territory of the "land" of Israel. Once again, it appears that such an image of the land could not have existed before the united kingdom. At issue is the development of the beliefs in the existence of a trans-local territory which belonged to a trans-tribal people, and in a God and his law the jurisdiction of which was such that it facilitated the existence of the territory and the people, the nation.

Wellhausen and durch das Blut

Let us turn to the work of Julius Wellhausen to whom we owe so much for our understanding of the history of ancient Israel and its religion. Wellhausen also thought that the basis of the character of ancient Israel as a nation consisted in the unification of the tribes, albeit a religious unification.

> Der Grund, auf dem zu allen Zeiten das Gemeinbewußtsein Israels beruhte, war der Glaube: Jahve der Gott Israels und Israel das Volk Jahves.[33]

Despite this correct appreciation of religion in the formation of ancient Israel as a nation, there exists a difficulty with the succinct phrase, "Jahve der Gott Israels, Israel das Volk Jahves." The phrase obscures what is precisely meant both by the worship of Yahweh and "Israel" at any particular time. It especially obscures the territorial element in the worship of Yahweh. Is it not more illuminating for our understanding of the history of pre-exilic Israel and its religion to append "Israel das Land Jahves" (Josh 22:19; Hos 9:3; Isa 14:2; Jer 2:7; Ezek 36:20; Joel 4:12) to Wellhausen's phrase, "Jahve der Gott Israels, Israel das Volk Jahves"? It would appear that Wellhausen, followed by Alt and Noth, did not consider that a constituent referent in the image of the "people" is the image of a territory, the "land."

The consequence of the separation of the belief in being related by blood from the kinship attributed to co-residence in a territory for the understanding of the development of ancient Israel as a nation becomes clear from the following counterposition of Wellhausen.

---

33. Wellhausen, *Geschichte*, 28.

Je größer die Gemeinschaft ist, um so mehr wird sie nicht durch das Blut, sondern durch die religiöse Idee ihrer Heiligkeit zusammengehalten.[34]

Now, the problem is what is meant by "durch das Blut." It would seem that Wellhausen thought the smaller and historically earlier community arose out of the natural biological relationship. (Recall Noth's use of the phrase "reine Stammesgötter," and Alt's assumption of the origin of the apodeictic law.) However, and this cannot be emphasized enough for our understanding of ancient Israel as a nation, it is apparently with the relatively late reforms during the reign of Josiah (and his größere Gemeinschaft!) and the book of Deuteronomy that we find such an emphasis on the attribution of kinship.[35] Consider also the emphasis on kinship in the books of Ezra and Nehemiah.

Wellhausen was correct to emphasize the ethical teachings of the prophets for the development of the worship of Yahweh. However, accompanying this ethical development (Amos 3:2; Isa 10:1-5; Jer 9:24-26) was also the belief in a trans-tribal people, "Israel," putatively related in biological descent, to whom belonged the land from "Dan to Beersheba," "Israel."[36] It apparently did not occur to Wellhausen that the saliency of the images of the trans-tribal "people" and of the "land," from Dan to Beersheba, of "all Israel" might be a relatively late development within the traditions of pre-exilic ancient Israel.[37] One must not overlook the extension of the corporate character of the worship of Yahweh through the development of the quasi-primordial[38] beliefs in a trans-tribal people and a trans-local land under the influence of the (more ethically oriented) prophetic

---

34. Ibid., 23.

35. G. von Rad, *Das Gottesvolk im Deuteronomium*, BWANT III, 11 (1929) 12-13, "Es ist ferner sicher kein Zufall, daß bei den drei ebengenannten, aus dem Bb. übernommenen Gesetzen mit der deut. Formulierung—hinausgehend über die ursprüngliche Vorlage—je das Wort ʾaḥ = Volksgenosse, eingefügt ist (Exod 21:2 = Deut 15:12; Exod 21:16; = Deut 24:7; Exod 22:24 = Deut 23:20f.)." Note the contrast between Exod 21:16 and Deut 24:7: Exod 21:16, "Anyone who abducts a man—whether he has sold him or is found in possession of him—must die"; Deut 24:7, "If anyone is found abducting one of *his brothers, one of the sons of Israel*, whether he makes him his slave or sells him, that thief must die."

36. W. Zimmerli, "Das 'Land' bei den vorexilischen und frühexilischen Schriftpropheten," in *Das Land Israel*, 39, ". . . theologisch relevanten Gesamtnamen Israel von dem Restisrael in Juda. . . ."

37. For a late date of Passover as a national festival, J. B. Segal, *The Hebrew Passover—From the Earliest Times to A.D. 70* (1963).

38. By "quasi-primordial," I mean the attenuation or extension of primordial attachments beyond their original reference to locality and blood-line; for example, the use of Heim, beyond its original reference, in Heimatland. Similarly, in ancient Israel, the use of "House" beyond its reference to the *bet ʾab* in the "House of David."

and Deuteronomic circles. That corporate character was extended through the attribution of a putative kinship of relation by blood, the lineage of Abraham-Isaac-Jacob, to the worshipers of Yahweh, and the belief in a territorially circumscribed national *bĕrît* with Yahweh.

In other words, the development of the theology of the *bĕrît*[39] may not only have effected a decisive change in the understanding of God's relationship with Israel,[40] but also may have been the essential factor in the constitution of the very images of the "land" and the "people," the nation of ancient Israel.[41] This is especially probable if we are correct to interpret this development as monolatrous;[42] for as such, it would have been a programmatic ideal[43] postulating the existence of a bounded land and a bounded people,[44] both made uniform through the jurisdiction of the law of Yahweh, the "god of the land." Perhaps we may consider, with all the necessary reservations appropriate to historical analogy, this "programmatic ideal" or "idea" of the nation as somewhat similar to the idea

---

39. W. Eichrodt, *Theology of the Old Testament* (1933; 1961); L. Perlitt, *Bundestheologie im Alten Testament*, WMANT 36 (1969); E. W. Nicholson, *God and His People* (1986).

40. Nicholson, *God and His People*, 192, 202.

41. Eichrodt, *Theology*, II, 254, "Because the concept of the nation was in this way detached from the empirical present, and made into an element in the hope of salvation, it exerted a distinctive effect on the formation of the community." It must not be overlooked that the images of a "people" and a "territory" are not "given" in the "empirical present"; but are themselves transcendent, albeit a "this-worldly" transcendence.

42. The existence of a consort of Yahweh (W. G. Dever, "Asherah, Consort of Yahweh? New Evidence from Kuntillet ʿAjrud," *BASOR* 255 [1984] 21-37) is not decisive evidence against the development of monolatry during the seventh century B.C. Decisive is that the "House of Yahweh," so to say, was supreme within the bounded land. For the term "monolatry" in the description of periods in the history of the worship of Yahweh, J. Wellhausen, *Prolegomena to the History of Ancient Israel* (1883; reprint 1973) 231-32; W. Robertson Smith, *The Old Testament and the Jewish Church* (New York, 1881) 282; S. R. Driver, *Deuteronomy* (³1902) xxviii; Weber, *Ancient Judaism*, 133.138.157.340; T. J. Meek, *Hebrew Origins* (1936; reprint 1973) 206-16; G. von Rad, *Theologie des Alten Testaments*, I (1957) 224; H. Ringgren, *Israelitische Religion* (1963) 58; V. Nikiprowetzky, "Ethical Monotheism," *Daedalus* 104 (1975) 69-89.

43. Perlitt, *Bundestheologie*, "Der Austausch des programmatischen Namens Israel . . . ," 274; Wellhausen, *Geschichte*, 37, "Israel ist nur eine Idee."

44. In addition to the putative lineage of Abraham-Isaac-Jacob, probably representing also a territorial amalgamation, note Exod 12:48, "Should a stranger be staying with you and wish to celebrate the Passover in honor of Yahweh, all the males of his household must be circumcised: he may then be admitted to the celebration, for he becomes as it were a *native-born*." Recall Joshua 5, the requirement of circumcision for residing *in the land.*

of the nation of Poland before 1919; or the idea of Germany in the *Reden* of Fichte.[45]

This ideal of ancient Israel as a nation represents a fundamental departure from the patrimonial state consisting of various Rechtsgemeinschaften, of various "peoples" with their respective gods in the land; and it was viewed precisely in this manner by the Deuteronomic circles, although often not without some difficulties.[46] There was to be only one people and one land—one legal (to be sure, religious) community: the people of Israel, understood to be holy, chosen, and descended from Abraham-Isaac-Jacob, and the land of Israel, understood to be holy, promised, and bounded. Not only would both be holy; but, as such, there would also be a "special relation,"[47] a "special affinity" between them such that the people would have their land and the land would have its people. This "special affinity"[48] between a particular trans-tribal people and a bounded, trans-local land is a constitutive characteristic of nationality.[49] The existence of any nation is predicated upon the Gemeinbewußtsein that a land has its people and a people has its land.

At some point in the history of the worship of Yahweh, perhaps coincident with the collapse of Assyrian power during the seventh century B.C., the constituent referents of the religious collectivity were also the constituent referents of a national collectivity.[50] This consolidation of the images of the "people" and the "land" of "all Israel," this "programmatic ideal" of Israel as a nation, may have been predicated upon the elimination of northern Israel as an object of loyalty of the Yahweh (and Baal!) worshipers of the north, and, concomitantly, the emergence of Jerusalem as the unrivaled, authoritative center of an "all Israel" perspective.

Antonin Causse continued this same dichotomy between territoriality and lineage.

---

45. Note an image of "Germany" propagated from Prussia, as an image of "all Israel" was propagated from Judah.

46. The "two Solomons," M. Noth, *The Deuteronomistic History* (1981); *Überlieferungsgeschichtliche Studien* (1948) 57–58; 2 Kgs 23:13; the anachronistic reference to Josiah in 1 Kings 13; the evasion of the true meaning of Jerubbaal, Judg 6:30–32.

47. Rost, "Die Bezeichnungen," 135, "ein Aufeinanderbezogensein."

48. Indicative of this "affinity," Ezek 7:2–7 where Yahweh addresses "Israel" as both the land and the people. One observes this "special affinity" or conceptual "conflation" in modern nationality as well: the word Deutsch refers to the German people, die Deutschen, and to the land, Deutschland.

49. E. Shils, "The Constitution of a Nationalilty," Foreword to D. Schnapper, *Jewish Identities in France* (1983).

50. Perlitt, *Das Land Israel*, 55, the "nationalreligiöse Tonfall des früheren Deuteronomismus," "Motive und Schichten der Landtheologie im Deuteronomium."

Le lien du sol tend à remplacer le lien du sang . . . le groupement territorial tendait à se substituer au groupement de parenté, et le clan finissait par se confondre avec le village.[51]

It did not occur to Causse that the "anciennes solidarités"[52] could also be territorial in nature.[53] He also apparently did not realize that kinship could be attributed by virtue of co-residence in an extensive territory.[54] Such an attribution occurred in the development of the conception of the "people" of Israel especially if Niels Lemche is correct that the system of tribal boundaries of Joshua 13–19 was derived, as a system, from the time of Josiah.[55]

However, a difference with Lemche is that the tribal system was not a program of "national renewal," as he described it; but one of national formation, albeit predicated upon previous events, above all the brief existence of the united kingdom, and the changing memories of those events. This is how such passages as Isa 11:13–14 (Jer 3:18) should be understood.

> Then Ephraim's jealousy will come to an end and Judah's enemies be put down; Ephraim will no longer be jealous of Judah nor Judah any longer the enemy of Ephraim. They will sweep down westward on the Philistine slopes, together they will pillage the sons of the East, extend their sway over Edom and Moab, and make the Ammonites their subjects.

As David had extended his sway over Edom and Moab, so "Israel" "today" (Deut 12:20; note the possessive suffix of *gĕbûl*), a new and different Israel (2 Kgs 23:17, 21–23), would, with the blessings of Yahweh, smite its enemies. We observe in Hos 3:2,

---

51. A. Causse, *Du Groupe Ethnique à la Communauté religieuse–Le Problème Sociologique de la Religion d'Israël* (1937) 18, 25.

52. Ibid., 36.

53. The "Israel" of the Merneptah stele may refer not only to a "people," a confederacy of clans, but also to a territory, G. W. Ahlström, *Who Were the Israelites?* (1986) 39–42. G. Fohrer noted that the Israelite population of sheep herders "von der Steppe immer wieder ins Kulturland wechseln und zu ihm in reger Beziehung stehen," *Geschichte der israelitischen Religion* (1969) 15. Consider Judg 6:3–4; Num 32:16; Deut 28:3–4. See also I. Finkelstein, *The Archaeology of the Israelite Settlement* (1988) 324–56; Lemche, *Early Israel*, 152. M. B. Rowton, "Autonomy and Nomadism in Western Asia," *Or* 42 (1973) 256–57, "it is not uncommon . . . for town and tribe to share a name in common . . . there is even an indication that . . . the Assyrian scribes may have thought that most tribal names were town names."

54. The geographical referents in the tribal names of Yehudah, Ephraim Naphtali, and, of course, Benjamin, Noth, *History*, 56–57; phrases as "Negev of the Kenites" (1 Sam 27:10) and "Negev of Caleb" (1 Sam 30:14).

55. Lemche, *Early Israel*, 287.

The sons of Judah and Israel will be one again and choose themselves one single leader. . . .

An image of the past (the united kingdom and the united monarchy: Isa 11:1, "A shoot springs from the stock of Jesse"; Jer 23:5; 33:14-26; Ezek 37:15-28, "My servant David will reign over them, one shepherd for all"), this element of temporal depth in the formation of the nation of ancient Israel, the common memories of a past collectivity as a part of the present collectivity, may be observed in the repeated references in Deuteronomy to the (previously separate, now unified) tradition of Abraham-Isaac-Jacob (Deut 1:8; 6:10; 9:6, 27; 29:13; 30:20). One characteristic of nationality, ancient and modern, is that it is a collectivity of temporal depth,[56] although circumscribed by the referents to the primordial images of the land and the people.

Conclusion

There are two conclusions to be drawn here important for our understanding of the history of ancient Israel and the worship of Yahweh. The attachments formed to both land and lineage may be constitutive of small collectivities, i.e., *mišpāḥâ* and *šēbeṭ*, and large collectivities, i.e., "all Israel." These attachments may be constitutive of historically earlier collectivities, i.e., the semi-nomadic clan or tribe, and later collectivities, i.e., the nation.

Second, the saliency (and the stability it presupposes) of the very conceptions of a "people" and of a "land," the former intimately connected with the latter, the image of ancient Israel as a nation, may be a relatively late development in the history of pre-exilic ancient Israel. Let us not forget that ancient Israel as a polity the territory of which encompassed more or less southern Judah and northern Israel existed for approximately no more than 80 out of 620 years, from the approximate date of the Merneptah stele (1208) to the fall of Jerusalem (587). If Alt was correct that the united kingdom was not a nation and if we are justified to doubt the saliency of the conceptions of the trans-tribal people, Israel, and the trans-local land, Israel, in that period or before, then when did such conceptions become constitutive of the nation? Perhaps the saliency of the very images of a people, Israel, and a land, Israel, although dependent upon previous events and collectivities (the united kingdom) and the (changing) memories of those events and collectivities, cannot be disassociated

---

56. For the interpretation of the past as part of, and, as such, legitimating the present, E. Shils, *Tradition* (1981).

from the monolatrous theology of the *bĕrît*. If so, then it is appropriate to speak of ancient Israel as a nation relatively late in its history when those conceptions became dominant in the collective consciousness (the Gemeinbewußtsein, the description of which Wellhausen, Alt, and Noth most properly set as their—and our—task) of the worshipers of Yahweh, i.e., the seventh and sixth centuries B.C.[57]

---

57. This paper examines briefly the use of the concept of nationality and the factors implicit in that concept, namely kinship, territory and common traditions, in the historiography of ancient Israel. The problem as to when is it justified to consider ancient Israel a nation is the particular focus of this paper. Too often examinations in the Gemeinbewußtsein of nationality separate kinship from territory as factors in its constitution. Such a separation often leads to taking for granted the very images of the "people" and the "land."

Chapter 3

Sociological Implications of the Distinction between "Locality" and Extended "Territory"

with Particular Reference to the Old Testament

I wish to examine how the variation in the bounded, spatial structure from a circumscribed locality, or, in particular, a sacred place, to an extended territory corresponds to a variation in the attributed significance to these structures. Specifically, I wish to examine the variation in both the nature and the jurisdiction of life-giving, life-sustaining, and life-ordering power. The question is whether an extended territory can possess any sacrality. If it can, then what might be the nature of that sacrality in an extended territory, how might it differ from that of a circumscribed locality, and what might be the prerequisites for its expression?

When we look into this structural variation, there arise a number of associated questions. In what way might the relations between the worshipers of a deity to each other and to the deity itself vary according to this distinction between these different spatial structures, the sacred locality and an extended territory? Above all, what are some of the constitutive, conceptual prerequisites and their corollary patterns of relation implied by the very existence of a territory?

Much has been written in the history of religion on the existence of localities or sacred places.[1] The belief in the generative power of the soil and, thus, its bearing on the present and future life of the family have been widely observed. The attribution of sacrality to the location where one's ancestors—those who gave life to you—are buried has also been widely recognized. These are the life-giving and life-sustaining matters of

---

1. For example, E. B. Tylor, *Primitive Culture*, 6th ed. (New York: G. P. Putnam & Sons, 1920) 204; W. Robertson Smith, *Lectures on the Religion of the Semites* (London: Adam and Charles Black, 1894), the local *Baalim*, pp. 91–139, the Arabian *hima*, p. 156, sacred trees and waters, pp. 165–97; M. P. Nilsson, *A History of Greek Religion* (Oxford: Clarendon, 1949), sacred waters, p. 80, *daimones*, pp. 109–15, local gods, pp. 149–50; W. Burkert, *Greek Religion* (Cambridge, Mass.: Harvard University Press, 1985), local cults, sacred sites, pp. 84–87.

nativity, of "blood" and "areal" descent, of the vim mirabilem seminum as Saint Augustine described it.[2]

People perceive life-generating, life-determining, and life-ordering power in that with which they are familiar. Indeed, in the English language, the common etymology of "familiar" and "familial" underscores people's proclivity to attribute life-generating sacred power through the idiom of kinship to immediate, familiar relations, both lineage and areal. It is not phenomenologically clear what is the nature of one's connection to a person, or a thing, or a locality such that these objects become "familiar" and, hence, sometimes "familial." However obscure the elements of this attribution are, even more obscure is the evident propensity of people to be familiar with, to consider as their "own," and, hence, to attribute sacrality to an environment which is considerably more extensive than that recognized by the relatively more immediately actions of the family and of the locality, for example, the nation. In contrast to the ample consideration in the study of the history and the phenomenology of religion of both the attribution of sacrality to lineage (e.g., ancestor worship) and the nature of the sacred place, the nature of the significance of a territory has been relatively ignored and, thus, requires elucidation.

A number of years ago, Edward Shils argued that the transition from the significance attributed to and constitutive of a locality to the significance attributed to and constitutive of a territory was a consequence of the "dispersion" or the "attenuation" of charisma.[3] Despite numerous and compelling examples of this "dispersion" or "attenuation" of sacrality, for example, monolatry in the ancient Near East, the existence of national churches in Christianity, the vox populi, vox dei of liberal democracy, or the evident and historically persistent willingness of citizens to die for their respective countries—the very phenomenon of patriotism, Shils's arguments and his imprecise formulations of "dispersion" and "attenuation" have by and large been neither pondered on nor followed up.

In contrast to Shils's arguments, the emergence of a designated area of land wider than a locality, that is, the emergence of a territory, has often been said to be associated with a process of secularization or *Entzauberung.* When Ernst Troeltsch and Max Weber employed these characterizations, they did not mean simply or primarily the expropriation of the property of the Church by the State. Influenced by the work of Henry

---

2. Saint Augustine, *Civitas Dei,* Book 22, Chapter 24.
3. Edward Shils, "Charisma, Order, and Status," *ASR* 30 (1965) 199f.

Sumner Maine and Ferdinand Tönnies, they thought that the emergence and stable existence of large territories, characteristic of European history especially since the Reformation, meant that there was no longer an attribution of sacrality to the land; they thought that such an attribution had been effectively undermined by a ubiquitous, egoistic calculation of utilitarian advantage required by the market. The continuing existence of patriotism has shown Troeltsch's and Weber's characterizations to be too simplistic. Indeed, even the consolidation of the image of the territory of ancient Israel was described by Martin Buber and Albrecht Alt as a process of secularization.[4]

In order to clarify some of the implications of the distinction between sacred place and territory and the varying nature of the significance attributed to both of these spatial structures, I will turn to the evidence provided by the Old Testament. I do so because the Old Testament provides an abundance of literary evidence indicating not only the existence of sacred-places and a territory, but also the differences between them. Specifically, this evidence is conveyed through the use of the following terms: *māqôm* (locality, sacred place), *kol hā'āreṣ* and *kol gĕbul yiśrā'ēl* (all the land, the territory of Israel), *kol yiśrā'ēl* (all Israel) and *gôy* (nation).[5] The

---

4. M. Buber, *The Prophetic Faith* (New York: Macmillan, 1977) 169, ". . . the absolute centralization [of the cult during the reign of Josiah] takes from the religious life of the people much of its simple continuity and thereby of its naturalness: hitherto meal and offering were bound up together, now they are to be separated, *hitherto there was everywhere holy soil, now it is in Jerusalem only*" (my emphasis); A. Alt, "Die Heimat des Deuteronomiums," *Kleine Schriften* II (München: C. H. Beck, 1953) 254.

5. In briefly examining the use of these terms in the Old Testament, I make no rigorous attempt to establish the precise *Sitz im Leben* of either the contrasting patterns of relation indicated by the respectively contrasting terms *māqôm*, locality or sacred place, and *kol hā'āreṣ*, all the land or territory, or of the image of the trans-tribal collectivity of *kol yiśrā'ēl*, all Israel. As to the emergence and consolidation of this image of "all Israel," I note three general possibilities: (1) an origin in the north before 721 B.C.; so G. von Rad, *Studies in Deuteronomy*, SBT 9 (London: SCM, 1953) 60–69; Alt, op. cit., 251–75, n. 4; E. W. Nicholson, *Deuteronomy and Tradition* (Oxford: Basil Blackwell, 1967); (2) a product of the court of Josiah (2 Kgs 23:1–3; 1 Kgs 13:2); or (3) an idealized image of either a first or second Deuteronomistic editor (so, F. M. Cross, *Canaanite Myth and Hebrew Epic* [Cambridge, Mass.: Harvard University Press, 1973] 274–89), at Mizpah (2 Kgs 25:23, Jeremiah 40) or in Babylon. Neither do I undertake a rigorous analysis of how the meanings of these terms vary according to the different literary strata in which they appear within the Pentateuch. Numerous analyses of such variations exist. For one, see the appropriate citations in G. Johannes Botterweck and Helmer Ringgren, eds., *Theological Dictionary of the Old Testament* (Grand Rapids: William B. Eerdmans). I do not deny the importance of recognizing these strata nor the attempt to describe historically what may or may not have occurred during, for example, the reign of Josiah. However, the fact of the matter is that, given the current

abundance of this linguistic evidence only confirms Adolf Harnack's observation that "die alttestamentliche Religionsgeschichte bietet den Schlüssel zum Verstandis vieler allgemeiner religionsgeschichtlicher Probleme, die ohne sie ungelöst bleiben müssten."[6]

Harnack's recognition that the Old Testament provides the keys to our understanding of many problems may be more suggestive than even he intended it to be. The individual's attachments to the nation of which he or she is a member and to the territory in which he or she lives appear to have been and continue to be historically ubiquitous, albeit with variation. These attachments may be observed even very early in Buddhist civilization, for example, in the account of Duṭṭhāgamaṇi in the Mahā-vaṃsa.[7] I note in passing that it was believed that in order for Lanka to become a territory proper for Buddhism, the "Canaanites" or Lanka, the Yakkahs, had to be first put under the *herem*. These attachments may be observed in ancient Egypt, for example, as expressed in the song of Sinuhe. They may be observed in Christian France during the Middle Ages, where significantly enough, there were recurrent references to the images of the Promised Land and the chosen people of Israel.[8] Of course, these attachments are also to be found in the history of Japan. Given the historical and cross-civilizational ubiquity of these attachments, we must

---

state of our sources, both historical and literary, nothing definitive can be said about even the probable *Sitz im Leben* of the development of these contrasting patterns and especially of these images of "all the land" and "all Israel." What can be said with confidence is that there are these contrasting patterns of relation and most definitely this image of a territory, "all the land," and its apparent sociological corollary, "all Israel." Consequently, it is the conceptual elements, both constitutive and derivative, of the beliefs implied by these contrasting patterns and, in particular, by this image of a territory of ancient Israel which will concern us. I acknowledge that to proceed in this manner may be overly inferential. Such a procedure is not to be shunned. It is, however, to be undertaken in a disciplined way, that is, undertaken with attention to the state of our historical understanding and the analysis of the sources, but not equivalent to that attention.

6. A. Harnack, "Die Aufgabe der theologischen Fakultäten und die allgemeine Religionsgeschichte," *Reden und Aufsätze* (Giezen: J. Ricker, 1904) 2.169.

7. The question of the historical reliability of the Mahāvaṃsa does not in any way invalidate this point.

8. J. Strayer, "France: the Holy Land, the Chosen People, and the Most Christian King" in *Medieval Statecraft and the Perspectives of History*, ed. John F. Benton and Thomas N. Bisson (Princeton: Princeton University Press, 1970) 312-13. See also the more recent studies, Bernd Schneidmüller, *Nomen Patriae–Die Entstehung Frankreichs in der politisch-geographischen Terminologie (10.-13. Jahrhundert)* (Sigmaringen: Jan Thorbecke, 1987); Thomas Eichenberger, *Patria–Studien zur Bedeutung des Wortes in Mittelalter (6.-12. Jahrhundert)* (Sigmaringen: Jan Thorbecke, 1991).

also raise the question whether the distinction between the spatial structures of sacred place and territory found within the Old Testament may be indicative of patterns of spatial relation which are fundamental to human existence.

1. Māqôm, *the Sacred or Local Place*

The Old Testament reveals a belief in the existence of numerous, apparently spatially circumscribed sacred sites of narrow radius. For example, Gen 12:6 describes how having arrived in the land of Canaan, Abraham stopped at the *māqôm* of Shechem. Here, *māqôm*, often translated simply as "place" or "site," should be translated as the "sacred place" of Shechem.[9] The sacred place was not the city as such, but a venerated spot of narrow radius within it or nearby.[10] The tradition explains that the location was sacred because it was there that Yahweh appeared to Abraham, and where, as a consequence, Abraham built an altar. For the purpose at hand of examining different images of the land, it matters little what may have been the actual historical kernel behind this tradition, for example whether an altar was built to the local numen of the "God(s) of the Fathers"[11] or to a local manifestation of El.[12] Indeed, it may be possible that this tradition and the "J" stratum of the Pentateuch within which it is found are the product of a relatively late, post-Josianic redactor or even author.[13] In any case, there would seem to have been a belief that there were specific sacred localities of narrow radius where the deity was thought to have revealed itself and where one might seek access to it.[14] Furthermore, the Old Testament describes the actions

---

9. J. Skinner, *Genesis* (New York: Charles Scribner & Sons, 1910) 246; R. de Vaux, *Ancient Israel* (New York: McGraw Hill, 1961) 279, 289; S. R. Driver, *The Book of Genesis* (London: Methuen & Co., 1905) 146, "the corresponding Arabic word *makam* is used similarly."

10. E. A. Speiser, *Genesis*, AB 1 (Garden City: Doubleday, 1964) 86; C. Westermann, *Genesis 12-36, A Commentary* (Minneapolis: Augsburg, 1985) 153; J. Scharbert, *Genesis 12-50* (Wurzburg: Echter Verlag, 1986) 128.

11. So A. Alt, "The God of the Fathers," in *Essays in Old Testament Religion and History* (Oxford: Basil Blackwell, 1966) 1-77.

12. So O. Eissfeldt, "El and Yahweh," *JSS* 1 (1956): 25-37.

13. For example, John Van Seters, *Abraham in History and Tradition* (New Haven: Yale University Press, 1973); Thomas L. Thompson, *The Historicity of the Patriarchal Narratives: The Quest for the Historical Abraham*, BZAW 133 (Berlin: Walter de Gruyter, 1974).

14. Consider also the apparent requirement of being in the presence of the deity through possession of idols and other objects of the cult, as, for example, in 2 Sam 5:21; outside the OT, consider, for example, the Chronicle of Nabonidus, *ANET* 306.

required as one approaches the sacred location, for example the removal of one's sandals (Exod 3:5; Josh 5:15).[15] In both of these passages, one finds that the place (*māqôm*) where respectively Moses and Joshua were standing is described as holy (*qādōš*).

There are other examples of descriptions of specific, delimited sites which were believed to be sacred. In Gen 22:3, 9, Abraham is described as traveling to the place (*māqôm*) which God had pointed out to him. Specifically, it is the place where Abraham builds an altar and offers to sacrifice his son, Isaac. In Gen 28:11, 16, 17, 19, Jacob, having awakened at the place (*māqôm*) where Yahweh appeared to him in a dream, recognized as a consequence that "Yahweh is in this place (*māqôm*)." Thus, he knew the place to be "nothing less than a house of God," named it accordingly Bethel, and erected a monument and altar (Gen 35:1).

We find the plural, places (*mĕqōmôt*), in 1 Sam 7:16 and Deut 12:2. The first passage states that "each year he [Samuel] went on circuit through Bethel and Gilgal and Mizpah and judged Israel in all these places (*mĕqōmôt*)." We should understand this passage to indicate that justice was administered at the local sanctuaries at the respective sacred places (Bethel, Gen 28:19; 35:1; Gilgal, Joshua 4-5; Mizpah, Gen 31:49). That the *mĕqōmôt* were the local sites where relations with the deities were established is clear from Deut 12:2, "You must destroy completely all the places (*mĕqōmôt*), where the nations you dispossess have served their gods, on high mountains, on hills, under any spreading trees." This passage also indicates the different kinds of places where it was believed that the deities either could be approached or would reveal themselves.

This very brief examination of the use of *māqôm* in these passages permits us to conclude the following about one conception of the location of the sacred. In this instance, to adduce a spatial metaphor, the relationship between the community and its deity was understood to be "vertical." While there may be a number of sacred locations from which the deity is approached, sacrality was believed to be concentrated at those places. The pattern of relation between the worshiper and the deity implied by the existence of these *mĕqōmôt* was such that the holy was avail-

---

Moreover, despite the evident etymological intention of Gen 32:23-33, it seems to me that H. Gunkel was correct to argue that the deity in this passage has all the characteristics of a place numen of great antiquity: *Genesis* (Gottingen: Vandenhoeck & Ruprecht, 1977) 364.

15. For a general overview of purification ritual and sacred sites, see de Vaux, op. cit., 274-311, n. 9; W. Robertson Smith, *Lectures on the Religion of the Semites* (London: Adam and Charles Black, 1894), Note B 446-54.

able in a particular place, and in each place it was accessible to one group in a manner in which it could not be accessible to anyone situated elsewhere.[16]

Do these *měqōmôt* also imply a belief in numerous, local, perhaps pre-Josianic Yahwehs in Judah to which Deut 6:4 is a polemical response?[17] Do these local places also imply the relative independence from each other of the correspondingly local *Rechtsgemeinschaften*, whether village, town, or clan (*mišpāḥâ*), in contrast to a (perhaps idealized) conception of an ascendant (Deuteronomic) *lex terrae* of a nation (*gôy*)?

In any event, it is often argued in the history of religion and society that at some point—usually assumed to be historically early—the land was conceived to be sacred. Yet, what precisely is meant by the use of the word "land"? There is a sociological ambiguity here which must be avoided. From the above, very brief examination of the existence of these various *měqōmôt*, one may conclude that it is precisely these local, sacred places which imply, perhaps paradoxically, a conception of the "secularization" of the land in antiquity, that is, the profane land outside the spatially delimited sacred sites.

The belief in local concentrations of sacrality, each of which are surrounded by profane land, stands in contrast to a conception of sacrality which is dispersed throughout a wider territory. To begin with, this contrast presents a possibility for consideration. Does the very existence of not simply a wider area of soil or land but of an image of a "territory" presuppose this dispersion, the nature of which is to be sharply distinguished from "secularization"?

2. Kol ha'areṣ, *the Territorial Dispersion of the Sacred*

Instead of, or perhaps historically one should say in addition to the existence of a number of sacred locations each of narrow radius, indicated by the term *māqôm*, there existed the recognition of the territory of Israel, indicated by the terms *kol hā'āreṣ*, "all the land," and occasionally *běkol gěbul yiśrā'ēl*, literally "within all the borders of Israel."[18] What was implied by this territorial designation, "all the land," and to what extent

---

16. Peter Brown, *The Cult of the Saints* (Chicago: University of Chicago Press, 1981) 86.

17. So the inscription from Kuntillat ʿAjrud.

18. As a territorial designation, sometimes employed, especially in Ezekiel, is the phrase *'ădamat yiśrā'ēl*, "the land of Israel"; occasionally the phrase *nḥlt Yhwh*, the "inheritance of Yahweh"; and often the possessive adjective "my" (Yahweh's) as in "my land" or "my inheritance."

do the conceptual elements of this particular territorial designation indicate prerequisites for the existence of any territory?

We note that the territory, "all the land" (Josh 11:16, 23; Deut 19:8) was described as the possession of Yahweh (Josh 22:19; Hos 9:3; Isa 14:2).[19] The territory of Yahweh (Josh 22:19) was the land which was clean, "Do you think your territory unclean? Then cross over into the territory of Yahweh."[20] The various descriptions throughout the Old Testament of the borders of this territory, "all the land," indicate clearly that what is being designated is a relatively extensive area and not a sacred place of narrowly circumscribed radius. The existence of the image of this designated, relatively extensive area of land, the Promised Land "from Dan to Beersheba," is so well known that it need not be further established.[21] I simply wish to note here the existence of this territorial designation, sometimes referred to as "all the land"; that it was occasionally referred to as the possession of Yahweh; and, as such, that it was considered to be sacred.

In Joshua, there are also two other terms which are associated with this territorial designation and which require our attention. The territory is described as the possession of the "Israelites" (Josh 22:11). Two terms are used to designate "Israelites." The first and better known is the phrase "sons of Israel." The second is *kol yiśrā'ēl*, "all Israel." This transclan/tribal designation "all Israel" appears 16 times in Joshua. Let us note here that there is an association in usage between the term which designates a relatively extensive area of land, "all the land," and a term which designates a people, "all Israel."

We also observe that this territory, "all the land," was bounded. In Josh 22:11, the River Jordan is described as the eastern boundary of the land of the Israelites.[22] The borders of the territory were believed to be sacred as they distinguished that which was clean, "all the land" of Yahweh and the land of "all Israel," from that which was not. Ps 78:54 describes how the "Holy One of Israel" saved Israel "by bringing them [Israel] down to his sacred border."

Even this brief examination of the evidence above indicates a conception of the presence of the deity different from what was observed in the

---

19. See also Lev 25:23; Isa 14:25; Jer 2:7; 16:8; Ezek 37:22; 36:20; Joel 4:2; Deut 11:12.

20. See also Amos 7:17; Hos 9:1-6.

21. See, for example, W. D. Davies, *The Territorial Dimension of Judaism* (Berkeley: University of California Press, 1982).

22. See also Deut 11:31; 12:10; 27:2.

case of the *māqôm*. To return to our spatial metaphor, in "all the land" of "all Israel," the sacred is conceived as not being concentrated, "vertically," at a particular place or number of specific places; rather, it is conceived as being dispersed "horizontally," if you will, throughout a bounded territory.

Let us examine briefly two examples of this image of a horizontally dispersed sacrality. In Isa 11:9, there is a reference to the holy mountain of Yahweh. Note, however, that this phrase is immediately followed by the passage "for the country (*hā'āreṣ*) is filled with the knowledge of Yahweh."[23] Here, the establishment of the relation to Yahweh is apparently not restricted to the *māqôm*, but may occur throughout the country. The relation is assumed to have been established through "knowing" Yahweh, that is, through a proper understanding and execution of ritual and the cult, and, above all, understanding and obeying Yahweh's law with which the country is "filled."

The phrase "for the country is filled with the knowledge of Yahweh" is deserving of further consideration. The phrase may be understood to signify that the power of the deity, in this case embodied (or as Gerhard von Rad described it, "sublimated"[24]) in "the knowledge of Yahweh," the law, has flowed out of the sacred place to cover or fill the (bounded) land.[25] As a consequence of the belief in this flowing out or filling up, the outlying areas of the land are envisioned as participating in the sacrality of Jerusalem. As a consequence of this territorial participation in or communion through the law flowing out from the center, there is a unifying relation of sacrality between the periphery and the center, Jerusalem.[26] The existence of a center, from which the knowledge of the sacred flows, and this unifying relation of the center to its periphery are, as we shall see again, apparently two constitutive elements of territoriality.

This image of the evident territorial dispersion of the sacred may also be observed in the juxtaposition of *māqôm* and *'ereṣ* in Jer 7:7, "Then here in this place (*māqôm*) I will stay with you, in the land (*'ereṣ*) that long ago I gave to your fathers for ever." Whether or not *māqôm* here refers to the

---

23. "Country," the land of Israel, and not the whole earth; based on 11:4 and especially 11:13, "then Ephraim's jealousy will come to an end and Judah's enemies be put down; Ephraim will no longer be jealous of Judah, nor Judah any longer the enemy of Ephraim."

24. G. von Rad, op. cit., 39, n. 5; see 1 Kgs 8:27.

25. Here note also the relation between the power of the deity, the blessing of Yahweh, the gift of grace, charisma, and the bounded land in Deut 28:8; 30:19.

26. Here, consider Edward Shils, "Center and Periphery," *Center and Periphery—Essays in Macrosociology* (Chicago: University of Chicago Press, 1975).

temple, the entire chapter moves back and forth between references to the sanctuary (7:2, 4, 10, 11, 30), to the *māqôm* (7:3, 6, 7, 12, 14, 20), to the *'ereṣ* (7:7, 34), and to the people (7:2, 12, 16, 23, 28). What is particularly noteworthy about this passage is the recurring association of *māqôm*, the land, and the people. This recurring association and the discriminating use of the terms indicate a belief that the center (here, the *māqôm* of Jerusalem), the land, and the people are inseparably bound up with each other.

3. Some of the Consequences of the Territorial Dispersion of the Sacred

How does this evident territorial dispersion of the sacred power affect the manner by which the worshipers of Yahweh established the proper relations with Yahweh? Joshua 5 recounts how the Israelites, having completed the crossing of the boundary of the River Jordan, and having entered the Promised Land, are circumscribed at Gilgal. The meaning of this Deuteronomistic passage[27] is certainly more significant than simply an etiological narrative in the service of creating an "all Israel" tradition. Israel's taking possession of the land of Yahweh is depicted as being dependent upon the circumcision of the entire male population of Israel. Why is this so?

Recall again Joshua 22, "Do you think your territory is unclean? Then cross over into the territory of Yahweh." The entire bounded territory was believed to be the possession of Yahweh; thus, the Promised Land as a whole was believed to be sacred. In this structural relation of extended territory, the accessibility of the holy does not depend upon one's presence at a particular locality. The extent of the area in which human beings have access to the deity is simultaneously the extent of the area over which the deity rules. This extension of dominion may take different forms. In Protestantism, we know that the dispersed, yet bounded presence of the deity in a correspondingly territorially extended, yet bounded area resulted in a monolatrous asceticism; the believer sought to order all of his activities according to the commands of God, also the God of the temporal authority. In the worship of Yahweh, this ascetic self-discipline also took the form of each individual disciplining the desires of his (or her) heart. The ancient Israelites also recognized this extension in divine dominion "objectively"; that is, through the law.

The laws which required the clean and rejected the unclean were believed to pertain not only to the *māqôm* or to the people, but also

---

27. M. Noth, *The Deuteronomistic History*, JSOTSup 15 (Sheffield: JSOT, 1981) 37.

throughout "all the land," the territory. Consequently, the male population of Israel upon entering Canaan had to be circumcised to be rendered fit not for access to a particular *māqôm*, but for residence anywhere and everywhere in the sacred land. The failure to observe the law of cleanliness would have represented a violation of Israel's covenant with Yahweh. To violate their covenant with Yahweh was understood by the Israelites at some point in their history not only as a sin against Yahweh, but also as a pollution of the entire land of Israel. We tentatively conclude that it was believed that the proper relations with Yahweh should evidently have an extensive, yet bounded territorial location. In this sense, the *kol hā'āreṣ*, "all the land," the territory, was considered to be a *māqôm*, a sacred place.[28]

We may already observe a few consequences for those who live in the image of a territory. One, the establishment of proper relations with the deity was not limited to the restricted locality; rather, the existence of a territory meant that the proper relations to the deity were to be practiced throughout an area of land, thereby transforming that land into a territory. In contrast to the vertical relationship between the deity and his worshipers confined to the restricted local area, the dispersion of the power of the deity over a bounded territory, that is, the extension of the area of dominion of the deity, necessarily entails the regulation of relatively many more activities of life in accordance with the commands (law) of the deity. The consequence of this regulation is to establish a relatively more consistent unified pattern of life, a rationalization of the activities of life. The existence of both the conception of a consistent pattern of life and the image of a bounded territory were facilitated by and required the dispersion of the "knowledge of Yahweh." In ancient Israel, this included the codification and promulgation of the law.

In the ancient Near East, this law was the law of the God of the land. (Today, the extent of the power of a state is determined by the jurisdiction of the *lex terrae*.) The law would have to be relatively authoritative throughout the land; the *Rechtsgemeinschaften* would become a single *Rechtsgemeinschaft*; they would have to acknowledge the center as their center and its law as their law. We can, in fact, observe this conception of an ascendant *lex terrae* and its center with the "New Passover" (2 Kgs

---

28. Several other passages clearly indicate the belief that the proper relations with Yahweh should extend to the entire, bounded land, indicating that the latter was conceived to be "*māqôm*-like." In Deut 24:4, to do something which is detestable in the sight of Yahweh means to "bring guilt on the land that Yahweh your God gives you for your inheritance." See also Jer 3:1. In Jer 2:7, Yahweh says, "but no sooner had you [Israel] entered than you defiled my land." See also Jer 16:18; Lev 18:27–28.

23:21-22), the regulations concerning sacrifice (Deut 12:13-28), and legal appeal to the center (Deut 17:8-13).

There is another implication which we may observe from even this brief structural contrast between the restricted sacred place and the extended territory. If, in fact, the latter does imply a dispersion of sacrality over space, then what are the spatial limits to this dispersion? The dispersion is not limitless. The existence of a territory entails boundaries; the law of the land has a specified jurisdiction. We have already observed the importance of the boundary of the River Jordan as indicating one territorial limit to the dispersion of Yahweh's power. Note especially the description of the jurisdiction of the law in Deut 16:4, *běkol gěbulkā*, "throughout your borders." Recall also the remarkably precise designation of boundaries of the land in Num 34:2-12. The boundaries indicate the spatial limits of the life-generating and life-sustaining power. Stable boundaries also indicate the spatial limits of the jurisdiction of the law, which is the expression of the life-ordering power.

One cannot claim that territories ruled by states today are the possession of their respective deities. Nor does it appear that the law of the modern nation-state is the law of the god of the land. Yet, it is precisely here where we must proceed with caution and avoid accepting too quickly conclusions similar to those of Troeltsch and Weber. We observed in Ps 78:54 that Yahweh was the Holy One of Israel. W. Robertson Smith observed that "Israel" was constituted through its relation to Yahweh; this is the significance we may perceive in the possessive "of Israel" in the phrase, "the Holy One of Israel." That is, in antiquity, an element, perhaps the most important element in the constitution of a society, was the deity worshiped in common by that society. W. Robertson Smith also observed that in the worship of a deity there was necessarily involved not only the establishment of right relations between the individual worshiper and the deity but also, as a consequence, the establishment of the right relations, within the collectivity, among the worshipers themselves. The most obvious vehicles for the establishment of the right relations among the worshipers and, hence, constitutive of the people, were the cult and, above all, the law of the deity.

Hegel made a somewhat similar observation that the representation of God constitutes the general foundation of a people—both ancient and modern. [29] For both the ancient Israelites and societies today this foundation of the society is the law. Of course, for the nation-states of today this

---

29. G. W. F. Hegel, *Introduction to the Philosophy of History* (Indianapolis: Hackett, 1988) 53.

law, once again, is not usually described as the law of the "god of the land."[30] Nevertheless, all law expresses or stipulates "right relations" and, as such, presupposes a conception of the sacred as the central assumption of the law. This central assumption of a law code, in turn, determines the nature of the subsidiary, conceptually dependent laws. In a liberal democracy, this conceptual center of the establishment of right relations is the sacredness of the individual and the inviolability of private property. Moreover, these right relations among the people of a nation today are territorially bounded, just as they were conceived to be at some point during the history of the worship of Yahweh.

The existence of an ascendant *lex terrae* of a modern society means that a number of previously existing, various *Rechtsgemeinschaften* have become a single, territorially bounded *Rechtsgemeinschaft*. As is well known, this is precisely what historically took place with the "territorialization" of the law, and hence the emergence of more or less stable territories, during the Middle Ages in Europe. Once again, there is a sacred, conceptual center to the *lex terrae* of the respective modern nation-states. The modern world is partly a monolatrous world.

We have observed that the image of a stable territory implies: (1) the dispersion over that territory of the power of the deity; (2) the vehicle of that dispersion is the law; and (3) the existence of boundaries which indicate the extent of both that dispersion and correspondingly the jurisdiction of the law. We have also observed an association of usage of terms designating simultaneously this bounded area of land and a people. It is this association of usage of terms designating land and people which we must now examine.

4. Conflation and Participation

In the Old Testament, we are accustomed to recognizing the belief that the dispersion of the sacred extended to the "sons of Israel," making them a kingdom of priests (Exod 19:6), holy (Lev 11:45; 19:2), and a people consecrated to Yahweh (Deut 7:6; 14:2). Let us examine two passages which explicitly indicate a spatial dispersion of sacrality. In 1 Kgs 9:7–8, note the significance attributed to the land by the Israelites.

> . . . then I [Yahweh] will cut Israel off from the land I have given them, and I will cast out from my presence this Temple that I have consecrated for my

---

30. I shall not discuss but only note here such telling and important modern developments as *cuius regio, eius religio*, and those countries where there are still, more or less, god(s) of the land, e.g., Sri Lanka.

name, and Israel shall become a proverb and a byword among all the nations. As for this exalted Temple, all who pass by will be astounded; they
will whistle and say, "Why has Yahweh treated this county and this Temple
like this?"

Here, somewhat similar to what we observed in Jeremiah 7, there are described apparently three interrelated, constitutive elements of Israel. The
term "Israel" is linked to the land, and both Israel and the land are linked
to the Temple. However, the nature of this relation between the land, Israel and the Temple is more explicit here than in Jeremiah 7. Evidently,
without the land, Israel was "incomplete"; it became a proverb and a byword among all the nations. Evidently without the expression of the life-
sustaining and life-ordering power of the deity (the "presence of Yahweh"[31]) emanating from Solomon's Temple (the center), both Israel and
the land ceased to be what they should be.

The apparent constitutive dependency of Israel on the land may also
be observed in Deut 29:24-25. "Why has Yahweh treated *this land* like
this? Why this great blaze of anger? And people will say, 'Because *they* deserted the covenant of Yahweh. . . .'" Note here especially the apparent
conflation of the image of "this land" and the image of "they." Note also
the apparent existential dependency of the land and the people on the
covenant, that is, the expression of the life-ordering power of Yahweh,
the law.[32]

From these latter two passages, it seems reasonable to conclude that
the worshipers of Yahweh at some point in their history considered:
(1) themselves, as the "people" (all Israel) to have been chosen by Yahweh with the obligation to be holy; (2) their land, "all the land," to have
been promised to them by Yahweh and which must also be holy; and
(3) that the people were "incomplete" ("a byword among all the nations")
without their land.[33] Apparently, the possession of "all the land," the territory, of "all Israel" was considered necessary for the continued life of
"all Israel" as a nation, as a gôy.[34]

---

31. It is the precise nature of the manifestation of Yahweh as an organizing center
of the Israelites which differs so dramatically throughout the Old Testament and presumably throughout the history of ancient Israel and which has been an object of
scholarly debate, for example, the Judges, the prophets, kingship, and the law.

32. Similarly, Ezek 7:2-7.

33. So, L. Rost, "Die Bezeichnungen für Land und Volk im Alten Testament," in
Festschrift Otto Procksch (Leipzig: J. C. Hinrichs, 1934) 141, "Lösung vom Land bedeu-
tet den Untergang als goy." See also, for example, Ps 83:4; Ezek 36:12, 20; 37:20-28;
Dan 3:37-38.

34. Note Deut 30:16-20: "you will live . . . in the land . . . choose life, then . . . for
in this your life consists, and on this depends your long stay in the land."

This apparent relation of dependency among the conceptions of "all the land," "all Israel," life and *gôy* reminds one of an observation made many years ago by S. R. Driver. He observed that "the land is conceived by the Hebrews as in moral sympathy with the people living upon it, and is thus also personified."[35] This personification of the land, this moral sympathy between a people and a land, indicates a conceptual conflation of the animate and the inanimate (Deut 29:24-25; Ezek 7:2-7) as Lucien Lévy-Bruhl would have described it.

In everyday usage, we are familiar with this phenomenon of conflation of human beings and inanimate matter in our distinction between a house and a home. When a house is in "moral sympathy" with a family, it is a home. It has become a spatial focus of the past memories, present existence, and future expectations of the family. The home is the physical locus of the life-sustaining hearth of the family. Perhaps the home is the *locus classicus* of people's attribution of sacrality to that with which they are familiar, for, as such, it is the most obvious environment upon which their lives are dependent. Yet, this conceptual conflation is also constitutive of territoriality. When an area of land is in "moral sympathy" with a people, a "country" exists.

We have observed that this conflation, in this case a "sympathy" between a people and a wide area of land, was facilitated by the belief that the power of Yahweh was dispersed throughout both the land and the people; thus, his spirit, his law, unified both and to each other.[36] Perhaps this is the significance of the term *kol*, "all" in *kol hā'āreṣ*, all the land, and in *kol yiśrā'ēl*, all Israel—that it conveys this trans-local participation or "unifying." (I note in passing that in the Sefire Stele the term "all" in "All Aram" apparently designates a territory including "Upper Aram" and "Lower Aram."[37]) That "all the land" and "all Israel" were believed to be united to one another through the dispersion of the power of Yahweh is clear from Num 35:34, where Yahweh instructs Moses to tell the sons of Israel "You must not defile the land you [Israel] inhabit, this land in which I [Yahweh] live; for I, Yahweh, live among the sons of Israel." Note again that this description of this "animated" area occurs after the

35. S. R. Driver, *Deuteronomy*, ICC (Edinburgh: T. & T. Clark, 1901) 272.

36. A renewed appreciation of such earlier works as H. Wheeler Robinson, "The Hebrew Conception of Corporate Personality," *BZAW* 66 (1936): 49-62, is in order; however, freed from the assumptions of a "primitive mentality" and of an obfuscatory, historical contrast of group consciousness with individual consciousness.

37. J. A. Fitzmyer, *The Aramaic Inscriptions of Sefire* (Rome: Pontifical Biblical Institute, 1967).

detailed description of the boundaries of the land in Num 34:1-12. Territoriality is a structure of bounded, spatial communion.

It is this "moral sympathy" between the land and the people which justifies S. R. Driver's description of the land as "personified." In a more sociological vocabulary, what is meant by Driver's term of "moral sympathy" is the existence of common objectified symbolic configurations, for example, the image of the territory or the image of the people or the law, in which all, in varying degrees, participate.

The phenomenon of personification of inanimate objects, in this case land, is a consequence of possession. The land, having been possessed by the people, is a part of the people. The land is a spatial focus of the memories of the people and of the present and future existence of the people. As such, the image of the land is one of the constitutive referents of the image of the people. The land has become pervaded by the spirit of the people. Once again, in a more sociological vocabulary, there is a shared participation in an objectified symbolic configuration, in this case, in the image of the land.

For the ancient Israelites, this common spirit which pervaded the people and the land and in which the people participated was their history and, above all, as Hegel observed, the representation of their God, Yahweh, specifically the covenant and its law. That a territory is the spatial focus of the memories of a people indicates that a territory, like a people or a nation, is a spatial structure with temporal depth.

Through the act of possession of an area of land, and decisively through the inhabitants' reflection on that possession,[38] an area of land becomes *their* land, it becomes significant; it becomes a territory.[39] We observe an evidently similar phenomenon of the relation between possession, "participation," territory, and temporal depth in modern nationality by our use of such terms as "motherland," "fatherland," "homeland." It is precisely the belief in the kinship of "all Israel" which embraces not only the putative lineage of Abraham-Isaac-Jacob but also the land from Dan to Beersheba which indicates that at some point during the history of the ancient Israelites, the image of Israel had developed into the image of a national collectivity. This is yet a further justification for the translation of the term *gôy* as nation.[40]

---

38. Here, for example, the prominence of the land and its relation to the existence of the people in Ezekiel.

39. On "significance" and its bearing on spatial structure, see G. Van der Leeuw, *Religion in Essence and Manifestation* (New York: Harper & Row, 1963) 672.

40. For *gôy*, E. A. Speiser, "People and Nation of Israel," *JBL* 79 (1960): 157-63; A. Cody, "When is the Chosen People Called a *Goy*," *VT* 14 (1964): 1-6.

From a slightly different perspective, we may observe this relation of constitutive dependency between the image of a people and an image of a land or of its appropriate or corresponding territory by considering the beliefs in a "chosen people" and a "promised land." All Israel was understood as having become a people as a consequence of the common belief of all its members in having been chosen by Yahweh; a people was constituted through the relations established among them in the common worship of a deity. However, throughout the Old Testament, we do not observe simply the shared belief in the chosen people. To be sure, there are those who are described as having been chosen by Yahweh; but they were chosen to dwell in the land promised to them by Yahweh. Evidently, Israel was understood to be "fully" Israel only in the land promised to them, hence "their land." Here again we observe this constitutive function of the image of a land for the image of a people, or for an image of what the people should be in order to be a people. Nor was it any land; it was a land which was believed to have been promised by Yahweh, a particular, bounded land from Dan to Beersheba. The belief in a specific, bounded land, promised by Yahweh, entails an image of a relatively extensive contiguous area of land within designated boundaries, which, by virtue of its contiguity, should be considered one and the same. Just as a "people" was constituted through its relation to Yahweh, so a "territory," an extensive, yet bounded contiguous area of land, was constituted through its relation to Yahweh—it was designated by Yahweh. The belief in a people chosen by Yahweh to dwell in a land promised to them implies the belief that a particular people has its own specific land which is proper to it and a specific land has its own particular people. Thus, these beliefs in a chosen people and a promised land imply a relation of constitutive dependency, a conceptual conflation of the objects of these beliefs. This conflation of referents, or spatial animation, is constitutive of territoriality.

As a consequence of this conflation, one conclusion to be drawn here is that the characteristic Deuteronomistic phrase "all Israel" may be understood to refer not only to the people, but also implicitly often to "all the land" from Dan to Beersheba. The juxtaposition of the phrases "all Israel" and "from Dan to Beersheba" in 1 Sam 3:20 and 2 Sam 17:11 would appear to support further this possibility.[41] Similarly, given the previous

---

41. See also Judg 20:1, 2, 34 where the phrases "all the sons of Israel," "all the people," and "all the tribes" are modified by the phrase "from Dan to Beersheba." As is well known, the terms "Israel" and "all Israel" have different meanings. G. A. Danell, *Studies in the Name Israel in the Old Testament* (Uppsala, 1946); note the evident

observations, the phrase "in Israel" (Deut 17:4, 20), particularly "an infamy in Israel" (Deut 22:21; Josh 7:15; Judg 20:6, 10) is to be understood
as also implying a territorial reference. Not only had a sin been committed among the "sons of Israel," but also in the land of Israel.[42] It would
appear that we are justified in pointing to a constitutive dependency of
the image of the people, "all Israel," upon the image of the whole land
(*kol hā'āreṣ*) (Deut 19:8; Josh 21:43) and vice versa.[43]

This same terminological ambiguity arising from this phenomenon of
conflation or participation may be observed in modern nationality. For
example, the term "Canada" may refer to a geographical entity. Yet the
term "Canada" and especially the term "Canadians" may refer to the
people of (the land of) Canada.

5. Once Again, Law and the Territory

The Israelites believed that the laws of the clean and unclean, the establishment of the proper relations with Yahweh, were not restricted to
the *māqôm* but must be applied throughout "all Israel," i.e., throughout
all the sons of Israel and throughout the territory of Israel.[44] Thus, the sacred, the power of Yahweh, the knowledge of Yahweh, the blessing of
Yahweh, would be infused into the different families and villages, unifying both respectively into a "people" and into a bounded "territory." The
vehicle for this unifying dispersion was believed to be the Deuteronomic
law, which would be consistently applied throughout an expanded territorial jurisdiction (Deut 16:18-20; 17:1-13). Yahweh would be so near
to his people (Deut 4:5-8; 30:11-14; Jer 7:21-26) precisely because the
extension of his personality[45] was the law, the only law which would be

---

"archaic usage" (so J. W. Flanagan, "Judah in All Israel," in *No Famine in the Land*, ed.
J. W. Flanagan and A. W. Robinson [Missoula: Scholars, 1978] 103); for "all Israel" in
2 Sam 2:9; also the "Israel" described in 1 Sam 7:15-17, so G. W. Ahlström, *Who Were
the Israelites?* (Winona Lake, Ind.: Eisenbrauns, 1986) 80.

42. Regarding the infamy committed "in Israel" in Judg 20:10, note the modifying
phrases "from Dan to Beersheba" in 20:1 and especially "throughout all the territory"
in 20:6. As to "in Israel," note the expression in Lev 20:2; 22:18, "Any son of Israel or
any stranger living in Israel." See also 2 Sam 13:12-13.

43. Consider in this context Josh 13:1-2, "yet much of the country still remains to
be subdued. This is the country remaining." See also the phrase "enlarges your territory," Deut 19:8; 12:20. Recall Num 35:33-34; note especially that this passage follows a detailed description of the boundaries of the territory, 34:2-12.

44. Note Exod 13:7, "throughout your territory," contra Exod 12:19; again, Deut
16:4.

45. Continuing with Driver's description by adapting the phrase of Aubrey
Johnson, *The One and the Many in the Israelite Conception of God* (Cardiff: University of
Wales, 1942).

obeyed in and throughout the land (Deut 7:1-6; 12:29-31). Recall the image of the description of 2 Kgs 23:2-3 where Josiah is described as having read the book of the covenant before "all the people." Such passages assert a trans-local, yet bounded participation in or communion through the shared power of Yahweh. It was precisely the objectification of that power through the written and promulgated law which made that common participation possible.

Walther Eichrodt described the law in the following terms: "in the law the will of God becomes concrete and emerges from the transcendence of his personality into the world of the Here and Now. . . . In the law God's will becomes flesh and blood."[46] The law had emerged in the "here and now" in the perceptible character of the people as a whole precisely because it was to be obeyed by every individual as the law of Yahweh, the only god to be found in the land, hence as the law of the land, a *lex terrae*.[47] It would appear that the term *kol yiśrā'ēl*, all Israel, came to imply not only a bounded *kol hā'āreṣ*, a territory, but also a *lex terrae*. Territoriality is a bounded, spatial dispersion of life-giving, life-sustaining, and life-ordering power.

The consistent application of the law throughout "all Israel" was dependent upon the development of an image of a stable trans-local society at the (never absolute) expense of, for example, the legally particularistic "self-help" of the more restricted *Rechtsgemeinschaft*, the *mišpāḥā*, the clan. A bounded, relatively consistent pattern of the conduct of life over the whole territory was viewed as normative, which, in turn, permits us to speak of the existence of an image of a "people" (Deut 26:16-19). Deut 6:25 is explicit in describing this normative pattern, "right living," as obeying the laws of Yahweh: "For us right living will mean this: to keep and observe all these commandments before Yahweh our God as he has directed us." This development presupposes a belief in the dispersion of the sacred (the territorial extension of Yahweh's sacred qualities) up to its boundaries; this is what makes it monolatrous.

6. Center and Periphery

We have several times alluded to the belief that the periphery was envisioned as being a part of the center, Jerusalem. In other words, the

---

46. W. Eichrodt, *Theology of the Old Testament* (Philadelphia: Westminster, 1967) 1.411, 416.

47. One can hardly deny the explicit territorial jurisdiction of the Deuteronomic law, a law to be observed in the land (for example, Deut 6:1, 10; 17:14; 18:9; 19:1; 21:1; 23:20; 25:15; 26:1); a land on which Israel must not bring guilt (Deut 24:4). See also Eichrodt, op. cit., 1.416, 92, n. 46; Davies, op. cit., 19-20, n. 21.

jurisdiction of the center was believed to have been such that it should appropriately encompass the periphery. Indeed, the center designated the periphery as its periphery; and the periphery recognized the center as its center. This is the significance of the image of stable boundaries: they are regarded by members of the society contained within them as determining or properly determining the appropriate extent of the life-giving, life-sustaining, and life-ordering power (Deut 30:20) of the trans-local communion (Josh 22:25), of the territorial possession.

Is the emergence and continued existence of the belief in an authoritative center a necessary condition for this image of a trans-local communion? Was the centralization of the cult a prerequisite for the beliefs in the legal unification both of the various clans, the mišpāḥôt, into the "people" of Israel and of this land of Judah and northern Israel into the territory "from Dan to Beersheba"? Was the image of "all Israel" dependent upon the existence of an unrivaled ascendant center, Jerusalem? Such a center would not only have supplanted competing centers, e.g., Bethel, through the concentration of a unifying authority; but also, as such, it was free to develop as the source from which a consistent, unifying law emanated.

The Deuteronomic centralization of the cult must not be viewed as simply a means for the consolidation of the power of the southern monarchy of Judah over the remnants of the northern kingdom. The elimination of other, competing sacred places (above all if they were also sacred places for the worship of other gods, e.g., Baal) was necessary for the consolidation of the stable image of a territory. Their elimination rendered less pronounced a spatial and legal heterogeneity which was implied by the existence of the měqōmôt and which is an obstacle to the relative spatial and legal homogeneity of a territory within its boundaries.

The perspective of a codified, public (Deut 17:18-20; 27:1-8; 31:9-13; 2 Kgs 23:1-8) law (Deut 13:1; 26:16-19), consistently applied and obeyed, would render less pronounced the distinction between the political and hierocratic center(s), on the one hand, and the periphery, the various mišpāḥôt, on the other. It would thereby have been one element in the consolidation of the image of all Israel.

This perspective of a unified, trans-local legal community, where the periphery, rather than being "secularized," is considered to be part of, and hence shares, albeit less intensely, in the sacrality of the center, also results in the perspective of the periphery legitimately having claims against the center. These claims can be observed in the descriptions of the actions of the "people of the land" and the descriptions of the prophetic denunciations of the kings. This relation of center and periphery is the sociological significance of Deut 17:16-20.

7. Conclusion

Empirically, the contrast between the two bounded, spatial structures of circumscribed locality and extended territory and their respective patterns of relation are by no means absolute. Numerous sacred localities continue to exist within territories the populations of which have embraced for millennia universalistic religions, e.g., Christianity and Buddhism. Theoretically, one would have expected these universalistic and other-worldly religions to have swept aside what are, *de facto*, locations where the relationship between the worshiper and the deity is *do ut des*. Yet, they have neither been able to do so (e.g., the "spirit religion" of Sri Lanka[48]) nor sought to do so (e.g., the "cult of the saints" in Christianity[49]). It is likely that the persistence of these sacred localities only underscores the inexpungeable need of people to seek more immediate solace in the face of the uncertainty and burdens of human existence. People often believe that such deliverance is more likely in places where there is perceived to be a greater concentration of sacrality, thus rendering access to the deity more likely.

Because Protestantism recognizes the possibility of direct access to God for each and every individual, it calls into question why one particular locality should facilitate that access more than any other. Thus, it is likely that the sharpest antagonism towards this concentrated sacrality of locality is to be found in Protestant countries with their national churches, where the religiously egalitarian tendency of the "priesthood of all believers" undermines a plurality of loci of intense and concentrated sacrality within the borders of these countries. Yet, sacred locality and territory coexist even in these instances. Every territory requires an ascendant center. Moreover, as I observed earlier, the individual attributes significance and sacrality to the environment with which he or she is familiar, the primordial. However, what is familiar is subject to extension, or as Shils has formulated the phenomenon, attenuation. Why and how this extension is possible is the sociological and phenomenological puzzle of territoriality and its significance. Each individual of a nation considers the entire territory of that nation to be his or her "own" and, as such, integral to the existence of his or her own life.

In the examination of the terms of the Old Testament, *māqôm*, the sacred place, and *kol hā'āreṣ*, all the land, I have attempted to show that the

---

48. Richard Gombrich and Gananath Obeyesekere, *Buddhism Transformed* (Princeton: Princeton University Press, 1988).

49. Brown, op. cit., n. 16.

latter, territorial designation indicates the phenomenon of the dispersion of the sacred. This dispersion, in turn, required a center, a periphery, and a unifying relation of center and periphery. This dispersive and unifying relation was facilitated by the existence of a *lex terrae*, whose jurisdiction enveloped the periphery. Finally, this territorial relation between center and periphery requires boundaries.

The precise, pre-exilic history of the relation between the sacred places and the territory of "all Israel" is uncertain.[50] It appears that the perspective of the Deuteronomic centralization of the cult was to undermine the significance of the *měqōmōt*. It appears further that this perspective may be associated with the reign of Josiah and perhaps the ascendancy of an "all Israel" perspective. Concomitant with this perspective was what Martin Buber called the "great Protestantism of the Prophets."[51] By this phrase Buber was referring to theological developments conveyed in such ideas as the "circumcision of the heart" (Deut 10:16; 30:6; Jer 4:4) and especially the denunciation of the cultic practices at the *měqōmōt* (e.g., Hosea).

Our concern has been the influence of this Israelite "Protestantism" on the image of the land. It appears that with the sacredness of localities undermined, the ancient Israelites sought to establish the right relation with God in three ways: through their own consciences (the circumcision of the heart, e.g., Jer 17:9–10; Mic 6:8), through a theological emphasis on the Promised Land and the chosen people, i.e., the nation, and, finally, through the law. Do we not observe a somewhat similar development with Protestantism?

A most obscure element of territoriality is its constitutive conflation or participation, where the inanimate, the soil, becomes "animated." This attribution of life-giving, life-sustaining, and life-ordering power to an extended spatial structure is a characteristic of territoriality, ancient and modern. This animation is a consequence of possession. The image of what is possessed has two referents: one, the actual object; and two, the possessor. In this sense, the object which is possessed, the land, is a "part of" the possessor, the people of the land. Likewise, the people become a

---

50. Martin Noth, *Das System der zwölf Stämme Israels*, BWANT 4/1 (Stuttgart: W. Kohlhammer, 1930) 54–55, recognized that such a center was a functional imperative for the consolidation of a "people." He brilliantly, even if at times tendentiously, sought to account for such a center by the putative existence of a twelve-tribe amphictyonic center. If we doubt the existence of a twelve-tribe amphictyony, then such a concentrating as well as emanating center of this "all Israel" could only have been Jerusalem of the 7th, 6th, or perhaps 5th centuries B.C.

51. M. Buber, *Kingship of God* (New York: Harper & Row, 1967) 116.

"part of" the land. This collective interpenetration or participation is a consequence of the fact that the trans-local structure of a territory and the trans-individual structure of a people are both temporally deep. Yet, most important is that the structure of territory is meaningful precisely because it is perceived to embody life-generating, life-determining, and life-ordering power. The life of the people, *kol yiśrā'ēl*, of the nation, *gôy*, depends upon its possession of its land, *kol hā'āreṣ*.

If we are justified in drawing functional parallels between, on the one hand, the belief in this territorial dispersion, as manifested by the Deuteronomic legal code as well as the terms *kol yiśrā'ēl*, *kol hā'āreṣ*, and *gôy*, and, on the other, the beliefs constitutive of modern nationality, its *lex terrae* and its territory—as the translation of *gôy* would imply, then we must also object to Weber's description of the putative pervasiveness of the *Entzauberung* of modern life. The territory of the modern nation is also *geistgeladen*, or as Driver put it, "personified." Once again, this is implied by the concept of territory, ancient and modern.

Chapter 4

The Chosen People of Ancient Israel and the Occident:
Why Does Nationality Exist and Survive?

When considering the significance for the Occident of the image of ancient Israel as the chosen people of Yahweh, one must clarify the nature of the evidence to which one appeals. Important facts have been established about ancient Israel, including its early history, from archaeological discoveries. We know, for example, from the Merenptah Stela[1] that during the fifth regnal year of the pharaoh Merenptah (1208/7 B.C.E.) there existed, in the hills east of the city-state of Shechem, a people "Israel" (and possibly a territory "Israel" as well[2]) who were defeated by the Egyptians. We also know that there appear to have existed Israelite settlements of the twelfth century B.C.E. in the highlands to the east and west of Shechem (Finkelstein 1988; Finkelstein and Na'aman 1994). The existence of both these settlements and the Merenptah inscription may support a variation of the older arguments of the Old Testament scholars Albrecht Alt (1925) and Martin Noth (1930; 1960) that, contra the biblical account of Joshua's conquest of Canaan, the emergence of Israel was likely a result of a historically complex combination of the assimilation of the native population with a gradual infiltration of foreigners, and the military victories of Saul and, especially, David.[3] Nevertheless, despite such archaeological discoveries, our primary evidence for Israel's concep-

1. The Stela states, "Canaan has been plundered into every sort of woe; Ashkelon has been overcome; Gezer has been captured. Yano'am was made nonexistent; Israel is laid waste, his seed is not." Ashkelon, Gezer, and Yano'am were city-states in the area of Canaan, see Yurco (1997: 35). For a recent discussion of the stela and the origin of Israel, see Bimson (1991). The "Israel" referred to in the Merenptah Stela is not to be confused with the putative twelve-tribe Israel, from "Dan to Beersheba."
    2. For the possibility that the unpronounced, hieroglyphic determinative sign designating a people of Israel may also designate a territory, see Ahlström (1986: 39–42; 1993: 284–86).
    3. Noth's hypothesis of a twelve-tribe amphictyony, which owes much to the arguments of Max Weber's *Ancient Judaism*, has today been generally rejected. For a recent overview of the so-called conquest and settlement of the promised land, see Weinfeld (1993: 99–155). For the likelihood for the relatively late, that is, eighth–seventh century B.C.E., development of the conception of Israel's covenant with Yahweh, see the excellent treatment in Nicholson (1986).

tion of a chosen people tied to its God, Yahweh, hence, to one another, through covenant, remains the Old Testament. Perhaps this is as it should be; for our interest in Israel—its conception of a chosen people and a promised land, and its monotheism—as a key object of historical imagination within the Occidental tradition, lies in its conceptual uniqueness, a uniqueness manifested in the Old Testament itself.[4] A brief discussion of two more archaeological discoveries will clarify this standpoint, especially as it bears on the problem of the constitution of nationality.

The discovery, approximately twenty years ago, in southern Israel at Kuntillet ʿAjrud, especially the two jars from around the eighth century B.C.E. on which such inscriptions as "Yahweh of Teman and his Asherah" appear, confirm that parts of the northern Israelite and Judaean population worshiped the goddess Asherah, consort of Yahweh (Meshel 1979;

---

4. These introductory comments are not arguments against the achievements of historical-critical analysis and higher biblical criticism in favor of a variant of biblical literalism. Indeed, far from it. To think that to read with care the Old Testament out of respect for the text as it is and in its entirety requires abjuring higher biblical criticism is to engage in hypocrisy; for to read the Old Testament with care is to recognize innumerable textual problems and inconsistencies. For example, according to Gen 17:9-14, all male descendants of Abraham were commanded by God to be circumcised (Gen 34:14-16; Exod 12:43-49). Given this putatively historically early commandment, we are left wondering why Israelite males had to be circumcised "a second time" as they crossed the Jordan River into the promised land as recounted in Josh 5:1-8. The explanation for this second circumcision at Josh 5:4 has all the indications of being an interpretative redaction if ever there was one. One also wonders, to take another example, just how the worshipers of Yahweh understood why they observed the Sabbath. According to Exod 20:8-11, the Sabbath was to be observed because "For in six days the Lord made heaven and earth, the sea, and all that is in them, but rested the seventh day; therefore the Lord blessed the sabbath day and consecrated it." However, Deut 5:15 appears to give a different or additional reason for observing the Sabbath, "Remember that you were a slave in the land of Egypt, and the Lord your God brought you out from there with a mighty hand and an outstretched arm; therefore the Lord your God commanded you to keep the sabbath day." Clearly the reason given in Deuteronomy for observing the Sabbath emphasizes the element of historical, temporal depth in Israel's center, that is, its legitimating self-understanding; but why the difference in the first place? Finally, given that Aaron's words, upon finishing the golden calf at Mount Sinai, "These are your gods, O Israel, who brought you out of the land of Egypt" (Exod 32:4) are exactly the same as those spoken by King Jereboam of (northern) Israel, having erected the golden calves at Bethel and Dan (1 Kgs 12:28-29), who cannot wonder about the relation between the two passages, even to the point of speculating that this implied denunciation of the latter determined the final composition of the former? Because in this article I am concerned ultimately with the influence of ancient Israel and the Old Testament on the Occident, our primary object of examination is the ideal of Israel as (selectively) presented in the Old Testament, and not the dating or order of one tradition in reference to another.

Emerton 1982; Dever 1984).[5] The scholarly suspicion that Yahweh may have had a consort was aroused about a century ago by the discovery of the fragmentary papyri of the (Samaritan or Jewish) military colony at Elephantine at the First Cataract of the Nile in Egypt, because it appears from the papyri that the goddess Anath was worshiped there along with Yahweh (Meyer 1912; Porten 1968). The papyri date from the fifth century B.C.E., although the military colony may have been established earlier, perhaps by Pharaoh Psammetichus I in the late seventh century B.C.E. (Ahlström 1993: 870). This suspicion was certainly heightened when the clay tablets from approximately 1300 B.C.E. of the northern Syrian coastal city of Ugarit were discovered in 1928, because the biblical term Asherah appears frequently in Ugaritic mythology as the name of the wife of El, the head of the Ugaritic pantheon.[6] There can therefore no longer be any uncertainty—an uncertainty that can apparently be observed even in the second century C.E. Mishnah (Abodah Zarah 3.7)—as to what the term Asherah of the Old Testament signifies: a female goddess. It has thus become clear that fairly late in the pre-exilic and even exilic (at Elephantine) history of the worshipers of Yahweh, elements of that population worshiped not only Yahweh, but also his consort. In and of itself, there is nothing exceptional in this finding; for such worship follows the pattern found throughout the ancient Near East. What is exceptional is, of course, the biblical prohibition against the evident practices of sections of the Israelite population against the worship of any deity but Yahweh. Thus, there arises the likelihood that the repeated biblical denunciations of the Canaanites and their religious practices represent, in fact, polemics against sections of the Israelite population in the service of a territorially circumscribed, religious and necessarily legal, relative homogeneity that, in turn, may indicate the existence of a nation.

The conceptual innovation of an exclusive monolatry and eventually monotheism was most likely to have been a development relatively late in Israelite history, that is, as a consequence of the activity of the prophets and the policies of national consolidation carried out during the reign of King Josiah (640–609 B.C.E.). Josiah's policies of allegiance to the one Yahweh, in compliance with the newly discovered Book of Law (2 Kgs 22:8) containing Yahweh's words reportedly not obeyed by Josiah's ancestors, the "new covenant" (2 Kgs 23:2), that required Josiah to expel the images of Asherah from the temple in Jerusalem and destroy them

---

5. For a brief overview of the controversy over the interpretation of Asherah, see Smith (1990: 92–94).

6. The Ugaritic mythology appears in translation in Coogan (1978).

(2 Kgs 23:6, 14) are, according to scholarly consensus, the laws of the covenant of Deuteronomy.[7] There, too, the destruction of the Asherah was commanded (Deut 12:2), for "Yahweh is [Israel's] God, Yahweh alone" (Deut 6:4).

Understanding ancient Israel as a nation certainly involves the problem of historically dating the so-called monolatrous and monotheistic theology of the covenant between Yahweh and his people, Israel, chosen by him to dwell in a land promised to them by him. It involves the determination of the historical setting and reality of the biblical description of Josiah's policies (and before Josiah, those of Hezekiah and Jehoshaphat), and the religious innovations associated with them. The historical reality of those policies and innovations is not necessarily the same as their description; that is, there is likely a distinction between Josiah's national policies and their idealized, post-exilic description as we have it before us in 2 Kings 22–23. The putatively 300-year earlier prophecy of Josiah's policies (1 Kgs 13:1–3) makes the necessity of this distinction clear. Indeed, the Old Testament itself, especially the so-called Deuteronomistic history of Judges through 2 Kings (Noth 1981 [1943]) is clearly a theological statement (hence, inner-Israelite polemic) containing within it a considerable amount of exegesis.[8] However, because our concern here is the influence of the image of ancient Israel as a nation on the subsequent traditions of the Occident, we can afford the otherwise questionable standpoint of remaining primarily within the description itself.

A number of conceptual developments that indicate the consolidation of an image of a symbolic center capable of sustaining the nation of Israel can be discerned (Grosby 1991 [in this volume, pp. 13–51]). First, there is the propagation of what justifiably can be viewed as national traditions. In 2 Kgs 23:21, for example, Josiah is described as commanding "all the people [to] keep the passover to the Lord your God as prescribed in this [newly discovered] book of the covenant."[9] The passover is further described as being one which "had not been kept since the days of the judges" before the reign of David. It is likely that this new passover of the recently discovered book of the covenant represents the completion of the transformation of previously distinct, early agricultural festivals of

<hr>

7. For the relation between the Book of Law discovered during the reign of Josiah and Deuteronomy, see von Rad (1948), Nicholson (1967), Weinfeld (1972), and recently Levinson (1997).

8. For commentary internal to the Old Testament, see Fishbane (1985).

9. For an apparent earlier attempt at such a reformation during the reign of Hezekiah, see 2 Chr 30:1, 5–6.

the feast of the unleavened bread and the paschal slaughter by combining them into the national festival of the exodus from Egypt (Levinson 1997: 53–97). Such a radical transformation of both the passover and the exodus (Deut 16:1–8) receives its legitimacy by being sanctioned by Moses—this time, according to Deuteronomy, at Mount Horeb in the land of Moab, instead of at Mount Sinai. Second, Deuteronomy, in contrast to Exodus (Exod 20:24), commands a centralization of the cult, one consequence of which would have been a regularization of religious practices in the service of a consistent monolatry propagated by the center. For example, Deuteronomy (12:2–5, 13–14) states:

> you must demolish completely all the places where the nations whom you are about to dispossess served their gods, on the mountain height, on the hills, and under every leafy tree [note well, at those locations where Genesis describes Abraham, Isaac and Jacob erecting altars]. Break down their altars, smash their pillars, burn down their Asherahs with fire, and hew down the idols of their gods, and thus blot out their name from their places.[10] You shall not worship the Lord your God in such ways. But you shall seek the place [Jerusalem] that the Lord your God will choose out of all your tribes as his habitation to put his name there. . . . Take care that you do not offer your burnt offerings at any place you happen to see. But only at the place that the Lord will choose in one of your tribes. . . .

Third, there are several policies that, when taken together, represent a rationalization of a territorially expansive, yet bounded law: a national law of the land. The law of the land (Deut 12:1) was to be proclaimed every seventh year in public before "all Israel—men, women, and children, as well as the aliens residing in your towns" (Deut 31:11–12).[11] The law was to be written down "very clearly" (Deut 27:1–8) for all to read and know. One obvious consequence of committing the law to writing and its periodic proclamation in public was its stabilization such that a community of law might emerge. Further elements of the rationalization of the law are observed in rules of evidence (Deut 17:4) that include the requirement of two or more witnesses to sustain a charge of any crime or wrongdoing (Deut 19:15); and the establishment of what appears to have been a professional judiciary. Deuteronomy (16:18–19) commands the appointment throughout Israel of judges and officials who "must neither show partiality nor accept bribes."[12] Perhaps indicative of the establish-

---

10. For Josiah's actions corresponding to this commandment, see 2 Kgs 23:4–20.

11. Jehoshaphat is described, in 2 Chr 17:7–9, as sending his officials through all the cities of Judah teaching the law to the people.

12. See also the description of Jehoshaphat's appointment of judges in 2 Chr 19:5–11.

ment of a state judiciary with the attendant rationalization of evidentiary procedure (in contrast to the procedurally irrational trial by ordeal, as described in Num 5:16–22) are Deuteronomy's (1:13) qualifications for such judges that they be "wise, discerning, and reputable" and not, as in Exod 18:21, "god-fearing" (Fishbane 1985: 245). Moreover, cases that proved to be too difficult for the local courts to decide were to be judged at the center (Deut 17:8–9), a requirement indicating a judicial hierarchy.

These conceptual developments resulted in the image of a relatively uniform national culture by undermining the primacy of the legal and religious heterogeneity of the previously somewhat distinct local communities of the bêt 'āb (the house of the father) and the mišpāḥâ (the clan) through incorporating their traditions into that of the nation (e.g., the national kinship structure of Abraham-Isaac-and-Jacob) (Grosby 1993a [in this volume, pp. 52–68]; 1993b [in this volume, pp. 69–91]).[13] The depiction of the national center is made complete when the periphery is described in 2 Kgs 23:1–3 as being part of the center through no less than a national ratification of the covenant.[14]

> Then the king [Josiah] directed that all the elders of Judah and Jerusalem should be gathered to him. The king went up to the house of the Lord, and with him went all the people of Judah, all the inhabitants of Jerusalem, the priests, the prophets, and all the people, both small and great; he read in their hearing all the words of the book of the covenant that had been found in the house of the Lord. The king stood by the pillar and made a covenant before the Lord, to follow the Lord, keeping his commandments, his decrees, and his statutes, with all his heart and all his soul, to perform the words of this covenant that were written in this book. All the people joined in the covenant.

Focusing our attention on such conceptual developments lays the basis for pursuing a related problem: What might an examination of the center of the nation—suggestively referred to as the "navel" in a theoretically clarifying exchange (Gellner 1996; Smith 1996a; 1996b)—of Israel tell us

---

13. It seems likely that the absence of any reference to Abraham in, for example, the (archaic?) poetry of Gen 49:2–27, and the pre-exilic prophets (with the exception of Jer 33:26) points to a consolidation of the image of the kinship structure of Abraham-Isaac-and-Jacob relatively late in the history of ancient Israel. A critical study of the consolidation of the traditions constitutive of the Israelite center confirms in the most striking fashion Renan's (1996) point about the selective receptivity and transformation of tradition.

14. In this regard, attention should also be paid to the reference to the assembly in 2 Chr 30:2. The incorporation of all the people into the center, roughly suggestive of the modern conceptions of equality before the law and citizenship, is clearest in the national covenant ceremony as described at Josh 24:25–27.

about the constitution of nationality in general? To what extent are the conceptual developments contained within Deuteronomy prototypical for the constitution of nationality?

The second archaeological discovery has to do with the conception of the covenant itself. Archaeological research has uncovered numerous Hittite, neo-Assyrian, and Aramaic treaties and loyalty oaths between states and between king and vassal that appear to have a fixed structure: identification of the covenant giver; historical prologue; stipulations; provision for deposit of the covenant and periodic public reading; ratification ceremony; and imposition of curses. Many scholars think that this structure provided the pattern on which the central covenantal traditions and texts of the Old Testament between Yahweh and his people (Exodus 20-24; 34:10-28; much of Deuteronomy; Josh 24:1-28) were based; this is formulaically expressed as King-vassal: Yahweh-chosen people of Israel.[15]

Whatever similarities may exist between such ancient Near Eastern treaties and oaths and the covenantal texts of the Old Testament, our overriding interest in Israel is, once again, in the various ways it decisively departs from the traditions of the Egyptian, Hittite, and Mesopotamian civilizations, above all, in its innovative conception of a covenant between a god, and only one god, and his people chosen to dwell in a land promised by him to them. Nowhere is this departure clearer than in the magnificent rationalization of the conception of the covenantal relation between Yahweh and his people found in Amos 3:2: "You [Israel] only have I [Yahweh] known of all the families of the earth; therefore I will punish you for all your iniquities." This rationalization within the sphere of religion[16] consists in the fact that in the face of the military defeat of the northern kingdom of Israel by the Assyrians in 722 B.C.E. under Sargon II, Israel could consistently maintain its worship of Yahweh only if the unconditional (or as Julius Wellhausen [1973 (1881)] formulated it, "natural") covenantal relation between Yahweh and his people (e.g., Gen 12:1-3; 15:17-18; 17:7, 19; Exod 6:2-8; Deut 4:31; 2 Sam 7:8-29; cf. Lev 26:44-45) was now understood as being conditional upon the criterion

---

15. Of the enormous literature on this topic, I cite only McCarthy (1978), Weinfeld (1972), Davidson (1989), and the extensive, if contentious, overview by Mendenhall (1992). Mention should also be made of seemingly different, non-theocentric covenantal traditions in the history of ancient Israel, for example, 2 Sam 2:4, where the people of Judah first proclaim David king over the house of Judah (when Ishbaal—"man of Baal," note well—was king over Israel, 2 Sam 2:8-10); and especially 2 Sam 5:1-3, where David is subsequently proclaimed king over "all Israel."

16. For the conception of rationalization within different autonomous "worlds" of human activity, see Simmel (1918) and Weber (1946).

of whether or not Israel was righteous. If the conception of the covenantal relation had remained unconditional, then the military defeat of Israel could have only signified the defeat of its god, Yahweh, by the evidently more powerful Assyrian deities. For Amos, "to know" (to enter into covenant with) Yahweh was to recognize relational criteria that transcended, hence conditioned, Yahweh's choice of Abraham and his descendants.[17] Thus, it became possible to understand the Assyrians as Yahweh's rod (Isa 10:5) used to punish an unworthy Israel. Here we see that conceptually creative potential which has been described by various scholars as "the demagicalisation of the world" (Weber 1952 [1921]), "the axial age" (Jaspers 1949; cf. Eisenstadt 1986), "the great Protestantism of the prophets" (Buber 1967 [1932]: 116), and whose subsequent unfolding in the history of the Occident would result in such ideas as inscrutable Providence; the cunning of reason; and, in contrast to the recent, facile, and so grossly one-sided as to be inaccurate, description of the tradition of American liberal democracy as being "universalistic," the manifest destiny of the American nation (Grosby 1993c [[in this volume, pp. 213–234]]).

Considerable caution must be employed if one is to understand properly the significance of this innovative departure of the Israelite prophets from the covenantal tradition of the ancient Near East to the cosmological and ethical "transcendence" of human affairs as implied by Amos 3:2 and 9:7, and, of course, Gen 1–2:3 (and the apparent commentary on the latter at Isa 40:28; 45:18–19). The transcendence was never unequivocal, for the primordial beliefs in a chosen people and promised land were not forever shattered by this conceptual development; rather they continued to exist, indeed, were occasionally forcefully reasserted, as is clear from the emphasis on kinship found in Ezra, Nehemiah, and the very existence of Israel today.[18] This uneasy combination of primordial and universal beliefs has made the Israelite and later Jewish worship of Yahweh a conceptually rich element in the Occidental tradition, preoccupied, as it rightly has been, with the relation between the one and the many, the unique and the universal.

---

17. Further elaboration of the conditional covenant is observed in Deuteronomy 28–30, where Israel's life depends upon its choice to serve Yahweh's commandments, decrees, and ordinances.

18. And for the rabbinic period as well, as the Palestinian rabbis, who dwelt in the promised land, sought to undermine the authority claimed by the Babylonian rabbis whose life outside the land was, as such, considered by the former to be illegitimate, see Gafni (1997). Subsequently, there is also the well-known example of Judah Halevi's (1130–40 c.e.) argument for the primacy of the people and land of Israel (e.g., Halevi, 2.8–24; 5.23). On Halevi and the *Kuzari*, see Silman (1995).

This latter recognition raises again the nature of the center of Israel as we know it from the Old Testament. Earlier we observed, in passing, how one consequence of the activity of the prophets from Amos to Ezekiel (cf. Williamson 1989) and the Josianic reformation, was the consolidation of an image of a relatively homogeneous center out of previous (above all, the glorious, if brief, united monarchy of David and Solomon) and local traditions such that there existed a nation of ancient Israel. Now, however, we must also recognize that contained within this center are heterogeneous orientations: both primordial and universal. There are the primordial attachments to kinship and land coexisting with the rationalization of both law and religion. We are thus confronted with the following problems. What is the nature of these orientations and the relation between them such that there existed a stable center, capable of sustaining a relatively homogeneous national culture? What might the answers to these questions tell us about nationality in general? Are the heterogeneous orientations found within the Israelite center homologous to the relation between "ethnie" and state (the latter bearing the rationalization of the law such that citizenship exists) in the modern nation, as described by Anthony Smith (1986; 1998) and Dominique Schnapper (1998)?

Such questions are not new. The assumption running throughout the history of the human sciences is that there exists a symbolic complex that is constitutive of the center (or Geist) of the nation (Freyer 1998). There has been an unnecessary tendency in the human sciences to view this core symbolic complex as uniform; at least that is how I understand the most profound expression of that tendency, namely G. W. F. Hegel's introduction to the *Philosophy of History* (1956 [1837]) and his *Philosophy of Right*, where the orientations within the center are viewed as "moments" in the realization of reason. Once again, an examination of the Old Testament and the history of ancient Israel reveals, in contrast, that the Israelite center consisted of a plurality of heterogeneous orientations.[19] To the problem of examining further the orientations within the

---

19. Herder (1968: 100) appeared to have recognized this heterogeneous plurality of orientations as well, "Forms of government refer to a very different maximum [of greatness], from that of beautiful morals, or a pathetic oration; notwithstanding, at bottom, all things in any nation have a certain connection, if it be only that of exclusion and limitation." My concern here is not the commonplace recognition of a plurality of orientations among nations, nor the commonplace yet morally pressing problem of a relativism arising from them. Rather, once again, the concern is one of ascertaining the nature of the formative, heterogeneous orientations constitutive of the symbolic center, the relation between them such that a stable center exists, and the problems of life that each seeks to address.

Israelite center and the relations between them, we add the problem of clarifying the problems of life with which each is concerned.

To pursue such problems, especially the latter, is to raise the possibility of cognitive orientations that are fundamental to human existence— what Eichrodt (1967: 349) referred to as "the natural goods of life." To raise this possibility may present more of a problem than a solution. Nonetheless, if one is to understand better the significance of nationality, then it is a problem that demands consideration, rather than dismissal under today's fashionable opprobrium of being metaphysical or "essentialist." It is within this context that we consider Yahweh's choice of Abraham, that is, Israel as a chosen people.

II

How are we to understand the description of Yahweh's choice of Abraham, and what might it tell us about nationality in general? We know from Genesis 11 that Abraham was of the tenth generation in the line of Noah through Shem; and, from Genesis 5, that Noah was of the tenth generation descended from Adam. Thus, Yahweh's choice of Abraham was presented as indicating the cosmological significance of a particular lineage: Adam had received God's blessing of life ("to be fruitful and multiply," Gen 1:28); his descendant the "new Adam," Noah, had received the same blessing (Gen 9:1); and finally, Noah's descendant the "newer Adam," Abraham, did as well (Gen 12:2; 15:15; 17:6) (cf. Cassuto 1992: 291). Thus, the putative lineage of Adam-Noah-Abraham-Isaac-and-Jacob was distinct from other nations because it was understood as standing in unique relation to God as the recipient of God's blessing of life and that upon which life depends, a bountiful land. As such, Israel[20] was understood by the worshipers of Yahweh to be the focal point of creation and human history, the former described in the primeval, mythic account of Genesis 1 through 11, and the latter beginning with Abram in Genesis 12. Such a self-understanding, the collective self-consciousness constitutive of a nation's symbolic center, contains one of the elements characteristic of nationality, namely, an assertion that legitimates an existence distinct from that of other nations. It is the symbolic vehicle of the individual nation's will to existence (Eliade 1987; Smith 1986: 22–31; cf. Armstrong 1982).

---

20. Characteristic of nationality, the term refers to both people and land (Rost 1934: 135). This terminological conflation indicates that the image of a territory is a constitutive reference in the collective self-consciousness of a "people" (Grosby 1995 [in this volume, pp. 191–212]).

However, in the case of ancient Israel, the assertion of distinctiveness reaches its ultimate grounding by being understood as integral to the order of the universe. There appears to be a homology between Yahweh and Israel: as Yahweh had created the world and life out of the void, so Israel signifies the establishment of the salvific collectivity against the evil forces of chaos (the nation's enemies) and death (Levenson 1994; Fishbane 1985: 350-79). The homology is legitimated by Yahweh's choice of Israel, that is, the promise of life by the creator of life. This assertion of distinctiveness constitutive of self-consciousness, of self-legitimation, indicates that there is an element of sacrality in the constitution of nationality, of which the complex of the traditions of ancient Israel is the ideal-typical example in the Occident: the origin and transmission of the life of the national lineage is seen as being directly linked to the divinity, hence to the order and even the creation of the world. As the influence of Israelite traditions on Christendom is well known, it will suffice to refer to only a few examples: ancient Armenia as the descendant of Noah through Japheth and Gomer (Khorenats'i 1978: I.xii; cf. Gen 10:2-3); both the medieval kingdom of France (Strayer 1971: 311-13) and the English Puritans[21] as the chosen people of God; the North Americans as the nation chosen by God to fulfill its manifest destiny in the new promised land (Weinberg 1935); and, for a recent combination of the attachment to the concepts of chosen people, promised land and Christianity, the Mormons.[22] Examples of the assertion of distinctiveness from ancient societies are numerous as well, albeit with significant variation among them, and, given their polytheism, obviously different from the traditions of the Old Testament. In ancient Egypt, the so-called Memphite theology asserts the divinity of the Pharaoh, and the sacrality of both Egypt and especially its life-sustaining capital, Memphis ("granary of the God, through which the sustenance of the Two Lands [Egypt] is prepared"). In Mesopotamia, the creation epic, the *Enuma Elish*, recited each year during the festival marking the New Year, recounted how order was created out of chaos as Babylon became the home of the gods.

But why should the one chosen from the tenth generation descended from Noah have been Abraham? We are given no reason for the choice when it is first recounted in Gen 12:1-3; nor subsequently in Gen 12:7;

---

21. See, for example, Cromwell's speeches of 4 July 1653 and 4 September 1654.

22. It is worth emphasizing here, even if only in passing, that the primordial attachments to the perceived objects of the transmission of life—kinship—however attenuated, i.e., in the modern nation, have not been undermined by the doctrinal universality of Christianity (Grosby 1996 [in this volume, pp. 166-190]).

13:14-17; 15; 17 (with the possible exception of 17:1 which, in any event, appears to refer to Abraham's future actions). These accounts offer no indication that Abraham was deserving of having been chosen;[23] indeed, presumably his worthiness was in doubt, for he was tested (Gen 22:1-2). Only after Abraham's offer of Isaac and because of it are we given a reason for Yahweh's choice of Abraham and his blessing of descendants, land, and protection (Gen 22:16-18); and it is only after the death of Abraham that we learn that Yahweh will fulfill his side of the covenant because Abraham obeyed his laws (Gen 26:3-5). Thus, we face the possibility of something inexplicable or capricious in Yahweh's initial choice of Abraham.

This possibility evidently troubled the ancient, rabbinic interpreters of Gen 12:1-3. Because they knew, based on Josh 24:2-3, that Terah, father of Abraham, served other gods, they concluded that Abraham—now interpreted from his youth (indeed, even from his infancy!) as worshiping the only one god, Yahweh—did not leave, but was driven out of Mesopotamia, the land of his ancestors (*Judith* 5:6-9; *Jewish Antiquities* 1.154-57; *Genesis Rabbah* 38:13). Stories even arose about the child Abraham's monotheistic arguments with his idolatrous father (*Jubilees* 11:16-17; 12:1-3, 6-7).[24] Of course, there is no biblical support for these interpretations and stories; but they reveal a pressing desire to portray the choice of Abraham as being a consequence of Yahweh's reasonable recognition of Abraham's virtue.

The significance of this cognitive compulsion to explain the choice of Abraham as being justified is that it is indicative of the difficulty for theological rationalization and philosophy to account for the individuality of nations—these culturally distinctive eruptions in history—indeed, the capriciousness of life itself. Rather than being embarrassed by the distinctiveness of Yahweh's choice of Israel, Judah Halevi (1964) forcefully reaffirmed it in the *Kuzari* (1.25-27) as being definitive of Judaism.

> THE RABBI: In the same way God commanded the speech to the assembled people of Israel [note well: the first of the Ten Commandments, Exod 20:2, Deut 5:6]: "I am the God whom you worship, who has led you out of the land of Egypt," but He did not say: "I am the Creator of the world and your Creator." Now in the same style I spoke to thee, a Prince of the Khazars, when thou didst ask me about my creed. I answered thee as was fitting, and

---

23. Nor, for that matter, does Gen 18:19.

24. These accounts are conveniently collected in Kugel. For the account of the twenty-day-old Abraham acknowledging the one and only god, see Ginzberg (1909: 189-93).

is fitting for the whole of Israel who knew these things, first from personal experience, and afterwards through uninterrupted tradition, which is equal to the former.

AL KHAZARI: If this be so, then your belief is confined to yourselves?

THE RABBI: Yes, but any Gentile who joins us unconditionally shares our good fortune, without, however, being quite equal to us.

This insightful defense of historical uniqueness (the tradition of God's deliverance of Israel from Egypt that includes the image of genealogical descent)[25] as the key to Judaism may rightly be extended to nationality in general. The element of distinctiveness conveyed through historical reference is necessary for the existence of a nation. Every nation has a "navel" or "roots"; all nations have, to one degree or another, a self-understanding of having been chosen (Smith 1992).

While Halevi correctly recognized the historical and primordial components of Judaism, there are, of course, also various theological rationalizations to be found within the Israelite self-understanding, e.g., Gen 26:3-5, where Israel would remain the chosen people of Yahweh as long as it proved itself worthy by obeying God's commandments (Amos 3:2). Thus, two conceptions of covenant are found within Israel: an unconditional covenant (Gen 17:7, 19; 2 Sam 7:15-16) between Yahweh and Israel, where the historical uniqueness of the relation between Yahweh and Israel is affirmed in an everlasting covenant with the descendants of Abraham (David), that seemingly recognizes the sanctity of the lineage itself; and a conditional covenant, where Yahweh's fidelity to the lineage is dependent upon the latter's obedience to his commandments, where Noah and Abraham are favored because they are righteous (respectively, Gen 6:9 and Gen 26:5), where Israel is favored because it is a priestly kingdom and a holy nation (Exod 19:6). Indeed, the "cognitive compulsion" referred to above, the drive toward rationalization within the world of religion, reaches its logical conclusion, monotheism, in Israelite tradition, expressed in Genesis 1-11, and with impressive succinctness, albeit in tension with the primordial beliefs in a chosen people and a promised land, in both Amos 9:7, "Are you not like Ethiopians to me, O people of Israel? says the Lord. Did I not bring Israel up from the land of Egypt, and the Philistines from Caphtor, and the Arameans from Kir?" and Isa 19:25, "Blessed be Egypt my people, and Assyria the work of my hands, and Israel my heritage."

---

25. Halevi could have also drawn attention to how God first describes himself to Moses at Exod 3:5 and 6:3 as "the God of your father, the God of Abraham, Isaac, and Jacob"; and not as the "creator of the world."

In summary, heterogeneous orientations, both primordial and universal, are constitutive of the Israelite center. The primordial orientation of the transmission of life is borne by the traditions of historical uniqueness and unconditional covenant. A universal orientation is borne by the traditions of conditional covenant, other expressions of religious rationalization (e.g., Mic 6:8), and, ultimately, monotheism. Several passages within the Old Testament clearly indicate that its redactors were conscious of the tension between these two orientations, as they attempted to hold both simultaneously. At Deut 10:14-15, Moses asserts the monotheism of the worship of Yahweh; yet the universalistic assertion is succinctly and, perhaps we are entitled to say, uncomfortably combined with the particularism of the unconditional covenant:

> Although heaven and the heaven of heavens belong to the Lord your God, the earth with all that is in it, yet the Lord set his heart in love on your ancestors alone and chose you, their descendants after them, out of all peoples, as it is today.

The tension of holding these two orientations simultaneously is heightened at Exod 32:12-13, where Moses reasserts the unconditional covenant within the context of the conditional, that is, within the context of Yahweh's punishment of Israel for violating his law.

> Turn from your [Yahweh's] fierce wrath; change your mind and do not bring disaster on your people. Remember Abraham, Isaac, and Israel, your servants, how you swore to them by your own self, saying to them, "I will multiply your descendants like the stars of heaven, and all this land that I promised I will give to your descendants, and they shall inherit it forever." And the Lord changed his mind about the disaster that he planned to bring on his people.

How are we to understand the significance of the interplay between these two orientations, to the point where Moses is described as changing the mind of God? Can it be that both orientations were understood as fundamental to human existence?

If both orientations are fundamental to human existence, might this quality account for the resilience of the traditions that bear them, the ability to withstand reinterpretation over time, thus allowing the Israelite center to resist being shattered? In other words, Why has Israel survived? Why has it played such a fermentative role in the Occident? Another archaeological discovery, the so-called Bar Kokhba coins, poses these problems by raising for consideration the Israelite center itself, rather than the orientations within it.

III

The "Bar Kokhba" coins were minted or, more accurately, overstruck on coins previously in circulation in the vicinity of Jerusalem during the years 132–135 c.e.,[26] when the Jews, under the leadership of Bar Kokhba or, as he was also known, Shim'on (Yadin 1961), rebelled against Rome. Among the various inscriptions found on these coins appear "year one of the redemption of Israel," "year two of the freedom of Israel." The conception of time conveyed by these inscriptions is interesting, namely, the designation of the date "year one" as beginning in 132 c.e., with the "redemption of Israel." Evidently, the designation "year one" indicates a belief that a decisive transformation had taken place—for the Jews such that they were evidently no longer Jews, but, once again, Israelites; and perhaps also for the world. One is, of course, reminded of similar, millenarian changes of dating, for example, during the French Revolution.

As interesting as this shift in temporal emphasis is, what is remarkably curious about these inscriptions is the appearance of the word "Israel" on these coins. Why is this so curious? It is curious because the state of "Israel," that is, a polity whose territory and population roughly corresponded to the "Israel" of the United Kingdom of David and Solomon, had, at the time of the Bar Kokhba rebellion, not existed for 1,000 years. At no time during the period from 922 b.c.e., the approximate date of the fall of the United Kingdom, to 132 c.e., the inception of the Bar Kokhba rebellion, had the polity of Israel, "from Dan to Beersheba," existed. To be sure, during this period of 1,000 years, there was briefly a kingdom which was called "Israel"; but it was the northern kingdom of Israel that existed, at times belligerently, alongside the southern kingdom of Judah. Moreover, the city of Jerusalem was in Judah, and not in the (northern) kingdom called "Israel." While the northern kingdom of Israel was destroyed by the Assyrians in 722 b.c.e., the southern kingdom of Judah continued to exist as an independent kingdom from 722 b.c.e. to 586 b.c.e. when it was conquered by the Babylonians. From 538 b.c.e. to 332 b.c.e. there existed the province of Judah, under the domination of the Persians. After this period, Judaea existed as a province within the Seleucid and then Ptolemaic empires; achieved independence under the Hasmonaean dynasty in 141 b.c.e.; and finally submitted to the Romans in 63 b.c.e. Thus, from 922 b.c.e. to 132 c.e., there did not exist a polity named "Israel" with Jerusalem as its capital. Yet, after a period of more

---

26. The standard works on the "Bar Kokhba coins" are Meshorer (1967) and Mildenberger (1949). See also Kindler (1962).

than 1,000 years, there appears, in 132 C.E., on coins the word "Israel" in the phrases "the redemption of Israel," "the freedom of Israel." Whence "Israel"?

Just as curious is that, of the hundreds of coins discovered in this area whose dates range from the fifth century B.C.E.[27] up to the Bar Kokhba rebellion in 132 C.E., only a very few, excluding the Bar Kokhba coins, have the word "Israel" inscribed on them. On these few coins appear the inscription "shekel of Israel." Interestingly, those few coins with this inscription appear to have been struck in the years from 66 C.E. to 69 C.E., that is, during the period of the Jewish war of independence against Rome. On all the other coins during this approximately 500-year period from the fifth century B.C.E. up to 132 C.E., the beginning of the Bar Kokhba rebellion, the only other inscriptions which refer to a polity or a people are the inscriptions *yhd* for "Judah" or "Judaea," or *yehudîm* for "Jews." These latter inscriptions are typical and the coins on which they appear are found in abundance, including apparently during the period of the Hasmonaeans (Meshorer 1982). The appearance of the *yhd* and *yehudîm* on these coins is understandable, for they correspond to the existence of Judah or Judaea as either a province or an independent kingdom from the fifth century B.C.E. to the second century C.E. Once again, whence "Israel"?

The pressing relevance of the question, "Whence Israel?" becomes obvious upon a moment's reflection on recent events in Eastern Europe. One could just as well have asked a number of somewhat similar questions, for example, "Whence Macedonia?" or "Whence the Battle of Kosovo?" or "Whence the monastery at Czestochowa?" Why do such collective designations and references to past events exist and persist? What is the nature of their significance?

A crucial element in the existence of a stable collectivity, such as nationality, is the consistency of its self-designation. This self-designation, for example, "Israel," by being an object of attention unites the individuals, as members of the nation, to one another and to the nation itself, including to the nation's distinctive past, which is understood as, in some measure, determinative of its current distinctiveness. We may describe this temporally deep self-designation, this existential self-understanding, as the self-consciousness of the nation, the existence of which is dependent upon its recognition (acceptance) by the individual members of the

---

27. From the sixth to the early fifth century B.C.E., the inscription *yhd* = Judah appears on bullae, which are small lumps of clay used to seal letters and/or documents, see Avigad (1976).

nation. The assertion and reaffirmation, over the generations, of this self-designating, temporally deep symbolic complex is seen clearly in (indeed, is commanded by) Israelite tradition (Exod 13:14; 12:26-27; cf. Exod 10:2; 12:14, 17; 13:8; Deut 4:9; 6:7, 20-21).

> And when your son asks you in days to come, "What does this mean?" you will tell him, "By sheer power Yahweh brought us out of Egypt, out of the house of slavery." . . . And when your children ask you, "What does this ritual mean?" you will tell them, "It is the sacrifice of the Passover in honor of Yahweh who passed over the houses of the sons of Israel in Egypt. . . ."

Thus, the current generation (Deut 29:12) enters anew and reaffirms through acceptance Yahweh's covenant with the past, the fathers of Israel (Deut 29:13)—a covenant made to future generations as well (Deut 29:15, "with those who are not with us today").

The object or focus of attention which unites a number of individuals into members of a nation must necessarily bear within it a number of meaningful referents, specifically the criteria that determine membership in, and, thus, the boundaries of, the nation. One such boundary-generating referent is the reinterpreted image of a historically distinctive past that separates the nation from other nations. For Israel that past was the history of the putative kinship structure of Abraham-Isaac-and-Jacob, the Exodus tradition, and the traditions found from Joshua through 2 Kings. Another boundary-generating referent is the law. Just as the passover was a referent in the Israelite and Jewish collective self-consciousness through yearly affirmation, so, too, was the law, as it was commanded to be publicly promulgated every seven years in the hearing of all of Israel (Deut 31:9-11; cf. 2 Kgs 23:1-3); a law that, having been written down (Exod 24:3-4; Deut 27:1-8; Josh 24:25-27) was, as a consequence, made stable, and whose territorial jurisdiction was envisioned as being the promised land, as is surely the case for the Deuteronomic legal code.[28]

These observations, that nationality is primarily a structure of collective self-consciousness constituted by each generation's affirmation of the temporally deep, jurisdictional referents of the nation's symbolic center, tell us something about the nation's structure. The question, however, that remains is: What is being "designated" or "articulated" as the center such that it sustains the attention of the members of the nation? In addition, why does that self-designation or self-articulation convey a "drive"

---

28. As the democratic potential of the image of the public promulgation of a written law before all the people is obvious, as is the king being bound by that law (Deut 17:18-20) for freedom, I mention these here only in passing.

for sovereignty; that is, why does the nation evidently contain within itself the "drive" to become a national state? As to the latter question, recall the reappearance of the self-designation "Israel" particularly at times of campaigns for national independence, that is, from 66 to 69 c.e., and especially from 132 to 135 c.e. To be sure, the always prepared potential for that reappearance may have been possible because the beliefs of the "conceptual center," for Israel, in a promised land, a chosen people, and a law whose jurisdiction was that land and people, were embodied in or conveyed by any number of representative institutions, for example, the Sanhedrin and the Patriarchate in the case of ancient Israel in the period of the Second Temple and immediately thereafter (Alon 1989). Furthermore, that reappearance of "reactivation" was in large measure possible because of the "objectivation" or "embodiment" of those beliefs constitutive of the conceptual center of Israel in the Hebrew Bible. However, our questions do not revolve around the existence of representative institutions, necessary as they are for nations to exist, as concrete bearers of meanings or *Kulturträger*.

Rather, the questions are: Why are some temporally distant objects of attention so real that they influence (and continue to do so over the centuries) the perceptions and actions of the individual? Why does a particular "conceptual center" continue to exist? And what is it that is being "designated," "articulated," "objectified," or "embodied" such that nationality exists? These questions have to be dealt with if we are to penetrate the significance of such symbolic representation in the formation and maintenance of nationality. I have offered in a preliminary fashion a tentative answer to these questions: the self-designating traditions of historical distinctiveness are elements seemingly necessary for the existence of the nation. This answer is clearly not good enough; whatever its merit, it seems tautological. We must press further if we are to achieve a better understanding of both the Israelite center and the significance of nationality, including why individuals regard their position on the soil of the earth and their physical proximity to others as significant.

IV

What happens to the nation if the processes of sustaining life, for example, the provision of food, and various collectivities, above all the family, but also the village, town and city, that are necessary for the propagation and continuation of life, are threatened? What happens if and when these processes and structures of propagation are threatened by virtue of the nation's weakness, especially military weakness? In such instances, confidence in the nation is shaken; it may even be lost. If it is lost, the nation becomes extinct; it dies.

What does this mean? It means that a nation requires "animation," that is, its existence is dependent upon the acceptance or "activation" of the traditions that are constitutive of the temporally deep conceptual center of the nation. The traditions must be kept alive by reaffirmation, as was recognized in Exodus (the meaning of the passover) and Deuteronomy (the periodic promulgation of the law). For example, today there are not enough individuals who believe in the efficacy of Hammurabi's law code for it to be the law of the territory of Babylon; consequently, Babylon today is not a living reality. To be sure, Hammurabi's law code exists today as an objective symbolic configuration; it may be found in books in many libraries. However, this objective achievement of the human mind remains merely that. It is not "animated" or being constantly "reactivated" in the minds of a number of individuals such that it is a constitutive referent in the collective self-consciousness of a Babylonian people. It is not "alive" by being part of the shared "mental environment" of each of many individuals.

In contrast to Babylon, the beliefs constitutive of Israel remained "active" in the minds of a continuous stream of numerous individuals; they remained so even in the absence of the existence of the state of Israel. As a consequence, this continually existing potential for "activation" permitted the possibility for Israel to reemerge, albeit precariously in 132 C.E. and more firmly in 1948. In this sense there is merit to Renan's understanding that a nation is *un plébiscite de tous les jours* (1896).

When attachment to the conceptual center of a nation is shaken by military defeat and especially territorial conquest, the nation may face death because those beliefs constitutive of the center are on the verge of ceasing to be accepted. It faces death inasmuch as the collective self-consciousness faces extinction, because the belief in the power of their nation and its institutions to safeguard the processes of the propagation and maintenance of life, its vitality, has been shown to be insufficient.

The element of legitimation in the relation between the consciousness of the individual and the collective self-consciousness of the nation and its conceptual center rests upon this covenantal character of an instrumental *do ut des*. When in antiquity a nation was defeated, its gods were literally carried away by the conquering army. What did this action signify? It signified that the conceptual center of the nation had been broken. The power of the national deity to safeguard both the propagation and continuation of the lives of the individual members of the nation and the territory in which that propagation takes place and which makes that propagation possible, was discredited. In such an instance, the individual may withdraw from participating in the collective self-consciousness of the nation by ceasing to recognize the beliefs constitutive of the center (represented by the deity) of that collective self-consciousness as his or her own.

For the nation to be sovereign, to be a national state, is for the god of the land to be free, and, as such, to be effective. For the nation to be sovereign, to be a national state, is for it to be able to act freely in the world with regards to the protection of those properties, for example, the life-sustaining land, necessary for the propagation and continuation of the lives of its members. To be sure, for the nation to be able to act freely, that is, to have a "will," can only mean that the nation has a representative (or representatives) who can act freely through the institutions of the state on its behalf. Ultimately, it is that representative who, as such, must safeguard the nation from the disorders of the world external to its borders that threaten the generation and transmission of the lives of its members, hence the life of the nation. Thus, the lives of the individuals of the nation are dependent upon the existence of the sovereign national state, dependent insofar as the individuals, as members of the nation, continue to look to it as the protector of their lives.

Designations like "Israel" signify that part of life which demands to be free, to determine itself; for they clearly refer to sovereignty, that is, to the self-determination of the nation. The nation requires the unhindered ability to determine its own affairs, above all, to preserve itself; thus, the nation, in order fully to be a nation, must be encased within the protective apparatus of its freedom, namely the state. This freedom, albeit the freedom of the nation, is a part of what is implied in these collective representations and references to the past, and it in part accounts for their tenacity.

The ancient Israelite belief in the everlasting, unconditional covenant between Yahweh and Israel was an expression of confidence (or the attempt to instill confidence) in the center. It allowed the center to continue to exist as long as one believed in Yahweh's promise that eventually Israel would arise from its ashes. The conditional covenant served this purpose as well, although, of course, through the introduction of transcendental criteria that provided meaning for the historical context of Israel's (momentary) destruction; and it further allowed for a new generation to establish a new covenant (Jer 31:31–34).

This is one part of the significance of nationality. It is a configuration of traditions that are pervaded by vital life and that have as their referents territorially specific beliefs about the processes of the generation, maintenance, and protection of life. These referents are found within the conceptual center, that organizing focus of beliefs, of the collective self-consciousness of the national collectivity: for Israel, the beliefs in the promises of descendants, bountiful land, and, eventually, national sovereignty. The reason why the (not necessarily factually accurate) memories of the united monarchy of David and Solomon were such a focal point in the national historiography and monolatrous beliefs of ancient Israel is that that period was putatively when those promises were fully realized.

These recognitions of the life-sustaining and life-protecting significance of nationality and the sovereignty or freedom required for that sustenance and protection are some of the reasons for the persistence and resilience of the attachments of the individual members of the nation to one another and to the nation. These collective designations and references to the past are significant because they are expressions of two orientations that are fundamental in human affairs: the transmission of life, and the freedom of life.

The beliefs that are constitutive of the conceptual center of the nation and that account for much of the significance of nationality do not only refer to the transmission of life and the freedom of life, they also refer to the order of life. The order of life is realized in law. Law, the promulgation of norms of right relations in the conduct of life, is also a necessary element of the conceptual center of the nation because it is through the law that the conceptual center of the nation is capable of being an organizing focus of the collectivity; the law asserts right relations throughout its territorial jurisdiction. This is to say that contained within the law is a core conception of right relations which, in turn, determines the nature of the subsidiary postulates of the law; contained within the law is the nature of the ordered relationship between the periphery and the center. The law is the vehicle by which the periphery participates in the center and through which the nature of that participation is determined (Deut 17:8–13).

Ultimately, the foundation of the conception of right relations is expressed in the conception of God. That is what Hegel (1956 [1837]: 50) meant when he observed that "religion is the sphere in which a nation gives itself the definition of that which it regards as the True." For the nation "to regard" a proposition to be true is for it to be recognized as a central tenet of the law. To be recognized as a central tenet of the law is to determine the order of the nation. That is why Hegel was also right to observe that "the conception of God constitutes the general basis of a people's character." This is also part of the significance of nationality, namely, that, in addition to being a collectivity for both the transmission of life and the freedom of life, it also orders life.

All three of these fundamental orientations in human affairs are found within the conceptual center of the nation. A relatively stable combination of these heterogeneous orientations is what is being "designated" or "articulated" in such collective designations of nationality as "Israel."

Do these three fundamental orientations in human affairs exist harmoniously with one another? Is their relation to one another within the conceptual center always the same from nation to nation, from civilization to civilization? The answer to these questions is "no." The order of a particular nation depends upon the weight accorded to one of these orientations at the expense of the other two within its conceptual center. Moreover, irrespective of the stability of a particular combination of these three orientations in a particular nation, it is a combination whose internal elements exist in tension with one another. (For example, for Israel, the interplay between unconditional and conditional covenants, or the ubiquitous potential for tension between hierocratic authority and political authority.) The elements within the conceptual center of the nation are heterogeneous; that is, each of these three postulates is fundamental. This heterogeneity in the fundamental orientation of human affairs is what, in part, accounts for the "natural" pluralism in human affairs.

Each of these orientations can be viewed in Deuteronomy. We observe repeatedly in Deuteronomy one of these orientations, the freedom of nationality in the many references to Israel being brought out of the "house of slavery," the kingdom of Egypt. In this regard, recall once again the inscriptions on the "Bar Kokhba" coins, "year one of the redemption of Israel" and "year two of the freedom of Israel." The nation of Israel was to be sovereign, and theologically formulated, the deliverance or redemption of that people chosen by Yahweh to dwell in that land promised to them by Yahweh.

The second orientation accounting for part of the significance of nationality, the propagation and transmission of life, is also quite evident in Deut 30:9:

> Yahweh your God will give you great prosperity in all your undertakings, in the fruit of your body, the fruit of your cattle and in the produce of your soil. For once again Yahweh will take delight in your prosperity as he took delight in the prosperity of your fathers.

Here, we observe that the propagation and continuation of the lives of the individual members of the nation is an expectation constitutive of

Israel. This expectation is an expression of the covenantal *do ut des* element within the conceptual center of nationality.

Yet, this orientation in human affairs, the transmission of life through the generations, was understood by the prophets to be dependent upon a sacred order of life; that is, conditional upon obedience to the law (earlier referred to as rationalization within the sphere of religion, conveyed through the Israelite conception of the conditional covenant). This third fundamental postulate in human affairs, the order of life, is expressed in Deut 30:16–20:

> If you obey the commandments of Yahweh your God that I enjoin on you today . . . if you keep his commandments, his laws, his customs, you will live and increase, and Yahweh your God will bless you in the land. . . . Choose life, then, so that you and your descendants may live . . . for in this your life counts, and on this depends your long stay in the land. . . .

Thus, in Deuteronomy, we observe a particular combination of the three orientations (the freedom of life, the propagation of life, the order of life) which exists within the conceptual center of the nation of Israel.

These are the answers, even if provided only sketchily, to the questions: Why is it that nationality exists and survives? What is the significance of nationality? Left unanswered is the question, why do some nations, for example, Israel, persist while others fade away?

V

It is worth considering the possibility that the answer to this last question may lie in the nature of the combination of the three orientations in human affairs which exist within the conceptual center of a nation. Do nations which accord greater weight to the order of life within their conceptual center continue to exist, while those which do not fade away? One way to understand the decline of paganism is to recognize that ascendant within the conceptual center of its societies was the primordial postulate of the propagation and transmission of life. However, the result of this ascendancy was that the conceptual centers of the pagan nations were discredited when those nations were militarily defeated, because those nations were no longer capable of safeguarding the propagation and transmission of the lives of their members. In contrast, does the significance of the conditional covenant lie in the fact that monolatrous, and, later, monotheistic "Israel" subordinated the postulate of the pagan "nature religions" to the postulate of the order of life, that is, to the law (or will) of Yahweh, thus allowing the belief in Israel to survive military destruction?

Can this mean that reason does in some way operate through history? Here, the Hegelian answer to this question must be resisted, for the rationalization that took place within the worship of Yahweh, namely, the subordination of the propagation and transmission of life to the law (the order of life), did not do away with the primordial attachment to kinship and land. The persistence of the latter, borne explicitly by the unconditional covenant, adds support to our assumption that it, too, is fundamental to human affairs.

The above observations lead us to consider briefly the relation between the monotheistic religions of the Occident and these three fundamental orientations in human affairs. Because the propagation and transmission of life, the sovereignty or freedom of the nation that they require, and the order of life are all fundamental, each finds its expression in the monotheistic religions of the Occident, albeit in various combinations. If Judaism, Protestantism, or Catholicism had consistently ignored one of these orientations, then they would have done violence to human existence. If they had done so, they would have discredited themselves; they would have lost their adherents; they would have faded away.

In Judaism, there is a clear recognition of the transmission and protection of life in the overtly primordial beliefs in a chosen people and a promised land. Any realistic interpretation of Judaism must appreciate the significance of these beliefs, that is, the primordiality of nationality.[29] However, the recognition accorded by Judaism to these primordial elements is by no means exclusive; for it coexists, as it were, with monotheism in ways that are conceptually fertile, provocative, and contradictory (for example, two conceptions of the covenant).

Protestantism is, of course, doctrinally universal; yet its tradition of national churches has meant that it accords weight to the primordiality of nationality. Protestantism represents the homage explicitly paid by the order of life, the ethical consistency of the Gospels, to the transmission and protection of life, that is, to the territory and territorial sovereignty of the nation.

Catholicism doctrinally accords almost an exclusivity to a universal order of life over against the primordial transmission and protection of life (see, for example, Luke 14:26-27). One need only recall the quasignostic dichotomy between the flesh and the spirit in the Gospel of John

---

29. The significance of the primordial elements in Judaism was faced squarely by Zeitlin (1943-44), and, recently, by de Lange (1986).

to see that this is so. Indeed, in John 12:25, it is asserted that those who hate their life in this world will keep it for eternal life. Nevertheless, as ethically compelling as the rationalization of universal Catholicism may be, it, too, has recognized that Caesar, whose ultimate charge is the protection of life in this world, must be given his due. This is to acknowledge that, despite the universalism of Christianity, the Occident is, in fact, made up of monolatrous societies. That this is so only again raises the problem of the significance of the concepts of the chosen people and the promised land, and of nationality in general.

References

Ahlström, G. W. 1986. *Who Were the Israelites?* Winona Lake, IN: Eisenbrauns.
_____. 1993. *The History of Ancient Palestine.* Minneapolis: Fortress.
Alon, Gedaliah, 1989. *The Jews in Their Land in the Talmudic Age (70-640 c.e.).* Cambridge, MA: Harvard University Press.
Alt, Albrecht. 1967. "The settlement of the Israelites in Palestine," in *Essays in Old Testament History and Religion,* 1st ed. 1925. Garden City, NJ: Doubleday & Co.
Armstrong, John A. 1982. *Nations Before Nationalism.* Chapel Hill: University of North Carolina Press.
Avigad, Nahman. 1976. *QEDEM–Monographs of the Institute of Archaeology–The University of Jerusalem,* no. 4. Jerusalem.
Bimson, John J. 1991. "Merneptah's Israel and recent theories of Israelite origins," *Journal for the Study of the Old Testament* 49: 3-29.
Buber, Martin. 1967. *Kingship of God.* 1st ed. 1932. New York: Harper & Row.
Cassuto, Umberto. 1992. *A Commentary on the Book of Genesis.* 1st ed. 1949. Jerusalem: Magnes.
Coogan, Michael David. 1978. *Stories From Ancient Canaan.* Louisville: Westminster.
Davidson, R. 1989. "Covenant ideology in ancient Israel," in *The World of Ancient Israel,* ed. R. E. Clements. Cambridge: Cambridge University Press.
Dever, W. G. 1984. "Asherah, consort of Yahweh? New evidence from Kuntillet ʿAjrûd," *Bulletin of the American Schools of Oriental Research* 255: 21-37.
Eichrodt, Walther. 1967. *Theology of the Old Testament* vol. II. 1st ed. 1933. Philadelphia: Westminster.
Eisenstadt, S. N. 1986. *The Origins and Diversity of Axial Age Civilizations.* Albany, NY: State University of New York Press.
Eliade, Mircea. 1987. *The Sacred and the Profane.* New York: Harcourt Brace.
Emerton, J. A. 1982. "New light on the Israelite religion: the implications of the inscriptions from Kuntillet ʿAjrud," *Zeitschrift für die alttestamentliche Wissenschaft* 94: 2-20.

Finkelstein, I. 1988. *The Archaeology of the Israelite Settlement.* Jerusalem: Israel Exploration Society.

Finkelstein, I. and N. Na'aman. 1994. *From Nomadism to Monarchy: archaeological and historical aspects of early Israel.* Jerusalem: Israel Exploration Society.

Fishbane, Michael. 1985. *Biblical Interpretation in Ancient Israel.* Oxford: Oxford University Press.

Freyer, Hans. 1998. *Theory of Objective Mind: an introduction to the philosophy of culture.* 2d ed. 1928. Athens, OH: University of Ohio Press.

Gafni, Israel M. 1997. *Land, Center and Diaspora: Jewish constructs in late antiquity.* Sheffield: Sheffield Academic.

Gellner, Ernest. 1996. "Do nations have navels?" *Nations and Nationalism* 2, 3: 366–70.

Ginzberg, Louis. 1998. *The Legends of the Jews*, vol. I. 1st ed. 1909. Baltimore: Johns Hopkins University Press.

Grosby, Steven. 1991. "Religion and nationality in antiquity: the worship of Yahweh and ancient Israel." *Archives Européennes de Sociologie* 32, 2: 229–65.

_____. 1993a. "Kinship, territory, and the nation in the historiography of ancient Israel," *Zeitschrift für die alttestamentliche Wissenschaft* 105: 3–18.

_____. 1993b. "Sociological implication of the distinction between 'locality' and extended 'territory' with particular reference to the Old Testament," *Social Compass* 40, 2: 179–98.

_____. 1993c. "The nation of the United States and the vision of ancient Israel," in *Nationality, Patriotism, and Nationalism*, ed. R. Michener. St. Paul: Paragon.

_____. 1995. "Territoriality: the transcendental, primordial feature of modern societies," *Nations and Nationalism* 1, 2: 143–62.

_____. 1996. "The category of the primordial in the study of early Christianity and second-century Judaism," *History of Religions* 36, 2: 140–63.

Halevi, Judah. 1964. [1130–40 C.E.]. *The Kuzari: an argument of the faith of Israel.* New York: Schocken.

Hegel, G. W. F. 1956. *The Philosophy of History.* 1st ed. 1837. New York: Dover.

Herder, Johann Gottfried von. 1968. [1784–91]. *Reflections on the Philosophy of the History of Mankind.* Chicago: University of Chicago Press.

Jaspers, Karl. 1953. *The Origins and Goal of History.* New Haven, CT: Yale University Press.

Khorenats'i, Moses. 1978. *History of the Armenians.* Cambridge, MA: Harvard University Press.

Kindler, Arie. 1962. "The Eleazar coins of the Bar-Kokhba War," *The Numismatic Circular* 70: 27–29.

Kugel, James L. 1997. *The Bible As It Was.* Cambridge, MA: Harvard University Press.

Lange, Nicholas de. 1986. *Judaism.* Oxford: Oxford University Press.

Levenson, Jon. 1994. *Creation and the Persistence of Evil.* Princeton, NJ: Princeton University Press.

Levinson, Bernard M. 1997. *Deuteronomy and the Hermeneutics of Legal Innovation.* Oxford: Oxford University Press.

McCarthy, D. J. 1978. *Treaty and Covenant. Analecta Biblica* 21A. Rome: Biblical Institute.

Mendenhall, G. E. 1992. "Covenant," in *Anchor Bible Dictionary,* ed. David Noel Freedman. New York: Doubleday.

Meshel, Z. 1979. "Did Yahweh have a consort? The new religious inscriptions from the Sinai," *Biblical Archaeology Review* 5, 2: 24–35.

Meshorer, Yaᶜakov. 1967. *Jewish Coins of the Second Temple Period.* Tel-Aviv: Am Hassefer.

_____. 1982. *Ancient Jewish Coinage.* Vol. I: *Persian Period through Hasmonaeans.* Dix Hills, NY: Amphora.

Meyer, Eduard. 1912. *Der Papyrusfund von Elephantine.* Leipzig: J. C. Hinrich.

Mildenberg, L. 1949. "The Eleazar coins of the Bar-Kokhba rebellion," *Historia Judaica* 11: 77–108.

Nicholson, Ernest W. 1967. *Deuteronomy and Tradition.* Oxford: Basil Blackwell.

_____. 1986. *God and His People: covenant and theology in the Old Testament.* Oxford: Clarendon.

Noth, Martin. 1930. *Das System der zwölf Stämme Israels. BWANT* 4, 1.

_____. 1960. *The History of Israel.* London: A. and C. Black.

_____. 1981. *The Deuteronomistic History.* Sheffield: JSOT.

Porten, B. 1968. *Archive from elephantine: the life of an ancient Jewish military colony.* Berkeley: University of California Press.

Rad, Gerhard von. 1953. *Studies in Deuteronomy.* London: SCM Press.

Renan, Ernst. 1896. "What is a nation?" in *The Poetry of the Celtic Races and Other Studies.* London: W. Scott.

Rost, L. 1934. "Die Bezeichnungen für Land und Volk im Alten Testament," in *Festschrift O. Procksch.* Leipzig: A. Deichert.

Schnapper, Dominique. 1998. *Community of Citizens: on the modern idea of nationality.* New Brunswick, NJ: Transaction.

Silman, Yochanan. 1995. *Philosopher and Prophet: Judah Halevi, the Kuzari, and the evolution of his thought.* Albany, NY: State University of New York Press.

Simmel, Georg. 1918. *Lebensanschauung, Vier metaphysische Kapital.* Munich: Duncker & Humblot.

Smith, Anthony D. 1986. *The Ethnic Origins of Nations.* Oxford: Basil Blackwell.

_____. 1992. "Chosen peoples: why ethnic groups survive," *Ethnic and Racial Studies* 15, 3: 436–56.

_____. 1966a. "Nations and their pasts?" *Nations and Nationalism* 2, 3: 358–65.

_____. 1996b. "Memory and modernity: reflections on Ernest Gellner's theory of nationalism," *Nations and Nationalism* 2, 3: 371–88.

_____. 1998. *Nationalism and Modernism.* London and New York: Routledge.

Smith, Mark S. 1990. *The Early History of God.* San Francisco: Harper & Row.

Strayer, Joseph. 1971. "France: the Holy Land, the chosen people, and the most Christian king," in *Medieval Statecraft and the Perspectives of History: essays by Joseph Strayer,* ed. John F. Benton and Thomas N. Bisson. Princeton, NJ: Princeton University Press.

Weber, Max. 1946. "Religious rejections of the world and their directions," in *From Max Weber*, ed. Hans Gerth and C. Wright Mills. New York: Oxford University Press.

_____. 1952. *Ancient Judaism*. New York: Free Press.

Weinberg, Albert K. 1935. *Manifest Destiny*. Baltimore: Johns Hopkins University Press.

Weinfeld, Moshe. 1972. *Deuteronomy and the Deuteronomic School*. Oxford: Oxford University Press. [Repr. Winona Lake, IN: Eisenbrauns, 1992]

Weinfeld, Moshe. 1993. *The Promise of the Land*. Berkeley: University of California Press.

Wellhausen, Julius. 1973. "Israel," *Encyclopaedia Britannica*, reprinted as an Appendix to *Prolegomena to the History of Israel*. 1st ed. 1881. Gloucester: Peter Smith.

Williamson, H. G. M. 1989. "The concept of Israel in transition," in *The World of Ancient Israel*, ed. R. E. Clements. Cambridge: Cambridge University Press.

Yadin, Y. 1961. "More on the letters of Bar Cochba," *Biblical Archaeologist* 24: 86–95.

Yurco, Frank J. 1997. "Merenptah's Canaanite campaign and Israel's origins," in *Exodus: the Egyptian evidence*, ed. Ernest S. Frerichs and Leonard H. Lesko. Winona Lake, Ind.: Eisenbrauns.

Zeitlin, Solomon. 1943-44. "Judaism as a religion," *Jewish Quarterly Review* 34: 1-40, 207-41; 35:85-16, 179-225, 303-49.

Chapter 5

Borders, Territory, and Nationality in the Ancient Near East and Armenia

Examination of evidence from the ancient Near East and Armenia, spanning a period of more than a thousand years, indicates the existence of conceptions of relatively precise boundaries, territories, and perhaps also nations. This evidence may not be sufficient enough to put to rest the assumption, found repeatedly throughout the social sciences, that in antiquity there were geographically imprecise frontiers but not bounded territories and, further, that nationality with its bounded, extended territory is exclusively a modern phenomenon. It should, nevertheless, be sufficient enough to require a more nuanced understanding of not only certain collectivities of antiquity and their respective territories, but modern nationality as well.

The evidence for the existence of various conceptions of bounded territory constitutive of respectively various collectivities in antiquity is by no means limited to the well known, but complicated example of the nation of ancient Israel.[1] There are a number of other examples among which are Edom, ancient Aram and ancient Armenia, the objects of our examination here. An examination of these three collectivities poses point blank both the question of whether or not nations existed in the ancient Near East and, correspondingly, the problem of the application of the category of nationality to these collectivities. An analysis of these three cases further reminds us that in reality the boundaries separating the categories which we employ in our investigations of various collectivities, both ancient and modern, are permeable. Rarely does a collectivity correspond with exactitude to a particular analytical category. This is true not only for the collectivities of antiquity, but for the modern national state as well.

---

1. I gratefully acknowledge the comments of Klaas Veenhof in the preparation of this article, which is part of a series of articles examining conceptions of boundaries, territory, and nationality in antiquity. Regarding ancient Israel, see Grosby 1991 [[in this volume, pp. 13–51]]; 1993a [[in this volume, pp. 52–68]]; 1993b [[in this volume, pp. 69–91]].

A constitutive characteristic of nationality, ancient and modern, is the existence of a relatively extensive, yet bounded and sociologically relatively homogeneous territory. There are a number of apparently constitutive elements to the existence of such a territory, for example, as an indication of its relative, sociological homogeneity, a name common to both the territory and the people who are related by inhabiting the territory, for example "all Israel."[2] In addition, this terminological conflation of the image of an extensive, yet bounded area of land and the image of "its" people usually has, as one of its elements, the fiction that the people are related by blood-tie, the classic example of which is the putative lineage of Abraham-Isaac-Jacob for ancient Israel.

In contrast to the boundaries of a nation which are conceptually fixed or stable, those of an empire are in flux, being often a consequence of the calculation as to whether or not the increased revenues gained from any further territorial expansion beyond the momentarily established frontier would be greater than the military and administrative expenses required for the effort.[3] Such a flux undermines the possibility for the consolidation over time of a stable, trans-local territorial referent in the mutual recognition—that is, a territorially bounded, shared tradition—through which a sociologically relatively homogeneous "people" is formed. To be sure, in antiquity such a territorially extensive, yet bounded mutual recognition or shared tradition was not among legally equal citizens of the land as in the case of modern nationality; rather, insofar as it existed, it was more likely derived from the common worship of the god of the land and subjection to the king of the land who, in turn, received the authority to rule that land and the people of the god from that god. In contrast to a nation, an empire's absence of stable boundaries means that its territory and inhabitants are sociologically heterogeneous: an empire contains within it many different peoples and many different territories.

The territories of city-kingdoms, in contrast to those of nations, are of qualitatively delimited area: there is, for example, the city-kingdoms, no extended, bounded territorial relation of center to periphery, the latter consisting of any number of towns which, in the case of nationality, are substantially related to the territorially relatively distant center. Thus, while there are numerous instances in antiquity of the god of the royal house becoming a god of the land, for the city-kingdom, the areal jurisdiction of the god of the land is that of the city and its immediate

---

2. For an introductory overview of the terms "Israel" and "all Israel," see Zobel 1977, pp. 397–420.

3. Lattimore 1979, p. 38. See also Tadmor 1975, pp. 37–38.

environs, e.g., Pallas Athene of Athens. In contrast are those instances where the territorial jurisdiction of the god is decisively trans-local, yet still bounded, for example, Horus-Seth (and later Amen-Re) of Egypt. How are we to understand these latter, territorially extensive, yet bounded collectivities?

The categorial nature of our problem may be further elucidated by briefly contrasting the apparently different territorial conceptions found, on the one hand, in the emergence of the Greek city-state from approximately the ninth century B.C. with, on the other, those of the Assyrian empire of the eighth century B.C. It may very well be that the birth of the territorially based community known as the *polis* was a consequence of gathering into a single decision-making body all the local *basileis* who had previously been more or less independent of one another.[4] This consolidation or territorial solidarity may have been facilitated not only through military subjugation, but also especially through the worship of a common deity, which, in turn, would have allowed the emergence of a bounded religious territory. Indeed, for many of the Greek city-states, the boundaries of their respective territories were marked by nonurban sanctuaries.[5] In these instances we observe a degree of sociological homogeneity that Francois de Polignac has suggestively described as a religious citizenship. Nevertheless, such a sociologically relative, territorial homogeneity derived from the common worship of the god of the land as distinct from the god of the royal house is not yet the problem before us; for in ancient Greece, the territorial jurisdiction of these gods was not trans-city-state, despite the adumbration of complicating, quasi-national developments such as the existence of both a pantheon which encompassed the otherwise territorially delimited and heterogeneous Greek city-states and the trans-city-state designation *Hellenes*.

In contrast to the delimited territorial distinctiveness of the Greek city-state is the territorial expansiveness of an empire, for example, Assyria during the eighth century B.C., especially beginning with the reign of Tiglath-pileser III. Nonetheless, despite Assyria's evident, opportunistic territorial expansion and contraction which is characteristic of an empire, there are here as well a number of complications for our analysis; for example, there is evidence not only for the belief at various points in Assyrian history that the land (of both the city Ashur and the empire) belonged to the god Ashur, but also for Assyrian conceptions of bound-

<hr>

4. For a recent treatment of the problem, see de Polignac 1995, p. 58; 1994, pp. 3-18.
5. De Polignac 1995, pp. 32-88.

aries. Quite common are such inscriptions as "I [Tiglath-pileser III] pursued him [Sarduri of Urartu] up to the causeway of the Euphrates, the border [*miṣir*] of his land,"[6] or "I [Sargon II] captured all of their lands and brought them within the borders of Assyria."[7] It is obvious enough that many of the boundaries referred to in such inscriptions are those of a sociologically heterogeneous, territorially expanding and contrasting empire. Nevertheless, one still wonders if there was a conception of a territorially stable, hence sociologically relatively homogeneous core to the empire.[8]

Perhaps these complications of both the Greek city-state and the Assyrian empire for our analysis only underscore the permeability of our categories—complications which, in turn, require a comparative and historical investigation into those factors which facilitate the existence of the relative sociological homogeneity of a bounded, trans-local territorial relation that is suggestive of nationality, for example, the ascendancy of the god of the land within a pantheon, or even monolatry. In any event, the intention of the ensuring analysis is more modest, being merely to present the categorial problem as represented by Edom, all Aram, and ancient Armenia.

Edom and Edomites

Our interest in Edom cannot be a result of an abundant amount of evidence which indicates the existence of a nation of Edom, for the evidence is much too limited.[9] Rather, our interest in a brief examination of Edom is in laying the groundwork for certain approaches in evaluating the terminological evidence pertaining to the determination of the nature of other collectivities of the ancient Near East and antiquity, in particular "all Aram" and ancient Armenia.

---

6. Calah Annal 17, line 11, Tadmor 1994, p. 52. For the use of *miṣru* as "border," "borderline," see CAD, vol. M, part II.

7. Luckenbill vol. II, 92. Note also the uses of *taḫūmu* in both the Antakya Stele (Donbaz 1990, p. 7), lines 4-5, "the boundary [*taḫūmu*] which Adad-nerari, king of Assyria, and Samsi-ilu, the commander in chief, established between Zakur of the land of Hamath and Atarsumki, son of Adramu"; and the Pazarcik Stele (Donbaz 1990, p. 9), "Boundary stone of Adad-nerari . . . ," where a boundary stone was evidently used to settle a border conflict.

8. So recently Machinist (1986, p. 186), ". . . one god, Ashur, remained the head of the pantheon throughout Assyrian history and that his name was identical with that of the state as a whole and the capital city as its core"; and similarly, Tadmor (1986, p. 205), ". . . in Assyria the unity of city, god and people was never broken. . . ."

9. For an exhaustive analysis of this limited evidence, see Bartlett 1989.

From Egyptian sources and the Hebrew Bible, there can be little doubt that the term "Edom" designated a trans-local territory. In the Papyrus Anastasi VI (end of the 13th century B.C.), there appear the following lines, "We have finished letting the Bedouin [shōsu] tribes of Edom pass the Fortress of Merne-Ptah Hotep-hir-Maat...."[10] The term "Edom" here contains the determinative "foreign hill country," thus indicating that the term refers to a geographical location.[11] The evidence from the Hebrew Bible also suggests that the term "Edom" designated a territory, for example, in 1 Kgs 22:47 and Jer 40:11 where the locational preposition bě, "in," is prefixed to Edom. Moreover, such phrases as "on the edge of your [Edom's] border [territory, gebulkā]" (Num 20:16) and "at the border [gebul] of the land ['ereṣ] of Edom" (Num 20:23) indicate clearly that Edom was a territorial designation.

The existence of a trans-local territorial designation itself points to a problem in determining the nature of the particular designated collectivity. The categories "tribe" and "city-kingdom" are not applicable categories by which such collectivities can be described, for there evidently existed a trans-local/tribal/city territorial designation; nor obviously does the category "empire" suffice, for the territory was deliminated. Corresponding to this problem of classification, indeed, confirming it, are indications that there was a "people" that was designated by the name of the territory. In the Hebrew Bible, we find numerous instances of the term "Edomite," 'edômî (as distinct from "Edom," 'edôm), for example, in Deut 23:7. Perhaps our classificatory quandary is best exemplified by 2 Sam 8:14, "throughout *all Edom* he [David] put garrisons, and *all the Edomites* became David's servants" (my emphasis). In point of fact, the Hebrew term for "all Edom" and "all the Edomites" is the same, kol-'edôm. In the first instance of "all Edom," the preposition bě, "in" or "throughout," is prefixed to Edom suggesting a geographical location. In the second instance, "all Edom" is modified by the masculine plural of the word "servant," thus justifying its translation not as "all Edom" but as "Edomites." Just how are we to understand this evident terminological conflation between a term designating a territory and a term designating a "people"? The conflation is, of course, characteristic of modern nationality; but what did it mean to be an Edomite?

Were the worshipers of Qaush—apparently the god of Edom—Edomites?[12] If the criterion for being an Edomite was the worship of Qaush,

10. ANET 1969, p. 259; Caminos 1954, pp. 293-94.
11. Bartlett 1989, p. 77.
12. See Vriezen 1965, pp. 330-53.

was one also an Edomite by the recognition of the fact of birth and/or residence in Edom? The evidence is lacking for reaching a definitive conclusion, although the two criteria of worshiping Qaush and residence in Edom would converge if Edom had become a monolatrous society during the late eighth and seventh centuries B.C. as had Judah (Israel) during the same period (if, in fact, that is what occurred in the period encompassing the reigns of the Judaean kings Hezekiah and Josiah). We do know, however, from Assyrian sources that during this period the names of the kings of Edom contained the divine name "Qaush," for example, Qaushmalaka ("Qaush has become king," from the reign of Tiglath-pileser III, 744-27 B.C.),[13] Qaushgabri ("Quash is powerful," from the reign of Esarhaddon, 680-69 B.C.).[14] Is this appearance of Qaush as a prefix to the names of these two Edomite kings similar to the increasing frequency of appearance of Yahweh as a prefix ("Ja," "Jo") to the names of the Judaean kings during the same period?[15] In any event, we have a graphic example of the development of monolatry in Herodotus' description (1.172) of the Caunians of Asia Minor. Certainly the development of monolatry would have contributed decisively to an increased degree of sociological uniformity of the territory and its inhabitants such that we may speak of the existence of a nation. It would have done so through the creation of a territorially bounded religion and legal code common to all who dwelled within the territory. Are the "new Passover" (2 Kgs 23:21-23), the regulations concerning sacrifice (Deut 12:13-28), legal appeal to the center (Deut 17:8-9), and the evident territorial jurisdiction of Deuteronomy 12-26 to be understood as a *lex terrae*?

Let us turn to "all Aram" and ancient Armenia in order to investigate further what this conflation between a term designating both a land and a people and other factors might indicate for their understanding of the nature of different collectivities of the ancient Near East and antiquity.

"All Aram": A Nation of Aram?

The evidence for the existence of the territorially bounded collectivity of "all Aram," the Sefire Stele, also does not permit us to draw definitive conclusions about its precise nature. Nevertheless, the inconclusiveness of the evidence should not prevent a further examination of it in the attempt to clarify the applicability of the category of nationality—as distinct

---

13. Calah Summary Inscription 7, reverse, line 11, Tadmor 1994, p. 170.
14. ANET 1969, pp. 291, 294.
15. For the latter, see Noth 1928.

from a city-kingdom with villages or towns as its vassals, a tribal confederacy, or an empire—to different societies of antiquity.

The Aramaic inscription of the Sefire Stele[16] begins by stating that it is "the treaty of Bir-Ga'yah, king of KTK, with Matiᶜel, the son of ᶜAtarsumki, the king [of Arpad]."[17] We do not know the location of the kingdom of KTK,[18] but we do know that Arpad was an Aramean city-kingdom to the north of Aleppo in northern Syria. Arpad appears several times in Assyrian documents during the ninth and eighth centuries B.C.[19] As far as the date of the treaty with which the Sefire Stele begins, it had to have been

---

16. Unless otherwise noted, the translation is Fitzmyer 1967.

17. [ ] indicates editorial restorations of lacunae. The correct spelling of Atarsumki is from Assyrian inscriptions (Parpola and Watanabe 1988, pp. 8–13).

18. A detailed evaluation of the arguments for the determination of the location of KTK is beyond the scope of this investigation. For the different possibilities, see Fitzmyer 1967, pp. 127–35; and Gibson 1975, p. 22. More recently, Parpola and Watanabe (1988, p. xxvii) have argued that Bar-ga'yah ("son of majesty") is a pseudonym for Ashur-nerari V and, thus, KTK stands for Assyria. In favor of their argument is the list of Mesopotamian gods of Bar-ga'yah from lines 8–10 of face A of Stele I, and especially "Ashur" at line 25. Thus, they think that the Sefire treaty is the Aramaic version of the treaty of approximately 754 B.C. between Ashur-nerari V and Matiᶜil of Arpad. But why the use of KTK as a pseudonym for Assyria? If, in fact, Dupont-Sommer's (1958) restoration of Urartu at line 4 of face A of Sefire Stele I is correct—and the anti-Assyrian alliance (see Tiglath-pileser III's Stele IB from Iran and Calah Summary Inscription 1, Tadmor 1994, pp. 100, 124) between Urartu and Arpad in 743 B.C. favors this possibility—then Bar-ga'yah would be Sardur III of Urartu, and KTK possibly a vassal of Urartu to the north of Arpad. If so, this would clarify the territorial jurisdiction of the Sefire treaty from lines 9–10 of face B of Sefire Stele I (see below). Na'aman (1978, pp. 220–39) has offered a third possibility that KTK might be a province of Hamath, based on the conclusion that the territory outlined by the border points from lines 9–10 of face B was that of Aram-Damascus. However Na'aman's analysis is not without its own problems; for example, it is difficult to see how Jair ("Yauru": Na'aman's rejection, decisive for his analysis, of the reading of Ya'di at line 9, where he reads a resh, hence "Yauru," instead of dalet, hence Ya'di) fits into the treaty. Furthermore, why would Hamath/Hadrach be referred to as KTK and why, in a treaty between Arpad and KTK, would there be a detailed description of the boundaries of Aram-Damascus? On the other hand, the apparent absence of any explicit reference to Hamath is one of the many puzzles of the Sefire inscriptions.

19. For the ninth century, presumably "Arame, man of Gusi," mentioned in a text of Shalmaneser III (ANET, p. 278), and the "Gusi from Ishani," mentioned in a text of Ashurnasirpal II (ANET, p. 276) may be understood as referring to Arpad—so one concludes from the Bny [restored, possibly Byt] Gs from line 16, face A of Sefire Stele I and Bny Gs from line 3, face B of Sefire Stele I, and the description of Matiᶜil as both of the Bit-Agusi in the Calah Summary Inscription 3, lines 16–17 (Tadmor 1994, p. 132) and King of Arpad at line 3 of face A of Sefire Stele I. In any event, Arpad is listed as the first city of the land of Bit-Agusi in the Calah Summary Inscription 5 (Tadmor 1994, p. 146). For the treaty of approximately 754 B.C. between Ashur-nerari V of Assyria and the same Mati'ilu of Arpad, see Parpola and Watanabe 1988, pp. 8–13.

before 740 B.C. for that is when Tiglath-pileser III conquered Arpad and incorporated it into the Assyrian empire. Perhaps the date of the treaty may be placed in the period between approximately 754 B.C. when Matî'el made a treaty with Ashur-nerari V (which was presumably repudiated by Matî'el possibly at the death of Ashur-nerari V in 745 B.C.) and 740 B.C. We must now examine those sections of the treaty which may indicate something about the nature of the collectivity designated as "all Aram."

The first point for our consideration occurs in a further description of the jurisdiction of the treaty. On face A of Stele I, from lines three to six we read

> and the treaty of KTK with [the treaty of] Arpad; and the treaty of the lords of KTK with the treaty of the lords of Arpad; and the treaty of the un[ion of . . .]W with *all Aram* and with ⟨the king of⟩[20] Muṣr and with his sons who will come after [him], and [with the kings of] *all Upper-Aram and Lower-Aram* and with all who enter the royal palace. [my emphasis]

Note that not only is the city-kingdom of Arpad included in the treaty, but so also is "all Aram," *'Aram kulloh*. What are we to make of the designation "all Aram"?

It would appear from the terms "Upper-Aram" and "Lower-Aram" which follow the reference to "all Aram" that the term "all Aram" may designate a territory which includes "Upper-Aram" and "Lower-Aram."[21] Nevertheless, it is still far from obvious how that territory was conceived. Were there two separate regions of "all Aram," whatever that latter term may signify; and, if so, in what way were they separate? We know that the terms "Upper Egypt" and "Lower Egypt" designated (corresponding to the flow of the Nile from its source to the Mediterranean Sea) respectively the southern and northern regions of a single collectivity with relatively stable boundaries.[22] In a similar manner, was there a territory unified under the leadership of the city-kingdom of Arpad known as "all Aram" which encompassed Upper and Lower Aram? Most importantly, what kind of unity was it?

An examination of Face B of Stele I may provide some answers to these questions; but the answers remain tentative. In the first five lines of Face B we read

---

20. ⟨ ⟩ indicates editorial additions.

21. For the Aramaic term "all," see Fitzmyer 1979, pp. 205–17.

22. For the terms Upper and Lower Egypt, the territory, and the boundaries of ancient Egypt, see Grosby 1991, note 25 [[pp. 30–31 in this volume]].

[The treaty of Bir-Ga'yah, king of KTK, with Matî'el, son of 'Atarsumki, the king of Ar]pad; and the treaty of the son of Bir-Ga'yah with the sons of Matî'el; and the treaty of the [grandsons of Bir]-Ga'yah with the offspring of Matî'el and with the offspring of any king who [will come up and rule] in his place, and with the Benê-Gush and with Bêt-ṢLL[23] and with [all] Ar[am; and the trea]ty of KTK with the treaty of Arpad; and the treaty of the lords of KTK with the trea[ty of the lords of Ar]pad and with its people. . . .

Based on the parallel occurrence of the terms "all Aram" and "Arpad" in these lines, Joseph Fitzmyer concluded that the title of Matî'el was actually "king of Arpad and of all Aram."[24] Such a conclusion, if warranted, might signify that "all Aram" was a relatively unified collectivity. This conclusion might have merit if, based on the restoration of Damascus at line 10 on face B of Stele I (see below), one accepts that Damascus, or at least the area immediately to its north was part of "Lower Aram" and presumably, as a part of "all Aram," under the control of Arpad; and one further assumes that Damascus was greatly weakened by its defeat in approximately 773 B.C. at the hands of Shalmaneser IV as described in lines 6-10 on the reverse side of the Pazarcik Stele, "the tribute of Hadiyani, the man of Damascus—silver, gold, copper, his royal bed, his royal couch, his daughter with her extensive dowry, the property of his palace without number—I received from him."[25] Further support for understanding Damascus as being greatly weakened at this time might also be found in 2 Kgs 14:25, 28 where Jeroboam II of Israel (782-748 B.C.) is described as having brought Damascus and perhaps a part of Hamath,

---

23. Unfortunately, the location and nature of Bêt-ṢLL is uncertain. Benê-Gush (Stele I, face B, line 3) = Bêt-Gush (Stele II, face B, line 10) = Arpad (see also note 19). It is precisely this equation or terminological conflation which is indicative of our categorial problem, namely, the attribution of presumed kinship, Benê-Gush, to a territorial collectivity, Bêt-Gush/Arpad. This attribution is often obscured by the use of the term "tribe," the latter implying a relation of blood, because for most collectivities the blood relation is a fiction. Examples of a territorial referent as the basis for the fiction of blood relation would appear to be the "tribes" (Banu)yamina from Mari and Benjamin from Israel, "those from the south." This is precisely where the work of M. B. Rowton is most relevant, see below. Our problem is ascertaining the existence of territorially more extensive kinship structures than that of Benê-Gush/Bêt-Gush. Perhaps the classic example of such a structure is Israel = House of Israel = sons of Israel (putative lineage of Abraham/Isaac/Jacob). The attribution of blood relation to a territorial collectivity through reference to an eponymous ancestor is also evident in Armenian history, see below. Also indicative of this categorial problem are such terms as *gayūm* from Mari and *gôy* from Israel which Malamat (1989, pp. 38-39) describes as being "ethno-geographic terms." For the Hebrew *gôy* as "nation," see Speiser 1960; Cody 1964. "Nation" is also an ethno-geographic term.
24. Fitzmyer 1967, p. 60.
25. Donbaz 1990, p. 9.

the Aramean kingdom situated between Damascus and Arpad, under the control of Israel, thus leaving the rest of the area of "all Aram" open to the control of Arpad. Still, even if this conclusion has merit, we do not know what is meant for Matîʿel and Arpad to be in control of "all Aram," especially given the widely accepted restoration of "the kings" at the end of line five of face A of Sefire Stele I, "[with the kings of] all Upper Aram and Lower Aram." If this restoration is accurate, then its implication may run counter to Fitzmyer's conclusion; for it would seem to imply the continued existence of independent city-kingdoms in an alliance with Arpad as its head. This, in turn, would indicate that "all Aram" should perhaps be understood as resembling more a military confederation than a unified state with Matîʿel as its king. The nature of "all Aram" still remains uncertain: does "all Aram" refer to a relatively unified collectivity; or does it more likely refer to not much more than yet another example of the numerous military alliances of city-kingdoms which were formed in the face of the military threat of Assyria during the ninth and eighth centuries B.C.? Was Arpad the lead city-kingdom of two otherwise distinct Aramean power blocs, "Upper Aram," under its direct control, and "Lower Aram," dominated by Damascus, with Arpad's rival, Hamath, in the middle;[26] or was it, after the relative decline of Damascus, the center of an emerging Aramaic nation, "all Aram"?

There is evidence from the Sefire Stele which may provide some understanding of the nature of the city-kingdom of Arpad and, hence, "all Aram." On Face A of Stele I at lines 35–36, we find the following curse against any possible violation of the treaty, "Just as this wax is burned by fire, so may Arpad be burned and [her *gr*]*eat*[27] [daughter-cities]! May Hadad sow in them salt. . . ." The restoration of "daughter-cities" appears reasonable particularly given the lines which appear just before the one quoted above (lines 32ff.).

> And may Arpad become a mound to [house the desert animal]: the gazelle and the fox and the hare and the wild-cat and the owl and the [ ] and the magpie! May [this] ci[ty] not be mentioned ⟨anymore⟩, [nor] MDRʾ nor MRBH nor MZH nor MBLH nor Sharun nor Tuʾim nor Bethel nor BYNN nor [. . . nor ʾAr]neh nor Ḥazaz nor ʾAdam!

Apparently this concluding list of proper nouns designated the smaller towns which were dependent upon the more powerful city-kingdom of

---

26. For the conflict between Hamath and Arpad, see the Antakya Stele (Donbaz 1990, p. 7) where Adad-nerari III is described as establishing the boundary between Zakur of the land of Hamath and Atarsumki [father of Matîʿel]; and the Zakir Stele (Gibson 1975, pp. 8–13) where "Bargush" at line 5 is to be understood as Arpad.

27. Italics indicate uncertain readings.

Arpad. We know from Tiglath-pileser III's Calah Summary Inscription 5 that both Sharun and Ḥazaz were considered by the Assyrians to be "towns of the land of the Bit-Agusi (Arpad)."[28] Sharun was located about 50 km northeast of the general vicinity of Arpad; Ḥazaz was about 13 km to the north northwest of Arpad; and ʾArneh could be 20 km to the southwest of Arpad.[29] If Tuʾim is modern Taʾum,[30] which is approximately 45 km southwest of Aleppo, then the territorial jurisdiction of Bit-Agusi/Arpad itself would have extended not only to the east to include an area formerly of the Bit-Adini, but also to the south into north central Hamath. Were these smaller towns, each with its own "sheikh," which were together centered on Arpad, also, as such, incorporated into the kinship structure of Bit-Agusi/Benê-Gush? In any event, if these towns listed on Face A of Sefire Stele I are expressive of the territorial jurisdiction of the land of Bit-Agusi/Arpad, as Tiglath-pileser III's Summary Inscription would seem to indicate, then they might be further evidence for understanding Bit-Agusi/Arpad as the expanding, lead city-kingdom of the military block of "Upper Aram" and possibly "all Aram" rather than the capital of a unified state of "all Aram." Even so, we are still faced with the problem of how to understand the apparent territorial designation "all Aram." It would seem that the weight of this briefly examined evidence, uncertain though it is, points to understanding the term "all Aram" as indicating the existence of what Martin Noth described as a "Sammelstaat," which externally has the appearance of a unity, but internally consists of individual, relatively independent parts, some of which were still ruled by their own dynasties, though all were subordinate (in a military alliance) to a central kingdom, in this case possibly Arpad under Matīʿel and previously Damascus under Ben Hadad I, Hazael, and Ben Hadad II.[31]

The problem with the characterization of the Arameans as respectively an episodic military confederation or a federated state is the very existence of the apparent, territorial designation "all Aram." The existence of this territorial designation points to a collectivity which might have been something more than a military confederation, for it implies a greater

---

28. Tadmor's correct reading (pp. 146–47, notes 5–7) of Bit-Agusi in place of Bit-Adini indicates that Arpad's power had extended to the north and east, incorporating territory previously part of Bit-Adini.

29. Fitzmyer 1967, 51. For the location of Ḥazaz (modern ʿAzaz) as north northwest of Arpad (modern Tell Rafad) see Dussaud 1927, map XII, and Hawkins 1973, p. 240. It seems unlikely that Bethel could have been the Israelite Bethel.

30. For the identification, see Astour 1963, p. 237; Dussaud 1927, Map X. MDRʾ might be Madyara to the east of Douma (Dussaud 1927, p. 305), and, if so, approximately 25 km northeast of Hamath.

31. Noth 1962, pp. 233–34.

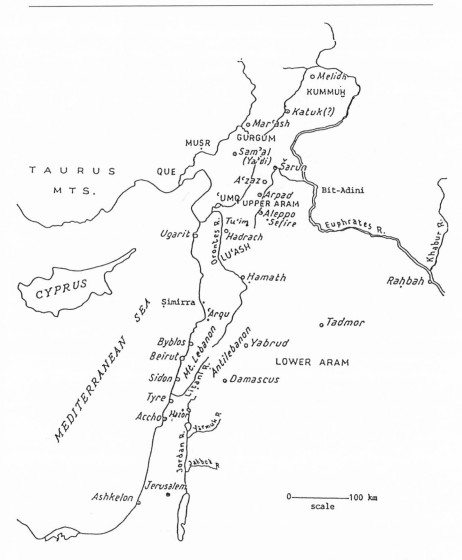

MAP 1. The ancient Near East with reference to the Sefire inscriptions. Adapted from Joseph Fitzmyer, *The Aramaic Inscriptions of Sefire* (Rome, 1967).

degree of sociological homogeneity than such an alliance. Moreover, if, in fact, "all Aram" had rather clearly designated boundaries, then the case for "all Aram" as a territorial unit, and not just a military alliance of city-kingdoms, the membership of which often changed, will be strengthened. However, a careful analysis of Aram's boundaries as described in lines nine and ten of Face B of Sefire Stele I only raises further problems. The lines describe the extent to which "the words of the concluded treaty are to be heard."

> ... from] ʿArqu to Yaʾd[i and] BZ, from Lebanon to Yab[rud, from Damas-cu]s to ʿAru and M..W., [and fr]om the Valley to KTK . . .

Joseph Fitzmyer thought that the phrase "from ʿArqu to Yaʾd[i and] BZ" designated respectively the southern and northern limits of the jurisdiction of the treaty. ʿArqu is probably the city Arqa on the coast of the Mediterranean mentioned several times in the inscriptions of Tiglath-pileser III.[32] It is, along with Ṣimirra directly to its north, also described there as a city of Hamath.[33] Yaʾdi is to the north of Arpad where one assumes the uncertain BZ is also located.[34] It is, however, more likely, depending upon how one understands the rest of lines 9-10, that the phrase "from ʿArqu to Yaʾdi and BZ" describes the territorial extent of Upper Aram with ʿArqu being its southwestern corner and Yaʾdi its northern limit, an area which would have encompassed much of Hamath. As to the phrase "from Lebanon to Yabrud," if Lebanon is Mt. Lebanon, then this designation may indicate the northwestern border between Upper and Lower Aram, with Yabrud being the northeastern limit of Lower Aram.[35] The likelihood of this latter possibility is strengthened if, in fact, the restoration of Damascus in line 10 is justified; for the phrase "from Damascus to ʿAru and M..W" might then indicate part of the southern border of Lower Aram, leaving open the question as to whether or not Damascus was actually a part of Lower Aram.[36] In any event, it must be admitted that the

---

32. The Calah Annal 13, line 6; Calah Summary Inscriptions: 4, line 2; 5, line 17; 6, line 22.

33. Calah Summary Inscription 5, lines 20-24, Tadmor 1994, p. 148. Does the reference to ʿArqu indicate that Arpad had gained control over Hamath at this time? For Arqa and Ṣimirra, see Oded 1974, pp. 42-45.

34. For the relation between (the land?) Yaʾdi and (its capital?) Samʾal, the latter is mentioned in the inscriptions of Tiglath-pileser III (Calah Annal 13, line 12; Annal 27, line 4; Stele IIIA from Iran, line 17; and Summary Inscription 7, line 8) with Panammu as its king; while in the Hadad inscription (Gibson 1975, pp. 65-86), Panammu is known as the king of Yaʾdi.

35. For Mount Lebanon as one of the border points of Aram-Damascus, see Tiglath-pileser III's Calah Summary Inscription 9, reverse, line 3 (Tadmor 1994, p. 186).

36. Such an interpretation is likely if ʿAru is the ʿArʿaru (Aroer) near, so one presumes, Damascus as mentioned in Isa 17:1-2, Biblica Hebraica (and, thus, not the Aroer in the Transjordan), "Behold Damascus shall cease to be a city; it shall become a heap of ruins. The towns of Aroer shall be deserted." Nonetheless, it must be acknowledged that this one line from Isaiah, which is not in the Septuagint, is the only evidence for this Aroer. For the textual difficulties involved in such a restoration, see Fitzmyer 1967, p. 64. Fitzmyer's location of ʿAru south of Aleppo seems odd. It is

uncertainty of both the restoration of M..W (perhaps Mansuate, and thus part of the southern boundary of Lower Aram) and ʿAru greatly complicates the geographical analysis. The final phrase, "and from the Valley to KTK," would then evidently refer to the territorial extent of the treaty, presumably from the Beqaʿ Valley in the south to KTK in the north if, in fact, KTK is a border region of Urartu; that is, the phrase describes the entire territorial extent of the area of "all Aram."[37] If this is how the last phrase is to be understood, then it is more likely that the first phrase, "from ʿArqu to Yaʾdi and BZ" indicates the jurisdiction of "Upper Aram." One tentatively concludes that the boundary points of these phrases probably designate the territorial extent of an Aramean military coalition, for example, from point A to point B, rather than as a detailed description of the boundaries of a unified state "all Aram."[38]

Nonetheless, once again, the very existence of the term "all Aram" cannot be easily dismissed. Indeed, even if the boundaries discussed above delineate the territorial extent of an Aramean military coalition, it was still Aramean. Here, again, is the problem: how to understand our apparently

---

based on ʿAru = Ara of north central Hamath (perhaps modern Maʿarret en-Noʿman, see Dussaud 1927, pp. 182, 188; Weippert 1973, p. 43) mentioned in the Calah Summary Inscription 5 of Tiglath-pileser III (Tadmor 1994, p. 148).

37. Are lines 20–23 of Tiglath-pileser III's Calah Summary Inscription 6 (Tadmor 1994, p. 152) confirmation of the territorial extent of "all Aram"? "Over Unqi in its entirety and Bit-Agusi to its full extent I ruled; I placed my eunuchs over them as governors. From the city of Kashpuna on the shore of the Upper Sea, the cities of Ṣimirra, Arqa . . . as far as Anti-Lebanon."

38. As to the latter possibility, see Mazar 1962, pp. 116–20. Mazar understood these lines to designate the "detailed boundaries of all Aram which were patterned after parallel biblical description that delineated the boundaries of Canaan and the land of Israel." For example, according to Mazar, "from Lebanon to Iabrud, and Damascus, and Aroer and Mansuate" are the names of four provinces of "Lower Aram" which provided the detailed extent of the territory of "Lower Aram." The primary objections to Mazar's analysis are that it rests upon both the doubtful assumption of the existence of a unified Aramean state in the mid-ninth century B.C., whose area reached from Mansuate in the south to Yaʿdi in the north, as a basis for the historically subsequent "all Aram" of the Sefire Stele; and the (perhaps idealized) description of the boundaries of Israel as a pattern for "all Aram." Nevertheless, the use of both *piḫatu*, "district," in lines 6–7 of Tiglath-pileser III's Calah Annal 19 (Tadmor 1994, p. 60 and note 7, p. 61) and *nagu*, "district," "province" (used in inscriptions of Assyrian kings from Tiglath-pileser III on, see CAD, vol. N, part 1) at, for example, line 17 of Calah Annal 23 (Tadmor 1994, p. 80), "the 16 districts of Damascus," makes one wonder if provinces or districts were, in fact, being described in lines 9–10 of face B of Sefire I, irrespective, of course, of any biblical parallel. Pitard (1987, p. 179) believes that "all Aram" and "Upper and Lower Aram" refer to an Aramean state dominated by Arpad, but that it did not contain Damascus.

justified use of the adjective Aramean, as implied by the term "all Aram?"
Our investigation of what "all Aram" might have designated becomes
more intriguing when we reconsider the previously quoted lines 4–5
from face B of Stele I.

> . . . and with [all] Ar[am; and the trea]ty of KTK with the treaty of Arpad; and
> the treaty of the lords of KTK with the trea[ty of the lords of Ar]pad *and with*
> *its people*. . . . (my emphasis)

Here we observe that the treaty was made not only between KTK and "all
Aram," not only between the kings of KTK and Arpad (line 1, face B), not
only between the lords, *b'ly*, of KTK and Arpad, but also with the people,
'mh. Of course, by including not only the king, but also "the people,"
everyone was understood to be bound by the sworn oaths. Still, one wonders if there is greater significance to the inclusion of "its people." Such a
formulation reminds us of 2 Kings 23 where Josiah is depicted as having
made a covenant not only in the presence of the elders, but also in the
presence of "all the people," *kl h'm*. Was the inclusion of "with its people"
in the Sefire treaty in some way an anticipation of, or an indication of certain political and religious ideas emerging at that time in the ancient
Near East which we find so developed in the theology of the covenant
between *kol yiśra'el*, "all Israel," and Yahweh in Deuteronomy? Furthermore, is there particular sociological significance, indicating some kind
of uniformity, to the use of "all"? Does the use of "all" as in "all Aram" indicate an anticipation of, or the early stages in the formation of a
bounded, territorial collectivity both more extensive and more sociologically uniform than a city-kingdom with its dependent towns and more
stable than a transient military alliance? In the case of ancient Israel, it
appears that the term "all" of "all Israel" emphasized a unity of the land,
"all Israel from Dan to Beersheba," which was inseparable from the unity
of the people, "all Israel."[39]

Perhaps with time, "all Aram" would have developed into a more
definite territorial entity other than the apparent areal jurisdiction of a
military alliance. Perhaps with time, "all Aram," that is, a collectivity encompassing the territory from the Beqa' Valley to Ya'di, would have developed an ascendant center capable, as such, of unifying the relatively
heterogeneous city-kingdoms of Damascus, Hamath, and Arpad into a
relatively homogeneous nation. However, such a development was cut
short by the final victory of the Assyrians. What can be said of the people

---

39. Consider, for example, 1 Sam 3:20; 2 Sam 16:21, 22; 17:11; 24:2; Ezek 11:15.

of the area of "all Aram" beyond presumably being Aramaic speaking? We do not know for certain of any developing belief in an ancestry common to "all Aram" similar to the putative genealogy of Abraham-Isaac-Jacob for "all Israel." Nevertheless, Martin Noth was probably correct when he stated that the Arameans apparently remained aware of being ethnically related (that is, where there is a fiction of relation by ties of blood); for even where they divided themselves structurally into several city-states, the names of these states maintained the common general designation of Aram—at least that is how they were viewed by the Israelites: the Hebrew Bible mentions Aram-Naharaim, Aram-Zobah, Aram-Beth-Rehob, and Aram-Damascus.[40] While the latter three designated areas fall within the domain of "Lower Aram," Aram-Naharaim was located around the great bend of the Euphrates, that is, in the general vicinity east of Arpad. Thus, at least from the perspective of the Hebrew Bible, some kind of ethnic similarity was perceived to exist throughout a geographical area stretching from Bit-Adini, east northeast of Arpad, to Aram-Beth-Rehob, southwest of Damascus. Perhaps one basis of this perceived similarity was the apparently common use of the Aramaic language throughout a geographical area encompassing Ya'di in the north to Damascus in the south, so one concludes on the basis of, respectively, the Hadad Stele erected by Panammu and the Barhadad Stele.[41] Mention should also be made of the curious designation found at line 1 in Stele IIIA from Iran of Tiglath-pileser III, "The kings of the land of Hatti (and of) the Aramaeans of the western seashore."[42] Does this use of the term Aramaeans refer to the inhabitants of the area of Kashpuna, Ṣimirra, and Arqa? Does it indicate that the Assyrians also recognized a trans-local relation "Aramean"? An answer to this last question is, of course, greatly complicated by the numerous Assyrian references to Arameans far to the east of "all Aram," including in the general vicinity of Babylonia.[43] In any event, it would appear from the terms of the Sefire Stele that at least the Arameans of Arpad perceived some kind of similarity between the "Aram" of Ya'di, Sharun, ʿArqu, Yabrud, and probably Damascus. This common designation of "Aram" in the terms "all Aram," "Upper Aram," and "Lower Aram" would appear to indicate the developing sociological uniformity of a

---

40. Noth 1962, p. 220.

41. Gibson 1975, pp. 3, 65. For an overview of the controversy surrounding the Barhadad Stele, see Pitard 1987, pp. 138–44.

42. Tadmor 1994, p. 106, where the determinative for land modifies *A-ri-me*, Aramaeans.

43. For an overview of the problem, see Forrer 1932.

collective self-consciousness of a nation.[44] An element of this uniformity may also be seen in the fact that Hadad appears to have become the leading god of the Aramean pantheon.[45]

In conclusion, it would appear from the Sefire Treaty that around 745 B.C. the Aramean city-kingdom of Arpad emerged as the leader of "all Aram." The emergence of Arpad as the leader of an anti-Assyrian military alliance may have been predicated upon the relative decline of Damascus as the prominent Aramean power in the first quarter of the eighth century B.C., especially following the defeat of Damascus in 773 B.C. at the hands of the Assyrian Shalmaneser IV. The emergence of "all Aram" may also have been predicated upon a century and a half long history of military alliances of different city-kingdoms in opposition to the western expansion of Assyria.[46] As to the diffusion of the Aramaic language among these different kingdoms as well as the nature of and salience of the self-designation of "Aram" among them, not much can be said other than that it respectively occurred and apparently existed. This linguistic diffusion and terminological self-designation are indicative of what Friedrich Meinecke called a *Kulturnation*,[47] and what Benjamin Mazar called an "ethnic-territorial" collectivity.[48] Neither term is satisfactory for distinguishing between empire, nation, and city-kingdom, and especially their apparently different constitutive territorial referents. In any event, we lack the evidence to investigate further the extent to which the different military alliances of the ninth and eighth centuries B.C. may have over-

---

44. The sociological problem of the significance of the term "all Aram" remains even if one follows Naʾaman (1978) in interpreting the borders described in lines 9–10 on face B of Stele I as those of an "all Aram" to the south of Hamath.

45. For Hadad, see Greenfield 1987. Note that the names of the kings Barhadad and Hadadezer of Damascus contained the divine name Hadad; Hadad is called upon by Matiʿel of Arpad to carry out the curses of the Sefire Treaty; and the inscriptions of Zenjirli (Gibson 1975, p. 65), where Hadad is described as having given to Panammu of Yaʾdi authority to rule. Thus, it would appear that Hadad had become the god of Damascus, Arpad, and Yaʾdi. However, in the Barhadad Stele (Gibson 1975, p. 3), the god Melqart is referred to as Barhadad's lord; and in the Zakir Stele (Gibson 1975, p. 9), Zakur of Hamath is described as having received his authority to rule from Baalshamayn. [In the new inscription from Tel Dan, the king (presumably Hazael of Damascus) names Hadad as the god who made him king and went in front of him into battle (A. Biran and J. Naveh, *Israel Exploration Journal* 45 [1995] pp. 1–18).

46. Based on 1 Sam 14:47 and 2 Sam 8:3, Malamat (1973, p. 141) concluded that as early as 950 B.C. the Aramean Hadadezer of Damascus had unified Aram-Beth-Rehob with Aram-Zobah.

47. Meinecke 1970.

48. Mazar 1962, p. 119.

come previous conflict between Aramean city-kingdoms, thereby facilitating the emergence of an "Aramean people" and a territory of "all Aram."

Although it appears from our reading of the Sefire Stele that Arpad was the leader of a military coalition, the terms "Upper Aram" and "Lower Aram" as part of "all Aram" may indicate that a territorially bounded nation of Aram may have been in the process of emerging before that process was cut short by the final victory of the Assyrians. However, if this were the case, the stability of the image of a bounded territory of "all Aram" was still to be achieved. To describe Aram and the Arameans as merely an alliance of city-kingdoms or tribes, as is usually the case, is to ignore the apparent territorial designations discussed above. On the other hand, to describe "all Aram" as a national state is evidently to go too far. Here we have an example of the permeability of our categories of analysis in the face of actual reality. This permeability is to be observed for modern collectivities as well; consider such modern societies as Germany before unification under Bismarck, the confederated nations of Belgium or Switzerland, or the "national," "tribal" societies of Africa.

Ancient Armenia

The evidence for the existence of a bounded Armenian territory and, indeed, a nation of Armenia (Greater Armenia) of the fourth century A.D. is to be found in abundance in the following works: Faustus' *Epic Histories* which, while covering the history of Armenia from the death of King Trdat III in 330 to the division of the country in 387 between Rome and Iran, was probably written or revised during the last half of the fifth century;[49] Agathangelos's *History of the Armenians* which, while describing the conversion of Trdat to Christianity (circa A.D. 314) and the missionary work of St. Gregory the Illuminator in Armenia, was probably written in the last half of the fifth century;[50] Elishe's *History of Vardan and the Armenian War* which, while recounting the unsuccessful Armenian revolt of 450/51 against Sasanian Iran and the subsequent fate of the Armenian prisoners, was probably written at the end of the sixth century;[51] and Moses Khorenatsʿi's *History of the Armenians* which, while covering the history of Armenia from primeval times down to the death of Mashtotsʿ, the missionary responsible for the invention of the Armenian script

---

49. See Garsoian's introduction to Pʿawstos 1989, p. 41.
50. See Thomson's introduction to Agathangelos 1976, p. xvi.
51. See Thomson's introduction to Elishe 1982, p. 29.

(circa A.D. 400), was possibly written as late as A.D. 750.[52] The evidence provided by these various early histories of ancient Armenia for the existence of a nation of Armenia with its bounded territory is so abundant and incisive that Cyril Toumanoff was fully justified to refer to these works as being nothing less than "national literary monuments."[53]

Despite the abundance and clarity of this evidence, which we will examine in a moment, it is of questionable reliability; for the image of single, unified Armenia of the fourth century is primarily the idea of Armenian Christian historiography, characteristic of all these works, and not necessarily historical fact.[54] Even though the boundaries of Arsacid Armenia (Greater Armenia) remained more or less the same for over four hundred years, from 95 B.C. to A.D. 363/87, the actual structure of Armenia during this period was feudal; it consisted of a network of relatively independent territorial units or separate principalities known as the *naXarar* system.[55] Even the structure of the early Armenian church was dominated by the *naXarar* system: its leadership was, for several generations, drawn from the family of Gregory as if the office of chief bishop was a hereditary fief.[56] Moreover, western Armenia (Lesser Armenia) was annexed to the Romans in A.D. 72, while the eastern part (Greater Armenia) was much influenced by Persia—a division only accentuated by the formal division of Greater Armenia between Rome (Constantinople) and Persia after A.D. 387.[57] Nonetheless, the dynastic lords or princes (the *naXarars*) of these relatively independent territorial principalities or "satrapies" were presided over by the "superdynastic" king of (Greater) Armenia. Thus, with Armenia, certainly after Trdat I ascended the Armenian throne (circa A.D. 50), there was a remarkable symbiosis of centrifugal tendencies—above all, the relatively independent territorial units of the *naXarars*—and centralizing tendencies—above all, the dynastic royal house and the emergence of a trans-local nobility.[58] This remarkable

---

52. See Thomson's introduction to Khorenats'i 1978, pp. 59-60.

53. Toumanoff 1963, p.106. Three other works in English on the social history of ancient Armenia are particularly important: the incomparable Adontz 1970; Garsoian 1985; and Garsoian's introduction, commentary, and various appendices in P'awstos 1989. See also Hewsen's commentary and appendices to Ananias 1992.

54. Garsoian 1985a, p. 342. For example, Faustus never acknowledges the existence of the Persian influenced southern principalities which were independent of Greater Armenia during the fourth century.

55. Adontz 1970, p. 235.

56. Toumanoff 1963, pp. 138-39.

57. For the influence of Persia on Armenia, see Strabo 1854, Book XI, Chapter XIV.

58. See Adontz 1970, pp. 235, 307-10; Toumanoff 1963, p. 112.

symbiosis properly reminds us of feudal Europe; thus, our analysis of the boundaries and territory of (Greater) Armenia during this period should also provide conceptual insights for ascertaining the existence of nationality during the European middle ages.[59]

The evident partiality of the early, Christian Armenian historiography by no means invalidates its usefulness for providing evidence for the existence of conceptions of boundaries and an Armenian territory. Even if the accounts of the early Christian Armenians are to some degree tendentious, the terms which they employed may be taken as reliable evidence for the existence of the conceptions of their day; for language and terminology are not the creations of a single individual. They have their own history; their existence is itself fact for our analysis. It is to an examination of these terms that we now turn.[60]

There appears repeatedly throughout these early histories of Armenia the phrase "land of Armenia," *erkir* (land) *Hayocʿ* (of Armenia/Armenians). The significance of this term may initially be seen by considering what it is not: it is not a geographical term explicitly signifying the areal possession of the royal house; nor does the term explicitly signify primarily a polity, for the latter is designated repeatedly by the term "realm of Armenia," *asXarh* (realm, kingdom or state) *Hayocʿ*, or "realm of the land of Armenia," *asXarh hayastan erkin*.[61] The term *erkir Hayocʿ*, "land of Armenia," appears to signify the territory of Armenia, that is, it appears to signify a relation, one of whose referents is a bounded locational proximity. It should be noted here that the existence of separate terms, "land of Armenia (of the Armenians)" and "realm (of the land) Armenia" may prefigure our own terminological and conceptual distinction between "nation" and "state."

Certainly in antiquity, the existence of a trans-local territorial designation in contrast to a description of the geographical possession of the king, for example, the "land of Israel from Dan to Beersheba" in contrast to the land of the "House of David," does not, *ipso facto*, indicate the existence of a nation; nonetheless, it is certainly suggestive of a degree of trans-local cultural homogeneity or relation. Once again, an element in ascertaining the existence of a nation is a designation common to both a

---

59. For recent discussions of nationality in the middle ages, see Reynolds 1984, and the fine series *Nationes, Historische und Philologische Untersuchungen zur Entstehung der europäischen Nationen im Mittelalter* (Sigmaringen: Thorbecke-Verlag).

60. For much of this analysis, I am indebted to Garsoian's superb appendices to Pʿawstos 1989.

61. Pʿawstos 1989, p. 524, "astan" of *hayastan* is the locative suffix.

"people" and an area of land. Why is this so? It is because this common designation indicates that the image of an area of land has become one of the referents around which the image of a "people" has been constituted; that is, it indicates that there exists a bounded territorial relation, a territorial collectivity of nativity, a nation. We find such a designation throughout early Armenian historiography. As indicated above, the term *Hay/Hayk'* (singular/plural) meant the territory Armenia;[62] yet, the term is also repeatedly used to designate "Armenians."[63]

> And after this, there was a bitter contest between the Persians and the Armenians (*Hayk'*), because the former had collected an army and came to seize the realm of the land of Armenia (*hayastan erkin*). (Faustus, *Histories*, III.xi)

Indicative of this "conflation" between terms signifying a land and its people,[64] characteristic of nationality, are passages like the following from Faustus' *Histories* (V.xliii).

> For seven years after that, the Persian army did not dare to enter again into the Armenian borders (*sahman*), and there was peace in the land. . . . And the entire land of Armenia lived in peace. . . . All the people of the land of Armenia favored these days. . . .

The intention of these observations, in particular this dual implication of *Hay* (*Hayk'*) referring to both the land of Armenia and the people of Armenia such that the term Armenia signifies both—reminiscent of the terminological conflation (*kol*) *yiśrā'ēl*, *'ereṣ yiśrā'ēl*—is not meant to deny the actual, heterogeneous nature of Armenian society, namely, once again, the centrifugal, feudal *naXarar* system, and the existence of a Roman Lesser Armenia, a Greater Armenia, and southern Armenian areas independent of both. Nonetheless, this terminology, and, as we shall observe, much more, does indicate that, despite this heterogeneity, it is appropriate for one to speak of the existence of an Armenian nation, however nebulous that nation might have been. These comments are equally relevant to an analysis of nationality in Europe during the middle ages.

---

62. *Mec Hayk'* refers to "Greater Armenia." Faustus uses the term *Hayk'*, "Armenia," and *Mec Hayk'* as synonyms, with no reference to the Roman Lesser Armenia, see P'awstos 1989, p. 480.

63. P'awstos 1989, p. 379. *Hayk'* is singular nominative; *Hayoc'* is plural nominative and genitive.

64. This terminological conflation can also often be seen with clans and tribes, for example, the clan and its territory were both called *naXararut'iwn* by Khorenats'i, see Adontz 1970, p. 371. To repeat, such a terminological conflation indicates that this fiction of a trans-local kinship of blood relation has as its basis a territorial referent. Once again, a similar conflation can be seen in the ancient Near East, see note 23.

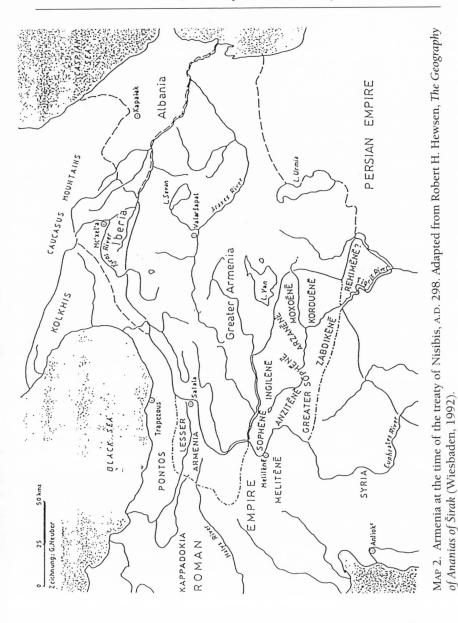

MAP 2. Armenia at the time of the treaty of Nisibis, A.D. 298. Adapted from Robert H. Hewsen, *The Geography of Ananias of Širak* (Wiesbaden, 1992).

In addition to the use of *Hay* (*Hayk⁽*), there are other indications of the existence of a cultural homogeneity constitutive of Armenia. There appears to have been not only a language common to the territory of

Armenia,[65] but also the awareness that it was constitutive of that territory. This may be seen in the term "land of Armenian speech," *erkir haykakan lezui*.

> And all the *azats* (the lower nobility) and peasants from one border (*sahman*) to the other of the entire territory (plural of *sahman*) of the land of Armenia mourned—the *azats* and all the peasants and all the dwellers in the house of T'orgom alike [all the speakers]-of-the-Armenian tongue. (Faustus' *Histories* V.xxx)

One presumes that the reference of the term "land of Armenian speech" encompassed Lesser as well as Greater Armenia.[66]

We have observed, so far, terms that would appear to indicate the existence of two referents of the collective self-consciousness constitutive of a nation of Armenia, a relation of a bounded areal jurisdiction, a territory, and a language (and after A.D. 400 an Armenian script common to "Roman" Armenia and "Persian" Armenia[67]) which was seen as common to Armenians and their territory.

A third referent in the formation of an Armenian collective self-consciousness was a belief in an ancestry common to all Armenians. In the above quotation from Faustus' *Histories*, reference is made to "all the dwellers in the house of T'orgom." We learn from Khorenats'i's *History* (I.xii) that Hayk, the term used to designate both Armenia and Armenians, was "son of T'orgom, son of T'iras, son of Gomer, son of Yapheth, [and] the ancestor of the Armenians." Clearly, Khorenats'i's description not only follows biblical models, but it actually places Armenia (Hayk) within biblical genealogy (see Gen 10:3).[68] The tendentiousness of such a description is obvious; less obvious is its significance.[69]

The bounded, trans-local territorial relation characteristic of nationality appears to engender, in varying degrees of saliency, the fiction of a kinship of ties of blood. Why this should be so is difficult to say. Perhaps there are two factors: (1) the land is life-sustaining and (2) a nation ceases to "live" if it does not have its own territory or references to a territory believed to be its own (including, usually, sovereignty over that territory). Both factors lie behind the connection between the idiom of

---

65. Strabo 1854, Book XI, Chapter XIV, "they [the Armenians] all speak the same language."

66. P'awstos 1989, p. 524.

67. Thomson 1994, p. 38.

68. See also Agathangelos 1976, p. xvi.

69. For the probable etymology of *Hayk* and its relation to the term Armenia, see the various discussions in Toumanoff 1963.

family relations through blood ties (the most obvious expression of the factors affecting the generation and sustenance of life) and their attribution to territorial relations. In any event, in antiquity, the obvious parallel example to Hay/Hayk is "Israel," the term applying to both the fictitious ancestry and the nation. Having observed three elements evidently constitutive of Armenian society, let us turn briefly to the existence of conceptions of the territorial boundaries of that society.

We have already seen examples of use of the terms "border" (*sahman*) and "territory" (where the plural of *sahman* is used) in ancient Armenian historiography. Characteristic of the many uses of these terms is the following excerpt from Faustus' *Histories* (V.xx).

> Morning and night he [Mušeł, commander of the Armenian forces] was at work, striving and straining to go to war, and he did not allow any—not one handful—of soil to be taken away anywhere from the confines (limits, boundaries) of the land of Armenia.[70]

The tumultuous history of the area, in particular Armenia being situated between the Roman and Persian empires, was not conducive to the establishment of stable borders encompassing the entire "land of Armenian speech." Nevertheless, there did exist relatively precise conceptions of the bounded territory of Greater Armenia. In Faustus' *Histories* (III.vii), we read that enemies of Armenia (possibly Iberians)

> scattered and spread altogether over [Armenia's] territory all the way to the small city of Satal and to Ganjak, [which is] the border of Atrpatakan.

Satal was at the far northwestern end of Greater Armenia and Ganjak was its far southeastern end, thus marking the borders of Greater Armenia at the time. A more detailed description of the territory is provided in Agathangelos' *History* (dcccxlii) in the discussion of the geographical extent of the missionary work of Gregory.[71]

> Thus throughout the whole land of Armenia, from end to end, he extended the labor of preaching the gospel. From the city of Satala to the land of Khaltikʿ, to Kalarjik, to the very borders of the Massagetae, to the gate of the Alans, to the borders of the Kaspkʿ, to Pʿaytakaran the city of the Armenian kingdom; from the city of Amida to the city of Nisibis he passed along the borders of Syria, the land of Nor-Shirakan and Kordukʿ, to the secure land

---

70. Note also the reference to "native land" in Elishe 1982, p. 131, "Their general himself took responsibility for the rear ranks; posting guards to the front and rear and the sides, he brought the army back safe and sound in thirty days near to the borders of their native land."

71. See also the detailed description of the borderlands of Greater Armenia in Pʿawstos 1989, IV.1.

of the Medes, to the house of the prince of Mahk'r-tun to Azerbaijan—he spread his gospel-preaching.

Another description of the territorial boundaries of Greater Armenia is to be found in Ananias of Širak's *Geography*. Ananias described in great detail how Greater Armenia was composed of fifteen areas. Each of the fifteen areas was further analyzed by Ananias in considerable detail, specifically the borders of each area were given and, then, each area's constitutive districts were listed and described. Unfortunately, even though Ananias' *Geography* was modeled after various ancient geographies and, as such, is most certainly not an example of Christian historiography, its description of Greater Armenia is still unreliable. Written probably in the early seventh century,[72] Ananias' *Geography* appears to conflate descriptions of Greater Armenia from two different eras, one being Greater Armenia before its division in 387, and the second being Armenia after 591. Indicative of the artificiality of Ananias' image of Greater Armenia is the fact that at no period of time did the fifteen areas of Greater Armenia, as listed and described by Ananias, exist at the same time.[73] Nonetheless, it is of some significance that there existed such a relatively precise geographical conception of the territory of Greater Armenia.

Needless to say, boundaries in antiquity were often provided, as it were, naturally, for example, the Euphrates was the boundary between Lesser and Greater Armenia before 387 and the Nymphios River marked the border between Roman and Persian Armenia after the division of 387.[74] However, any conclusion that boundaries in antiquity were only established by such physical markers as rivers or mountain ranges is unwarranted.[75] Note, for example, Khorenats'i's (II.lvi) description of the borders established by Artashes.[76]

> And he established markers for the borders in the following way: he ordered four-sided stones to be hewn, their centers to be hallowed out like plates, and that they be buried in the earth. Over them he had fitted four-sided obelisks, a little higher than the ground.

---

72. See Hewsen's introduction to Ananias 1992, pp. 15, 33.
73. Ananias 1992, pp. 59, 146–50.
74. For the "natural" boundaries of Armenia, see Strabo 1854; Pliny 1942, Book VI, chapter 10; Ptolemy 1932, pp. 123–25.
75. Recall the boundary established between Hamath and Arpad as described by the Antakya Stele (Donbaz 1990, p. 7), and the boundary stone, *tahūmu*, of Adadnerari III as described in the Pazarcik Stele (Donbaz 1990, p. 9).
76. See also, for example, Agathangelos 176, p. xxxvi, where ditches were dug to fix the borders, and P'awstos 1989, IV.i for the setting of the boundary line marking the division of Armenia of A.D. 387.

Furthermore, it would appear that the Armenians may have also distinguished conceptually a more precise boundary from a more imprecise frontier. As we have observed, the word *sahman* designated a boundary, and its plural indicated the relatively precise jurisdiction of the area within a set of boundaries, i.e., a territory. However, there is another term *marz* which, in contrast to *sahman*, may have meant "border district" or perhaps "frontier."

The recognition of a territorially bounded shared language and the belief in a common ancestry of those who speak that language and dwell in that territory are not the only examples of a relation of relative sociological uniformity characteristic of nationality to be found in the ancient historiography of (Greater) Armenia.[77] Another striking example of such a relation occurs in Faustus' *Histories* (III.xxi) when an Armenian "council" meets in the aftermath of the Persian kidnapping of the Armenian king, Tiran.

> Then the men of the realm of the land of Armenia—the *naXarars* (noble-"dukes"), magnates, nobles *kusakals* (governors), *asXarhakals* (administrators), and *azats* (retainers), the army leaders, judges, chieftains, and princes, not to mention the army commanders and even [some/many?] of the *ramik* (ordinary people) and *sinakan* (peasantry)—gathered together in a council of still greater accord.

Faustus appears here and in other places to be describing an institution which resembles a national assembly.[78] This description of the assembly of the Armenian people is also reminiscent of descriptions indicative of the existence of other nations, for example, once again, Josiah before all the people of Israel as portrayed in 2 Kings 23.

Conclusion

In the cases of Edom, and especially "all Aram" and ancient Armenia, there are terms which, as Nicholas Adontz put it, are themselves "the best witnesses and interpreters of historical life." The difficulty is, of course, the conceptions which we employ in our attempt to understand these philological kernels of historical significance. The unavoidable fact is that in these three examples, spanning a period of more than a thousand

---

77. Consider also the apparent recognition that certain beliefs and actions were appropriate only for Armenian soil, Pʿawstos 1989, IV.liv.

78. See also especially Pʿawstos 1989, IV.li, where the council is described as meeting without the king and in opposition to him. For other references to the council, *zolov*, in the ancient Armenian histories, see Garsoian 1985b, note 46.

years, there exist terms signifying bounded, trans-local territorial relations. How are we to understand them?

Whatever ambiguities surround these terms and however limited is the evidence, this much is clear: there existed in the ancient Near East and Armenia terms that indicate the existence of bounded territorial relations spanning locality and "tribe." If we restrict our use of the term "tribe" to indicate a collectivity the membership of which is based primarily on familial descent, then clearly it is insufficient as a descriptive category for the territorially trans-local societies of Edom, "all Aram," and Armenia. To recognize that the fiction of relation by blood is attributed to relatively extensive, yet bounded territorial co-residence—as was the case for ancient Israel and Armenia, and apparently for Edom and perhaps "all Aram"—should mean to leave behind the category of "tribe" and enter into the category of nationality. Territorially constituted tribes of limited locality in the ancient Near East, as described by M. B. Rowton a number of years ago,[79] represent an analytical, transitional category between tribe and the bounded, territorially more extensive nation. Rowton described such polities, when sovereign, as dimorphic states, where there is a tribal confederation which is centered on a town and a dynasty within a tribal territory. One of the implications of the argument of this article is to clarify whatever ambiguity exists in Rowton's use of the term "centered." It would seem that the use of "centered" in Rowton's description of dimorphic states indicates the presence of a territorial referent in the traditions constitutive of a collectivity—a referent which, in turn, is at the basis of a (fictitious) trans-local kinship of blood relation. Such a "centering" is what accounts for the conflation between those terms that designate both a bounded area of land and a "people."

Our understanding of the fact of the very existence of these terms of extended, yet bounded territorial relation will be advanced if certain anachronistic assumptions are laid to rest. One such assumption is that nationality is exclusively a modern phenomenon. One of the purposes of this admittedly brief and schematic analysis is to show the usefulness of analyzing the existence of these terms of territorial relation from the perspective of the category of that territorial collectivity of nativity, nationality. To be sure, there are good reasons, especially in the case of "all Aram," to qualify the application of the classificatory concept of nationality. Yet, even with "all Aram," it is helpful to consider in what ways "all Aram" was and was not a nation, in particular, in what ways "all Aram" had apparently not yet achieved a constitutive territorial stability. These and

---

79. Rowton 1974.

other qualifications do not invalidate the merit of applying this category of analysis to certain ancient collectivities. Moreover, such an application is an example of the contribution that the study of the ancient Near East and Orient can make to the study of medieval and modern Europe by deepening our understanding of nationality. A nation is a relation, a form of collective self-consciousness, of a large number of individuals with an image of a bounded, trans-local territory as a constitutive referent of that relation. As a relation, a nation is a living entity, requiring continual reanimation of the forms of the relation, that is, requiring adherence to its existence through reaffirmation of the conceptual referents around which the relation of collective self-consciousness is constituted. As a living relation, any nation is complete with heterogeneous, centrifugal as well as centalizing tendencies. That this is so was obvious in the case of ancient Armenia. It is also certainly the case with the modern national state.

Bibliography

Adontz, Nicholas. 1970. *Armenia in the Period of Justinian* (Lisbon: Calouste Gulbenkian Foundation), originally published in 1908.

Agathangelos. 1976. *Agathangelos, History of the Armenians*, trans. R. W. Thomson (Albany: State University of New York Press).

Ananias. 1992. *The Geography of Ananias of Širak (ASXARHAC'OYC')*, trans. Robert Hewsen (Wiesbaden: Reichert).

Astour, Michael. 1963. "Place-Names from the Kingdom of Alalah in the North Syrian List of Thutmose III: A Study in Historical Topography." *Journal of Near Eastern Studies* XXII: 220–41.

Bartlett, John R. 1989. *Edom and Edomites* (Sheffield: JSOT Press).

Caminos, Ricardo A. 1989. *Late-Egyptian Micellanies* (London: Oxford University Press).

Cody, Aelrud. 1964. "When is the Chosen People Called a Goy." *Vetus Testamentum* 14: 1–6.

Donbaz, Veysel. 1990. "Two Neo-Asyrian Stelae in the Antakya and Kahramanmaras Museums." *Annual Review of the Royal Inscriptions of Mesopotamia Project* 8: 5–24.

Dupont-Sommer, A., and Starcky, J. 1958. "Les inscriptions araméennes de Sefiré." *Mémoires présentées par divers savants à l'Académie des inscriptions et belles-lettres* XV: 197–351.

Dussaud, Rene. 1927. *Topographie Historique De La Syrie Antique Et Médiévale* (Paris: Librairie Orientaliste Paul Geuthner).

Elishe. 1982. *Elishe, History of Vardan and the Armenian War*, trans. R. W. Thomson (Cambridge: Harvard University Press).

Fitzmyer, Joseph. 1967. *The Aramaic Inscriptions of Sefire* (Rome: Pontifical Biblical Institute).

_____. 1979. "The Syntax of *kl, klh*, 'All' in Aramaic Texts from Egypt and in Biblical Aramaic." In J. Fitzmyer, *A Wandering Aramean* (Missoula: Scholars Press), pp. 205-17.

Forrer, E. 1932. "Aramu." *Reallexikon der Assyriologie* 1: 131-39.

Garsoian, Nina G. 1985. *Armenia between Byzantine and the Sasanians* (London: Variorum).

_____. 1985a. "Armenia in the Fourth Century. An Attempt to Re-define the Concepts 'Armenia' and 'loyalty.'" In Garsoian 1985, pp. 341-52.

_____. 1985b. "Prolegomena to a Study of the Iranian Aspects in Arsacid Armenia." In Garsoian 1985, pp. 1-46.

Gibson, John C. L. 1975. *Textbook of Syrian Semitic Inscriptions*, Vol. 2 (Oxford: Oxford University Press).

Greenfield, Jonas C. 1987. "Aspects of Aramean Religion." In Patrick D. Miller, Jr., Paul D. Hanson, and S. Dean McBride, eds. *Ancient Israelite Religion* (Philadelphia: Fortress Press), pp. 67-78.

Grosby, Steven. 1991. "Religion and Nationality in Antiquity." *Archives Européennes de Sociologie* XXXII: 229-65.

_____. 1993a. "Kinship, Territory and the Nation in the Historiography of Ancient Israel," *Zeitschrift für die alttestamentliche Wissenschaft* 105: 3-18.

_____. 1993b. "Sociological Implications of the Distinction Between 'Locality' and Extended 'Territory' with Particular Reference to the Old Testament." *Social Compass* 40: 179-98.

Hawkins, J. D. 1973. "Ḫazazu." *Reallexikon der Assyriologie* 4: 240.

Khorenatsʿi, Moses. 1978. *Moses Khorenatsʿi, History of the Armenians*, trans. R. W. Thomson (Cambridge: Harvard University Press).

Lattimore, Owen. 1979. "Geography and the Ancient Empires." In M. T. Larsen, ed. *Power and Propaganda—A Symposium on Ancient Empires* (Copenhagen: Akademisk Forlag), pp. 35-40.

Luckenbill, Daniel David. 1926. *Ancient Records of Assyria and Babylonia* (Chicago: University of Chicago Press).

Machinist, Peter. 1986. "On Self Consciousness in Mesopotamia," In S. N. Eisenstadt, ed. *The Origins and Diversity of Axial Age Civilizations* (Albany: State University of New York Press), pp. 183-202.

Malamat, Abraham. 1973. "The Aramaeans." In D. J. Wiseman, ed. *Peoples of Old Testament Times* (Oxford: Oxford University Press), pp. 134-55.

_____. 1989. *Mari and the Early Israelite Experience* (Oxford: Oxford University Press).

Mazar, B. 1962. "The Aramean Empire and its Relations with Israel." *The Biblical Archaeologist* 25: 98-120.

Meinecke, Friedrich. 1970. *Cosmopolitanism and the National State* (Princeton: Princeton University Press), originally published 1928.

Naʾaman, Nadav. 1978. "Looking for KTK." *Die Welt des Orients* IX: 220-39.

Noth, Martin. 1928. *Die israelitischen Personennamen in Rahmen der gemeinsemitischen Namengebung*, BWANT 10 (Stuttgart: W. Kohlammer).

_____. 1962. *Die Welt Des Alten Testaments* (Berlin: Alfred Töpelmann).

Oded, B. 1974. "The Phoenician Cities and the Assyrian Empire in the Time of Tiglath-pileser III." *Zeitschrift des Deutschen Palästina-Vereins* 90: 38–49.

Parpola, Simo, and Watanabe, Kazuko. 1988. *State Archives of Assyria*, Vol. II (Helsinki: Helsinki University Press).

P'awstos. 1989. *The Epic Histories Attributed to P'awstos Buzand*, trans. N. Garsoian (Cambridge: Harvard University Press).

Pitard, W. T. 1987. *Ancient Damascus: A Historical Study of the Syrian City-State from Earliest Times until its Fall to the Assyrians in 732 B.C.* (Winona Lake, Ind.: Eisenbrauns).

Pliny. 1942. *Natural History* (Cambridge: Cambridge University Press).

Polignac, François de. 1994. "Mediation, Competition, and Sovereignty: The Evolution of Rural Sanctuaries in Geometric Greece." In Susan E. Alcock and Robin Osborne, eds. *Placing the Gods–Sanctuaries and Sacred Space in Ancient Greece* (Oxford: Clarendon Press), pp. 3–18.

_____. 1995. *Cults, Territory and the Origins of the Greek City-State* (Chicago: University of Chicago Press), first published in 1984.

Ptolemy, Claudius. 1932. *Geography of Claudius Ptolemy* (New York: New York Public Library).

Reynolds, Susan. 1984. *Kingdoms and Communities in Western Europe 900-1300* (Oxford: Oxford University Press).

Rowton, M. B. 1974. "Enclosed Nomadism." *Journal of the Economic and Social History of the Orient* 17: 1–30.

Speiser, E. A. 1960. "People and Nation of Israel." *Journal of Biblical Literature* 79: 157–63.

Strabo. 1854. *The Geography* (London: H. C. Bohn).

Tadmor, Hayim. 1975. "Assyria and the West: The Ninth Century and its Aftermath." In Hans Goedicke and J. J. M. Roberts, eds. *Unity and Diversity–Essays in the History, Literature and Religion of the Ancient Near East* (Baltimore: Johns Hopkins University Press), pp. 36–48.

_____. 1986. "Monarchy and the Elite in Assyria and Babylonia: The Question of Royal Accountability." In S. N. Eisenstadt, ed. *The Origins and Diversity of Axial Age Civilizations* (Albany: State University of New York Press), pp. 203–24.

_____. 1994. *The Inscriptions of Tiglath-Pileser III King of Assyria* (Jerusalem: The Israel Academy of Sciences and Humanities).

Thomson, R. W. 1994. "Mission, Conversion, and Christianization: The Armenian Example." In R. W. Thompson *Studies in Armenian Literature and Christianity* (Aldershot: Variorum), pp. 28–45.

Toumanoff, C. 1963. *Studies in Christian Caucasian History* (Washington: Georgetown University Press).

Vriezen, Th. C. 1965. "The Edomite Deity Qaus." *Oudtestamentische Studiën* 14: 330–53.

Weippert, Manfred. 1973. "Menahem von Israel und seine Zeitgenossen in einer Steleninschrift des assyrischen Konigs Tiglathpileser III aus dem Iran." *Zeitschrift des Deutschen Palästina-Vereins* 89: 26-53.

Zobel, H.-J. 1977. "Yiśra'el." In G. J. Botterweck and H. Ringgren, eds. *Theological Dictionary of the Old Testament* (Grand Rapids, Mich.: Eerdmans), pp. 397–420.

Chapter 6

'Aram Kulloh and the Worship of Hadad: A Nation of Aram?

The question posed by the title to the following considerations is not an unreasonable one despite the prevailing historiographical prejudice that insists that the ethno-geographic collectivity known as nationality is exclusively a modern phenomenon; for there appears in line five of Face A of Sefire Stele I the apparent self-designation "all Aram"—a self-designation that seemingly refers to a relatively extensive, yet bounded territorial collectivity.[1] It would appear from the inscriptions of the Sefire Stele that "all Aram" was understood by "all Aram," or at least by Mati'el of Arpad (IA, line 1), to encompass "Upper and Lower Aram" (IA, line 6). It is not exactly clear what was meant by the evidently geographical designation "Upper and Lower Aram." It is possible that "Upper Aram" referred to Syrian Aram, while "Lower Aram" referred to an area in the vicinity of Babylonia.[2] However, it is more likely that "Upper Aram" and "Lower Aram" referred to some kind of a division of a Syrian "all Aram"; that is, a bounded area (and its population) stretching from the Beqa' Valley/Damascus in the south to Bet-Gush/Arpad and perhaps Ya'di/Sam'al in the north (IB, lines 9-10).[3] As is well known, the restoration of lines 9-10 of Face B of Stele I is disputed, resulting in an uncertain interpretation of those border points apparently marking the territorial extent of the trans-city-state formation of "all Aram." Indeed, much remains uncertain about

Author's note: Revision of paper presented to "Who were, or are, the Arameans?" conference of The ARAM Society for Syro-Mesopotamian Studies, Department of Near Eastern Languages and Civilizations, Harvard University, 9-11 June 1996.

1. Of the enormous literature on the Sefire Stele, I cite here only B. Mazar, "The Aramean Empire and its Relations with Israel," *The Biblical Archaeologist*, XXV (1962) 98-120; J. Fitzmyer, *The Aramaic Inscriptions of Sefire* (Rome, 1967); N. Na'aman, "Looking for KTK," *Die Welt des Orients* IX (1978) 98-120; H. Sader, *Les États Arameens de Syrie* (Beirut, 1987).

2. For references to Arameans in the vicinity of Babylonia around the time of the Sefire Treaty, see Tiglath-pileser III's Summary Inscription 7, lines 5-9, H. Tadmor, *The Inscriptions of Tiglath-pileser III, King of Assyria* (Jerusalem, 1994) 158-61; J. A. Brinkman, *A Political History of Post-Kassite Babylonia 1158-722 B.C.* (Rome, 1968) 268-72.

the inscriptions of the Sefire Stele, including most obviously, who and what was, respectively, Bir-Ga'yah and KTK–Bir-Ga'yah, king of KTK, being one of the contracting parties to the treaty preserved on the Sefire Stele; Matî'el, king of Arpad, being the other (IA, line 1; IB, line 1). No attempt is made here to reanalyze or to discuss in detail what appears to me, given the current state of the evidence, to be the insurmountable uncertainties of the Sefire Stele. Rather, in what follows, I wish to consider some of the implications of that evidence which is certain, or at least relatively certain.[4]

The qualifier "all" in "all Aram" is clearly of some sociological significance; it implies a certain kind of collective unity. One is immediately reminded of the Deuteronomistic use of "all" in "all Israel (*kol yiśrā'ēl*) from Dan to Beersheba."[5] In the case of Israel, the Deuteronomistic use of "all" underscores the (hoped for) unity of both all the land of Israel and all the people of Israel—the unity of one believed to be inseparable from the unity of the other. While this use of "all Israel" may have represented a programmatic goal for what Israel was supposed to become; it, nevertheless, also reveals the terminological conflation embodied in the very designation "Israel"—a term referring both to all the land "from Dan to Beersheba" and all the people, *běnê yiśrā'ēl*. This terminological conflation is

---

3. So A. Alt, "Die syrische Staatenwelt vor dem Einbruch der Assyrer," *Zeitschrift der deutschen morgenländischen Gesellschaft*, 88 (1934) 254, n. 2, "Aber die dortigen [along the course of the Euphrates, including the vicinity of Babylonia] Gebiete und Staatengebilde der Aramäer befanden sich zur Zeit unserer Stele längst in den Händen der Assyrer und kamen infolgedessen als Vertragsteilnehmer für Arpad kaum mehr in Betracht. Es wird sich daher mehr empfehlen, den Ausdruck hier auf Syrien zu beziehen; dann bezeichnet "Oberland" entsprechend der Höhenlage am ersten das Reich von Damaskus, "Unterland" die nördlicheren Aramaerreiche in der Umgebung von Arpad, und das unseres Wissens niemals zu Aram gerechnete Gebiet von Hamath legt sich trennend dazwischen." For an overview of the problem, see Fitzmyer, *Sefire*, 31; and, more recently, Sader, *Les États Araméens*, 145, "Les limites géographiques données dans IB 9-10 nous semblent englober les territoires de tous les rois membres de la coalition [du haut et du bas Aram], puisque les clauses du traité devaient être appliquées sur tout le territoire ainsi délimité." Mention should be made that Na'aman, "Looking for KTK," has challenged the widely accepted restoration of the dalet in Ya'di, thus calling into question Ya'di as a point marking the northern boundary of "all Aram."

4. The intention of this article is to develop further a few of the points referred to in passing in S. Grosby, "Borders, Territory, and Nationality in the Ancient Near East and Armenia," *Journal of the Economic and Social History of the Orient*, 39/4 (1996) 1-29 [[in this volume, pp. 120-149]].

5. Consider, for example, 1 Sam 3:20; 2 Sam 17:11; 24:2; Deut 11:6; 13:11. As is well known, the object of the designation of "all Israel" varied; for an apparently "archaic usage" of the term, see 2 Sam 2:9.

indicative of what takes place in the structure of kinship known as nationality: there is a relation of kinship attributed to a relatively extensive, yet
bounded territorial co-residence. When that kinship is described in the
idiom of blood relation, usually with reference to an eponymous ancestor,
for example, Jacob/Israel (Gen 32:28; 35:10), it is, of course, fictitious.
This is obvious enough. What, however, deserves to be emphasized is the
territorial referent in the relation.

In modern nationality, the territorial referent in the mutual recognition of relation around which the collectivity is constituted is usually explicit, as may be seen in the *jus soli* as a determinant for membership in
the national state. Nonetheless, the imagery of blood relation may be
found in modern collectivities as well, for example, in both the idiom of
the "founding fathers" of the country and the *jus sanguinis* as a determinant for membership in some national states. In ancient collectivities, the
territorial referent is implicit, as may be seen in the more frequent recourse to the idiom of blood relation. In the ancient Near East, this
"ethno-geographic" phenomenon may be concretely seen not only in the
use of such terms as the Hebrew *gôy*, but also in the use of the designation "house" (*bêt*), for example, in the Hebrew Bible, "the whole house of
Israel" (Ezek 11:15) to refer to the nation of Israel, and in the Sefire Stele,
"the house of Gush," *Bêt-Gush* (IIB, line 10), to refer to both the territorial
jurisdiction of the house, the city-state of Arpad,[6] and the inhabitants of
the house, the *Běnê-Gush* (IB, line 3)–this latter ethno-geographic conflation[7] mediated through the reference to the eponymous ancestor "Gusi"
who is described as having paid tribute to Ashurnasirpal a little more
than a century before the approximate date of the Sefire Treaty of 750
B.C.[8] Finally, I note in passing that the tribe, usually understood to be
constituted by beliefs about actual kinship in blood, may also be an
ethno-geographic collectivity. Martin Noth drew attention to this possibility in the history of ancient Israel when he recognized that the names
of the tribes Judah, Ephraim, Benjamin, and probably Naphtali were

6. The list of towns in lines 34–35 of Sefire IA are those included within the immediate jurisdiction of Arpad. See also the list of towns in Summary Inscription 5, Col. II,
line 7, of Tiglath-pileser III, a list that concludes with the phrase "cities of the land of
Bit-Agusi," Tadmor, *Inscriptions*, 146–47.
7. Is the repeated phrase, "the people of the land of Matiʾ-ilu" in the treaty of
Ashurnerari V with Matiʾ-ilu (S. Parpola and K. Watanabe, *Neo-Assyrian Treaties and
Loyalty Oaths* [State Archives of Assyria, II; Helsinki, 1988] 8–13) also indicative of
this conflation?
8. D. Luckenbill, *Ancient Records of Assyria and Babylonia*, Vol. 1 (Chicago, 1926)
477.

most likely originally names of locations.[9] In these instances, was it the persistence over time of a territorial referent in the mutual recognition—that is, the shared tradition—of those who dwelled in these respective areas which was at the basis of the fiction of blood relation? Is the same phenomenon at work in "enclosed nomadism," as described by M. B. Rowton, where territorial location, the town, and the individuals putatively and actually related by blood, the tribe, share a name in common?[10] Needless to say, these two referents, blood and location, in territorially small structures of kinship would, over time, converge.[11] In any event, we are concerned here with a territorially more extensive structure of kinship than either the Israelite *šēbeṭ* or the city-state of *Bêt-Gush/Bĕnê-Gush*. What do we know about the nature of the terminological conflation of the apparent ethno-geographic term "all Aram"?

Evidence from the Hebrew Bible, inconclusive though it is, could be understood as confirming the ethno-geographic and perhaps national character of "all Aram." We find there references to Aram-Beth-Rehob (2 Sam 10:6), Aram-Zobah (2 Sam 10:6), Aram-Damascus (2 Sam 8:5), and Aram-Naharaim (Gen 24:10; Judg 3:8; Ps 60:2). On the face of it, the prefix "Aram" would seem to indicate that the Israelites recognized some kind of relation among the people of Beth-Rehob, Zobah, Damascus, and Naharaim. This relation is often described in the scholarly literature as "ethnic"; but the use of this term may obscure more than it clarifies. As to the nature of the relation, it would appear that the Israelites (Judaeans) recognized at least a linguistic distinction between themselves and the "Arameans"; for, in 2 Kgs 18:26, Eliakim, the person in charge of King Hezekiah's palace, is described as telling the Rabshakeh of King Sennach-ereb of Assyria, "Please speak to your servants in the Aramaic language, for we understand it; do not speak to us in the language of Judah within the hearing of the people who are on the wall [of the city of Jerusalem]." Common language is usually one of the indicators of an ethnic group. However, how the Arameans themselves viewed the use of Aramaic is a different matter; especially how, for example, someone from Damascus

---

9. M. Noth, The History of Israel (London, 1959) 53–84.

10. M. B. Rowton, "Autonomy and Nomadism in Western Asia," *Orientalia*, N.S., 42 (1973) 256–57. Brinkman, *A Political History*, 271, goes so far as to say that some of the descriptions of Arameans as tribes may have been an Assyrian fabrication or simplification.

11. This of course does not mean that for nationality, both ancient and modern, there are not other structures of kinship existing within or alongside of the larger, essentially territorial collectivity, e.g., the Israelite *bêt 'āb* viz. *gôy*, as may clearly be seen in Josh 7:14–18.

would have viewed the dialect of someone from Sam²al. Unfortunately, we have no evidence about such matters.

Happily, the Hebrew Bible makes explicit another characteristic of ethnicity; namely, the territorial referent also at the basis of the ethnic designation: in this case, the apparent relation indicated by the prefix "Aram" spans a geographic area from Beth-Rehob in the southern Lebanon Valley to Naharaim in the general vicinity of Bit-Adini east of the Euphrates. The probability of a territorial referent in the recognition of the relation "Aram" reminds one of repeated scholarly speculations that the early Assyrian references to *Aḫlamū-Armaja* and, later, *Arumu/Aramu* referred to those who dwelled in the west.[12] As to the latter possibility, one notes with interest the phrase *māt Arime*, land of Aram, with the determinative *KUR* often modifying Aramean.[13]

Does this evidence support Benjamin Mazar's conclusion that "all Aram" was an "ethnic-territorial concept"?[14] Does the term indicate the existence of a territorial collectivity of nativity, a nation? The answer to this question must be a qualified "no" for the following reasons all of which call into question the saliency of the self-designation "all Aram," hence, its national character. First, from lines 1–6 of Face A of the early eighth century Zakir Stele, there is clear evidence not only for an independent Hamath and Luʿath, but also for considerable "inter-Aramean" strife over its actions.[15]

> The Stele, which Zakir, king of Hamath and Luʿath, set up . . . and Baalshamayn made me king in Hadrach. Then Barhadad son of Hazael, king of Aram, organized against me an alliance of [six]teen kings—Barhadad and his army, Bargush and his army, the [king] of Kue and his army, the king of

---

12. See, for example, Brinkman, *A Political History*, 277–81, especially n. 1799; G. M. Schwartz, "The Origin of the Arameans in Syria and Northern Mesopotamia: Research Problems and Potential Strategies," in *To the Euphrates and Beyond*, ed. O. M. C. Haex, H. H. Curvens, and P. M. M. G. Akkermans (Rotterdam, 1989) 275–91; R. Zadok, "Elements of Aramean Pre-history," in *Ah, Assyria . . . Studies in Assyrian History and Ancient Near Eastern Historiography Presented to Hayim Tadmor*, ed. M. Cogan and I. Ephʿal (Scripta Hierosolymitana, 33; Jerusalem, 1991) 104–17; W. T. Pitard, "Arameans," in *Peoples of the Old Testament World*, ed. A. J. Hoerth, G. L. Mattingly, and E. M. Yamauchi (Grand Rapids, 1994) 207–30.

13. For early examples, see the "Broken Obelisk" of Ashur-bel-kala. A. K. Grayson, *Assyrian Royal Inscriptions*, Vol. 2 (Wiesbaden, 1976) 235; and perhaps from Tiglath-Pileser I, "Assyrian Chronicle Fragment 4," *Assyrian and Babylonian Chronicles* (Locust Valley, 1975) 189.

14. B. Mazar, "The Aramean Empire," 119.

15. John C. L. Gibson, *Textbook of Syrian Semitic Inscriptions*, Volume 2 (Oxford, 1975) 9.

Umq and his army, the king of Gurgum and his army, the king of Sam'al and his army. . . .

If, in fact, the "all Aram" of the Sefire Stele does encompass roughly an area from the Beqa' Valley in the south to Ya'di in the north, then these lines from the Zakir Stele would indicate such a marked heterogeneity that it is difficult to speak of a nation of "all Aram"; for Hamath was located midway between Damascus of Barhadad in the southern part of "all Aram" and Arpad of Bargush in the northern part of "all Aram."

This apparent lack of the relative uniformity characteristic of a nation is confirmed by lines 4–5 of the early eighth century B.C. Antakya Stele.[16]

The boundary which Adad-nērārī, king of Assyria, (and) Šamšī-ilu, the commander in chief, establish between Zakur of the land of Hamath and Atar-šumki, son of Adramu: . . .

We know from the Pazarcik Stele[17] and from lines 1 and 3 of Sefire IA that Ataršumki was king of Arpad, the Bargush of the Zakir Stele. For our purposes, we need not concern ourselves with determining the historical circumstances surrounding the inscriptions of the Zakir and Antakya Stele. It is sufficient to observe from the Zakir Stele that there was such hostility between the military coalition, under the leadership of Damascus and Hamath that it led to war; and from the Antakya Stele that there were distinct and disputed boundaries between Hamath and Arpad. Evidently Hamath was a real and lethal thorn in the flesh of its neighbor to its south, Damascus, and its neighbor to its north, Arpad.

This apparent heterogeneity more characteristic of city-kingdoms and coalitions of city-kingdoms would seem to be further confirmed by the inscriptions of Tiglath-pileser III. From both Annal 19 and Summary Inscription 5, it would appear, as Hayim Tadmor describes the situation, that there were defined borders between states and within states in northern and central Syria which were firmly established in local tradition and which were taken over by Tiglath-pileser III in setting up his administration in these newly conquered and densely populated areas.[18] Lines 7–10 of Annal 19 provide a delineation of the borders of Hamath.[19]

the city of Hatirikka, the district of Nuqudina, [Mount Hasu] together with the cities of its environs, the city of Ara [. . .], both sides of them, the cities of their environs, all of Mount Sarbua, the cities of Ashhani (and) Yatabi, all of Mount Yaraqu, . . . the cities of Ellitarbi, Zitanu, up to the city of Atinni . . . ,

---

16. V. Donbaz, *Annual Review of the Royal Inscriptions of Mesopotamia*, 8 (1990) 7.
17. Donbaz, *Royal Inscriptions*, 9–10.
18. Tadmor, *Inscriptions*, 61, n. 7.
19. Tadmor, *Inscriptions*, 61–63.

the city of Burname—19 districts of Hamath together with the cities of their environs. . . .

Summary Inscription 5 contains a fragmentary list of towns arranged by city-kingdom. Preserved there are separate lists of the towns within the respective jurisdictions of both the land of Bit-Agusi (Column II, line 7) and the land of Hamath (Column II, line 24). Given the apparent history of conflict between Hamath, on the one side, and Damascus and Arpad, on the other, as conveyed by the Zakir and Antakya Stele, one concludes that the borders and towns described by Annal 19 and Summary Inscription 5 of Tiglath-pileser III were not of provincial areas within "all Aram"; but rather, they designated the jurisdiction of distinct city-kingdoms.

This conclusion certainly calls into question the saliency of a tradition of "all Aram." If there was such a tradition (and there must have been given the existence of the term "all Aram"), it would appear to have been subordinate to the various, heterogeneous traditions of city-kingdoms—a situation perhaps somewhat similar to what occurred in ancient Greece. Perhaps there was a tradition of a southern military coalition with Damascus at its head, incorporating Aram-Zobah and Aram-Beth-Rehob, and a tradition of a northern military coalition with Arpad at its head as indicated by lines 11-12 of the Pazarcik Stela, "I [Adad-nērārī] fought a pitched battle with them—with Ataršumki, son of Adramu, of the city of Arpad(da), together with eight kings who were with him. . . ." Perhaps these two traditions correspond to the two designations "Lower Aram" and "Upper Aram" of line 6 of Sefire IA, with Hamath in the middle. Whatever merit such possibilities might have, one is still faced with the designation "all Aram"—a designation, the very existence of which certainly indicates that any conclusion as to the unequivocal distinctiveness of the city-kingdoms is evidently avoiding a number of complications. These complicating factors deserve one's attention.

Given this evidence for territorial heterogeneity with attendant heterogeneous structures of kinship, curious is the description found in line 1 of Stele IIIA from Iran of Tiglath-pileser III, "the kings of the land of Hatti, (and of) the Aramaeans of the western seashore."[20] Is it possible that the use of the term "Aramaeans" in this phrase refers to the inhabitants of such cities of the western seashore as Ṣimirra and Arqa which in Summary Inscription 5 of Tiglath-pileser III are described as cities of the land of Hamath? Most curious is the appearance of the city Arqa (= ʿArqu) at line 9 of Sefire IB as one of the boundary points marking the jurisdiction of the Sefire treaty and, one assumes, part of the territory of "all Aram."

---

20. Tadmor, *Inscriptions*, 106-7.

Let not one of the words of thi[s] inscription be silent, [but let them be heard from] ʿArqu to Yaʾd[i and] BZ, from Lebanon to Yab[rud, from Damas]cus to ʿAru and M..W, [and from] the Beqaʿ to KTK.

Is one to conclude from this reference to ʿArqu that Hamath had become a part of "Upper Aram" under the leadership of Arpad, especially if ʿArqu and Yaʾdi represent respectively southern and northern boundary points of "Upper Aram" and Lebanon and M..W (Mansuate?) represent the southern boundary points of "Lower Aram"? Is it possible that based on the three Assyrian campaigns against Hamath of 772, 765, and 755, as recorded in the Eponym Chronicle,[21] that one should conclude that both Hamath had clearly undertaken an anti-Assyrian policy and that it, as a result of these campaigns, had become greatly weakened, thus permitting Arpad to take the lead of the military bloc of "Upper Aram"?[22] Is it also possible that Damascus had also become greatly weakened as a result of its defeat both at the hands of Shalmaneser IV in approximately 773 B.C.[23] and, subsequently, at the hand of Jeroboam II,[24] thus allowing Arpad to take the lead of "all Aram"?

Such a possibility still begs the question of the nature of the unity of "all Aram." No doubt, the renewed military threat of Tiglath-Pileser III's Assyria was a good enough reason to form a military coalition. However, the problem before us is the pursuit of those *gemeinschaftliche* elements at the basis of, or running parallel to, the formation of such a military coalition of otherwise apparently distinct city-kingdoms or blocs of city-kingdoms—elements as, once again, implied by the very term "all Aram." The problem may be reformulated in the following manner. One assumes that the earlier coalition of Damascus and Arpad against Hamath as described in the Zakir Stele may have been a result of either the pro-Assyrian policy of Zakir (although it should be noted that there is no evidence internal to the Zakir Stele to confirm this suspicion) or Zakir's growing territorial ambitions as indicated by having become king of Hadrach/Luʿath (lines 3-4 of IA). Yet, the particular problem before us, in light of the designations of "Upper Aram," "Lower Aram," and "all Aram" of the Sefire Stele, is the determination of elements of relatedness present in the alliance between Damascus and Arpad against Hamath.

---

21. Luckenbill, *Ancient Records*, Vol. II 1195.

22. Regarding this possibility, note that the town Tuʾim listed in line 34 of Sefire IA appears to be of *Bêt-Gush*; while the same town (as seems likely) Tuʾammu which is listed in the geographically ambiguous lines 9-14 of Tiglath-pileser III's Stele IIB from Iran might be understood to be of the land of Hamath. Tuʾim/Tuʾammu = modern Taʾum, 10 km northeast of Idlib.

23. See lines 6-10, reverse, of the Pazarcik Stele, Donbaz, *Royal Inscriptions*, 9-10.

24. Consider 2 Kgs 14:25, 28.

Benjamin Mazar had an interesting solution to this problem. He postulated that a generation earlier Hadadezer of Aram-Damascus had created
a "unified Aramean state," "officially named Aram, with its capital at Damascus."[25] An initial stage in the formation of this single, unified state
would apparently have been the anti-Assyrian coalition under the leadership of Hadadezer which fought Shalmaneser III at the battle of Qarqar in
853. The coalition was maintained for about a decade. Mazar further
thought that a comparison of 1 Kgs 20:1 with 1 Kgs 20:24 would reveal
the political and administrative reforms carried out by Hadadezer necessary for the creation of this putatively unified Aramean state.[26] The existence of such a state would certainly help explain the degree of relatedness
characteristic of nationality implied by the phrases "all Aram," "Upper
Aram," and "Lower Aram" of the Sefire Stele; for it would have provided
the existence of a period, however brief, out of which a victorious, indeed
glorious, tradition of "all Aram" could have become common to those
who initially participated in the anti-Assyrian coalition and who later
dwelled within the territory of this putatively, previously unified state.
Such a tradition would have been a focal point or conceptual center for
subsequent generations which, as such, would have provided a degree of
relatedness for those who recognized that center or tradition as their
own. Such a possibility is not farfetched; for one need only recall how the
relatively brief period of King David's Israel provided the focal point for a
subsequent tradition of "all Israel from Dan to Beersheba," spanning,
however tenuously, the territorial (and religious) heterogeneity of northern Israel and southern Judah. The difficulty with Mazar's argument is
that there is no evidence which would suggest that Bêt-Gush/Arpad was,
in any way, subordinate to Damascus.[27]

Even if Mazar's argument for the existence of a unified "all Aramean"
state during the middle of the ninth century B.C. is doubtful, it nonetheless properly focuses our attention on the problem of ascertaining those
conceptual elements and traditions held in common among the "Aramean" city-kingdoms such that there was a degree of relatedness parallel
to the evident traditions of distinctiveness. It would seem that three such
elements may be observed, two of which have already been mentioned.
First, as discussed above, there apparently was an awareness of an Ara-

---

25. Mazar, "*The Aramean Empire*," 112, 116.
26. Mazar, "*The Aramean Empire*," 108.
27. Moreover, it would appear that Arpad paid tribute to Shalmaneser III in 853,
indicating that it was not part of the anti-Assyrian "Aramean" coalition under the leadership of Damascus; see Luckenbill, *Ancient Records*, Vol. 1, 610.

mean language, at least according to the Judaean perspective based on 2 Kgs 18:26. Second, there was a tradition of common military action among the "Aramean" city-kingdoms against the Assyrians, most notably the coalition at the battle of Qarqar.[28] That this coalition was maintained for about a decade, facing the Assyrians in 853, 849, 848 and 845, is surely of some sociological significance.[29] It is difficult to imagine some degree of relatedness or brotherhood not arising out of such a sustained alliance (and the memories of such a sustained alliance) where the members of one city-kingdom died in battle while defending the land of a contiguous city-kingdom when both city-kingdoms were confronted by a common enemy. In this regard, one should recall Julius Wellhausen's observation about the origin of ancient Israel, "Das Kriegslager, die Wiege der Nation, war auch das älteste Heiligtum."[30] Is it not also likely that such a "relatedness" would have been also fostered among the "Aramean" city-kingdoms by a military and geographical situation of Assyria to the east, Israel to the south, and the land of Hatti to the north?

According to Assyrian records, as early as 1300 B.C. the Sutu and Aḫlamû formed military coalitions against the Assyrians.[31] If we entertain the possibility of an overlap of the populations of the Sutu, Aḫlamû, and Arameans,[32] then we have a more than five-hundred-year-long tradition of "Aramean-like" polities forming anti-Assyrian coalitions. Indeed, given this framework, what is remarkable is the persistent heterogeneity of city-states in this area within an apparently increasingly "Aramean" *Umwelt*—a situation somewhat reminiscent, albeit of a lesser magnitude, of Mesopotamian history before the time of Sargon. Furthermore, other evidence supports the idea that Sutu was also an ethno-geographic term. As early as the end of the sixteenth century B.C., in an inscription on the statue of Idrimi, king of Alalaḫ, Sutu is modified by the determinative KI,

---

28. For an overview of the history of such coalitions, see N. Naʾaman, "Forced Participation in Alliances in the Course of the Assyrian Campaigns to the West," in *Ah, Assyria*, 80–98; and H. Tadmor, "Assyria and the West: The Ninth Century and Its Aftermath," in *Unity and Diversity, Essays in the History, Literature, and Religion of the Ancient Near East*, ed. H. Goedicke and J. J. M. Roberts (Baltimore, 1975) 36–48.

29. It appears that Arpad opposed the Assyrians in 847/46, see Luckenbill, *Ancient Records*, Vol. 1, 653, 655.

30. J. Wellhausen, *Israelitische und Jüdische Geschichte* (Berlin, 1905) 24.

31. Luckenbill, *Ancient Records*, Vol. I, 73.

32. M. Heltzer, *The Suteans* (Naples, 1981), especially chapter VI, 74–98, for a detailed examination of the evidence; Brinkman, *A Political History*, 277–87. George Mendenhall's analysis of the Amorites should also be considered in light of this possibility, "Amorites," in *Anchor Bible Dictionary*, Vol. 1 (New York, 1992) 199–202.

thus indicating that it designated a concrete territory.[33] In the thirteenth century, there is evidence for both the existence of Suteans in an area stretching from west of Karchemiš to the region of Damascus (that is, roughly equivalent to the apparent territorial extent of "all Aram") and the existence of a certain Sutean country in the same region.[34] The significance of this observation for our deliberations becomes clear when one keeps in mind that traditions with locational referents are necessary, constitutive elements of a territory, for example, the "land of Sutu." We do not know anything about such probable Sutean traditions and how they, in turn, might have influenced the subsequent emergence of an Aramean *Umwelt*. Nonetheless, one can observe how such temporally deep traditions may contribute to the formation of a territory by considering the phenomenon at work in Judges for (northern) Israel and in Genesis, especially according to the analysis of Hermann Gunkel[35] (a part of which surely remains valid), for "all Israel."

The third element which might allow us to speak of an Aramean cultural environment was religious. Jonas Greenfield observed that, in contrast to the repeated combining of Baal with Hadad in the earlier Ras Shamra texts, by the beginning of the first millennium B.C. a clear bifurcation had taken place in the use of the names Baʿlu and Hadad.[36] According to Greenfield, the worship of Baal had apparently become confined to the Phoenician cities and their colonies, while Hadad had become the head of the Aramean pantheon. If this were so, then the worship of Hadad would certainly have been a constitutive element in the formation of an Aramean relatedness. Nonetheless, our confidence in Greenfield's observation must be tempered by the sparseness of the evidence on the Aramean side. Moreover, it appears that it was Baalshamayn, and not Hadad, that was the god of Zakir of Hamath (lines 2–3, 11 of Zakir IA). On the other hand, the subsequent emergence of Dea Syria would seem to imply a territorially bounded, relative uniformity of an Aramean culture.[37] Fortunately, there is more to consider here, namely the cult of Hadad of Aleppo and its probable significance for "all Aram."

---

33. Heltzer, *Suteans*, 80–81.
34. Heltzer, *Suteans*, 83.
35. H. Gunkel, *Genesis* (Göttingen, 1901).
36. J. Greenfield, "Hadad," in *Dictionary of Deities and Demons in the Bible*, ed. K. van der Toorn, B. Becking, and R. W. van der Horst (Leiden, 1995) 716–26; "Aspects of Aramean Religion," in *Ancient Israelite Religion: Essays in Honor of Frank Moore Cross*, ed. P. D. Miller, P. D. Hanson, and S. D. McBride (Philadelphia, 1987) 67–78.
37. For Dea Syria, see H. J. W. Drijvers, "Dea Syria," *Lexicon Iconographicum Mythologiae Classicae* (Zurich, 1981).

At line 36 of Sefire IA, it is Hadad that is called upon to carry out the curses of the treaty. Based upon the reasonable restoration of "Hadad of Aleppo" at line 10 of Sefire IA, and the appearance of Aleppo at line 5 of Sefire IIIC, it is surely Hadad of Aleppo that is referred to at line 36. This is rather curious because it suggests that the chief deity of Matīʿel of Arpad was to be found in Aleppo—a geographical duality which, in turn, implies some degree of division between political and hierocratic authority. What was so special about Aleppo that such an apparent division would have been tolerated by Matīʿel? Perhaps the most intriguing lines 4–5 of IIIC provide an answer.

> If any of my officers flees from me as a fugitive or any of my kinsmen or any of my eunuchs or any of the people who are under my control, and they go to Aleppo. . . .

In answer to the question as to why one should flee to Aleppo and not Arpad, John C. L. Gibson thought that these lines indicated that Aleppo, as a shrine of Hadad, may have been an international or at least inter-Aramean place of refuge.[38] If this were so, then this would not only help explain the apparent division between Arpad and Aleppo, but it would also have meant that the cult of Hadad of Aleppo would have been an obvious focal point for Aramean relatedness. The evidence below may suggest this possibility, but it is by no means decisive.

The determination of whether or not the cult of Hadad of Aleppo was a religious center for "all Aram" would depend upon its recognition as such by Damascus. There would seem to be no direct evidence for such a recognition. Nevertheless, there is one piece of indirect evidence which might suggest some kind of relation between Damascus and Aleppo (Arpad). At the end of the treaty between Ashurnerari V of Assyria and Matīʾ-ilu of Arpad, there appears a list of the deities of the treaty.[39] Not only does Hadad of Aleppo appear in the list, as one would fully expect given that Matīʾ-ilu is party to the treaty, but there may also appear Rammān (biblical Rimmon, 2 Kgs 5:18) of Damascus.[40] One assumes that Rammān, "the thunderer," was a Damascene epithet for Hadad, especially given the reference to Hadad-rimmon in Zech 12:11 and the repeated

---

38. Gibson, *Syrian Semitic Inscriptions*, Vol. 2, 53. See also J. C. Greenfield, "Asylum at Aleppo: A Note on Sfire III, 4–7," in *Ah, Assyria*, 272–78.

39. Parpola and Watanabe, *Neo-Assyrian Treaties*, 13.

40. As read by Parpola, see note to lines 22f. and the reference to the collation, Parpola and Watanabe, *Neo-Assyrian Treaties*, 13. The reading is not certain.

presence of Hadad as part of the names of the kings of Damascus.[41] If the reading of Rammān is correct, then there arise several questions: why should the god of Damascus appear in a treaty between Assyria and Arpad, and what might have been the relation between Rammān/Hadad/Hadad-rimmon of Damascus and Hadad of Aleppo? Does the appearance of Rammān in the treaty imply the recognition by Damascus of the cult of Aleppo as also its cult—a recognition which, in turn, might indicate a degree of relatedness between Damascus and Arpad?

There can be little doubt about the widely recognized sanctity of the cult of Aleppo.[42] On his way to the battle of Qarqar, Shalmaneser III offered sacrifice there.[43] Indeed, as early as the 18th century B.C., Aleppo, chief city of Iamḫad, was recognized as an important cult center, for Zimrilim, king of Mari, had dedicated a statue to Hadad of Aleppo,[44] even though, as Wolfram von Soden put it,[45] he was, like Shalmaneser III much later, not king of Aleppo. No doubt, both Zimrilim's recognition of and his trips to the cult of Hadad of Aleppo had a political component to it; nonetheless, clearly George Dossin was correct to note that "a la vérité, le but de ces voyages est religieux."[46] Thus, the evidence would seem to indicate that for no less than one thousand years, the cult of Hadad of Aleppo was recognized to be particularly important. This, of course, does not necessarily mean that it was either the chief cult of "all Aram" or recognized as such by Damascus; nonetheless, given the cult's impressive history, it is difficult to imagine that it would not have been a key constitutive element of both this putative "bifurcation" between Baal and Hadad, as postulated by Greenfield, and an emerging Aramean *Umwelt*.

The recent publication of the Antakya Stela raises once again the problem of the nature of boundaries in the ancient Near East; for there appears at both lines 4 and 10 the Assyrian word *taḫūmu* along with *miṣir* (*miṣru*) at line 14. It would seem from this use of *taḫūmu* that, in fact,

---

41. Relevant here are lines 4–5 of the Tel Dan inscription, "[And] Hadad made me [Hazael] king. And Hadad went in front of me . . . ," A. Biran and J. Naveh, "The Tel Dan Inscription: A New Fragment," *Israel Exploration Journal*, 45/1 (1995) 1–18.

42. See H. Klengel, "Der Wettergott von Ḫalab," *Journal of Cuneiform Studies*, XIX (1965) 87–93.

43. J. B. Pritchard, ed., *Ancient Near Eastern Texts* (Princeton, 1955) 278–79.

44. See M. Burke, *Textes administraitifs de la salle III du Palais* (ARMT, XI; Paris, 1963) 113, p. 47.

45. W. von Soden, "Das altbabylonische Briefarchiv von Mari," *Die Welt des Orients*, 3 (1948) 200.

46. G. Dossin, "Les Archives Épistolaires du Palais Mari," *Syria*, 19 (1938) 115, n. 3. See especially B. Lafont, "Le Roi de Mari et les Prophètes du Dieu Adad," *Revue d'Assyriologie*, 78 (1984) 7–18.

conceptions of boundaries, in contrast to the geographically more imprecise conception of "frontier," in the ancient Near East could be rather precise. Moreover, the use of the boundary stone also appears to indicate
that such boundaries need not have necessarily corresponded to natural
markers like mountains and rivers. The problem of these considerations
into the nature of "all Aram" has also been one of boundaries—not primarily those of Sefire IB, lines 9-10, but the boundaries marking the
categories that we employ in our analysis of ancient and, for that matter,
modern collectivities.

It does not seem that "all Aram" was a nation. Yet, it is difficult to re-
frain from using the adjective "Aramean" when discussing the various
city-states within the area of "all Aram." It would seem that we have here
an entity which, in our attempt to analyze its nature, requires that we violate the boundaries of our categories of analysis. A somewhat similar categorial problem was recognized by J. N. Postgate a number of years ago
when he complained about the difficulty of translating the Aramaic term
bīt PN (and its Assyrian equivalent *bītu* PN).[47] The term clearly indicates,
through the use of the personal name of usually an eponymous ancestor,
a belief in being related by blood; hence, the term suggests an entity resembling a tribe or a coalition of tribes. However, as Postgate recognized,
the term also indicates the existence of an entity which was clearly something more than a tribe or a coalition of tribes; for it also has a geographical connotation. One wonders, once again, whether or not it is this
geographical element which is, in fact, at the basis of the fiction of being
related by blood: where all who dwell within the geographical jurisdiction of the "house" are described as being related to the founder of his
and their house. While the term "house of [all] Aram" does not appear in
the Sefire Treaty, it is perhaps not to assume too much that a synonym for
"all Aram" would have been the "whole house of [all] Aram," just as an
apparent synonym for "all Israel" was "house of [all] Israel." Perhaps it is
this territorial element at the basis of the fiction of being related by blood
which accounts for some of the difficulty in understanding not only the
term *bīt* PN, but also such ethno-geographic terms of kinship as *gôy* and,
indeed, that territorial collectivity of nativity, the nation.

Whatever difficulties exist in understanding various, relatively large
structures of kinship, this much is clear: one must not be content to refer
to "all Aram" as merely a geographical expression with little, if any,

---

47. J. N. Postgate, "Some Remarks on Conditions in the Assyrian Countryside,"
Journal of the Economic and Social History of the Orient, 17/3 (1974) 234.

gemeinschaftliche (or, if one prefers, ethnic) connotation.[48] To be sure, the city-kingdoms of Damascus, Hamath, Arpad and Ya'di exhibit considerable heterogeneity. On the other hand, a geographical self-designation indicates more than location. It indicates how one conceives of oneself in relation to others. It often indicates an attribution of kinship to those others included in the geographical self-designation.

---

48. So the conclusion of Sader, *Les États Araméens*, 278–81.

Bibliography

Alt, A. "Die syrische Staatenwelt vor dem Einbruch der Assyrer," *Zeitschrift der deutschen morgenländischen Gesellschaft*, 88 (1934) 233–58.

Biran, A., and Naveh, J. "The Tell Dan Inscription: A New Fragment," *Israel Exploration Journal*, 45/1 (1955) 1–18.

Brinkman, J. A. *A Political History of Post-Kassite Babylonia 1158-722 B.C.* (Rome, 1968).

Burke, M. *Textes administraitifs de la salle III du Palais* (ARMT, XI) (Paris, 1963).

Donbaz, V. *Annual Review of the Royal Inscriptions of Mesopotamia*, 8 (1990).

Dossin, G. "Les Archives Épistolaires du Palais Mari," *Syria*, 19 (1939) 105–26.

Drijvers, H. J. W. "Dea Syria," *Lexicon Iconographicum Mythologiae Classicae*, III/1 (Zurich, 1981) 355–56.

Fitzmyer, J. *The Aramaic Inscriptions of Sefire* (Rome, 1967).

Gibson, John C. L. *Textbook of Syrian Semitic Inscriptions*, Vol. 2 (Oxford, 1975).

Grayson, A. K. *Assyrian Royal Inscriptions*, Vol. 2 (Wiesbaden, 1976).

_____. *Assyrian and Babylonian Chronicles* (Locust Valley, 1975).

Greenfield, J. "Hadad," in *Dictionary of Deities and Demons in the Bible*, ed. K. van der Toorn, B. Becking, and R. W. van der Horst (Leiden, 1995) 716–26.

_____. "Asylum at Aleppo: A Note on Sfire III, 4–7," in *Ah, Assyria . . . Studies in Assyrian History and Ancient Near Eastern Historiography Presented to Hayim Tadmor*, ed. M. Cogan and I. Eph'al (Scripta Hierosolymitana, 33) (Jerusalem, 1991) 272–78.

_____. "Aspects of Aramean Religion," in *Ancient Israelite Religion, Essays in Honor of Frank Moore Cross*, ed. P. D. Miller, P. D. Hanson, and S. D. McBride (Philadelphia, 1987) 67–78.

Grosby, S. "Borders, Territory, and Nationality in the Ancient Near East and Armenia," *Journal of the Economic and Social History of the Orient*, 39/4 (1996) 1–29.

Gunkel, H. *Genesis* (Göttingen, 1901).

Heltzer, M. *The Suteans* (Naples, 1981).

Klengel, H. "Der Wettergott von Ḥalab," *Journal of Cuneiform Studies*, XIX (1965) 87–93.

Lafont, B. "Le Roi de Mari et les Prophètes du Dieu Adad," *Revue d'Assyriologie*, 78 (1984) 7–18.

Luckenbill, D. *Ancient Records of Assyria and Babylonia* (Chicago, 1926).

Mazar, B. "The Aramean Empire and its Relations with Israel," *The Biblical Archaeologist*, XXV (1962) 98–120.

Mendenhall, G. "Amorites," in *Anchor Bible Dictionary*, Vol. 1 (New York, 1992) 199–202.

Naʾaman, N. "Forced Participation in Alliances in the Course of the Assyrian Campaigns to the West," in *Ah, Assyria . . . Studies in Assyrian History and Ancient Near Eastern Historiography Presented to Hayim Tadmor*, ed. M. Cogan and I. Ephꜥal (Scripta Hierosolymitana, 33) (Jerusalem, 1991) 98–120.

Noth, M. *The History of Israel* (London, 1959).

Parpola, S., and Watanabe, K. *Neo-Assyrian Treaties and Loyalty Oaths* (State Archives of Assyria, II) (Helsinki, 1988).

Pitard, W. T. "Arameans," in *Peoples of the Old Testament World*, ed. A. J. Hoerth, G. L. Mattingly, and E. M. Yamauchi (Grand Rapids, 1994) 207–30.

Postgate, N. J. "Some Remarks on Conditions in the Assyrian Countryside," *Journal of the Economic and Social History of the Orient*, 17/3 (1974) 225–43.

Pritchard, J. B., ed. *Ancient Near Eastern Texts* (Princeton, 1955).

Rowton, M. B. "Autonomy and Nomadism in Western Asia," *Orientalia* N.S., 42 (1973) 247–58.

Sader, H. *Les États Araméens de Syrie* (Beirut, 1987).

Schwartz, G. M. "The Origin of the Arameans in Syria and Northern Mesopotamia: Research Problems and Potential Strategies," in *To the Euphrates and Beyond*, ed. O. M. C. Haex, H. H. Curvens, and P. M. M. G. Akkermans (Rotterdam, 1989) 275–91.

Tadmor, H. *The Inscriptions of Tiglath-pileser III, King of Assyria* (Jerusalem, 1994).

_____ . "Assyria and the West: The Ninth Century and Its Aftermath," in *Unity and Diversity, Essays in the History, Literature, and Religion of the Ancient Near East*, ed. H. Goedicke and J. J. M. Roberts (Baltimore, 1975) 36–48.

von Soden, W. 1948. "Das altbabylonische Briefarchiv von Mari," *Die Welt des Orients*, 3 (1948).

Wellhausen, J. *Israelitische und Jüdische Geschichte* (Berlin, 1905).

Zadok, R. "Elements of Aramean Pre-History," in *Ah, Assyria . . . Studies in Assyrian History and Ancient Near Eastern Historiography Presented to Hayim Tadmor*, ed. M. Cogan and I. Ephꜥal (Scripta Hierosolymitana, 33) (Jerusalem, 1991) 104–17.

Chapter 7

The Category of the Primordial in the Study of Early Christianity and Second-Century Judaism

> Jesus said in reply, "I was sent only to the lost sheep of the House of Israel." (Matt 15:24)
>
> These twelve Jesus sent out, instructing them as follows: "Do not turn your steps to pagan territory . . . go rather to the lost sheep of the House of Israel." (Matt 10:5)

I

Examinations of selected passages from the New Testament, like the two above from Matthew, have led an increasing number of scholars of the New Testament and historians of early Christianity to conclude that Jesus lived as a Jew. Moreover, the life and work of Jesus are to be understood as having taken place clearly within a framework of Jewish eschatological expectation;[1] that is, Jesus intended Jewish restoration.[2] In support of these conclusions, E. P. Sanders in his impressive work *Jesus and Judaism* points to a number of what he takes to be historical facts, among which two are the call of the twelve apostles, the number "twelve" representing indirectly the twelve tribes of the nation of all-Israel,[3] and the turning over of the tables of the money changers in the temple (Matt 21:12). The latter historical fact, according to Sanders, is not to be interpreted as a rejection

---

1. E. P. Sanders, *Jesus and Judaism* (Philadelphia: Fortress, 1985), p. 91.

2. Ibid., p. 116. In contrast, see, e.g., C. F. D. Moule, *The Origin of Christology* (Cambridge: Cambridge University Press, 1977).

3. On the use of "twelve," see Matt 19:28 and, of course, the Epistle of Saint Barnabas VIII, in *The Genuine Epistles of the Apostolic Fathers*, trans. William Wake (Philadelphia, 1846): "To whom the Lord gave authority to preach the gospel: being at the beginning twelve, to signify the tribes, because there were twelve tribes of Israel." For "all-Israel" as a term of national restoration, see S. Grosby, "Religion and Nationality in Antiquity," *Archives Européennes de Sociologie* 2 (1991): 229-65 [reprinted in this volume, pp. 13-51], "Kinship, Territory and the Nation in the Historiography of Ancient Israel," *Zeitschrift für die alttestamentliche Wissenschaft* 1 (1993): 3-18 [reprinted in this volume, pp. 52-68], and "Sociological Implications of the Distinction between 'Locality' and Extended 'Territory' with Particular Reference to the Old Testament," *Social Compass* 40, no. 2 (1993): 179-98 [reprinted in this volume, pp. 69-91].

of either the temple or Israel; rather, Jesus' action represents a demand for the purification of the temple of a renewed all-Israel. As such, the demand stands squarely within Jewish tradition (see 2 Kgs 18:4, 22:3-23; 1 Macc 4:36-60; 2 Macc 10:1-8).[4] Furthermore, Jesus' instructions to the twelve apostles in Matt 10:5, "Do not turn your steps to pagan territory," reminds us of what was expected by the restoration of all-Israel as expressed in, for example, Bar 2:34-35: "Then I [Yahweh] will bring them [Israel] back to the land I promised on oath to Abraham, Isaac and Jacob, and make them masters in it. . . . I will be their God and they shall be my people. And I will never again drive my people Israel out of the land that I have given to them." In other words, the eschatological expectation was the reestablishment of the primordial integrity of the nation of all-Israel; that is, the land from Dan to Beersheba would once again belong to its only appropriate possessor, the putative descendants of Abraham, Isaac, and Jacob.

There were, of course, other elements in the work of Jesus, for example, the belief in eschatological miracle in the establishment of the kingdom and the salvation of the individual as an individual. As is well known, these elements were further developed by Paul, albeit not without exacerbating the ambiguities and potential conflicts in Jesus' Jewish eschatological expectation. Nevertheless, if the life and work of Jesus took place in the context of his idea of Jewish restoration, then our understanding of the dispute between Paul and James as indicated in such passages as Gal 2:11-12 becomes clearer. In point of fact, the increasing scholarly acceptance of conclusions similar to those of Sanders only adds credibility to Adolf von Harnack's conclusion, prompted by his consideration of such passages as Gal 2:11-12, on the organizational structure of the early church in Palestine. Approximately eighty-five years ago, Harnack observed, "The fact that it was Jesus' relations, however, who were pushed to the front, cannot have been merely the consequence of the high esteem in which James 'the Just' was held, and his reputation with all sections of the community, but the idea that blood relationship with Jesus conferred on these descendants of David a right to rule must have been a contributing factor."[5]

The intention of these foregoing remarks is not to reexamine the considerable difficulties surrounding the quest for the historical Jesus. It is

---

4. See W. D. Davies, *The Gospel and the Land* (Berkeley: University of California Press, 1974), pp. 339, n. 10, and 190. Unless noted otherwise, English translations of the Bible are from the Jerusalem Bible (Garden City, N.Y.: Doubleday, 1968).

5. Adolf von Harnack, *The Constitution and the Law of the Church in the First Two Centuries* (London: Williams & Norgate, 1910), pp. 33-34.

rather to bring into the foreground the element of primordiality in early Christianity and the Judaism of that period. The purpose in doing so is by no means merely to reassert the significance of primordiality in Jewish eschatology (i.e., the beliefs in the lineage of Abraham, Isaac, and Jacob and the land of all-Israel) or in the constitution of the early Church (i.e., the apparent criterion of *Sippen-* or *Erbscharisma* for leadership of the early Palestinian church). As important as primordial relations are for the sociological study of early Christianity, in particular for our under-standing of the boundaries of the different communities, the intention of these foregoing remarks is to point to the possibility of a different and broader point of departure in the consideration of the significance of pri-mordiality for the study of early Christianity.

II

By "primordiality" I mean beliefs about the significance of nativity, that is, about the life-giving and life-determining connections formed through both birth to particular persons and birth in a specific territory. These are beliefs that attribute significance to the creation and transmis-sion of life; they are the cognitive references to the objects around which various structures of kinship, from the family to the nation, are formed.[6] That Christianity attempted doctrinally to sweep away the significance of primordial relations is so well known that it need not be elaborated on here in any detail. It will suffice merely to refer to Gal 3:27-29, "All are baptized in Christ, you have all clothed yourselves in Christ, and there are no more distinctions between Jew and Greek, slave and free, male and female, but all of you are one in Christ Jesus." Furthermore, the con-stitution of the early church quickly abandoned the criterion of relation by blood—assuming Harnack was correct—for hierocratic office.[7] All of

6. E. Shils, "Primordial, Personal, Sacred and Civil Ties," *British Journal of Sociol-ogy* 8 (1957): 130-45; Clifford Geertz, "Primordial Sentiments and Civil Politics in the New States," in *Old Societies and New States*, ed. C. Geertz (New York: Free Press, 1963); S. Grosby, "The Verdict of History: The Inexpungeable Tie of Primordiality," *Ethnic and Racial Studies* 17, no. 1 (1994): 168-74, "Territoriality," *Nations and Nation-alism* 1, no. 2 (1995): 143-62 [[in this volume, pp. 191-212]].
7. Although for over a century the primacy of the Armenian church remained in the family of Saint Gregory the Illuminator, passing frequently from son to son; see Charles Burney and David Marshall Lang, *The Peoples of the Hills: Ancient Ararat and Caucasus* (London: Weidenfeld & Nicolson, 1971), p. 224. Malachia Ormanian, in *The Church of Armenia* (London: Mowbray, 1955), p. 14, wrote that "the retention of the patriarchate in the family of St. Grigor was at the wish of the nation, either as a de-sire to do homage to the great Illuminator, or as an unconscious compliance with the

this is well known and obvious, but does this rejection of primordiality settle once and for all the matter of its role in early Christianity?

To consider Matt 10:35-38 (see also Mark 3:33-35) in the context of this question, even briefly, is to recognize a far more complicated situation: "For I [Jesus] have come to set a man against his father, a daughter against her mother, a daughter-in-law against her mother-in-law. A man's enemies will be those of his own household. Anyone who prefers father or mother to me is not worthy of me. Anyone who prefers son or daughter to me is not worthy of me." Here we see that the primordial relations constitutive of the family evidently pose obstacles for the universalistic ties of the Christian community. If for no other reason, they do so because they raise the following question: Who has the power of the gift of life, the parents or God?[8] The obviousness of the alternatives suggested by this question appears to indicate that human beings recognize two diverse and distinctive loci of power bearing on the existence and conduct of life; that is, human beings are responsive to two sources of the sacred, one being the universally valid norms ordained by a transcendental god about the right order of life and the second being the generation and transmission of life itself.

The continuing recognition of the ever-present potential for the challenge of the primordial relations of the family to universal Christianity may be seen in the insistence of Augustine that "in regard to natural generation, it may be said: Neither the wife nor the husband's part is anything, but it is God who fashions the form of the offspring; nor is the mother who bears and brings the child to birth anything, but it is God who gives the growth."[9] The consequences of this ever-present potential

---

influences of a pagan custom." Nina G. Garsoian, in "Secular Jurisdiction over the Armenian Church (Fourth–Seventh Centuries)," and "Prolegomena to a Study of the Iranian Aspects in Arsacid Armenia," both in her *Armenia between Byzantium and the Sasanians* (London: Variorum, 1985), pp. 234-35, 9-10, 24, n. 45, has attributed the practice to the influence of earlier Iranian tradition in which all offices of the realm were the hereditary prerogatives of certain noble lineages.

8. The differences between Matt 10:35-38 and Mic 7:6 are so striking that the former should not be considered in the context of the latter. See also Matt 19:29. Note Celsus's accusation that the Christians demand that children disobey their parents (the father); *Origen: Contra Celsus*, ed. Henry Chadwick (Cambridge: Cambridge University Press, 1953), pp. 165-66.

9. Saint Augustine, *City of God*, ed. V. J. Bourke (New York: Doubleday, 1958), bk. 22, chap. 24. Note also bk. 12, chap. 26: "Nor do we look upon a woman as the creator of the child she bears . . . whatever bodily or seminal causes may play a part in reproduction . . . by the intermingling of the two sexes . . . nevertheless every nature as such is created wholly by the Supreme God."

may be seen in the historically recurring denunciation of carnal relations and marriage as unclean ("since sex is always a danger" [1 Cor 7:2]) by various Christian sects, albeit heretical ones, for example, the Montanists, the quasi-gnostic Bogomili of the Eastern church, and the Cathari of the West.[10] Of course, only such sects could interpret Matt 5:28 ("But I say this to you: if a man looks at a woman lustfully, he has already committed adultery with her in his heart") in such a fashion that it ascetically sets itself against the persistent, primordial relations of humans. In contrast, the church has avoided directly confronting the primordial relations of the family—a confrontation that would do violence to persistent human sensibilities—by seeking to sanctify those relations (1 Corinthians 7; 1 Tim 4:3) and thus place them under its jurisdiction. By so doing, the church has sought to bring the primordial relations of the family into harmony with the universalistic Christian community so that the family becomes a constitutive component of that community. Where the church's subordination of the primordial relations of the family has not proven adequate to abrogate the conflict for very pious, ascetic Christians between being one with Christ and the primordial ties of the family, it has segregated those individuals into the holy orders of the church.

The intention of these remarks is not to reopen a sociological investigation of the relation between male and female members of the various Christian communities during the first and second centuries of their existence, however important such an investigation continues to be. The significant point is the recognition of historically persistent, heterogeneous loci of sacrality that indicate the existence of historically persistent, heterogeneous sacral patterns of transcendence. From our very brief consideration of Matt 10:35–38, we have not merely observed the well-known strain between the universalism of the Christian community and the primordial relations of the family. We are further interested in the fact that despite this tension, the primordial relations of the family have persisted. Moreover, and of special importance, this persistence is true not only for the family, which for us was but an example, albeit a marked one, of the persistence of a primordial locus of sacrality, but also for the primordial relations of other structures of kinship, namely, nationality and its constitutive element of territoriality. It is the continued presence and influence of especially these other structures of kinship, even after the emergence of the universalism of the world religions, that substanti-

---

10. See, e.g., S. Runciman, *The Medieval Manichee* (Cambridge: Cambridge University Press, 1947). For an interesting work on the background of the Bogomili, see Nina G. Garsoian, *The Paulician Heresy* (The Hague: Mouton, 1967).

ates the merit of the category of the primordial for historical investigation into human affairs. That merit has been implicitly challenged in various ways, perhaps the most interesting of which is the historicism of Karl Jaspers. Before examining the influence of territoriality and nationality on early Christianity, we must turn our attention to Jaspers's argument.

III

In *The Origin and the Goal of History*, Karl Jaspers described the axial age as the period of human history when humanity took the step into universality in every sense.[11] This step into universality was embodied in the emergence of what Max Weber had earlier called the "world religions," in contrast to the primordial religions of a particular people and locality. In the West, the charismatic breakthrough that provided the foundation for the subsequent establishment of the world religion of Christianity was accomplished by the Israelite prophets in their formulation of an ethical, monotheistic religion.[12] The latter was characterized by an increased rationalization in understanding cosmic events that otherwise resisted a consistently ethical explanation. The primordial religions could not provide such a relatively coherent view of the world, for example, a rational explanation of the defeat of one's country in war. For the primordial collectivity and its religion, the defeat of one's country necessarily signified the defeat of its national god. In other words, a characteristic of the world religions of the axial age is the ascendant recognition of universal, otherworldly criteria and principles by which to judge the affairs of this world. Concomitantly, beliefs in the ability to manipulate the deity through magic were, if not entirely swept aside,[13] certainly subordinated in the world religions to beliefs in a deity who demanded righteousness and obedience to his law by all.

---

11. Karl Jaspers, *The Origin and Goal of History* (New Haven, Conn.: Yale University Press, 1953), p. 2. See also *The Origins and Diversity of Axial Age Civilizations*, ed. S. N. Eisenstadt (Albany: SUNY Press, 1986).

12. Max Weber, *Ancient Judaism* (New York: Free Press, 1952), pp. 297-335.

13. One should certainly not overlook the importance of either the magical character of the sacraments or the beliefs in the exorcism of demons for early Christianity (e.g., Gregory the Wonder Worker; Saint Gregory the Illuminator, who putatively freed the king of Armenia, Tiridates, of demoniacal possession; etc.). This is a common enough recognition. For examples, see Morton Smith, *Jesus the Magician* (San Francisco: Harper & Row, 1978); Ramsay MacMullen, *Christianizing the Roman Empire A.D. 100-400* (New Haven, Conn.: Yale University Press, 1984), pp. 27-29, 60, 108-9.

Another characteristic of the world religions of the axial age was their ability to migrate, that is, to become established outside the territory of their origin and separate from the population of their origin, for example, the expansion of Buddhism from India to China, the expansion of Confucianism and Buddhism across East and Southeast Asia, and, of course, the expansion of Christianity and Islam throughout the world. In other words, for the world religions, or, as A. D. Nock called them, "prophetic religions," conversion was possible, in contrast to primordial religions.[14] With regard to this ability to expand through conversion, it is of interest to note Seneca's bitter complaint about the subversion of Roman religion as being a result of "the conquered having given laws to the conquerors."[15] No doubt, the ability of the religion of the conquered—in this case, the ethical monotheism of early Christianity—to subvert the primordial religion of the conquering Romans was a consequence of the former's significantly more rationalized doctrine.

Now from a slightly different context, we pose again our previous question: Has the expansion of the world religions at the expense of primordial collectivities and their religions settled once and for all the matter of the significance of primordiality? Jaspers thought that the axial age represented the step into universality in every sense. He thought that in the new creations of the *Geist*, as embodied in the world religions of the axial age and, above all, in their greater potential for explaining the inescapable misfortunes of life, "there had developed qualities that progressed to the free personality founded on existence as an autonomous individual."[16] Clearly there is much merit to Jaspers's observations, for the prophecy of the world religions assumes the existence of the conscience of the individual and addresses itself to that conscience. The emphasis in the work of Jesus on the salvation of the individual as an individual is unmistakable. Yet, as was observed earlier with the problem presented to Christianity by the primordial properties of the family, the situation is far more complicated than what Jaspers's sharp disjunction would suggest, and, for that matter, more complicated than those catego-

---

14. A. D. Nock, *Conversion* (Oxford: Clarendon, 1933). By conversion I mean, following Nock, a thorough reorientation of the soul from the old wrong to the new right. The contrast between primordial religions and world religions is, of course, ideal-typical (i.e., it is based on historically abstract categories of a pure type, the justification for which is heuristic), with numerous religious movements, e.g., Orphism, Mithraism, and the territorially expansive cult of Isis, representing transitions between these two poles.

15. Saint Augustine, bk. 6, chap. 11.

16. Jaspers, p. 57.

ries of historical analysis that rest on this disjunction, for example, "modernity." Indeed, the persistence of nationality is evidence enough to indicate that a far more complicated relation exists between the ethical universalism of the world religions and those territorial collectivities of nativity, nations.

It is obvious enough that the world religions have undermined various primordial religions and their respective collectivities, but they have not undermined primordiality. The world religions have sought and established in various ways a modus vivendi with the significance of primordiality. Numerous and historically varied examples of the complicated interrelationship between these two patterns of transcendence, the primordial and the universal, may be adduced: the primordial structures of kinship and territory providing jurisdiction for the postprophetic laws of Deuteronomy (see Deut 15:12, 23:20, 24:7);[17] the crusades of the thirteenth century, undertaken in the name of universal orthodoxy against the Albigenses, resulting in the incorporation of Toulouse into the territory of France; the papal recognition of Poland as a distinct Catholic province in the attempt to safeguard the territorial integrity of Poland, in particular her western border, from the Order of Teutonic Knights;[18] and the assertion of the primordial boundaries of the collectivity constituted, in part, by the universalistic beliefs in the liberty of the individual as expressed in John Jay's Federalist Paper no. 2.[19]

The persistence and resilience of the primordial ties of distinctive, territorially constituted and delimited cultural traditions, as seen in the above examples, indicate that the "free personality" of "an autonomous individual" of which Jaspers wrote is an abstraction with only limited

---

17. For the classic treatment of the Deuteronomic laws as postprophetic, see Julius Wellhausen, *Prolegomena to the History of Ancient Israel* (1878; Gloucester, Mass.: Smith, 1978). For a more recent treatment, see E. W. Nicholson, *God and His People* (Oxford: Clarendon, 1986).

18. See Norman Davies, *God's Playground: A History of Poland* (New York: Columbia University Press, 1982); Konstantin Symmons-Symonolewicz, *National Consciousness in Poland: Origin and Evolution* (Meadville, Pa.: Maplewood, 1983).

19. "With equal pleasure I have as often taken notice that Providence has been pleased to give this one connected country to one united people—a people descended from the same ancestors, speaking the same language, professing the same religion, attached to the same principles of government, very similar in their manners and customs, and who, by their joint counsels, arms, and efforts, fighting side by side throughout a long and bloody war, have nobly established their general liberty and independence. . . . This country and this people seem to have been made for each other" (Alexander Hamilton, James Madison, and John Jay, *The Federalist Papers*, ed. Clinton Rossiter [New York: Mentor, 1961], p. 38).

empirical support. The universalistic breakthrough of the axial age did not obliterate primordiality; most individuals are members of collectivities not because of a voluntary exercise of conscience but because of the significance that is attributed to the fact that they are born into them. As such, the distinctive cultural tradition of such a collectivity is a constitutive element in the development of the character of the individual as he or she matures from infancy into adulthood; the distinctive cultural tradition has a bearing on the thoughts and actions of the individual. This fact, and the above examples, indicate not only that the universality of the world religions has dramatically transformed various primordial collectivities, but also that primordial relations have had a bearing on the historical expressions of universality, indeed, often providing the structural jurisdiction for that transcendence. This is certainly obvious in the paradoxical combination of primordiality and universality of Eastern Orthodoxy and Protestantism: the national, Christian church. In these two instances, the distinctive cultural traditions constitutive of the primordial collectivity circumscribe the universality of the Christian doctrine.

In matters such as these, one should abjure conceptions of the unilinear and unequivocal progress of one pattern of transcendence over all others. It is more in keeping with the facts to recognize a complicated and shifting interplay between various patterns of transcendence, each of which appears to be persistent in human affairs. The ethical monotheism of the world religions is the result of the rational pursuit of humanity for answers to the problem of what is the right order of life. This entails the pursuit of universal sacrality, which is one pattern of transcendence, but it does not exclude the attachment to other patterns of sacrality. The existence of beliefs constitutive of primordial collectivities like the national state appears to be the result of the attachment to patterns of primordial sacrality having to do with the propagation and protection of life. This is a second pattern of sacrality. These are two differing loci of the sacred—the one cosmic, the other primordial. They correspond to two different sets of beliefs: those about what is the right order of life and those about the propagation and protection of life.

IV

What significance does the recognition of the persistent existence of heterogeneous loci of sacrality have for the sociological understanding of early Christianity? In particular, how might that heterogeneity be manifested in the organizational structure of the early church? Primordial relations are often considered to have had little or no bearing on the activities and structures of the early church. In support of such conclusions, references are often made to the equality among the members of the local communities (as expressed in, e.g., such practices as the *agapae* or dogmatic propositions such as Gal 3:28, 5:6, 6:15; 1 Cor 12:13) and between the local communities themselves (at least before the triumph of the principle of the monarchical episcopate). Insofar as references to locality have been factors in these considerations, they have been restricted to observations such as (the now-mystical) Jerusalem as the eschatological center of the universe. Nevertheless, as with the persistence of the primordial ties of the family so, too, primordial attachments to locality have persisted. Beliefs in the existence of those sites where access to the deity was perceived to be more efficacious were not entirely undermined.[20] Such sites were believed to be more efficacious for contact with the deity because these sites, in contrast to others, were perceived to be sacred; that is, recognitions of the spatial heterogeneity of the sacred continued even in the context of a Christian equality and universalism that, at least dogmatically, implied a spatial homogeneity of this world. At the basis of this spatial heterogeneity of the sacred often rests a continuing significance attributed to territorially distinct cultural traditions.

Evidence for the existence of this locational parochiality of the sacred in early Christianity is, as we shall see, rarely explicit. Nevertheless, when the following examples of Montanism, Donatism, the separatism of the Copts and Armenians, and the cult of Theotokos are considered together, we perceive the influence, however indirect, of primordial relations on the otherworldly universality of Christianity. Let us consider briefly here Montanism, the least self-evident of the above examples.

While the second-century heresy of Montanism doctrinally shared much with the Christianity of that time, it was nonetheless distinguished by its chiliasm, its hostility to sexual relations and marriage, and its insistence that the "spiritual man," the prophet, as the embodier of Spirit, was alone the true church capable of pardoning transgressions, while the "organizational men," the bishops and priests, did not have this capacity.[21]

---

20. See, e.g., Maurice Halbwachs, *La topographie légendaire des évangiles en terre sainte: Étude de mémoire collective* (Paris: Presses Universitaires de France, 1941); Peter Brown, *The Cult of the Saints* (Chicago: University of Chicago Press, 1981).

21. The oracles, writings, and references to Montanism have been conveniently collected into one volume (Ronald Heine, *The Montanist Oracles and Testimonia*, Patristic Monograph Series 14 [Macon, Ga.: Mercer University Press, 1989]). I have used Heine for reference, rather than J.-P. Migne's *Patrologiae Latinae* and *Patrologiae Graecae*. With regard to its chiliasm, note the second- to third-century anonymous polemic

"But," you say, "the Church has the right to pardon sins." This I recognize more than you [yet] this right will pertain to those who are spiritual, either to an apostle or prophet. For indeed the Church itself is properly and principally the Spirit itself. . . . And for this reason the Church indeed will pardon transgressions; but it is the Church of the Spirit, done by means of a spiritual man, not the Church which consists of a number of bishops. For the right and the decision belongs to the Lord, not to the servant; it belongs to God himself, not to the priest.[22]

In this last characteristic, Montanism anticipated Donatism and elements of Protestantism as well. With such characteristics, Montanism represented, generally speaking, a more radical, ascetic rejection of the world than what one typically finds in the increasingly accommodating Christianity of that time. What is remarkable about Montanism, especially in such an otherworldly context, was the belief that "Jerusalem would descend from heaven" in the Phrygian home town of Montanus, Priscilla, and Maximilla, Pepuza.[23] Indeed, the accusation is repeatedly made that Montanus and his prophetesses renamed Pepuza "Jerusalem." Typical of these accusations is the one by Filastrius of Brescia: "The Cataphrygians proclaim certain prophets of their own, that is, one named Montanus, and Priscilla, and Maximilla. . . . They apply the name Jerusalem to their village Pepuza . . . where Maximilla and Priscilla, and Montanus himself are recognized to have spent their useless and fruitless lives."[24]

That Christ's kingdom was to be located in Phrygia was for Harnack an indication of Montanus's pretentiousness.[25] No doubt, Harnack was right, but surely the significance of the Montanist reversal of Gal 4:26 ("the Jerusalem that is above"), such that Phrygia was proclaimed to be the promised land, rests elsewhere. This is not to say that by such a proclamation Montanus was a nationalist or that Montanism was a nationalist movement. Nonetheless, Montanus's statement that his Phrygian

---

against Montanism: "For there have been more than thirteen years to this day since the woman [the prophetess Maximilla] died, and there has been neither a local nor a general war in the world, but by mercy of God there is rather an enduring peace even for Christians" (ibid., p. 19). On its hostility to sexual relations and marriage, see Apollonius's assertion that Montanus "taught the dissolution of marriage" (ibid., p. 23) and Tertullian's exhortation to chastity, "Seize the opportunity not to be obligated to anyone in conjugal matters . . . for by continence you will gain a great store of holiness" (ibid., p. 65). Note also Tertullian's contrast of spirit to flesh (ibid., pp. 77, 79).

22. Ibid., p. 93. The quotation is from Tertullian.
23. Ibid., p. 5. The oracle is attributed to Priscilla by Epiphanius.
24. Ibid, p. 139. See also the accusations of Apollonius (ibid., p. 23), Cyril of Jerusalem (ibid., p. 113), Epiphanius (ibid., p. 131), and Augustine (ibid., p. 163).
25. Adolph von Harnack, *History of Dogma* (1885; New York: Dover, 1961), 1:168.

home was the new Jerusalem indicates, even if only indirectly, the possibility of a geographical parochiality of the sacred coexisting with the universal transcendence of Christianity.

The influence of primordial relations on early Christianity, as in the case of Montanus's attachment to his Phrygian home of Pepuza, is by no means limited to the attribution of sacrality to specific localities. More significant for the history of Christianity has been the influence of the attachments constitutive of more extensive, bounded territories on Christianity. What was the sociological expression of this influence?

In *The Constitution and the Law of the Church in the First Two Centuries*, Harnack provided a more suggestive point of departure for the consideration of the significance of the historically profound primordial tie of territory on the organization of the early church.

> There is another important point in the organization of the Churches in the earliest period which needs attention. . . . We have repeatedly emphasized the fundamental antinomy and tension which controls the historical development of the constitution [of the early Church]; on the one hand we saw the community as a missionary community, as the creation of an apostle, as his work, and in this aspect it appeared a universal obligation; on the other hand we saw the community as a self-contained local community. . . . But from the beginning a third factor intervened, at first almost imperceptibly and then more and more clearly, in the situation caused by this tension and the opposition between the universal and local organization. . . . We allude to the inner and outer connecting ties subsisting between the communities situated in one province. . . . The consequence of this state of affairs was two-fold. In the first place, the division of the empire into provinces, and consequently the provincial spirit, gained an influence over the church. . . . Between the more or less ideal universal church and the local church there comes in the provincial church. . . . And this again is a proof of how absolutely dependent everything here is on the political organization.[26]

By these remarks, did Harnack miss the significance of his suggestive references to the existence of both the "inner and outer connecting ties subsisting between the communities situated in one province" and "the provincial spirit"?

The provincial spirit of the second and third centuries to which Harnack referred indicates the existence of distinct cultural traditions that have "settled" in territories, and, as such, constitute them. The justification for this observation is by no means merely theoretical. Only a few centuries after the appearance of the apostolic, missionary community,

---

26. Harnack, *Constitution* (n. 5 above), pp. 156–60.

we are confronted with the existence of more or less national churches—for example, the Armenian and the Coptic—and community-bound assertions—for example, that made by Gregory of Tours, that the Franks are a special people chosen to defend Christianity.

Armenia of the fourth century, as described in the fifty-century work *The Epic Histories* by Faustus of Byzantium, provides a good example of what Harnack meant by the existence of "the inner and outer connecting ties subsisting between the communities situated in one province," resulting in a "provincial spirit." During the middle part of the fourth century, Tiran, the king of Armenia, satiated with food and drunk with wine at the table of his Persian guests, was kidnapped by the Persians and subsequently blinded by them.[27] As is to be expected from the Christian historian, Faustus explained the blinding of Tiran as God's retribution for Tiran's earlier executions of Saint Daniel and the Christian patriarch Yusik. What is especially noteworthy for our purposes is Faustus's description of the Armenian response to the kidnapping of their king: "Then the men of the realm of the land of Armenia—the magnates, nobles, governors, lords, and retainers, the army leaders, judges, chieftains, and princes, not to mention the army commanders and even [some/many?] of the non-noble people [ṙamik] and peasants [šinakan]—gathered together in a council [or assembly] of still greater accord. Then they began to speak to one another and said, '. . . Let us protect our realm and ourselves, and let us avenge our own "true-lord." ' "[28] In this description we observe not only the existence of what could legitimately be called a national council but also a conception of an Armenian territory, "the realm of the land of Armenia," constituted by a recognition of the geographical jurisdiction of the dominion of the royal house and the extent of Armenian cultural tradition and language.[29]

The analytical problem is to describe the relation and probable causal factors between a provincial spirit and the universal mission of Paul, with respect to the "territorialization" of the church. Harnack was certainly correct to focus our attention on the early, provincial division of the church. However, the implication of his remarks is blunted by his reducing the significance of the provincial division to the historical realities

---

27. *The Epic Histories Attributed to Pʿawstos Buzand*, trans. Nina G. Garsoian (Cambridge, Mass.: Harvard University Press, 1989), bk. 3, chap. 20.

28. Ibid., bk. 3, chap. 21.

29. For Garsoian's discussion of the technical terms *erkir* (land) and *erkir haykakan lezui* (land of Armenian speech), see ibid., p. 524.

of either a mere matter of administrative convenience or a mere continuation of, or accommodation to, Roman practices.[30]

In *The Mission and Expansion of Christianity in the First Three Centuries*, Harnack was correct to insist that, in the controversy over Easter between the Greeks and the Romans, the differences were not national.[31] Yet this appropriate observation, once again, does not settle the matter: the differences were expressive of the persistence of differing traditions in the face of the otherwise expansive universalism of Catholicism. The tenacity of these differences was confirmed by subsequent events. Those differences retarded the expansion of a consistent universalism. But it is not enough to recognize the retardation; it is not enough to recognize the weight of tradition. We wish to know why a consistent expansion was thwarted; what is the significance of the weight of those traditions constitutive of a territory? Do the answers to these questions exist in heterogeneous loci of sacrality?

Harnack's comments are, for us, but an example. One could just as well have pointed to A. H. M. Jones's criticisms of E. L. Woodward's arguments about the putative national character of the disputes of the early Church.[32] It is most certainly not the intention of this essay to argue that disputes over dogma are reducible to differences between nationalities. It is to say too much to argue that Donatism was an explicitly national movement, yet it did become a largely Numidian, separatist movement.[33] It would clearly be wrong to argue that the disputes over the nature of Jesus Christ were nationalist in intention, yet there arose a separate, Coptic

---

30. For the Roman provinces, see A. H. M. Jones, *The Later Roman Empire, 284-602* (Oxford: Blackwell, 1964), app. 3.

31. Adolf von Harnack, *The Mission and the Expansion of Christianity in the First Three Centuries* (1902; Gloucester, Mass.: Smith, 1972), p. 65. But note the later comments: "The every-increasing dependence of the Eastern Church upon the redistributed empire (a redistribution which conformed to national boundaries) imperiled by degrees the unity of the church and the universalism of Christianity. The church began by showing harmony and vigor in the sphere of action, but centrifugal influences soon commenced to play upon her, influences which are perceptible as early as the Paschal controversy of A.D. 190 between Rome and Asia, which are vital by the time of the controversy over the baptism of heretics, and which finally appear as disintegrating forces in the fourth and fifth centuries" (ibid., p. 442, n. 1). Our problem is, what were these centrifugal tendencies?

32. A. H. M. Jones, "Were Ancient Heresies National or Social Movements in Disguise?" *Journal of Theological Studies*, n.s., 10 (1959): 281-98; E. L. Woodward, *Christianity and Nationalism in the Later Roman Empire* (London: Longmans, 1916).

33. W. H. C. Frend, *The Donatist Chuch* (Oxford: Oxford University Press, 1952).

Monophysite church.[34] It is certainly incorrect to reduce religious disputes to conflicts between social or national groups—the achievements of
the mind acquire a relative independence from their creators. They have
a life of their own; once created, they follow their own logic.[35] This is, after
all, how we are to understand the increasingly rational pursuit for the
meaning of life as expressed in the emergence and consolidation of the
world religions—a pursuit that follows the logic of the beliefs themselves.

Nevertheless, it is also incorrect to proceed as if differing territorial or
national traditions were irrelevant as factors influencing the structure of
the early church or affecting the substance of certain religious beliefs. To
be sure, the evidence for indirect influence may be inferential. Let us consider, for example, the matter of language. It is generally assumed that
the Hussite translation of the Bible contributed to and was an expression
of the existence of a separatist, Hussite movement. If so, what conclusions, if any, should we draw for the development of the Coptic church
from the translation by the end of the third century of the Bible into Sa-
hidic? What conclusions should we draw from the fact that, in the Egypt
of the sixth and early seventh centuries, outside the Greek-speaking area
of Alexandria, the Coptic church reigned supreme?[36] What conclusions
should we draw from the fact that the Libyan/Berber-speaking areas of
North Africa were mainly Donatist in contrast to Latin-speaking pro-
consular Africa and Carthage?[37] No doubt, distinctive languages are expressions of and vehicles for distinctive cultures. But why should the
existence of various languages be a factor in the retardation and deflection of a consistent universalism of Christianity?

It is interesting that mathematics, in contrast to religious doctrine,
maintains a consistent notational system. The significance of the difference between the consistent notational system of mathematics and the
translation of the Bible into the languages of distinct communities may
point to varying kinds of knowledge. This is not merely a matter of the
well-known, technical difficulty of translating one term from the Bible
into the language of another culture and period.[38] Our considerations

---

34. E. R. Hardy, *Christian Egypt: Church and People* (Oxford: Oxford University
Press, 1952).

35. See Hans Freyer, *Theorie des objektiven Geistes* (Leipzig: Teubner, 1928).

36. Hardy, p. 163. See also W. H. C. Frend, "Nationalism as a Factor in Anti-
Chalcedonian Feeling in Egypt," in *Religion and National Identity*, ed. Stuart Mews (Oxford: Blackwell, 1982), p. 32.

37. Frend, *Donatist Church*, pp. 52, 57.

38. For example, certain Hebrew terms such as ṣedeq or rûaḥ have various meanings in the Hebrew Bible and are notoriously difficult to translate. The word ṣedeq can

thus far point to the underlying significance of that very difficulty. Is it the case that the difficulties arising from the translation of the universalistic doctrine of the church into various languages represent indirectly the confrontation between the universalistic, sacral pattern of the right order of life, namely, the Gospels, and the parochial, sacral pattern of the generation and protection of life, namely, the distinct cultural tradition of the primordial collectivity? This possibility appears likely if we keep in mind that since language is an expression of and a vehicle for the life of a distinct cultural community, then, as such, it would be a factor in the deflection of the attempt to organize that life along universalistic lines.

The indirect bearing of distinct cultural traditions on universalistic Christianity may, of course, be expressed in other ways. Why were two areas, Phrygia and Numidia, which were traditionally resistant to classical influence, territories of religious dissent, respectively, Montanism and Donatism? Were there protonational, anti-Roman sentiments at play in these instances? Returning to Egypt, one cannot help but notice that throughout the fifth and sixth centuries there was competition between Constantinople and Alexandria. Were there protonational, pro-Egyptian, anti-imperial sentiments at play in this competition? The imperial policy to enforce Chalcedonian orthodoxy on Egypt would have set such sentiments into motion. In any event, W. H. C. Frend struck the right note when he wrote that "it will be no longer adequate to label the African Donatists 'schismatics' and the Egyptian Monophysites 'heretics' without further ado. Conflicts over orthodoxy have rarely been simple conflicts over truth and error. Both now and then they have in part been the outcome of clashes of cultures, themselves represented by deep-rooted territorial . . . traditions."[39] One element underlying this territorial expression of the conflicts over universal orthodoxy appears to be that one locus of the sacred—the geographical, bounded dispersion of the primordial tie constitutive of a territory—reasserted and extracted its due from another locus of the sacred, the doctrinal universality of Christianity.

---

mean "right relations" either in terms of measures and weights or in terms of proper sacrifice. It can also mean, and is usually translated into English as, "righteousness" in the sense of an ethical attribute. The Hebrew *ṣédeq* is usually translated into Greek as *dikaios* and into Latin as *justus*. Just a glance at Deut 33:19 will suffice to indicate the difficulty of translating *ṣedeq* as *dikaios, justus*, or "righteousness." In Deut 33:19 of the Jerusalem Bible, *ṣedeq* is translated as "success." The word *rûaḥ* can mean "breath," "wind," or "spirit." It is usually translated into Greek as *pneuma* and into Latin as *spiritus*. Just a glance at 2 Sam 22:16 indicates that, at least in this instance, the Greek and Latin terms are not quite appropriate for *rûaḥ*.

39. W. H. C. Frend, *The Early Church* (Philadelphia: Fortress, 1982), p. 2.

V

The existence of what Frend called the "deep-rooted territorial traditions" is, especially in light of subsequent developments, the most salient primordial factor influencing early Christianity. There are, of course, other factors, for example, infant baptism (the incorporation of the infant into the ethically universal church on the compulsory basis of the primordial criterion of birth into a particular family). There is also another primordial factor, associated with territoriality, which is particularly significant for Christianity, given the religious prominence of Constantinople.

In the sixth and early seventh centuries, Constantinople was besieged by the Avars and the Persians. During the siege the Virgin Mary, Theotokos, "she who gave birth to God," emerged as the special protectress of Constantinople.[40] It was believed that she had fought alongside the defenders of the city in the battle before the very walls of her church at Blachernae.[41] As a consequence, the Virgin's hymn, the Akathistos, was adopted as the city's special hymn of thanksgiving to Theotokos, whom the inhabitants clearly envisaged as their own special mediator.[42]

> Unto you, O Theotokos, invincible champion,
> Your city, in Thanksgiving ascribes the victory for
>   the deliverance from sufferings.
> And having your might unassailable,
>   free me from all dangers, so that I may cry
>   unto you: "Hail! O bride unwedded. . . . [43]
>
> Hail! O defense against invisible foes.
> Hail! To you, who opened the gates of paradise . . .
> Hail! To you, through whom Hades was dispoiled.
> Hail! To you, through whom we are vested in glory.[44]

---

40. Averil Cameron, "The Theotokos in Sixth-Century Constantinople," *Journal of Theological Studies*, n.s., 29 (April 1978): 79–108; Vasiliki Limberis, *Divine Heiress: The Virgin Mary and the Creation of Christian Constantinople* (London: Routledge, 1994). For a defense of the Catholic belief in the cult of the Virgin Mary, see John Henry Newman, *Certain Difficulties Felt by Anglicans in Catholic Teaching* (1864; London: Longmans, Green, 1920), pp. 27–118, esp. pp. 68–76 on the intercessory power of Theotokos.

41. Cameron, p. 80.

42. Ibid.; see also N. Baynes, "The Supernatural Defenders of Constantinople," in *Byzantine Studies* (London: Athlone, 1955), pp. 248–60. For this translation of the Akathistos hymn, see Limberis, pp. 149–50.

43. From the early seventh-century prologue (Limberis, p. 149).

44. From verse 7 (ibid., p. 152).

Hail! O unshakable tower of the Church.
Hail! To you, through whom trophies of victory are assured.
Hail! To you, through whom enemies are vanquished.[45]

Of course, this paganization, if you will, of Mary, that she was now seen as the defender and champion of her city, Constantinople, was a consequence of a particular convergence of historical factors. Approximately two hundred years earlier, the sister of the emperor Theodosius II, Pulcheria, herself a virgin, established at Constantinople a festival celebrating virginity. Central to this festival was the worship of the Virgin Mary. Pulcheria was also responsible for having built the church dedicated to Theotokos, Blahernae, in which Mary's shroud was placed. Thus, while it appears that Pulcheria was a pious ascetic, there can be little doubt that Pulcheria intended a convergence of the veneration of the Virgin Mary as Theotokos and the virgin empress, Pulcheria.[46] Such a convergence was a corollary to the assertion of imperial authority into the affairs of the church, especially at the expense of the troublesome head of the Constantinople church, the anti-Marian and anti-Pulcheria Nestorius. In any event, by the seventh century, the Virgin Mary, Theotokos, had become for the Christians of Constantinople their wall of defense, their all-victorious general, their supernatural champion of earth, and their mediator in heaven.[47]

The belief that there exists a special relation between a locality and a deity is a feature of primordial religions. One is reminded of the preeminent armed goddess of the city of Athens, Pallas Athena.[48] It will be remembered that Athena, too, was a virgin.[49] As with Mary two hundred years later at Constantinople, Athena, according to Zosimus, was seen walking about the walls of Athens as she successfully defended her city against Alaric in 396 c.e.: "While Alaric with his entire force was approaching the city he spied Athena Promachos patrolling the wall just as she can be seen in statue form, armed and looking capable of withstanding the invaders. . . . Alaric could not bear the sight of her, but put a stop to any attempt against the city and offered terms of peace through heralds."[50] Is it possible that even as late as the sixth century the Athenian

---

45. From verse 23 (ibid., p. 158).
46. Ibid., pp. 47–61.
47. Baynes, p. 260.
48. See Walter Burkert, *Greek Religion* (1977; Cambridge, Mass.: Harvard University Press, 1985), p. 140.
49. Ibid., p. 143.
50. *Zosimus: Historia Nova*, trans. J. Buchanan and Harold Davis (San Antonio: Trinity University Press, 1967), p. 198.

tradition still exerted influence, transfigured, to be sure, on the Christians of Constantinople? Even if there was such an influence, we are still compelled to ask why the tradition was "reactivated," albeit indirectly. This paganization of Mary has often been described as a consequence of the merging of imperial cult with ecclesiastical worship.[51] The obvious location for such a convergence between political and religious authority would have been Constantinople, the seat of imperial power. Whatever merit there may be to such a description, we must press further in order to understand the significance of the cult of Theotokos.

One element of that significance is a spatial heterogeneity of the sacred: the area of Constantinople was different from other areas; it had a special relation to Mary and, hence, to the divine. This idosyncratic spatial relation to the divine also meant access to special powers at Constantinople, access that was made more possible because Mary's shroud was located there. This spatial heterogeneity of the sacred is characteristic of primordiality. However, in this case, it is not just the fact that Mary's Constantinople was believed to have had a bearing on the generation of the life of the city and its inhabitants that gives it its primordial character. In this case, the primordial locus of the sacred is constituted not only by beliefs about the generation of life but also by beliefs about the protection of that generation.

The cult of Theotokos in sixth- and seventh-century Constantinople is a categorical, primordial incursion into universal Christianity in the face of the realities of life, that is, war, and the necessity to protect the life of both the individual and the collectivity in the face of it. This is similar to the case of the Polish Mary, Black Madonna of Częstochowa, the miraculous savior and protectress of Poland. The cults of Theotokos in sixth- and seventh-century Constantinople and the Black Madonna of Częstochowa are expressions, in the context of universalistic Christianity, of the primordial deflection of the beliefs in the equality of all human beings, as the children of God, and the spatial uniformity of the goodness of the earth, as the creation of God. This deflection arises from the primordial imperative for the self-preservation of life, including the life of territorially distinct cultures.

The significance of the categorical, primordial incursion—the recognition of the categorical necessity to protect the life of the collectivity, patriotism—into the universalism of Christianity is minimized by relegating it

---

51. See, e.g., Sabina MacCormick, *Art and Ceremony in Late Antiquity* (Berkeley and Los Angeles: University of California Press, 1981); Kenneth Holum, *Theodosian Empresses* (Berkeley and Los Angeles: University of California Press, 1982); Limberis.

to a problem of church-state relations, although church-state conflict may be an expression of this significance. For example, the understandable opposition of early Christianity to beliefs in the apotheosis of man, that is, its opposition to the worship of the caesars, may be understood as the resolute protest of Christianity against the blending of religion and patriotism and, as such, an expression of the conflict between church and state.[52] As Harnack observed, "One of the cardinal aims and issues of the Christian religion was to draw a sharp line between the worship of God and the honor due to the state and its leaders."[53] But, if primordiality is a persistent orientation in human affairs, then the matter of its significance, and the significance of patriotism, surely must exist beyond the problem of church-state relations. Its persistent significance may be observed in the very continuation of the beliefs in the apotheosis of man in Christianity: by the third century, Christianity permitted the belief in the apotheosis of man, for example, in the worship of saints—and not only saints, but national saints. Certainly the cult of Theotokos is a variation of apotheosis. Other examples of Christian apotheosis as a vehicle of primordial attachment are so numerous that it will suffice to refer only to, in the East, Saint Sava of Serbian orthodoxy and, in the West, Saint Louis, the tutelary saint for the Capetians.[54] Even if these examples are less dramatic than the worship of Theotokos in Constantinople, they nevertheless represent the worship of (lesser) deities who are believed to be the champions and protectors of the life of particular people and their territory.

For the world religions of the axial age, the relation between these two evidently inexpungeable patterns of sacrality, the primordial and the universal, is filled with tension. Perhaps the belief in the apotheosis of the individual in Christianity is one way this tension was relaxed.

This is the significance of the belief in the apotheosis of the individual and its typical expression in Christianity, the recognition of national

---

52. On opposition to the worship of the caesars, see E. Bickerman, "Die Römische Kaiserapotheose," *Archiv für Religionswissenschaft* 27 (1929): 1-34; A. Momigliano, "How Roman Emperors Became Gods," in *On Pagans, Jews, and Christians* (Middletown, Conn.: Wesleyan University Press, 1987). On opposition to the blending of religion and patriotism, see Harnack, *Mission and Expansion* (n. 31 above), p. 295.

53. Harnack, *Mission and Expansion*, p. 295.

54. On Saint Sava, see Stella Alexander, *Church and State in Yugoslavia* (Cambridge: Cambridge University Press, 1979), pp. 3, 16. On Saint Louis, see Elizabeth M. Hallam, "Philip the Fair and the Cult of Saint Louis," in Mews, ed. (n. 36 above), p. 204; Joseph Strayer, "Philip the Fair," in *Medieval Statecraft and the Perspectives of History* (Princeton, N.J.: Princeton University Press, 1971), pp. 208-9. For a most interesting discussion of death masks and puppets, see the excursus to Bickerman, entitled "Zum Bestattungszeremoniell Beim Französischen Hofe," pp. 32-34.

saints: it is the homage paid by otherwise universalistic Christianity to
the sacrality of the primordial ties of territoriality and nationality; it is the
recognition by the representatives of a perceived right order of life—the
church—of the categorical necessity of the generation, transmission, and
protection of life itself. This is to say that one expression of the modus
vivendi established between universalistic Christianity and the primordial collectivity is the canonization of national saints. A classic example
of this phenomenon is the case of Saint Stanisław, the patron saint of Poland, whose dismembered body was miraculously reconstituted, just as a
divided Poland would one day be restored.

VI

As mentioned above, a characteristic of primordial religions is the special relation between a deity and a locality, a people, or both. The ethical
monotheism of the Israelite prophets shattered the certainty of that special relation by making it conditional on Israel's righteousness and its obedience to the law of God. Perhaps it would be more accurate to describe
this break as an ethically monotheistic monolatry, despite the conceptual
contradiction in such a description, for the Judaism of the Diaspora preserved the primordial beliefs in a land promised to a people chosen to
dwell in it.[55] However contradictory such a characterization of Judaism
might be, it is no more so than the recognition that the societies of the putatively universalistic Christian Occident are, in fact, monolatrous.

After the destruction of the second temple, there was no longer a Jewish state. Yet, there continued to exist a collective entity known as the
Jewish people. Gedaliah Alon referred to this entity as the *ethnos*, a so-
cially distinct group with certain rights to administer its own internal affairs.[56] I see no good reason not to consider the Jewish people of the first
and second centuries who dwelled in what they considered to be their
own land (Matt 10:5)—*'ereṣ yiśrā'ēl*—to be a nation. To be sure, the existence of a nation without its own state is an unstable predicament that the
Jews sought to resolve during the so-called Bar Kokhba war of 132 C.E.

---

55. This contradictory situation was caught well by Solomon Zeitlin, "Judaism as
a Religion," a book-length article that runs for a number of issues of the *Jewish Quarterly Review* (34 [1943/44]: 1–40, 207–41, 321–64; 35 [1944]: 85–116, 179–225,
303–49). See also Nicholas de Lange, *Judaism* (Oxford: Oxford University Press,
1986), pp. 4, 19–20.

56. Gedaliah Alon, *The Jews in Their Land in the Talmudic Age (70–640 C.E.)* (Cambridge, Mass.: Harvard University Press, 1989).

Why a nation is compelled to seek its own state is a complicated question requiring a careful and lengthy explanation. Here, a few of these complications will be suggested. Perhaps the primordial collectivity of the nation is compelled to create its own state in order to have the instruments of power to safeguard its existence. This is to recognize that a structure of kinship, the nation, is as such a structure of the generation and transmission of life (that is what a primordial collectivity is) that, seeking to preserve itself (as do all forms of life), requires the means—the state—to do so. If this is so, then when the nation seeks to be a national state, it is seeking no less than its self-completion. Perhaps there is more to this relation between nation and state. It is often observed in phenomenological analyses that consciousness must have an object. A theological expression of that observation is that spirit seeks material representation. A sociological expression of that observation is that the spirit of the nation seeks the state so that the nation, through its representatives, might act in the world.

It is sometimes argued that after the destruction of the second temple—indeed, it is sometimes argued even after the destruction of the first temple—Judaism emphasized its universalistic elements. There is truth in such an argument, as can be observed even from this brief quotation from Josephus's *Contra Apionem*: "There ought also to be one temple for one God. . . . This temple ought to be common to all men, because he is the common God of all men."[57] "It will be also worth our while to see what equity our legislator would have us exercise in our intercourse with aliens. . . . All those that have a mind to observe our laws should be allowed to do so [in] a true union which not only extends to our own nation, but to those that would live after the same manner with us."[58] Nonetheless, such an argument requires significant qualification.

Before the destruction of the temple in 70, the Jewish Christians—those who rejected the doctrines of Paul but still believed that Jesus was the Messiah—were considered to be part of the nation of all-Israel. The Jews called the Jewish Christians *Minim*, and the Christians called them Ebionites. But after the destruction of the temple, the sages declared them to be outside of all-Israel. Also excluded at that time were the *Netinim*, the descendants of foreign slaves.[59] Concomitant with the narrowing of the criteria for membership in all-Israel were laws restricting the transfer of

---

57. Josephus, *Contra Apionem*, in *The Works of Josephus*, trans. William Whiston (Peabody, Mass.: Hendrickson), 2.24.

58. Ibid., 2.29.

59. Alon, pp. 26–28.

property in the land of Israel. Certain *halakhot* of tannaitic origin forbade the sale or lease of land or houses in *ʾereṣ yiśrāʾēl* to non-Jews.[60] For example, the Mishnah states, "No one may sell to the heathen [non-Jews] anything which is attached to the soil, but after severing it from the soil the sale is allowed. . . . In the land of Israel no one may let houses to them nor (needless to say!) fields."[61] The underlying motivation for such prohibitions in the second century was to forestall the permanent settlement of foreigners in the land of Israel by preventing them from acquiring land.[62] Pisḳa 80 of the Sifre Deuteronomy makes clear this continuing primordial attachment to land: "It once happened that R. Judah ben Betherah, R. Mattiah ben Heresh, R. Hananiah ben Ahi, R. Joshua, and R. Jonathan were going abroad. When they reached Platana and remembered the Land of Israel, they raised their eyes (heavenward) and wept, rent their garments. . . . They said: '(The duty of) dwelling in the Land of Israel is equivalent to all the other commandments of the Torah put together.' . . . Thereupon they returned to the Land of Israel."[63] Evidently, during the first and second centuries, we find a reassertion of the primordial boundaries of all-Israel.

Ps 137:4–5 states, "How could we sing one of Yahweh's hymns in a pagan country? Jerusalem, if I forget you, may my right hand wither." Such recognitions of primordial attachment of a people to their own territory in the Hebrew Bible (see also, e.g., 1 Kgs 9:7–8) point to another problem in the consideration of primordiality. What are the constitutive elements of a people or a nation? Can, in fact, a people exist separately from actual possession of their land or, in the case of an ethnic group, without reference to the land of its ancestors? When a nation or an ethnic group ceases to exist as such, is it because the attachment, whether actual or ideal, to a particular territory has been dissolved? If this is the case, and if a nation does continue to exist—to be sure, precariously—separate from the (sovereignty over the) land, the image of which is a constitutive ele-

---

60. Ibid., p. 285.

61. *ʿAboda Zara*, ed. W. A. L. Elmslie (Cambridge: Cambridge University Press, 1911), p. 15.

62. Alon, p. 286. See also Herbert Danby, *The Mishnah* (London: Oxford University Press, 1933), p. 438, n. 4. One is reminded of similar restrictions on the sale and leasing of property in England, where, as late as 1870, no alien could hold real property or inherit land (see Sir Frederick Pollock and Frederick William Maitland, *The History of English Law before the Time of Edward I*, 2 vols. [London: Cambridge University Press, 1968]).

63. *Sifre: A Tannaitic Commentary on the Book of Deuteronomy*, trans. Reuven Hammer (New Haven, Conn.: Yale University Press, 1986), pp. 134–35.

ment of its existence as a nation, then is not such a nation incomplete? If there is merit to this train of thought, then there is likewise some merit to Max Weber's imprecise and often criticized characterization of that people, chosen to dwell in a land promised to them, of the Middle Ages as a "pariah people." This is also why W. D. Davies was correct when he observed that "Jewish sanctity is only fully possible in the land. . . . The exiled life is, therefore, an emaciated life, even though, through suffering, it atones."[64]

VII

In Romans, Paul champions the universality of the Gospel by contrasting a righteousness consisting in faith to submission to the Law. In so doing, Paul has not set Christianity against Judaism, for the Israelite prophets had also elevated righteousness, the circumcision of the heart, above mere obedience to the Law. Even the most superficial knowledge of, for example, Jeremiah and Micah makes this clear. The contrast between Christians, on the one hand, and Jewish Christians and Jews, on the other, is made when Paul asserts that it is faith alone that is necessary for salvation and, moreover, that it is a gift of an all-merciful God, equally attainable to all mankind. However, from the perspective of the significance of primordiality, perhaps there is a different judgment to be made on the relation between the Hebrew Bible and the New Testament. Such a reevaluation seems to be required given the territorial and national divisions in Christendom, divisions that represent a compromise between two loci of the sacred, one primordial and the other universal.

As was observed, Harnack drew attention to the incursion of the provincial spirit into the structure of Christianity that began in the second century. In *The History of Dogma*, Harnack repeatedly referred to this incursion on the "secularizing of Christian life and the Church." Whatever merit such a description may have regarding the organizational solidification of the church hierarchy, the division of that organizational structure into various territorial jurisdictions should not be understood as merely a process of secularization or routinization. Rather, that territorial division represented the accommodation of an otherworldly, universal sacrality to this-worldly, territorial structures and to the primordial sacrality that they bear. This provincial spirit was, in fact, the bearer of

---

64. W. D. Davies, *The Gospel and the Land* (Berkeley: University of California Press, 1974), p. 60. See also H. Parzen, "The Ruaḥ Haḳodesh in Rabbinical Literature," *Jewish Quarterly Review* 20 (1929): 51–75.

primordiality. It was the vehicle by which the primordial tie of territoriality, and all that implies, was carried into the church.

We may reformulate a theological consequence and complication, albeit unintended, arising from universal Christianity's accommodation to the evidently inexpungeable tie of primordiality. Recent papal pronouncements have affirmed the belief of the church that the covenant between God and the Jews remains intact. There are difficulties—difficulties that have dogged the church from early in its history, such as the Marcionites—for the church, arising from such an affirmation of primordial loci of sacrality, that is, beliefs in a chosen people and a promised land. The church has sought to minimize these difficulties, as it has from its very beginning, by incorporating the Hebrew Bible into its dogma by subordinating it to the New Testament. This incorporation and subordination of the Hebrew Bible to the New Testament has often been expressed theologically in earlier Christian scholarship by repeated attempts to discover the New Testament in the Old. An excellent example of such scholarship is Sigmund Mowinckel's *He That Cometh*.[65] However, if there is merit to Harnack's observation about the provincial spirit, and if we are correct to see greater significance in that spirit—that is, the primordial tie of territoriality as a locus of sacrality—is it possible that there is a dogmatic and historical irony at play here? Rather than observe the New Testament in the Old, Mowinckel not withstanding, is it the Old Testament, with its beliefs in a promised land and a chosen people, that haunts the New? The likelihood of such a possibility is a theological expression of the merit of the primordial as a category of historical analysis.

---

65. Sigmund Mowinckel, *He That Cometh* (1951; Oxford: Blackwell, 1956).

Chapter 8

Territoriality

I

In the so-called secular and individualistic twentieth century, millions and millions of human beings have given their lives for a land and a country which they believe to be their own. These and other events, especially recent ones in Eastern Europe, tragic though they are, vividly indicate that territorial integrity and territorial sovereignty remain extremely important in the organization of human society. Indications of this importance may be seen in the continuing emasculation of the Maastricht Treaty and the continuing attacks on the increasingly irrelevant European monetary system; or in the recent victory of the queen of Poland, the Virgin Mary, against her mortal enemy, Russia (Davies 1982: 401); or in events in the former Soviet Union or in what was once Yugoslavia; or in events in Sri Lanka, India, or Quebec; or in the establishment of the state of Israel; and in many, many other events—not to mention two world wars. Such events indicate that the significance which is attributed to territoriality remains a fundamental, constitutive element of modern society. As such, territoriality calls into question the widely held assumption of the complete secularization and individualism of our time as described, for example, by Constant (1988), Tönnies (1940), Simmel (1971; 1978), Troeltsch (1986; 1991), and Weber.[1]

Critics might object to my initial observations with the claim that these recent events to which I have referred are, in fact, "responses" to both the secularization and the utilitarian calculation required by the modern market. It is my belief that such an objection is little more than a sleight of hand; for what requires explanation is precisely the "unmodern" nature of these all too pervasive "responses." Even as responses,

Author's note: An earlier version of this article was presented to the Department of Geography, University of Wisconsin-Madison. I gratefully acknowledge the financial assistance of the John M. Olin Foundation in the preparation of this article.
    1. See, for example, Weber's (1946) use of the term "secularization," and, of course, his general treatment (1930) of the *Entzauberung* of the world.

191

these events have something to do with the fundamental order of society and the resistance of that order to the "twisting of the tails of the sacred cows of society."

One of these "sacred cows" is the primordial attachment to one's own country, one's own land, and one's own way of life. By the term primordial, I do not mean a racial or genetic predisposition; rather it refers to the significance of vitality which man attributes to and is constitutive of both nativity and structures of nativity, whether that structure be the relation of lineage, for example, the family, or the relation of area, for example, the locality in which one is born and in which one is sustained.[2] Man has recognized and continues to recognize these two relations or lines of descent as life-giving and life-determining structures of nativity; or as Saint Augustine acknowledged the phenomenon, those relations which bear "the miraculous power of the seed."[3]

The sociological, anthropological, and phenomenological puzzle of territoriality and its related phenomenon of nationality is that the attachments to the territory of the national state is to a structure considerably more extensive than that of a family or a locality. Nevertheless, the fact is that throughout history man has considered, albeit with variations, environments which are considerably more extensive than those of the family and the home to be his "own," hence, integral to his life. It is this historically persistent primordial pattern of attachment to relatively extensive environments, for example, to the territory of the national state, which is my concern here.

How is the continuing significance of territory as shown in recent events to be understood? The eminent geographer, Robert Sack (1980: 193; 1986) apparently thinks that "the attachment to nation-states in fact may be the clearest expression of mythical-magical consciousness (what Lévy-Bruhl [1985] called primitive mentality) of place in the twentieth century." However, if Sack is correct, and given the continuing significance of territoriality and nationality, what does his observation say about the nature of the territorially bounded societies of our time? This question poses a number of problems for us to consider. The particular problem I wish to consider is the nature of territory or, for lack of a better term, "territoriality."

---

2. My use of the term *primordial* follows the earlier and somewhat similar use of Edward Shils (1957) and Clifford Geertz (1963). See also Grosby (1994).

3. Saint Augustine, *De Civitate Dei* (1955), Book 22, chapter 24, lines 7–8, "*vim mirabilem seminum.*"

II

One constitutive prerequisite for the existence of a territory is the existence of boundaries. These boundaries are not always precise and they do not always remain stable. How "stable" a boundary is and the reasons for its stability are important problems. Indeed, stability is a most important and most difficult historical, political, and sociological phenomenon to understand.

The existence of boundaries and the area, the territory, within those boundaries imply that this area is conceived as being relatively homogeneous in some way. This relative, internal homogeneity is an essential element of territoriality. By virtue of being designated as an area which exists within boundaries, the entire designated land is considered in certain respects to be relatively homogeneous or uniform—not, of course, topographically homogeneous, but sociologically homogeneous. Each and every particular, smaller area of ground within the boundaries is only a part of the more extensive territory; as such, these different areas within the boundaries are in certain respects relatively similar to each other in contrast to those areas which are outside the boundaries.

Often it has been argued that an area of land is a single, homogeneous area by virtue of the propinquity of its parts within natural topographical boundaries like seas, oceans, and mountains. That is, that different areas of land should be considered uniform, one and the same, by virtue of their being contiguous with one another. This was certainly one argument for the territorial expansion of the United States from the Atlantic to the Pacific under the banner of "manifest destiny."[4]

One problem with this argument is that we must account for the apparent deviations from the recognition of territoriality as a consequence of bounded propinquity. A striking exception was the Ottoman empire. Rather than the area of land within the Ottoman empire being considered uniform or homogeneous, it was in fact quite heterogeneous and was accepted as such. It was divided up into different communities, usually religious—the *millet* system—each with its own laws. As a matter of fact, it is precisely this heterogeneity which is implied by our very use of the term "empire." This heterogeneity is one of the essential characteristics which distinguish an empire from a national state.

---

4. Note Albert K. Weinberg's (1935: 43-71) suggestive phrase, "geographical Predestination." Note also the emphasis on territorial contiguity in Carl Schurz (1893), and the reference to territorial "propinquity" in "Progress in America," *The United States and Democratic Review*, February 1846.

Furthermore, we need only think of the recent examples of Lebanon, Sri Lanka, Cyprus, and now the Balkans where propinquity evidently has been less salient as a constitutive element of territoriality—or, as the case may be, a more circumscribed propinquity has been a factor in the attempt to constitute a new territory. Clearly, these examples force us to reconsider the constitutive elements of boundaries and in what way these elements influence the nature of the relative homogeneity, or lack thereof, of the area, the "territory," within those boundaries.

One of the things at stake here is the nature of and apparent limits to the expansion of familiarity—that is, the nature of and limits to what we consider to be our own; our own land and our own people. While it is clear that the scope of "interaction," influenced by modern means of communication and transportation, and the existence of extensive markets for agricultural and industrial goods are factors which affect the range and intensity of familiarity, they are most certainly not decisive.

The examples of the Ottoman empire, Cyprus, Sri Lanka, and the Balkans indicate that historical, sociological, anthropological—choose whatever term you wish, we can avoid this minor terminological difficulty by using the German *geistige*—factors have also influenced the distinctive features of the boundaries of a territory, hence, the distinctive features of any particular territory. Thus, territorial boundaries may also correspond to linguistic boundaries; or territorial boundaries may correspond to the boundaries of a religious collectivity; or territorial boundaries may indicate demographic cleavages (Watkins 1991: 112, 138); or, most importantly, territorial boundaries may indicate the extent of the jurisdiction of the *lex terrae*, the codified and promulgated law of the land.

Indeed, the law of the land, which implies recognition of a bounded uniformity in subjection to the law—that is, what has sometimes been referred to as the formal rationalization of the law (Weber 1954)—is a very important element in the establishment and, above all, the stability of the territorial boundaries of a society. This is the case because one element of the stability of a society is its consciousness of itself, that is, its self-image which guides its continual self-regulation and self-renewal. When a society is conscious of itself, the existence of that society is an object of the imagination and reflection of its individual members often through contemplation of the events of its territorially bounded history, but also especially through the recognition of the legitimacy of the territorially bounded law of the society.

It is precisely this formal rationalization of the law which historically has been an essential factor in the formation of a "people" with "their" territory. Because the *millet* system of the Ottoman empire recognized rather than undermined distinct legal communities, it was a retarding influence on the emergence of stable "peoples" with their own territories. That is, the *millet* system retarded rather than contributed to the existence of that relative homogeneity required for the existence of a territory, above all, a national territory. We are witnessing today in the Balkans the legacy of this legal heterogeneity of the Ottoman empire. In this sense, the *millet* system was relatively irrational, in contrast to the more rational territorial legal codes which emerged in and contributed—to be sure, often violently—to the formation of the various societies of Western Europe. The connection between the rationalization of the law and the consolidation of the relatively extensive primordial structures of a "people" and a territory is just one of the many paradoxes of territoriality and its related phenomenon of the national state. This connection may be observed in such historically diverse circumstances as the probable constitution of the putative lineage of Abraham, Isaac, and Jacob through adoption of the ancient Israelite covenant, or the continuing territorialization of the law during the Middle Ages in Europe. That such a connection exists between formal rationality (of the law) and primordiality is a cautionary reminder that human activity at any particular time cannot with any explanatory accuracy be subsumed under only one descriptive category of behavior. Perhaps this paradox has become sharpest in several democratic societies as they are constituted by both a recognition of the universal rights of man and a territorially delimited exercise of those rights.

The image of territorial boundaries also contains connections with the relations of center and periphery (Shils 1975); certainly stable territorial boundaries do, for such a stability indicates an achieved determination of what is appropriately the periphery. Here, I indicate only a few of the many possible *geistige*, or transcendental, factors which have influenced the nature of the boundaries of any particular territory and, thus, the distinctive features of that territory.

III

This brief digression into the different, possible constitutive elements of territorial boundaries, which in turn indicate the distinctive features of the society within those boundaries, means that these territorial boundaries do not merely imply territorial jurisdiction. They also imply the jurisdiction of distinctive patterns of human conduct. Now, the idiom commonly employed within the social sciences is that within territorial boundaries different individuals "interact." But is this so?

The term "interact" has overly behavioristic, atomistic connotations. It also suggests temporal simultaneity. That is, the use of the term implies a relation where there is nothing outside the two interactors which has any bearing on the interaction; it is as if each actor is entirely self-contained; it is as if each calculating actor only takes into account his or her own maximization of pleasure. Such an implication greatly misrepresents both the nature of human action and the mind of the individual. A great deal of human activity is rarely—almost never—a phenomenon of simply or primarily two or more persons "interacting." Individuals orient their actions in ways that are meaningful to one another; their actions are guided by the norms engendered by the shared benefits constitutive of the territorially bounded society. Territorial boundaries imply the existence and usually indicate the jurisdiction of such substantive orientations.

We do not interact, but we *participate* in patterns of activity which are valid within certain territorial boundaries. Thus, territory is not primarily the spatial location of interaction; rather, it is *in* the image of the territory, that is, in the substantive patterns constitutive of a territory, that the individual members of the collectivity participate. It is the distinctive features of this participation in this image of the territorially bounded community which indicates in what way the designated area within the boundaries is sociologically relatively uniform. It is a participation (to be sure with varying degrees of saliency across different strata of society at any particular time) in the territorially bounded customs, traditions, laws, historical knowledge and often even the language—what Durkheim referred to as the collective consciousness—of a society. It is precisely this phenomenon of participation in a realm of these symbolic objectivations which raises questions about the validity of the allegations about the pervasive "tremendous individualism" of modern society.

Rarely are these bounded patterns "negotiated," although often specific actions within these patterns are. These bounded patterns are given, rather than negotiated; they are there; they have a relatively independent, *a priori* existence. The force of life exists not only within the individual; there are relatively independent, stabilized expressions of life around the individual as well. That is precisely what these substantive orientations, these bounded patterns of action and beliefs, which are constitutive of a territory, are: language, custom, and law. They are all stabilized, objectified expressions of life in which the individual participates. As such, these beliefs and the patterns of human conduct which they imply are life-ordering and life-sustaining. By no means is this merely a recognition that these stabilized, objective patterns in which the individual participates function as ordering and sustaining channels of human activity. The very fact that these substantive orientations are life-ordering and life-sustaining means that they are likely to be recognized as containing charismatic properties. That is why most human beings revere their own language, customs, laws, and traditions in general. Because these life-ordering and life-sustaining stabilized patterns have charismatic attributes, they may be viewed as being somewhat similar to the powerful, life-determining "mana" of the primitive mentality, as described by Lévy-Bruhl, in which the individual participates.

I believe that Karl Popper (1972: 106-90; 1977) and Edward Shils (1981) were correct to characterize these bounded patterns in which we participate as having an "objective" existence. In addition to the recognition of their objectivity, these bounded patterns, once again, have charismatic attributes: they order and sustain life. Therein lies the key to our understanding the phenomenon of patriotism. Therein lies the key to our understanding the problem of why, during the twentieth century, millions of human beings have been willing to risk their own lives to defend their own countries, their own pattern of life. Thus, there would appear to be a suggestive parallel between Lévy-Bruhl's "law of participation" and Popper's and Shils' understanding of the participation of the individual psyche, constitutive of what Popper called "World Two," in the symbolic configurations and bounded patterns, constitutive of what Popper called "World Three." Of course, not all the symbolic configurations within World Three have charismatic properties, for example, a mathematical proposition does not; but many of those configurations constitutive of territoriality and nationality do. These all too brief remarks lead us to conclude that much of our use of the word "territory" refers not merely to a geometrically delineated space; it rather refers to the transcendental significance of that space; it refers to the life-ordering and life-sustaining significance of a space which makes that space into a meaningful structure.[5]

---

5. To be sure, territoriality does not imply, to employ Max Weber's categories, an "other-worldly" transcendence, but rather a "this-worldly" transcendence. The phrase "this-worldly transcendence" refers to the primordial objects of the shared beliefs, the collective self-consciousness, constitutive of a territory, namely the objects of a trans-local territory and a "related" people. There are numerous implications of paramount importance of the "this-worldly" transcendental character of territoriality which we must resist delving into here, for example, how the transcendental, primordial element of territoriality is influenced by especially an "other-worldly," universal transcendence, for example Christianity and vice versa, or why Protestant countries are more

IV

It will be helpful if we proceed by making a distinction between two general categories of factors constitutive of territoriality. On the one hand, the existence of a territory implies an area of the earth's surface, the physical characteristics of the land, etc. Moreover, it also implies, as we have observed, a bounded, intricate patchwork of patterns of relationships in which life is carried on. These two factors are both objective and may be studied with the appropriate scientific procedures; the former using many of the techniques employed in, for example, cartography and topography, the latter using techniques employed in demography and social surveys.

However, to turn to the second category of factors, territoriality also implies: (a) how the land is conceived by those who live within the territory, and (b) the consciousness of—or we may say the shared significance attributed to—these bounded patterns of relationships. This second aspect of territoriality is also objective, albeit its nature is more difficult to study. As this consciousness is a consequence of a complicated historical development, we may say that it is a product of the human imagination, but it is not imaginary. It has acquired reality. The recognition of this complicated historical development of this collective consciousness makes explicit what was implicit in our use of the term "participation"; namely, that territoriality is a phenomenon of bounded temporal depth—what Dilthey (1989) referred to as a structure of "duration." This is by no means merely to say that the collective self-consciousness constitutive of territoriality is an historical structure. It does mean that current elements of the structure of a territory are references to past events which provide

---

territorially homogeneous than Catholic, Hindu, and even, surprisingly, Buddhist countries. As to the territorial heterogeneity of Buddhist societies, see R. Gombrich and G. Obeyesekere (1988), specifically the discussion of the so-called spirit religion.

Such considerations eventually would lead us to contemplate the possible proclivities of the human mind, for example, man's ability to disengage himself from the immediate surroundings of the natural environment, that is, the environment he can see or touch, and the various directions that disengagement from these particular, immediate "interests" subsequently takes (Scheler 1928; Gehlen 1988). All that I am attempting to indicate here is that the pheomenon of territoriality is not a plain empirical fact; it has an "objective," transcendental character; and, further, there is a charismatic, primordial element to that character. This does not mean that territoriality or, for that matter, nationality is "imaginary" as Benedict Anderson (1983) incorrectly argues, but that it is, in part, a very real, objectively concrete consequence of an act of the imagination.

meaning to and, hence, order our activities in the present.[6] A territory is a temporally deep structure.

If we agree that these are both aspects of territoriality, then a number of further problems arise, in particular involving the relation between this bounded shared attribution, this collective consciousness, and the corresponding area of the earth's surface. If territoriality does imply the existence of collective self-consciousness (in fact, several collective self-consciousnesses, for those within the territory are recognized as such by those outside the territory and vice versa), then what is the nature of those attachments formed by the collectivity of human beings not only among themselves, such that they are a collectivity, but also to the inanimate space, such that the latter becomes a territory?

How does the animate—human beings and the connections between them, both cognitive beliefs and affectual feelings—"penetrate," as it were, the inanimate, the soil? That this, in fact, occurs seems clear from the phenomenon of "familiarization": in our common vernacular we rarely speak of a territory; rather, we often speak of "home," "homeland," even "fatherland."[7] Nor are these accidental or historically vestigial expressions; for one needs only to consider for a moment one's own continual use of the terms "house" and "home" and what makes a house into a home. Is it that when something is enveloped by the mind of man, when it has become "familiar" to us, we have turned our attention to the thing, made it some way our own, possess it; and by so doing "animate" the thing, "familiarize" it? Is the act of possession, both by the individual and the collectivity, of the inanimate an expression of the realization of the will to live (Van der Leeuw 1963)? If it is, then it is perhaps more understandable why we not only tend to "animate" the inanimate, but also tend to describe those inanimate things which we possess, with which we are familiar, and which have an explicit bearing on the ordering and sustaining of life in terms of familial relations—the latter being the most immediate, most familiar and obvious vehicle of life.

A territory is not simply an area within which certain physical actions are performed; rather, it refers to a structural, symbolic condition which

---

6. Numerous examples, varying in salience, of the temporal depth constitutive of territoriality may be adduced. For example, consider the Battle of Kosovo which remains significant for Serbs today, or Czeçstochowa for the Poles. That memories of such events and locations have been sustained through historiography is obvious enough. The more important problem remains as to the nature of the significance of these particular locations and the past events which are associated with them.

7. Jean Gottman (1973) referred to territoriality as a "psychosomatic phenomenon of the community." See also Tuan (1974).

has significance for those who act within it and towards it. Thus, the phenomenon of territoriality is not to be considered primarily within the context of such behavioristic categories as the "range" or the "habitat." In this regard, Hans Gadamer (1988: 402) was entirely correct when he observed that to have a "world," in this case, a territory, is to have an attitude towards it. However, as has already been suggested, one cannot be content merely to insist that what is significant to the individual and to the collectivity necessarily implies the existence of an attitude which shares in the meaning of the particular structure. What is the nature of the "attitude" involved in territoriality such that millions of human beings in the twentieth century have sacrificed and are willing to sacrifice their lives for their "own" land, their territory? It appears that in historically diverse situations, man has believed that his own life is dependent upon the continued existence of the territorial sovereignty of "his" country. Once again, the puzzle of territoriality is the attribution of this primordial, life-giving, and life-sustaining significance to an environment which is considerably more extensive than that recognized by the relatively more immediate actions of the family.

As a consequence of the various, historically conditioned, objective achievements of the mind which are constitutive of a territory and its boundaries, it has been noted that territoriality is a spatial structure of temporal depth. It has also been noted that the individual participates in the image of this temporally deep, that is historically produced and tradition-bearing structure.

There is a phenomenological vagueness to this use of the term "participation." The spatial structure of a territory and the objective image of that structure must not be viewed as being exclusively external to the individual who participates in that structure. To view participation in this manner is to adopt a misleading dichotomy which will never be able to help us understand why many different individuals believe a territory to be their own, and why, further, they are willing to sacrifice their lives for their territory and their country. In contrast, it must be emphasized that the image of the territory is also an object of the consciousness of the individual about the individual. The individual, too, has temporal depth—both physically, that is, developmentally—but also, and more relevant here, is the very constitution of his own image of himself, in the very constitution of his own "mental environment." There is an "intermingling" here between the objective image of the territory in which the individual participates, and the image which the individual has of himself. This "intermingling" may be observed in the fact that from the moment of birth the individual is never merely a member of the family into which he or she is born; the individual is also a member of the larger collectivity into which he or she is born.

Whatever phenomenologically takes place in this relation between the self-consciousness of the individual and the territorially bounded collective self-consciousness of the society, there appears to be an historically persistent, albeit with variations, tendency to describe different associations and relations even to inanimate objects in terms of biological connectedness—for example, through the use of certain adjectives like "home" and "father" in respectively "homeland" and "fatherland" or simply through the use of possessive pronouns and adjectives, male and female. This tendency to conflate the animate with the inanimate has often been described as an expression of "primitive mentality." The facts of the twentieth century demand that we conclude that an important part—I do not say all, but an important part—of the modern *Weltanschauung* is this so-called primitive mentality.

There is a wide variability in patterns of action; obviously not all activities are about the generation and sustenance of life, nor do they all include the phenomena of "animation" or "familiarization." Nevertheless, I doubt that any territory can exist that is not to one degree or another "animated." Employing the phrase of the geographers John Kirkland Wright (1966: 250-85) and Yi-Fu Tuan (1976), "geopiety" is an historically pervasive phenomenon. Now the specific task for historical and sociological research is to determine which factors facilitate a "familiarity" with an area of land such that it becomes a territory. How does the image of an extent of land become a constitutive part of what Max Scheler suggestively called the "mental environment" both of the individual and of the collectivity which the individually "falls in with" (Scheler 1954); or, as I, in an allusion to Lévy-Bruhl's "law of participation," have formulated the phenomenon, in which the individual "participates"? These are the extraordinarily difficult and perhaps overly ambitious questions before us. Here, I will limit myself to a few observations, primarily of a negative or cautionary nature.

V

Clearly there is much merit to Henry Sumner Maine's (1970: 165) conclusion that "the movement of the progressive societies has hitherto been a movement from status to contract," or in the terminology of

Talcott Parsons and Edward Shils (1951), a movement exhibiting an in-creasing emphasis on individual achievement at the expense of ascrip-tion with qualities derived from membership in primordial collectivities. I will even risk the hoary accusation of "evolutionism" by stating that the history of the Occident exhibits a development of the recognition of the distinction of the individual with rights and duties specific to himself. However, we must object to Maine's insistence that the first and sole pos-sible criterion for membership in the status-dominated collectivity was the attribution of kinship of blood and that only later when the status-bound society was a thing of the past did there arise a recognition of common locality—territoriality—as a basis for membership in society. Maine refused to acknowledge any territorial component in the constitu-tion of the collective self-consciousness of the historically earlier, status-dominated societies.[8] Apparently, it did not occur to Maine that the fic-tion of common ancestry, of an original brotherhood, could be attributed by the members of the status-dominated, primordial collectivity to those with whom they shared residence in a territory. In this regard, Robert Lowie's (1927: 51–73) criticism of Maine was definitive. The well-known existence of deities of locality and the "god of the land" of these relatively small societies, and their common worship indicate the existence of what Lowie called the "territorial tie."

Although Maine was correct about territoriality in modern contract-bound societies, that is to say, the recognition of membership based on co-residence, he did not see that territoriality is a limitation on the con-tractualism of modern society. I shall return to this point in a moment. Here, let us merely note the fact that there is a fiction of kinship implied in our use of the term "people."

The point I wish to emphasize here is that we cannot successfully seg-regate the phenomenon of territoriality historically, that is, under the rubric of a distinction between antiquity and "modernity." A more differentiated attempt than that of Maine to depict a historical cleavage and development of territoriality was presented a number of years ago by Marshall Sahlins (1968: 6). He argued that while territories clearly ex-isted in ancient and tribal societies, it was only in the modern era of the state where society was established as a territory. I believe this argument to be historically misleading.[9] For example, obviously territoriality was

8. As is well known, a conception of a congruence of territory, language, and people can be found in Genesis 10:5; 10:19–20; 10:30–31.

9. A careful reading of Sahlins' *Tribesmen* reveals a number of ambiguous formula-tions which, in turn, raise questions about his apparent historical or developmental

an essential, explicit component in the constitution of the society of ancient Israel (Grosby 1993 [[in this volume, pp. 52-68]]). This is especially
so if the system of the twelve tribes corresponds to and is a consequence
of the administrative, territorial division of ancient Israel under Solomon
(Lemche 1985: 285-88). In any event, the tribal names Judah, Ephraim,
Benjamin, and Naphtali clearly indicate that they refer to territorial location (Noth 1960: 56-67). Furthermore, the land of ancient Israel is described in Numbers 34 as having rather remarkably precise, designated
boundaries. We also find throughout the long history of ancient Egypt a
persistent conception of territorial boundaries—boundaries which were
understood to separate the Egyptians from the "Asiatics," "Sand-dwellers"
and "Nubians."[10] I note in passing that there are distinctive terms in hi-
eroglyphics for "the land of Egypt" and "the people of Egypt" (Morenz
1973; Gardiner 1916; Bullock 1978).[11] Many other examples could be
adduced.[12] In these examples from antiquity, we are justified in recognizing the existence and importance of territorial boundaries and not
merely frontiers.

We must reject any argument that insists that territoriality is a product
of post-Cartesian "modernity." However, modern means of communication and transportation, and markets for agricultural and industrial
goods have been factors which have facilitated the emergence and stability of territories larger than what typically existed in antiquity.

Regarding territoriality and the related phenomenon of nationality in
the Middle Ages, it is already a number of years since Ernst Kantorowicz
(1957: 232-72), Gaines Post (1953), and Joseph Strayer (1971: 312-13)
showed that by the early fourteenth century (1) custom, law, and descent
were assumed to go together; (2) that law had become territorialized; and
(3) "peoples" came to be perceived in territorial terms.[13] That is, medieval
ideas about kingdoms and peoples were very like modern ideas about nations (Reynolds 1984: 9, 262). This is abundantly clear from the four-

---

dichotomy. For example, formulations like: "so empowered in the district, *which is its
main focus*, the conical clan presents itself simultaneously as a descent group and a
unit of political order" (p. 50); "involved in this way as the *basis of territorial grouping*"
(p. 54); "membership is decided by a *combination of residence and descent*" (p. 54); "'descent' in major *residential* groups" (p. 55) (my emphases)—these formulations indicate
that even certain tribes were constituted as territorial societies.

10. Note that the territorial possessions of ancient Egypt outside these borders,
e.g. *Retenu* (Canaan), were considered by the Egyptians not to be a part of Egypt.

11. See also A. Erman and H. Grapow (1921) for "Egypt."

12. For example, see the description of the boundaries of Upper and Lower Aram
in the Sefire Stele, J. A. Fitzmyer (1967).

13. More recently, see Anthony D. Smith (1994).

teenth century English law definition of "alien" as someone not born in
the territory of England (Pollock and Maitland 1968). Moreover, recent research has indicated that the term *patria* was used as early as A.D. 700 as
a political term designating (1) a *regnum*, (2) the geographical area of the
regnum, and (3) even the name of the people of that area (Eichenberger
1991). Furthermore, it is surely significant that the images of the promised land and the chosen people of the Old Testament clearly and
repeatedly reappear in fourteenth-century France (Strayer 1971; Schneidmüller 1987) and, of course, seventeenth-century England.[14] The relevance of these latter observations is not merely that extended territoriality
is a phenomenon of the Middle Ages in Europe, but also that it has not
been undermined by universalistic Christianity. That the two coexist, ex-
erting influence on one another, is surely paradoxical; but it has been historically shown not to be a contradiction. That this is so is abundantly
clear from the existence of "national" Christian churches: the Gallican,
Anglican, and the entire history of Eastern Christianity.

For too long now much of the historical and sociological research on
territoriality and nationality has been marred by the adoption of obfuscatory and simplistic dichotomies. Typical of such an adoption are such
groundless assertions as that there was no conception of bounded territory in antiquity (Giddens 1985: 50-51), or that extended territoriality
or nationality are exclusively modern phenomena. In contrast to these
kinds of assertions found, for example, in the many works of Hans Kohn,
or in Ernest Gellner's *Nations and Nationalism*, or in Benedict Anderson's
Imagined Communities, or in E. J. Hobsbawm's *Nations and Nationalism
Since 1780*, stands the refreshing observation of the medievalist Susan
Reynolds (1984: 255-56).

> There is no foundation at all for the belief, common among students of
> modern nationalism that the word *natio* was seldom used in the middle
> ages except to describe the *nationes* in which university students were di-
> vided. It was used much more widely than that, and often as a synonym for
> *gens*. . . . There is no reason to believe that words of this kind [for example,
> *populus, natio, gens*] were used more precisely and consistently through the
> centuries than they are today . . . like a *gens* or a *natio*, a *populus* [a people or
> a country or a nation] was thought of as a community of custom, descent
> and government.

Her observations and the evidence which supports them (Eichenberger
1991; Schneidmüller 1987) have been ignored often as a consequence of
the adoption of a rigid distinction between antiquity and "modernity" or

---

14. See Cromwell's speeches of 4 July 1653 to the Nominated Parliament (the
Barebones Parliament) and of 4 September 1654 (Abbot 1945).

a variant of that distinction, between *Gemeinschaft* and *Gesellschaft*. One consequence of such an ill-founded approach is to assume that a territory of a nation exists only when there is some kind of "homogenized *Gesellschaft*."[15] If that homogeneity does not exist, so the argument goes, then a territory (or a nation) is said not to exist. Such a procedure is to erect a straw man only to knock it down.

Earlier, I argued that the existence of a territory assumed a *relative* homogeneity or uniformity. No territory can be sociologically completely homogeneous. For example, the relation between the center and the periphery, a necessary constitutive factor of extended territoriality, is a paradoxical relation of relative homogeneity. Often the periphery is resentful of the center; in any event, the periphery is different from the center. Yet while it is different, the periphery is nonetheless tied to the center in various ways which an area outside the boundaries of that territory is not. It was also observed earlier that individuals exhibit a primordial attachment to their family and to the locality in which they are born and in which they live. Yet, these attachments somewhat paradoxically and sometimes uneasily coexist with attachments to the larger, life-sustaining territory of the society in which those individuals also live. In this sense, many smaller "territories" may and usually do exist within a necessarily only relatively homogeneous, larger territory.

The relation between these smaller "territories" within a lager territory may be stable or unstable depending upon innumerable factors. The existence of the former does not deny the existence of the latter or vice versa. Sometimes the attachments to local areas may be and often are considerably more salient and intense than those to the larger area of that territory which encompasses the smaller areas. For example, the allegiances to locality in seventeenth- and eighteenth-century France were certainly powerful. Yet such allegiances coexisted with an awareness, sometimes very vague indeed, that there was a center, i.e., the king or Paris, and that the king merited one's deference. On the other hand, it may be only during a war that the patriotic attachment to the larger area of the territory clearly takes precedence over the attachment to the locality within that territory.

Of course, the ability to be aware of a center of a territorially extensive society has been heightened by education and by modern means of communication and transportation. However, in the absence of such technological developments, there still exists the possibility of allegiance to a geographically distant center. To take two, rather graphic examples: the

---

15. This is the essence of, for example, Gellner's argument in *Nations and Nationalism*.

Jews of the Diaspora of antiquity annually sent a half-shekel to Jerusalem; and for almost two millennia now, Catholics have looked toward
Rome. Moreover, Catholics have often done so while also, paradoxically,
worshiping local saints at local sacred sites.

Sometimes it is argued that the expression of territoriality differs dramatically depending upon the particular civilization. Although there appears to be some variability, for example, the relative lack of significance
of nationality in Islamic civilization (Lewis 1991), this argument must be
pursued with caution or risk being too facile. For example, we may certainly speak of an Egyptian nation; and the Palestinians have demanded
a land of their own so that they can live as a nation. Furthermore, one
may also observe territoriality in civilizations which have developed under the influence of one of the more "other-worldly" of all religions,
namely, Buddhism. This may be observed even very early in the history
of Buddhist civilization, for example, in the account of Duṭṭhagāmaṇī
(approximately 100 B.C.) in the Mahāvaṃsa (Geiger 1986). (The question of the historical reliability of the Mahāvaṃsa does not in any way invalidate this point.) In chapter 25 of the Mahāvaṃsa, the warrior-king
Duṭṭhagāmaṇī is described as having unified the land of Laṅkā, putatively in the service of spreading the doctrine of Saṃbuddha. In this account, we observe an image of Sri Lanka as a territory unified through
the adoption of the Buddhist religion. It is difficult to imagine the current
Sinhalese nationalist perspective in the absence of this 2,000-year-old
tradition. I note in passing that the Mahāvaṃsa (1.20) also states that in
order for Laṅkā to become a territory proper for Buddhism, the "Canaanites" of Laṅkā, the Yakkahs, had to be first put under the *herem*, the ban.
Were the mythological Yakkahs an allusion to the Tamils?

Territoriality is not by any means distinctive of modern times, or of advanced modern states. It is a fundamental feature of all human societies.
We may even observe rather stable territorial attachments in the phenomenon of nomadism. In a series of extraordinarily interesting articles, M. B.
Rowton examined the nomadism of Western Asia and particularly of the
ancient Near East. Drawing upon Lattimore's *Studies in Frontier History*
and Johnson's *The Nature of Nomadism* and the work of Fredrik Barth
(1961; 1981), Rowton (1974) concluded that what actually takes place in
this area is not nomadism, but "enclosed nomadism." The latter is characteristic of pastoralists who are a part of a tribe which includes a sedentary element, and who also seasonally migrate within sedentary regions.
Moreover, there is a link formed between nomad and sedent, between
tribe and town such that it was not uncommon in, for example, the an-

cient Near East for town and tribe to share the same name.[16] In these instances, while there may not be stable territorial boundaries, there is a clear, persistent attachment, probably constitutive of the collectivity, to locality. Territorial attachments may even be observed among the camel nomads of the Arabian Peninsula of the twentieth century. The nomadic Al Murrah, who sometimes travel 1,000 km looking for desirable water pasturage, have a tribal territory, *dirrat al murrah*. The Al Murrah even claim to have a home town, Najran in southwestern Saudi Arabia (Cole 1973).

VI

It is sometimes conceded that while there may have been expressions of extended territoriality in antiquity and in the Middle Ages, territoriality today is of a radically different nature.[17] Such an argument stresses the transformative significance of democratic citizenship on the emergence of a relatively more uniform territory. There can be no doubt that in this case, an even further development of the formal rationalization of the law has contributed mightily to the existence of a sociologically more homogeneous territory. Nevertheless, such an argument minimizes the past and continuing significance of "representation" as an essential factor contributing to the cohesion of a territorially extensive society—where an individual represents the collectivity and whose actions are attributed to the members of the collectivity. Of course, historically the king is the classic example of such representation—a king who is also subject to the law (Kern 1939).[18] In any event, to understand territoriality today as primarily a democratically acceptable, modern mechanism or "strategy" for the attribution of citizenship is to overlook its more profound and ethically often very troublesome aspects.

---

16. There is even some indication that the Assyrian scribes may have thought that most tribal names were town names (Rowton 1973a; 1973b).

17. Perhaps the most thoughtful argument along these lines is that of S. N. Eisenstadt (1973; 1987: 1-11). Briefly, Eisenstadt argues that what characterizes the uniqueness of modernity is, in part: (a) the secularization of the center and (b) a revolutionary shift in the relation between center and periphery, an expression of which is citizenship, which, in turn, indicates a congruence between cultural and political identities of territorial population.

18. An aspect of the significance of representation for the existence of a nation may be observed in the continuing fascination of the English people with the activities of the politically powerless royal family. For an analysis of the significance of the monarchy for the England of today, see Shils and Young (1956). It should also be noted

The question remains as to why human beings attribute significance to what outwardly seems like merely a physical fact. Even in societies of democratic citizenship, there is an important primordial element constitutive of these societies. For example, while it is of course obvious that economic considerations have been a factor in the recent French, German, and American[19] restrictions on immigration, there is still more to these restrictions than merely such considerations. Moreover, an attempt to account for these restrictions on immigration among Western, democratic countries as consequences of recent shifts in the political landscape of these countries is certainly much too facile. One ought to remember that the United States has had numerous restrictions on immigration for the past hundred years. On the contrary, the territories of these societies have never been nor are they now merely locations of residence. For better or for worse, these territories are "homes" for those who are born and dwell within them. The entire territory of the national state is recognized in some way to be your "own"; it is where you were born; it is the jurisdiction of that with which you are familiar: your customs and language—your way of life.[20] One saw an expression of this recognition when in 1989-90 thousands of Germans took to the streets demanding *Einheit*: one people, one land. Moreover, it must not be forgotten that membership in the territorially circumscribed society of the United States, which has assimilated so many immigrants, is, for the most part, determined by birth in the territory. The *ascriptive* criterion of birth, even if it is no more than birth in the territory, is a primordial criterion for the determination of membership in a collectivity.

I have raised objections to the widely accepted, putative historical sequence of first kinship or blood ties, then territoriality—the one "pre-modern," the other "modern." It must not be overlooked that, in many modern societies, kinship is attributed, in various ways, to those who are considered "related" by virtue of birth in and coresidence in a territory. It is not

---

that even the ruthlessly materialistic and scientistic regime of the Soviet Communist Party, whose putative aim was to eliminate all forms of superstition, recognized the importance of representation through such actions as the entombment and display of the body of Lenin.

19. Proposition 187 in the State of California—a proposal which would prohibit all social services to illegal immigrants and, further, which would make it a criminal offense not to report illegal immigrants to the authorities.

20. As is well known, the general citizenry of the United States remains strongly patriotic. Moreover, one should remember that the putative internationalists of the Soviet Communist Party marshaled support for the defense of Russia during the Second World War under the slogan "defense of the motherland."

quite accurate to assert as Simmel and Tönnies did that this modern relation, in contrast to earlier ones, is qualitatively different by virtue of its "impersonality," its *gesellschaftliche* quality. On the contrary, membership in the territorially extensive national state is *impersonally personal*. This quality of the "impersonally personal" can be readily observed by considering briefly one's own reaction to *your fellow* countrymen who were held as hostages. You have never met these individuals; you have never spoken to them; you have never had any "face to face" relations with them. To this extent, your relations with these people are, in fact, impersonal. Yet, you also experience a deeply felt sense of outrage because *your fellow* countrymen have been taken hostage—it is a rather "personal" affair, there is an aspect of a *gemeinschaftliche* relation. It is precisely in the above use of the possessive adjective "your" and the adjective "fellow" where we may observe the immediacy of the primordial attachment, and its extension.

Our understanding of modern society, above all of territoriality, will be improved if we put aside the distinction of a pre-modern *Gemeinschaft* and a modern *Gesellschaft* as a rigid analytical and historical dichotomy; and, instead, view both as patterns of activity which often interpenetrate one another in various ways throughout history. This is the conclusion I draw from the observation of the geographer Robert Sack with which I began. The time is long overdue to question the explanatory merit of what is in my view too simplistic a distinction between what is modern and what is not, irrespective of the obvious validity of some aspects of the distinction and irrespective of where one draws that distinction (for example, with Machiavelli or Hobbes, or with Bacon or Descartes or even Abelard (Kolakowski 1990)).

There is a fundamental, primordial feature in modern societies. Territory is life-sustaining. It sustains biologically the life of the individual and the life of that individual's collectivity by providing the necessary physical nutrients. It also sustains life by providing the locus for those memories and psychic patterns necessary for the ordering of life. As such, a territory is recognized by its inhabitants to be significant as a primordial structure of vitality. This is only one of the consequences of the consideration of the nature of territoriality.

References

Abbot, Wilbur Cortez. 1945. *The Writings and Speeches of Oliver Cromwell.* Cambridge, MA: Harvard University Press.
Anderson, Benedict. 1983. *Imagined Communities.* London: Verso.

Augustine. 1955. *De Civitate Dei*. Corpus Christianorum. Series Latina. Turnhout: Brepols.

Barth, F. 1961. *Nomads of South Persia*. Boston: Little, Brown.

_____. 1981. "A general perspective on nomad-sedentary relations in the Middle East," in *Process and Form in Social Life*. London: Routledge & Kegan Paul.

Bullock, R. 1978. *The Story of Sinuhe*. London: Probsthian.

Cole, D. P. 1973. "The enmeshment of nomads in Saudi Arabian society: the case of Al Murrah," in C. Nelson (ed.), *The Desert and the Sown*. Berkeley: Institute of International Studies.

Constant, B. 1988. "The liberty of the ancients compared with that of the moderns," in B. Fontana (ed.), *Benjamin Constant–Political Writings*. Cambridge: Cambridge University Press (first published in French in 1820).

Davies, N. 1982. *God's Playground*. New York: Columbia University Press.

Dilthey, W. 1989. *Introduction to the Human Sciences*. Princeton: Princeton University Press (first published in German in 1883).

Eichenberger, T. 1991. *Patria–Studien zur Bedeutung des Wortes im Mittelalter (6.-12. Jarhundert)*. Sigmaringen: Jan Thorbecke.

Eisenstadt, S. N. 1973. *Tradition, Change and Modernity*. New York: Wiley.

_____. 1987. "Historical traditions, modernization and development," in S. N. Eisenstadt (ed.), *Patterns of Modernity*. Washington Square: New York University Press.

Erman, A., and Grapow, H. (eds.). 1921. *Wörterbuch der ägyptischen Sprache*. Berlin: Akademie der Wissenschaften.

Fitzmyer, J. A. 1967. *The Aramaic Inscriptions of Sefire*. Rome: Pontifical Institute.

Gadamer, H. 1988. *Truth and Method*. New York: Crossroad (first published in German in 1960).

Gardiner, A. H. 1916. *Notes on the Story of Sinuhe*. Paris: Librairie Honore Champion.

Geertz, C. 1963. "Primordial sentiments and civil politics in the new states," in C. Geertz (ed.), *Old Societies and New States*. New York: Free Press.

Gehlen, A. 1988. *Man*. New York: Columbia University Press (first published in German in 1940).

Geiger, W. (trans.) 1986. *The Mahāvaṃsa or The Great Chronicle of Ceylon*. New Delhi: Asian Educational Services (first published in 1912).

Gellner, E. 1983. *Nations and Nationalism*. Ithaca: Cornell University Press.

Giddens, A. 1985. *The Nation-State and Violence*. Berkeley: University of California Press.

Gombrich, R., and Obeyesekere, G. 1988. *Buddhism Transformed*. Princeton: Princeton University Press.

Gottman, J. 1973. *The Significance of Territory*. Charlottesville: University of Virginia Press.

Grosby, S. 1993. "Kinship, territory, and the nation in the historiography of ancient Israel," *Zeitschrift für die alttestamentliche Wissenschaft* 105: 3-18.

_____. 1994. "The verdict of history: the inexpungeable tie of primordiality," *Ethnic and Racial Studies* 17: 164-71.

Hobsbawm, E. J. 1990. *Nations and Nationalism Since 1780*. Cambridge: Cambridge University Press.

Kantorowicz, E. 1957. "Pro patria mori" in *The King's Two Bodies*. Princeton: Princeton University Press.

Kern, F. 1939. *Kingship and Law in the Middle Ages*. Oxford: Basil Blackwell (first published in German in 1914).

Kolakowski, L. 1990. *Modernity on Endless Trial*. Chicago: University of Chicago Press.

Lemche, N. P. 1985. *Early Israel*. Leiden: E. J. Brill.

Lévy-Bruhl, L. 1985. *How Natives Think*. Princeton: Princeton University Press (first published in French in 1910).

Lewis, B. 1991. "Watan," in J. Reinharz and G. L. Mosse (eds.), *The Impact of Western Nationalisms*. New York: Sage.

Lowie, R. 1927. *The Origin of the State*. New York: Harcourt, Brace.

Maine, H. S. 1970. *Ancient Law*. Gloucester: Peter Smith (first published in 1861).

Morenz, S. 1973. *Egyptian Religion*. Ithaca: Cornell University Press (first published in German in 1960).

Noth, M. 1960. *The History of Israel*. London: Adam & Charles Black (first published in German in 1950).

Parsons, T., and Shils, E. 1951. *Toward a General Theory of Action*. Cambridge, MA: Harvard University Press.

Pollock, F., and Maitland, F. W. 1968. *The History of English Law*. Cambridge: Cambridge University Press (first published in 1895).

Popper, K. 1972. *Objective Knowledge*. Oxford: Oxford University Press.

Popper, K., and Eccles, J. 1977. *The Self and Its Brain*. London: Routledge & Kegan Paul.

Post, G. 1953. "Two notes on nationalism in the Middle Ages," *Traditio* 9: 281-329.

Reynolds, S. 1984. *Kingdoms and Communities in Western Europe 900-1300*. Oxford: Oxford University Press.

Rowton, M. B. 1973a. "Autonomy and nomadism in Western Asia," *Orientalia* N.S. 42: 247-58.

_____. 1973b. "Dimorphic structure and the parasocial element," *Journal of Near Eastern Studies* 32: 201-15.

_____. 1974. "Enclosed nomadism," *Journal of the Economic and Social History of the Orient* 17: 1-30.

Sack, R. D. 1980. *Conceptions of Space in Social Thought*. Minneapolis: University of Minnesota Press.

_____. 1986. *Human Territoriality*. Cambridge: Cambridge University Press.

Sahlins, M. D. 1968. *Tribesmen*. Englewood Cliffs: Prentice-Hall.

Scheler, M. 1928. *Die Stellung des Menschen im Kosmos*. Bern: A. Francke.

_____. 1954. *The Nature of Sympathy*. London: Routledge & Kegan Paul (first published in German in 1923).

Schneidmüller, B. 1987. *Nomen Patriae–Die Entstehung Frankreichs in der politisch-geographischen Terminologie (10.-13. Jahrhundert)*. Sigmaringen: Jan Thorbecke.

Schurz, C. 1893. "Manifest destiny," *Harpers New Monthly Magazine* 87: 731-46.

Shils, E. 1957. "Personal, primordial, sacred and civil ties," *British Journal of Sociology* 8: 130-45.

_____. 1975. "Center and periphery" in *Center and Periphery–Essays in Macrosociology.* Chicago: University of Chicago Press.

_____. 1981. *Tradition.* Chicago: University of Chicago Press.

Shils, E., and Young, M. 1956. "The meaning of the coronation," *Sociological Review* 1: 63-82.

Simmel, G. 1971. "The metropolis and mental life," in *Georg Simmel–On Individuality and Social Forms.* Chicago: University of Chicago Press (first published in German in 1903).

_____. 1978. *The Philosophy of Money.* London: Routledge and Kegan Paul (first published in German in 1907).

Smith, A. D. 1994. "National identifies: ancient, medieval and modern?," *Ethnic and Racial Studies* 17: 375-99.

Strayer, J. 1971. "France: The Holy Land, the Chosen People, and the Most Christian King," in John F. Benton and Thomas N. Bisson (eds.), *Medieval Statecraft and the Perspectives of History.* Princeton: Princeton University Press.

Tönnies, F. 1940. *Gemeinschaft und Gesellschaft.* New York: American Book (first published in German in 1887).

Troeltsch, E. 1986. *The Significance of Protestantism for the Rise of the Modern World.* Philadelphia: Fortress Press (first published in German in 1906).

_____. 1991. "The essence of the modern spirit" in *Religion in History.* Minneapolis: Fortress Press (first published in German in 1907).

Tuan, Yi-Fu. 1974. *Topophilia.* Englewood Cliffs: Prentice-Hall.

_____. 1976. "Geopiety: a theme in man's attachment to nature and to place," in D. Lowenthal and M. J. Bowden (eds.), *Geographies of the Mind–Essays in Historical Geography in Honor of John Kirtland Wright.* New York: Oxford University Press.

Van Der Leeuw, G. 1963. *Religion in Essence and Manifestation.* New York: Harper & Row (first published in German in 1933).

Watkins, S. C. 1991. *From Provinces into Nations–Demographic Integration in Western Europe–1870-1960.* Princeton: Princeton University Press.

Weber, M. 1930. *The Protestant Ethic.* London: George Allen & Unwin (first published in German in 1905).

_____. 1946. "The Protestant sects and the spirit of capitalism," in H. Gerth and C. Wright Mills (eds.), *From Max Weber.* New York: Oxford University Press (first published in 1920).

_____. 1954. *Max Weber on Law in Economy and Society.* Cambridge, MA: Harvard University Press (first published in German in 1921).

Weinberg, A. K. 1935. *Manifest Destiny.* Baltimore: Johns Hopkins University Press.

Wright, J. K. 1966. *Human Nature in Geography.* Cambridge, MA: Harvard University Press.

Chapter 9

The Nation of the United States and the Vision of Ancient Israel

It has become a commonplace in considerations of the nature of nationality and nationalism to distinguish between two different points of departure: the existence of a "people" whose traditions are grounded in a conception of citizenship, a liberal nationalism; and the existence of a "people" whose traditions are grounded in a conception of the *Volk*, an integrative nationalism. This distinction has been elaborated further as the difference between the nationalism of the West in contrast to the nationalism of the East; or, as the difference between a people whose constitutive traditions have been formed out of beliefs in individual, democratic rights and a people whose constitutive traditions have been formed under the influence of a fusion of romanticism and a variant of historicism. I do not wish to deny entirely any merit to such distinctions. Their merit can be immediately observed from comparing, for example, the writings of the friend of Thomas Jefferson and poet of the American revolution, Philip Freneau, with the works of such nineteenth-century Polish romanticists and patriots as Adam Mickiewicz and Juliusz Slowacki. Indeed, it is difficult to imagine any other nation but the Poles producing such works as *Konrad Wallenrod* or *Anhelli.*

On the one hand, we find proclaimed as self-evident the natural and universal rights of man: "all men are created equal; that they are endowed by their creator with inherent and inalienable rights; that among these are life, liberty, and the pursuit of happiness. . . ." Today, in the United States, "being an American" may, of course, mean many different things to many different people; but this much is certain: the vast majority of Americans understand the "American way of life" to include recognizing and defending another person's right to say what that person believes, irrespective of whether or not they may agree with the beliefs of that person. The acceptance of the Bill of Rights, often, to be sure, inchoately understood throughout the different strata of the population of the United States, is the essential foundation to the civility of the "American way of life."

In contrast, who else but a Polish nationalist would have referred to such disputes as whether or not to have one or two chambers of government, or the scope of the freedom of the press as the quarrels between the Pharisees and the Sadducees over what is *tref* and what is *kosher*?[1] Who else would have referred to Frederick the Second of Prussia, Catherine the Second of Russia, and Maria Theresa of Austria as the Satanic trinity?[2] A tradition of the inseparability of Polish nationalism and Polish Catholicism among Polish patriots continues today. Who would deny that the Polish Catholic church is an essential component of the "Polish way of life?" What Pole today needs to be reminded of the rescue of Poland at the monastery of Częstochowa?

Having briefly noted this typology of the different constitutive traditions of respectively different peoples, I now want to put this distinction aside as it is, for a number of reasons, flawed. This distinction also obscures the task before us of better understanding the problematic relationship between nationality and democratic rights. The limitation of this distinction becomes obvious when one recognizes that the desire for liberty and the recognition of the rights of the individual are to be found among the traditions of the so-called "nations of the East." For example, while in his description of America Mickiewicz used an idiom which someone like Thomas Paine would have found objectionable, namely that America was a "holy land," it was nonetheless a land which Mickiewicz thought holy precisely because it represented freedom not only for the nation but also for the individual. The desire for freedom is fundamental to human existence. An analysis of the expression of that desire ought not to be confined to the history of the people of England and of America—so one concludes from the *History* of Herodotus, the demands of the Israelite prophets for justice for the individual, and the recent events in Tiananmen Square.

There is another reason for abandoning this distinction and similar typologies of nationalism and nationality. When one considers the democratic liberties as expounded by Jefferson and Paine in their declaration of the universal, natural rights of man, there arise necessarily a number of questions in conjunction with these declarations, just as occurred at the founding of the United States regarding the question of slavery: who is a member of the people, where is that person a member, upon what basis is a person a member? In other words, and what these questions point

---

1. Adam Mickiewicz, *The Books of the Polish Nation* in *Konrad Wallenrod and other writings of Adam Mickiewicz* (Westport: Greenwood Press, 1975) 172.
2. Ibid., 139.

to is that every collectivity (except presumably heaven and the kingdom of God), including the nation which incorporates the declaration of the universal rights of man as a part of its own image of itself, has boundaries which determine who is and who is not a member of that collectivity. Thus, and even with the democratic rights of man embodied in the Constitution of the United States, one cannot escape considering the American nation in William Graham Sumner's categories of "in-group" and "out-group," of "we-group" and "others-group."

We need not go far to uncover here the problematic relationship between democratic liberties and nationality for it exists even within the doctrine of natural rights. We recognize as inalienable and natural the right of the individual to life, liberty, and the pursuit of happiness. However, one may also make the argument—and so it has been made during the history of the United States, including by Jefferson himself—for the natural right of the nation to its own security (the right to self-preservation). The exercise of this latter right may very well at times abrogate the natural rights of those individuals who are not members of the nation, who exist outside the boundaries of the nation. Moreover, the necessities required to maintain the security of the nation may also at times require restrictions in the exercise of the democratic rights of the nation's own citizenry.

Given the existence of scarcity (of economic resources, of knowledge, of ability), it is a functional imperative for the existence and preservation of any collectivity that it should be bounded. Despite the recent "discoveries" of several professors that we live in an age of "postscarcity," the kingdom of God on earth has not been realized. Consequently, competition remains inescapable, and humanity remains divided in numerously different ways—nationality being one of them.

From the perspective of a bounded collectivity, in this case the nation-state, the contrast between universality and exclusivity, which is implicit in the distinction between a nationalism of democratic citizenship and a nationalism of the *Volk*, loses some of its significance. Liberalism and liberal democracy, in particular the universalistic beliefs that all men are created equal and that they are endowed by their creator with inherent and inalienable rights, have never been realized in any collectivity but the nation-state. This fact presents us with an inescapable paradox: we may affirm noble, universalistic beliefs such as all men have been created equal; but as far as the implementation of these universalistic, inherent, and inalienable rights are concerned, they have a clearly particularistic application.

Once this paradox is recognized, the important political problem now becomes a matter of the proper mixture of universality and exclusivity; or, in the terms of how the problem is usually posed in the relation between liberal democracy and nationality, the proper mixture of, on the one hand, the rights of the individual, and, on the other, the duties of the individual to his nation. The establishment of this proper mixture is particularly problematic in the United States with its separation of church and state. Of course, that separation is a prerequisite for the freedom to worship in the manner one chooses, and is thus one of the underpinnings to civility in America. However, that separation also may invite disagreement as to what is of fundamental importance to the conduct of both the life of the individual as well as the life of the nation. Indeed, it may even invite dispute over the very definition of life as can be seen in the current controversy over abortion.

There is yet another reason for putting aside the distinctions with which this discussion began. These distinctions blur the difference between nationality and nationalism. In order for any nation to exist, there has to be a territory of the nation in which the people of the nation dwell or believe they have the "right" to do so. Thus, a nation has two boundaries: one determines the territory of the nation, and another determines the people of the nation. What is unique about nationality in contrast to a city-kingdom or an empire is that the image of a relatively extensive area of land is a constitutive ingredient of, or, in terms of Lucien Lévy-Bruhl, a "part of" the formation of the people of the nation. This conflation or conjoining of the image of a territory and the image of a people is accomplished in different ways. One way is the long development of often previously local and separate traditions into a common tradition of the people which, in turn, elicits the image of the territory. In other words, territoriality is an ingredient in those common memories. Another and most important factor is the existence of a *lex terrae* which unites a territory and the people throughout that territory into a nation. Thus, a constitutive characteristic of nationality is the shared belief that a particular people has its land and a particular land has its people. Essential to the constitution of nationality is the belief in the existence of a relatively extensive contiguous area of land within designated boundaries, which, by virtue of its contiguity, should be considered one and the same.[3] These are essential prerequisites for the existence of any nation.

---

3. This principle of contiguity may be justified in many different ways. For example, in ancient Israel, it was the belief in a promised land which was pervaded by

What is of particular interest here are the images of a territory and of a people who are in some way "related"—images without which no nation, however classified, could exist.

What must be considered as distinct from nationality is nationalism which is a set of beliefs about the nature of that "right" of a people to "their" land, the nature of the "people," and finally the nature of the land. There may be and usually are many different nationalisms expounded by many different members of the nation. Those different nationalisms represent different visions of the nation and its relation to other nations; nevertheless, the different proponents of these different nationalisms are in agreement as to the existence of the nation. Once this distinction between nationality and nationalism is clear in our minds, we can then better appreciate patriotism. Patriotism recognizes the necessity of the nation; it is affection for one's nation. It is the acknowledgment that the life of the individual is also dependent upon the life of the nation.

The Vision of Ancient Israel

Edward Shils has described the attachments formed to land and blood-tie as primordial.[4] Regarding nationality, we find the objects of these primordial attachments transformed from the local soil of the home to the territory of the nation and from the blood-tie of the family to the people of the nation. The example, *par excellence*, of the image of these transformed primordial objects of a land and a people in the formation of a nation is the "promised land" and the "chosen people" of the nation of ancient Israel. The issue before us is to what extent the image of ancient Israel and in particular the image of a chosen people and a promised land have been factors in the formation of different nations subsequent to the existence of the nation of ancient Israel. It is obvious that many other factors (which are sometimes described by many writers on the subject of nationality and nationalism as "interests") have contributed to the formation of nations. However, it seems that rarely has the vision of ancient Israel been considered a factor in the formation of nationality, including the nation of the United States.

---

the spirit of Yahweh manifested in the Deuteronomic code, which, in turn, was to be obeyed throughout that land. The principle of contiguity was an important element in the territorial expansion of the United States in the decade of the 1840s and was justified by the doctrines of Providence and manifest destiny.

4. Edward Shils, "Primordial, Personal, Sacred, and Civil Ties," in *Center and Periphery—Essays in Macrosociology* (Chicago: University of Chicago Press, 1975) 111-26.

We are accustomed, particularly from the writings of Max Weber and Ernest Troeltsch, to consider the influence of Christianity on the orientation of the conduct of one's activity. It is most curious (and certainly worthy of discussion at another time) that especially Max Weber, always an ardent German patriot,[5] should have paid so little attention as to how the Old Testament—that is, the evident persistence of the primordial beliefs in a chosen people and a promised land—may have influenced the formation of various collectivities, particularly the nation.

One expects that the image of a chosen people was a constitutive factor in the nationalism of the *Volk*. Here one recalls not only the various works of the Polish romanticists, but also Fichte's *Addresses to the German Nation*. However, as has already been stated, the image of a people is a constitutive factor of any nation. As early as the beginning of the fourteenth century and following the conflict between Boniface VIII and Philip the Fair, Pope Clement V in the bull *Rex Gloriae* (1311) compared the people of France to the people of Israel:

> . . . like the people of Israel . . . the kingdom of France, as a peculiar people chosen by God to carry out divine mandates, is distinguished by marks of special honor and grace.[6]

This is truly a remarkable comparison for any apostolic successor of Peter to have made. Less remarkable, but still revealing are the words of Nogaret, the Keeper of the Seals under Philip the Fair:

> . . . the kingdom of France was chosen by the Lord and blessed above all other kingdoms of the world.[7]

Parenthetically, I think one is justified to consider that it was during this period where the origins of Gallicanism are to be found,[8] almost four hundred years before the formal declaration of Gallican liberties. It is also to this period that we must look for the origins of the nation of France.[9]

---

5. See Wolfgang Mommsen, *Max Weber and German Politics 1890-1920* (Chicago: University of Chicago Press, 1984).

6. Joseph R. Strayer, "France: the Holy Land, the Chosen People, and the Most Christian King," in *Medieval Statecraft and the Perspectives of History: Essays by Joseph P. Strayer*, ed. John F. Benton and Thomas N. Bisson (Princeton: Princeton University Press, 1971) 312-13.

7. Ibid., 311.

8. So Joseph R. Strayer, *The Reign of Philip the Fair* (Princeton: Princeton University Press, 1980) 299-300.

9. See also, for example, Gaines Post, "Two Notes on Nationalism in the Middle Ages," *Traditio*, IX (1953): 281-329; Ernst Kantorowicz, *The Kings Two Bodies* (Princeton: Princeton University Press, 1957) 232-72.

The imagery of a chosen people and the comparison to ancient Israel occur so frequently during the English revolution of the seventeenth century that I need not provide many examples of it here. One need only recall the works of such writers as Foxe, Milton, and Cromwell. As Yahweh led Israel into war, so God was believed to have marched into battle on the side of Cromwell's army. Let us note here two speeches of Cromwell. In his speech of July 4, 1653 to the Nominated Parliament (the Barebones Parliament), Cromwell stated:

> This Scripture I shall remember to you, which hath been much upon my spirit, Hosea, xi, 12, "Judah yet ruleth with God, and is faithful among the Saints. . . ." Truly you are called by God to rule with Him, and for Him. . . . Thus God has owned you in the eyes of the world; and thus, by your coming hither have you owned him, as it is in Isaiah xliii, 21. It is an high expression, and look to your own hearts whether, now or hereafter, God shall apply it to you. "This people," saith God, "I have formed for Myself, that they may show forth my praise. . . ." You have been passive in coming hither, being *called*,–and that's an active work. This people have I formed: consider the circumstances by which you are called hither, through what difficulties, through what strivings, through what blood you are come hither,–where neither you nor I, nor no man living, three months ago, had a thought to have seen such a company taking upon them, or rather being called to take, the supreme authority of this nation. Therefore, own your call! . . . I say, you are called with a high call. And why should we be afraid to say or think, that this may be the door to usher in the things that God has promised; which has been prophesied of; while He has set the hearts of His people to wait for and expect? We know who they are that shall war with the lamb, against his enemies; they shall be a people called, and chosen and faithful. And God hath, in a military way–we may speak it without flattering ourselves, and I believe you know it–He hath appeared with them and for them; and now in these civil powers and authorities does not He appear? . . . [10]

On September 4, 1654 in his speech to Parliament, Cromwell could not have been more explicit as to the deliverance of the new Israel.[11]

> . . . the only parallel of God's dealing with us that I know in the world, which was largely and wisely held forth to you this day,–Israel's bringing out of Egypt through a wilderness, by many signs and wonders towards a place of rest[12] I say, towards it. . . . You were told to-day of a people brought out of Egypt towards the land of Canaan, but, through unbelief, murmuring, repining, and other temptations and sins, wherewith God was provoked, they were fain to come back again, and linger many years in the

---

10. Wilbur Cortez Abbot, *The Writings and Speeches of Oliver Cromwell*, Vol. III (Cambridge: Harvard University Press, 1945) 52-66.
11. Ibid., 434-43.

wilderness, before they came to the place of rest. . . . But this must be by knowing the true state of affairs, that you are yet like the People under Circumcision, but raw; your peace are but newly made.

A similar imagery appears throughout the history of the United States, especially in its formative stages. We shall turn to an examination of this material in a moment.

The point which I have attempted to draw attention to here from only a few, but dramatic examples is the presence of this primordial imagery in the history of the development of the collective consciousness (what Renan called the "common memories") of those peoples, American, English, and French, which have traditions, to one degree or another, of liberal democracy. To be sure, the nation of ancient Israel has not always been referred to; at times, the imagery has consisted of such descriptions as the rich, productive soil of the nation of "X," or the noble, brave ancestors of the country of "Y." The point at issue is the existence of the beliefs in a bounded territory and a people and the traditions which bear those beliefs, irrespective of any particular nationalism, without which no nation can exist.

We are concerned here with the existence of particular beliefs and the traditions which bear those beliefs which, in turn, become shared by, hence constitutive of a "people," a nation. The existence of this image of a people presupposes a stability over time of a constellation of shared beliefs within a society. Nationality is not to be understood as identical to the state, the latter, as Weber observed, being an association which monopolizes the legitimate use of physical force as a means of dominion within a territory. The point here is that the boundaries of the association must not be taken for granted, they must be accounted for. To be sure, the development of a particular nation may be dependent upon the earlier existence of numerous collectivities, including tribal confederacies, kingdoms, and states, and, above all, the memories of those collectivities.

---

12. The significance of the concept of "rest" in the Old Testament is clear from Deuteronomy 25:19, "Therefore when Yahweh your God has given you rest from all your enemies round about, in the land which Yahweh your God gives you for an inheritance to possess. . . ." About this Deuteronomic conception of "rest," Gerhard von Rad wrote, "We must not spiritualize any of this: this 'rest' is not peace of mind, but the altogether tangible peace granted to a nation plagued by enemies and weary of wandering. . . . The life of the chosen people in the 'pleasant land,' at rest from all enemies round about, the people owning their love for God and God blessing his people— this is the epitome of the state of the redeemed nation as Deuteronomy sees it," G. von Rad, "There Remains Still a Rest for the People of God: An Investigation of a Biblical Conception," in *The Problem of the Hexateuch and other essays* (Edinburgh: Oliver & Boyd, 1966) 95.

Moreover, the continued existence of a nation may be dependent upon its having its own state. However, the object of our examination into the essential nature of nationality is, for the lack of a better term, the "layer" of collective consciousness, those shared traditions, which exist within a society. That "layer" of collective consciousness, those traditions constitutive of a people, is not to be equated with or considered inseparable from either the economy or the state of a particular society. The image of a people, this shared awareness of a perceived common history, and those institutions and customs in which that image inheres have their own relatively independent existence. In addition to this relatively independent nature of nationality, these common memories of a perceived past, this "layer" of collective consciousness within a society, necessary for the existence of any nation, is a phenomenon which occurs over time. This indicates that nationality, a "people," is a collectivity of temporal depth. Understanding nationality and patriotism will be hindered greatly if one views these phenomena in the manner in which they are typically treated in the literature of the social sciences today, namely as essentially and simply *ad hoc*, instrumental "constructions" of the "elites" in the service of consolidating their power.

The Nation of the United States and the Vision of Ancient Israel

One would expect from their origins and from the brief examination of only a few of Cromwell's speeches that the American Puritans understood themselves as the people chosen by God to establish the American Israel. In many instances, the analogy between the Pilgrims and the Israelites was explicit and persistent; we need only recall Cotton Mather's *Magnalia Christi Americana* or Increase Mather's *The Day of Trouble is Near*. At times, there was only a general reference to the workings of Providence; here, for example, consider William Bradford's *Of Plymouth Plantation*. I do not want to give the impression that an image of a particular people believed to have been chosen by God to inhabit a specific land was the only concern on the minds of these courageous Europeans who settled in America during the sixteenth and seventeenth centuries. Some came in pursuit of economic advantage. Many came to America to escape religious persecution.

The ancient Israelites sought release from their bondage, that is, they sought the freedom of their people to live "at rest" in their own land. The Old Testament, and in particular the Deuteronomistic History of the

Books of Joshua through 2 Kings, is a message of redemption for a particular people in a designated territory of this world. The early settlers in America understood themselves in a similar manner, for many of them believed that it was from the soil of the promised land of the American continent that the freedom they sought was destined to grow. As we are considering the writings of deeply religious people who were very much aware of the rejection by Jesus and Paul of the Covenant of the Old Testament and its primordial particularism, we must not underestimate the significance of this "this-worldly" orientation.[13] That such primordial attachments reemerge, continue to exist, and indeed flourish (e.g., the nationalities in the Soviet Union today) indicates that they and the traditions which embody, preserve and reshape them are not historically residual phenomena overwhelmed by a putatively ubiquitous, individualistic utilitarianism of a disenchanted world.

Let us look briefly at just a few examples of how Cotton Mather portrayed the history of New England in *Magnalia Christi Americana* (1702). In the Introduction, we can observe how Mather, as it were, places Jesus within the context of the Old Testament:

> 'Tis possible, that our Lord Jesus Christ carried some thousands of Reformers into the Retirements of an American Desert, on purpose, that, with an opportunity granted unto many of his Faithful Servants, to enjoy the precious Liberty of their Ministry, tho' in the midst of many Temptations all their days, He might there, To them first, and then By them, give a Specimen of many Good Things. . . . But behold, ye European Churches, there are Golden Candlesticks [more than twice Seven times Seven!] in the midst of this Outer Darkness; Unto the upright Children of Abraham, here hath arisen Light in Darkness. . . . 'Tis very certain, that the greatest Entertainments must needs occur in the History of the People, whom the Son of God hath Redeemed and Purified unto himself as a Peculiar People. . . .[14]

Here Jesus is described as having brought the light of God to the "Peculiar People" of the "Children of Abraham" in America, on "the other side of the Atlantic Ocean." Mather continued his history with the description of William Bradford, governor of Plymouth-Colony, as "a Moses," "the leader of a People in a Wilderness."[15] Similarly, John Winthrop, governor

---

13. This primordial orientation is certainly not limited to the Puritans. Consider, for example, not only the above quoted bull *Rex Gloriae* of Clement V, but also the dispute over voting during the Council of Trent, the doctrine of *cuius regio, eius religio,* Gallicanism, and the various national churches of Eastern Orthodoxy.

14. Cotton Mather, *Magnalia Christi Americana* (Hartford: Silia Andrus & Sons, 1855) 27.

15. Ibid., 113.

of the colony of Massachusetts, was introduced in Mather's history in the following manner:

> Accordingly when the Noble Design of carrying a Colony of Chosen People into an American Wilderness was by some Eminent Persons undertaken, This Eminent Person was, by the Consent of all, Chosen for the Moses. . . .[16]

Indeed, for Mather, Winthrop was the "Nehemias Americanus." Discussing the articles drawn up under Winthrop, Mather further stated, "But whilst he thus did as our New-English Nehemiah, the part of a Ruler in managing the Public Affairs of our American Jerusalem, when there were Tobihahs and Sanballats enough to vex him . . . he made himself still an exacter Parallel unto that governor of Israel. . . ."[17]

As almost every discussant of the early history of the United States has pointed out, there of course was a rupture between the seventeenth century Puritans of New England and the leaders of the American Revolution. Surely, one will be hard put to discover anything in the Old Testament resembling the right of the individual to worship God in the manner one chooses. Indicative of this discontinuity is what I take to have been Thomas Jefferson's rather derisive reference to the "family God of Abraham, of Isaac and of Jacob, and the local God of Israel."[18] It is not my intention here to enter into a detailed discussion of American history and, in particular, the relation, or lack thereof, between, for example, the Puritans and Jefferson. Here, I am only interested in tracing briefly the beliefs in and imagery of the people of the nation and the land of the nation in the traditions of the American people. There is no question as to the fundamental importance of the belief in the natural rights of man and the democratic liberties embodied in the Bill of Rights in the formation of the "American way of life." This latter belief provides the continuity of the spirit of the nation of the United States from the revolution of 1776 up to today. However, co-existing, at times uneasily, with the recognition of these democratic rights of the individual as an embodiment of the American spirit is also, for lack of a better term, a "corporatist" tradition. It is within the shaping of this tradition in the collective consciousness of the American nation that we find reference to and comparison with ancient Israel, the chosen people and the promised land. Consequently, there is a continuity as well as a discontinuity in American history with the Puritan traditions and primordial themes of the Old Testament. The imagery of a

---

16. Ibid., 119.
17. Ibid., 121.
18. Jefferson's letter of August 4, 1820 to William Short.

chosen people and a promised land continues throughout American history. Indicative of this continuity is the doctrine of "manifest destiny,"[19] the doctrine of a continental United States whose "boundaries the God of nature had marked out"[20] for the American people. As Yahweh had set the boundaries of Israel from Dan to Beersheba, from the Great Sea to the Jordan River, so Providence had set the boundaries of the United States from the Atlantic to the Pacific.[21] Never mind that for a time there was uncertainty as to whether the northern border of the United States was the 49th parallel or 54,40.

In contrast to the territorial conceptions of a city-kingdom, an empire or the *millet* system of the Ottomans, nationality is predicated upon an image of a "homogeneous" territory and people within designated boundaries. As to the nature of this homogeneity, I have already referred to both the belief that contiguous tracts of land are in some way or another understood to "belong" together and the existence of a *lex terrae* which unifies that land over which it has jurisdiction. It was precisely this idea of contiguity which we find coming to the forefront during the first half of the nineteenth century when the territories of Texas and Oregon were incorporated into the United States. The doctrine of manifest destiny proclaimed the "mission" of the chosen "people" of America, as the bearers of democratic liberties, to spread those liberties through the extension of the borders of the United States throughout the contiguous territory of the continent of North America.[22]

Consider the ideas expressed in a poem about the manifest destiny of the American people, "Progress in America" which appeared in the Feb-

---

19. See John L. O'Sullivan, "The True Title," *New York Morning News*, December 29, 1845, ". . . by the right of our manifest destiny to overspread and to possess the whole of the continent which Providence has given us for the development of the great experiment of liberty. . . ."

20. Stephen A. Douglas, Congressional Session of January 31, 1845.

21. Albert K. Weinberg described the establishment of the continental boundaries of the United States as "geographical Predestination," *Manifest Destiny* (Baltimore: Johns Hopkins Press, 1935) 43–71.

22. The doctrine of manifest destiny was also prominent in the 1880s and 1890s but then it referred to the incorporation of territory which was outside the continent. Here, see Carl Schurz, "Manifest Destiny," *Harpers New Monthly Magazine* 87 (1893) 731–46, for an argument against "the new 'manifest destiny' precept [which] means, in point of principle, not merely the incorporation in the United States of territory contiguous to our borders, but rather the acquisition of such territory, far and near, as may be useful in enlarging our commercial advantages, and in securing to our naval facilities desirable for the operations of a great naval power [i.e., Hawaii, Cuba]." Note in this article Schurz' use of such terms as "national household," "family circle," and "our family" to describe the American people and the American nation.

ruary 1846 issue of the then influential *The United States Magazine and Democratic Review*:

> And thus we cover Texas! Thus we spell With deeds, the drowsy nations, as, of yore, The adventurous Spaniard crack'd th' Atlantic's shell. Though not for him to penetrate the core. The good old Norman stock will do as well, Nay, better; a selected stock of old, With blood well-temper'd, resolute and bold; Set for a mighty work, the way to pave For the wrong'd nations, and, in one great fold, Unite them, from old tyrannies to save! We do but follow our destiny,
>
> As did the ancient Israelite—and strive, Unconscious that we work out His decree, By Whom alone we triumph as we live! . . . The right depends on the propinquity, The absolute sympathy of soil and place, Needful against the foreign enemy, And for the due expansion of our race. . . .

Note the ascribed kinship of the American people as being of a putative "Norman stock" and the belief that the "destiny" of this people, like the ancient Israelite, is to complete the designs ("His decree") of God. In the final four lines quoted, there is stated a doctrine which asserts an inseparability of "propinquity," "sympathy of soil and place," and the "due expansion of our race."[23] The ancient Israelites believed that the bounded land of Israel belonged to them because Yahweh had promised it to them and their ancestors. The Americans of the mid-nineteenth century believed that Providence or God had given a particular people of "Norman stock" and propinquity a historic mission to possess a bounded, contiguous land which was "due" only to them.

Even Thomas Jefferson, while critical of the primordial covenant of the Old Testament, would nonetheless state in his Second Inaugural Address (1805),

> I shall need, too, the favor of that Being in whose hands we are, who led our forefathers, as Israel of old, from their native land, and planted them in a country flowing with all the necessaries and comforts of life. . . .

In the same speech, note how Jefferson defended the Louisiana Purchase to his critics:

> . . . and in any view, is it not better that the opposite bank of the Mississippi should be settled by our own brethren and children, than by strangers of another family?

Here, Jefferson resorted not to the doctrine of the natural rights of the individual, but to the primordial imagery of an American kinship and

---

23. This latter doctrine was put forward in opposition to Britain's claim to the Oregon territory based on first possession.

"Israel of old." To be sure, the primordial image of the family of the American nation is less salient than the Israelite belief in a common ancestry of "all Israel." One expects as much given that the United States in its brief history of approximately three hundred years has been a nation of immigrants. We shall return later to the question of the nature of the kinship of the people of the nation. The important point to note here is the evident resilience of primordial attachments, however attenuated, in the formation and continued existence of the nation.

This historic mission or manifest destiny of the American nation, in which the American people have in varying degrees of intensity believed, has had several aspects to it. In the nineteenth century, there was the territorial component of the occupation of the continental promised land of the new American Israel. Another component, already briefly referred to, was the mission of the American nation to be the bearer of democratic liberties to the world. During the twentieth century this latter aspect has been understood as the mission of the American people to make the world safe for democracy. One is reminded of the exilic prophets of ancient Israel who prophesied of a holy people and a new Jerusalem to which the rest of the world would look. I do not dispute that this second component of the American mission has at times been in the service of other ends, such as territorial aggrandizement or national security; nor, as I have argued earlier, is it surprising. However, even then, the nation has been thrown into debate and often deeply divided (e.g., policy toward the American Indians before 1830, and abolition of slavery or the preservation of union, whether or not the United States should have foreign territorial possessions, etc.).

When former president Ronald Reagan not too long ago described the Soviet Union as an evil empire, he, by doing so, alluded to a perceived historic mission of the United States of America and of the American people to oppose totalitarianism. His speech was ridiculed by a section of the American press; and perhaps it was somewhat manichean in tone. However, this speech has more in common with American tradition than have its detractors. Consider the poem of Philip Freneau, "The Rising Glory of America" (1772).

> ... By persecution wronged, And sacerdotal rage, our fathers came From Europe's hostile shores to these abodes, Here to enjoy a liberty in faith, Secure from tyranny and base control! ... And when a train of rolling years are past (so sung the exiled Seer in Patmos isle) A new Jerusalem, sent down from heaven, Shall grace our happy earth—perhaps this land, Whose ample bosom shall receive, though late, Myriads of saints, with their immortal king, To live and reign on earth a thousand years, thence called Millennium.

Paradise anew Shall flourish, by no second Adam lost, No dangerous tree with deadly fruit shall grow, No tempting serpent to allure the soul From native innocence–A Canaan here, Another Canaan shall exceed the old. . . . Groves shall adorn their verdant banks, on which The happy People, free from toil and death, Shall find secure repose. . . . Such days the world, And such America at last shall have When ages, yet to come, have run their round, And future years of bliss alone remain.

With such references to "New Jerusalem," the "Millennium" and "Canaan,"[24] one might think that Freneau was an erstwhile Puritan who yearned for a return to the life of New England of the previous century, or that he represents an anticipation of American nativism. On the contrary, Freneau is rightly considered to be the poet of the American revolution. Again, we want to note the existence of the imagery of the people and the land (and, at times, the historic mission or manifest destiny of both) in the collective, that is shared, self-perception of America by Americans.

One of the ways the nation is understood by the members of the nation is that it is a community. What can be and often is obscured by the many different typologies of nationality and nationalism is that membership in the *Gemeinschaft* of the nation of the United States not only conveys democratic rights to its members, it also entails duties. The appeal to ancient Israel as a community of historic mission and as a community of law emphasizes the obligations of not only the individual as a member of the nation to the nation, but also the nation itself. The United States has an obligation as the bearer of democratic liberties and an obligation to its own self-preservation. There has also been a long tradition in the history of the United States of the duty of the individual to his nation and the duty of the nation to preserve itself.

It was the question of the duties of the citizen to his nation and the necessities required for the preservation of the nation itself which increasingly occupied the attention of James Russell Lowell during and after the American Civil War. During this period, Lowell sought to balance what he perceived to be an exaggerated emphasis on the rights of the individual and the states at the expense of the right of the nation to its own preservation. Characteristic of this change in Lowell's thinking, this influential spokesman of American opinion (he was the founder of *The Atlantic Monthly*) now asserted "the best testimony to the virtue of coercion is the fact that no wrongdoer ever thought well of it" ("E Pluribus Unum," 1861).

---

24. See also Freneau's "The Jewish Lamentation" (1779) with its mention of the "nation" and "native soil."

The essay of "E Pluribus Unum" was written just before the outbreak of the Civil War; consequently, national unity was foremost on Lowell's mind. For our purposes, what is of particular interest are the arguments employed by Lowell.

> The United States are not a German Confederation, but a unitary and indivisible nation, with a national life to protect, a national power to maintain, and national rights to defend against any and every assailant, at all hazards. Our national existence is all that gives value to American citizenship. . . . The first and greatest benefit of government is that it keeps the peace, that is insures every man his right, and not only that, but the permanence of it. In order to do this, its first requisite is stability; and this once firmly settled, the greater the extent of conterminous territory that can be subjected to one system and one language and inspired by one patriotism, the better.

The first sentence quoted above and in particular the phrase "not a German confederation" is perhaps Lowell's response to the debate, which erupted during the 1830s, over the right of nullification, the right of one state (in particular South Carolina) to annul or to ignore the law of the United States. This right of nullification logically led to the recognition of the right of secession. The defenders of the right, for example Calhoun, sought to frame the debate as a question of liberty versus centralized power. In opposition, Daniel Webster and others such as Lowell and Carl Schurz stood for "Liberty and Union, now and forever, one and inseparable." Note Lowell's use of such terms as "national life," and that now it is national existence which gives value to American citizenship and not vice versa. In particular, note the significance attributed to "conterminous territory," "one language," and "one patriotism" for the existence of the American nation (and, we may add to the existence of any nation). Here, Lowell emphasized the duties of the individual citizen to the nation, as well he should have in 1861.

We are not surprised, then, to find in Lowell's "Ode Recited at the Harvard Commemoration" (1865) the use of primordial imagery and the comparison to ancient Israel. In the section of the ode on "our Martyr-Chief," Lincoln (and the United States?) is described as "New birth of our new soil, the first American." Lowell concluded the ode with these lines.

> O Beautiful! my Country! ours once more!
> Smoothing thy gold of war-dishevelled hair
> O'er such sweet brows as never other wore,
> And letting thy set lips,
> Freed from wrath's pale eclipse,
> The rosy edges of their smile lay bare,
> What words divine of lover or of poet

Could tell our love and make thee know it,
Among the Nations bright beyond compare?
What more our lives without thee?
What all our lives to save thee;
We will not dare to doubt thee,
But ask whatever else, and we will dare!

As if to complete the circle, Lowell now directed his attention to the Puritan origins of the American nation. He was, by no means, the first to do so. For example, thirty-five years earlier, Daniel Webster had delivered at Plymouth his speech on the "First Settlement of New England"—a speech which is remarkable for its sensitivity to and perception of the nature of patriotism and the influence of the Puritans on the development of the American nation. Lowell turned to the early history of New England in order to root his argument of duty to the nation in the tradition of the Puritans[25] and in the Old Testament. In his essay, "New England Two Centuries Ago" (1865), he wrote:

> Next to the fugitives whom Moses led out of Egypt, the little shipload of outcasts who landed at Plymouth two centuries and a half ago are destined to influence the future of the world. The spiritual thirst of mankind has for ages been quenched at Hebrew fountains. . . . Their [the Puritans'] view of human rights was not so limited that it could not take in human relations and duties also.

This call for the unity and duty of the entire people to the nation was in no way confined to Lowell. Consider the following note on nationality by Walt Whitman, certainly no New England brahman.[26]

> Indeed, what most needs fostering through the hundred years to come, in all parts of the United States, North, South, Mississippi Valley, and Atlantic and Pacific coasts, is this fused and fervent identity of the individual, whomever he or she might be, and wherever the place, with the idea and fact of American totality, and with what is meant by the Flag, the stars and stripes. We need this conviction of nationality as a faith, to be absorbed in the blood and belief of the people everywhere, South, North, West, East, to emanate in their life, and in native literature and art. We want the germinal idea that America, inheritor of the past, is the custodian of the future of humanity.

---

25. In his speech of October 7, 1864 Carl Schurz identified the cause of the North in the Civil War with the Puritans. "This [the Puritan influence] is the spirit to which the North owes her thrift and industry, her education, her liberty, her progressive enterprise, her prosperity, and her greatness. It was not so with the original settlers of the Southern country. . . ."

26. *The Complete Writings of Walt Whitman*, Vol. 5 (New York: G. P. Putnam's Sons, 1902) 263.

We take it for granted that Whitman would have been appalled by the recent decision of the majority of the U.S. Supreme Court protecting the burning of the American flag; for he, no doubt, understood by freedom of expression the rational exercise of the freedom of speech. Unfortunately, the recent Supreme Court decision appears to equate any form of expression, including purposeful acts of incitement to riot, with the freedom of speech. By so doing, it seems to me that the Court has blinded itself to the essential prerequisite for the existence of democratic liberties, namely, the maintenance of the public, civil realm of the nation which, in turn, recognizes as legitimate the existence of different beliefs each competing with one another within the context of rational discourse. That this prerequisite was the intention of the authors of the Constitution may be seen in the fact that the first amendment to the U.S. Constitution does not recognize the right of the people to assemble; rather, it recognizes the right of the people peaceably to assemble. No one has denied the right of the American communist who burned the flag or the American neo-fascist to disseminate their views in an orderly manner. However, is it not obscene to equate the right of the freedom of speech with the right of the American neo-Nazis to march through a predominantly Jewish community which is well known to contain numerous survivors of the concentration camps?

For Whitman, the unity of the nation required faithfulness to the essence, the sacred core, of the nation, and to the symbols representing that national essence.[27] Lowell sought to root that essence of the American way of life (both the democratic rights of the individual and the duty, inseparable from those rights, of the individual to the nation) in the experience of the ancient Israelites and American Puritans. The appeal to the ancient Israelites was certainly no coincidence, for the Deuteronomic legal code combined provisions for fairness and justice for the individual with the stated intention to put an end in the promised land to the practice of "everyone doing what seems right to himself."[28] As a matter of fact, the ancient Israelites believed that the promised land would belong to the chosen people only as long as that chosen people remained faithful to the law and the traditions of their ancestors. So the issue was also understood both in the War of 1812, the culmination of which was the miracu-

---

27. See also, for example, Whitman's lecture, "The Death of Abraham Lincoln," given fifteen years after the assassination, "Then there is a cement to the whole people, subtler, more underlying, than any thing in written constitution, or courts or armies—namely, the cement of a death identified thoroughly with that people, at his head, and for its sake. Strange, (is it not?) that battles, martyrs, agonies, blood, even assassination, should so condense—perhaps only really, lastingly condense—a nationality."
28. Deuteronomy 12:6.

lous—as it was understood at the time—victory of Andrew Jackson at New Orleans, and the American Civil War. In words strikingly reminiscent of the vision and the plea of the pre-exilic prophets of ancient Israel for a new unity and covenant between "all Israel" and God, Abraham Lincoln proclaimed a day of national fast (proclamation of March 30, 1863) in the following manner.

> ... may we not justly fear that the awful calamity of civil war which now desolates the land may be but a punishment inflicted upon us for our presumptuous sins, to the needful end of our national reformation as a whole people? ... We have grown in numbers, wealth, and power as no other nation has ever grown; but we have forgotten God. Let us then rest humbly in the hope authorized by the divine teachings that the united cry of the nation will be heard on high, and answered with blessings no less than the pardon of our national sins, and the restoration of our now divided and suffering country to its former happy condition of unity and peace.

In both the War of 1812 and the Civil War the promised land of liberty was saved from destruction; and both victories were catalysts for an outpouring of professed loyalty and rededication to the nation.

Conclusion

In the century after the Civil War, there have been three challenges to the idea and reality of the nation of the United States as one people, one land, one law. The latest and most significant challenge was whether or not all members of the nation were entitled to equal protection under the *lex terrae*; that is, the violation of the civil liberties of Black Americans. As we are all aware of the civil rights legislation of the last approximately thirty years, I shall not discuss this matter further. Neither of the other two challenges, the American Indian population and Black nationalism, have represented a significant threat to the existence of the nation. Nonetheless, both of these instances raise some interesting questions regarding nationality, and thus are worthy of brief consideration.

With the passage of the Indian Removal Bill (1830), the Indians within the territory of the United States were forced into territories which were designated as their own or were given legal right to their own existing tribal territories. As these territories are administered under tribal law, they constitute separate pockets of *Rechtsgemeinschaften* within the United States. In the last several years and especially after the passage of the Indian Child Welfare Act (1979), an interesting legal dispute has arisen as to the extent of the authority of an Indian tribe over the determination of who is entitled to adopt an Indian child. There have recently been cases involving the Navajos, Choctaws, and Apaches. In each of these cases, the state social service agency has found white parents to adopt the Indian babies. In each case, the respective tribal council of the tribe of which the mother is a member has challenged the adoption and sued for custody of the child based on the argument that the tribe has jurisdiction, even when the baby was born outside the reservation. These disputes raise the issue of the existence of legal communities of a distinct territory and people within the territorial boundaries of the United States. However, except for the unfortunate lives of these children (the preliminary judgments have tended to recognize joint custody even in the case of a fourteen-year-old Apache girl who was adopted by white parents when she was an infant), today such occurrences are mainly of theoretical interest. According to the 1980 census, only $6/10$ of 1% of the population of the United States was considered to be Indian; and of that $6/10$ of 1%, only 32% live on territories designated as Indian.

Regarding Black nationalism, quite clearly the vast majority of Black Americans within the United States desire and have desired integration into American society as citizens of the United States. The only exception to this fact was perhaps the Universal Negro Improvement Association of the Black Jamaican Marcus Garvey. During especially the period from 1915 to 1920 a number of factors converged such as a dramatic decline in immigration, increased demand for labor by the war industries, a significant migration of Black Americans from the South to the North and the participation of 400,000 Black Americans in the U.S. army during the First World War. One of the results of these converging factors was an increased hope among Black Americans for a better life in the United States; and there was a better life for many. However, with an end to the war, industrial production declined and many of the returning Black soldiers became unemployed civilians. In addition, racial prejudice continued, and the period also saw a dramatic increase in the membership of the Ku Klux Klan—an increase which was not reversed until around 1925. In 1917, race riots broke out in East St. Louis, and in 1919 the same occurred in Chicago[29] and Washington. Many of the previous hopes of Black Americans turned to despair. It was within this context of frustration and despair that Garvey caught the attention of many Black Americans. No doubt his popularity was due more to an expressed pride of many Black Americans in their race rather than a desire to become a separate nation or to return to Africa. Certainly there were also promi-

---

29. For the Chicago riot of 1919, see *The Negro in Chicago. A Study of Race Relations and a Race Riot in 1919. The Chicago Commission on Race Relations* (Chicago: University of Chicago Press, 1922).

nent Black Americans such as Philip Randolph and Robert Abbott who opposed the separatism of Garvey. In any event, whatever popularity Garvey's movement had at one time achieved, it was dissipated after a few years. Today, besides possibly a few professors of departments of Black Studies, the only people who believe in the existence of a Black nation within the territory of the United States appear to be Mikhail Gorbachev and his advisers who have been busy exhuming from some dustbin a few obscure, sixty-year-old pamphlets of the American Community Party on the so-called theory of the "Black Belt."

Membership in the nation has been determined by the attenuated primordial criteria of birth in the territory and territorial inhabitation. It has been these primordial attributes which have provided formal, democratically acceptable criteria for the determination of citizenship. These criteria have provided boundaries for the nation. Membership is not determined by a voluntary, conscious affirmation of, in the case of the United States, the U.S. Constitution—a kind of adult baptism. The argument could be made that a consistent embodiment of liberalism would require such a conscious and continual affirmation. However, many problems would arise as a result of such an argument. I mention only one here. Who would be the judge of the sincerity of such an affirmation? So much for consistency.

Once again, the primordial referents of the national collective consciousness reveal a certain paradox of the theory of universal natural rights—all men have inalienable rights, that is, all men within the same territorially (and often linguistically) defined nation-state. It is this paradox which is the foundation of much of the "tension" of the collective awareness of America of itself; that is, a particular nation chosen by Providence to be the bearer of natural, universal democratic freedoms. One may observe the consequences of the attempt to eliminate this "tension" in the swings in proposed immigration policy from hypocritical utopianism (open the borders), which denies the primordial reference in American nationality, to intolerance against the ethnically alien, which denies civil liberties.

Co-residence in the territory of the nation has provided the basis for the kinship of the "people" of the nation. For example, when an American is kidnapped and executed by terrorists one is outraged, to be sure, by the injustice done to a fellow human being. However, we also find that most Americans are outraged that a "fellow" American—one of "their own"—has been murdered. These other Americans probably have never had any face-to-face contact with the kidnapped victim, yet they consider this person to be part of their "American family." This phenomenon of kinship attributed to those who reside in the territory of the nation appears to be characteristic of many nations some of which have also, at times, further entertained the belief in a putative genetic stock common to the members of the nation. We should also note that this kinship of the nation is not exclusively a modern phenomenon as can be ascertained from the incorporation of Edomites, Calebites, and Kenites who dwelled in the land of Israel into the kinship structure of the descendants of Abraham, Isaac, and Jacob.

Fascism has attempted to undermine the boundary of territory for the determination of membership in the nation. America, too, has had its nativists; one need only recall the "Know-nothing" movement of the 1850s and such later figures as John Fiske, Father Coughlin, and George Lincoln Rockwell. Through a demagogic exploitation of the attachments to and beliefs in primordial objects, they attempted to undermine both the territorially generated kinship of the members of the nation and the territorially bounded realm of the public and civil society, which recognizes diversity of opinions, pursuits, and activities. For example, there have been occasional attempts to equate "true Americanism" with white Anglo-Saxon Protestantism.

The political conclusion to be drawn from the danger to liberal democracy posed by such attempts and movements is not to disavow or ignore the existence of primordial attachments in the conduct of the life of the individual and of the life of the nation. In any event, the significance of primordiality is persistent and resilient as we can observe from the continuing beliefs in a chosen people and a promised land, or some variation thereof. The problem posed in politics is not ignoring such primordial attachments; but rather, acknowledging them within the context of liberal democracy. It is, once again and as we began our discussion, a question of the proper proportion.

We seek knowledge through the exercise of reason, discussion, and debate. We seek to improve the life of man in this world. We stand for the democratic liberties of man. However, we also acknowledge—and political responsibility demands such acknowledgment—the legacy of the Old Testament. Edward Everett Hale, the author of the immensely popular *The Man Without a Country*, written in the midst of the American Civil War in the summer of 1863, put it quite well when he wrote in the preface of his novel, "... the tie which binds you and me to the country which takes care of us is a tie as real and it involves duties as distinct as the tie which binds a boy to his mother, to whom he owed his life and who always takes care of him."

Chapter 10

Nationality and Religion

In an effort to establish some order to remarks on a relation that is theoretically so complex and historically so varied as the one between nationality and religion, the following discussion of that relation is divided into two sections. The intention of the first section is to clarify analytically the distinction between nationality and religion. Such a clarification must also consider the difficulties in maintaining this distinction. The second section briefly presents a comparative sketch of the relation between religion and nationality in which the limitations of that sketch must also be admitted.

The Distinction between Religion and Nationality

There exists a theoretical muddle that has landed many considerations of the relation between nationality and religion in a thicket of confusion. The confusion is not unwarranted; for both nationality and religion are structures that order human cognition and action, each drawing upon and permeating the other. Nevertheless, the confusion threatens not only to obscure the complicated ways that religion has influenced nationality, but also to eliminate religion altogether as a factor of such influence. Especially two traditions of analysis of this relation have contributed to this confusion.

It has occasionally been argued that there is no real distinction between nationality and religion. The most articulate, early version of this argument by Emile Durkheim saw "in the Divinity only society transfigured and symbolically expressed" (1974: 52); that is, "the idea of society is the soul of religion" (1947: 419). Thus, religion was understood by Durkheim not only to arise out of social life itself, but also to be a system of ideas by which individuals collectively represented to themselves the society to which they belonged and their relations to it (Evans-Pritchard 1965: 57).

At stake in Durkheim's understanding of religion, which continues to exert a powerful influence on the social sciences, is whether religion is an independent variable in both the constitution of, and subsequent influence on, nationality; or, as with Durkheim, it is limited to being a consequence of the representation of society by society. It is difficult to know epistemologically what exactly "consequence" means within Durkheim's explanatory framework, a difficulty compounded by the frequent and fashionable recourse to the obfuscatory term "reflection," as in "the collective symbols are a reflection of solidarity." Ultimately, what is at stake is the imaginative capacity of the mind to transcend the social environment.

To acknowledge that one is not the master of one's life may, as Durkheim argued, lead one to recognize the power of society over the individual. However, as Alexander Goldenweiser (1922: 371-74) observed in his criticism of Durkheim's analysis of religion as the representation and worship of such power, the acknowledgment that one is not the master of one's life may just as well arise out of an awe before the magnificence and enormity of nature upon which the individual *and* society are dependent. The recognition of such dependency may, in turn, be directed to a search for a meaningful account of what otherwise may be meaningless, for example: for the individual, his or her own suffering and death; for the collectivity, its threatened or actual destruction. Such a search indicates that religion arises out of the rationalizing capacity of the mind, the direction of which follows the categorial principle or principles specific to the world of religion and those needs of human beings to which this world is a response. These include the assertion of meaning to the existence of human life, both individually and collectively, and the universe to counter the distress of life in this world and to protest against the annihilation of the personality of both the individual and the nation (Nilsson 1960: 419; see Weber 1978: 451).

This search for meaning in response to these religious needs has led to a recognition of varying kinds of power that, while believed to exist beyond this world—thereby indicating the necessity to distinguish religion from society—are also believed to have bearing on the affairs of this world—thereby indicating the possibility of a convergence of religion and nationality. Such a convergence is more likely insofar as the protest against the annihilation of the personality takes the direction of a belief in one's existence beyond death not in heaven but through the descendants of one's family and nation. In this case, the meaning attributed to death, specifically in war, is that it serves the continued existence of oneself through the continued existence of one's nation (see Weber 1946a: 335). In any event, Durkheim's restriction of the belief in a power or powers greater than that of the individual to the society upon which the individual is dependent represents an overly limited view of the mind's imaginative capacity.

The necessity of the analytical distinction between religion and nationality, indicating a weakness of Durkheim's analysis, irrespective of the latter's contribution to describing how religion and its rites and ceremonies contribute to maintaining the solidarity of society, may be seen in prophecy. It is often the case that there are competing prophetic visions (for example, in the history of ancient Israel, those of Jeremiah and Hananiah). The existence of competing prophecies appears inexplicable within Durkheim's explanatory framework, unless one assumes that such competing prophecies are in some way expressions of differing degrees of intensity of solidarity. This assumption does not seem plausible; for such visions do not differ in degree, but are opposed to one another. Moreover, prophetic statements such as Amos 3:2—"Only you [Israel] have I [Yahweh] known of all the families of the earth; therefore, I will punish you for all your iniquities"—can be reasonably understood to have been destructive of the solidarity of the *gôy* (nation) of ancient Israel.[1] Certainly Jeremiah's prophecies were viewed by many of the Judaeans as being so (Jeremiah 20; 26; 38)!

It is possible to understand Amos's prophetic denunciation of Israel's iniquities as serving to constitute a renewed national solidarity through a reinterpreted self-understanding of Israel as God's chosen, but now properly disciplined, people in light of the military defeat in 722 B.C.E. of the northern kingdom at the hands of what Isaiah believed was God's agent of Israel's spiritual rectification, Assyria (Grosby 1999 [in this volume, pp. 92–119]). A similar attempt to reinforce the faltering symbolic center of the defeated nation may be observed in Jeremiah's prophecy of a "new covenant" between Yahweh and Israel (Jer 31:31) either in anticipation of, or in light of, the destruction of the first temple at the hands of Babylonia in 587 B.C.E. The attempts to provide meaning to the defeat of one's nation has become standard fare, for example, during the dismemberment of Poland in the nineteenth century, Adam Mickiewicz's *Konrad Wallenrod* and especially Juliusz Slowacki's *Anhelli*.[2]

---

1. For the translation of *gôy* as a nation, see Speiser (1960), Cody (1964).

2. Another example, brought to my attention by Dr. Bruce Cauthen, the reinterpretation of the Confederacy as a saving remnant being disciplined by God for future vindication in light of its defeat in the American Civil War (Wilson 1980: 58–78). For the Islamic response to the defeat of the 1967 war with Israel, the explanation of idolatrous Arabism as the cause, see Sivan (1997).

Even if such a "Durkheimian" understanding of the prophecies of Amos and Jeremiah has merit, the conceptual turn by the Israelite prophets to a purpose or meaning to the events of this world, although it may have accounted for national defeat while maintaining a belief in the nation and its God, necessarily opened the door to a history that was understood as being the theater of one God (see Amos 9:7) whose existence and standards, insofar as they can be grasped, necessarily transcend this world. The classic, symbolic expression of the other-worldly origin of such standards are the Ten Commandments portrayed as being given to Moses *from* God above. The world religions that assert a fundamental distinction between two realms—the events of "this world," on the one hand, and the deity and its standards of the "other world" that provide meaning to those events, on the other (for example, in Christianity, that of Caesar and that of God; Matt 22:21)—are what Max Weber called the world religions of the book and what Karl Jaspers (1953; see Eisenstadt 1986) referred to as the *geistige* developments of the axial age.

The development of these religions has, in turn, caused innumerable difficulties for the solidarity of the national state—the stability of its self-understanding—for the events of this world unfailingly prove to be resistant to being brought into order with the perceived purpose to history, that is, the purpose of God. Such difficulties existed even for Israel, believed to be chosen by God, as can be seen in the anxious oscillation over what it meant to be chosen. Was the relation between Israel and Yahweh unconditional, conditional, or could Israel be rejected altogether by Yahweh and, hence, face annihilation, the possibility of which is posed in Exod 32:9-10? Eventually, the meaning of the corporate distress of this world for ancient Israel, in light of the massive defeats of 67-70 c.e. and 132-35 c.e., could only be maintained by situating it within an increasingly other-worldly messianic expectation.

This other-worldly realm, its deities and its standards are transcendent insofar as they cannot be seen or touched, but can be perceived only by an act of the imagination. While believed to be other-worldly in origin, such standards are appealed to in order to order the actions of individuals in this world through the expectation that they be conformed to; for example, in Confucianism the emperor must have the "mandate of heaven" to rule legitimately (Schwartz 1975). This religious appeal to transcendent standards by which to judge the affairs of this world has contributed to maintaining the solidarity of the national society through the assertion of a meaningful order in contrast to the chaos that was often understood to hold sway outside the borders of the nation (or civilization), hence among the barbarians (Eliade 1987: 20-65) or among the demons of the jungle, as formulated in the Hindu *Ramayana* (Pollock 1993). However, the belief in the existence of an other-worldly, ideal realm and especially the institutional expression of this belief—an institutional expression which has existed most notably in the Occident with its church and organized priesthood and which, as a result, has made the appeal to such standards more likely—has also meant an ever-present potential for societal discord and even revolution because this realm exists as a counter-factual ideal to be realized (see Lewy 1974). Even in China—where in contrast to the Occident, the consequences of the divergence between these two realms were relatively muted because the Confucians were organized not as a separate church and priesthood but as a state bureaucracy (Eisenstadt 1986: 291-98)—whether or not the emperor was entitled to the "mandate of heaven" could be questioned. This had revolutionary implications; to cite only two from many examples, the revolt of the Yellow Turbans in 184 c.e., and the Taiping Rebellion of 1850-64 which, despite Christian elements, drew upon this Confucian conception. That this was so was precisely the criticism of China and Confucianism made by the Japanese revivalists of Shinto during the eighteenth and nineteenth centuries (Yoshino 1992: 46-49; Bellah 1957: 100; Holtom 1947: 78-79).

Durkheim, of course, recognized the existence of societal discord. However, he did not, in contrast to Weber (1978: 1158-1211), view it as an inevitable consequence of conflicting orientations of the mind to the affairs of this world and to an other-worldly meaning attributed to those affairs. Rather, Durkheim understood discord to be a pathological consequence of the dislocations arising from the societal transition from mechanical solidarity (*Gemeinschaft*) to organic solidarity (*Gesellschaft*). However, the potential for discord that the world religions, "the city of god," pose for the "city of man" cannot so easily be historically located. It is thus more accurate to recognize, in contrast to Durkheim, the possibility of not only degrees of independence of the mind from the social environment, but also that this independence may manifest itself in qualitatively different directions. This latter possibility was the presupposition of Weber's analysis of the *eruption* of charisma—hence, the need to distinguish analytically these orientations of the mind that result in religion and nationality. More will have to be said about this distinction.[3]

---

3. Durkheim's analysis of religion as an idealization and intensification of the solidarity of the *conscience collective* is more complicated than the above summary might suggest for it recognizes: that cognition and action are individually centered (the principle of methodological individualism); the existence of collective consciousness

A second tradition of analysis, while seemingly recognizing a distinction between nationality and religion, has blurred the distinction, as indicated by this tradition's widely employed terms: civil religion, secular religion, political religion, and ideology.[4] Corresponding to these terms are the worthy attempts to describe the consensus or solidarity of the nation through such ultimately unsatisfactory yet nonetheless analytically suggestive categories as "the religious dimension," "religiosity," or, as Durkheim formulated it, "la vie sérieuse."

This tradition of analysis can be further differentiated into two objects of concern, the first being those patterns of belief, constitutive of the nation that incorporates religious traditions. Perhaps the best representative of this concern is the influential work of Robert Bellah on civil religion (1970; Bellah and Hammond 1980). Bellah drew attention to how aspects of a religious tradition could be constitutive elements in the image of the nation that became shared among its members, the collective self-consciousness. Examples are the Puritan self-understanding of being a new people chosen by God to settle in the promised land of America; or, following Tocqueville (1969: 287-301, 235-37), the individualism of Protestantism as an element of American self-understanding; or the Shinto revival of the shrine of the sun goddess at Ise as part of the restoration of the Japanese emperor to actual sovereignty in the service of consolidating a national body free from foreign influence (Bellah 1957: 81; see Blacker 1971: 529). Often this analysis focused attention on those events that were not part of a religious tradition per se, but rather were events that drew upon such a tradition, for example: drawing upon the Christian understanding of the death of Jesus, the portrayal of Abraham Lincoln as the slain saviour—sacrificial victim—of the nation; or the Thanksgiving holiday in the United States as a feast of national communion. (As a classic example of rites of national communion, see Edward Shils's and Michael Young's 1956 [1975] analysis of the coronation of Elizabeth II.) According to the Durkheimian tradition of analysis, since these national ceremonies

---

whose referents constitutive of the symbolic center of the collective consciousness are objects of contemplation of varying salience; and those objects exist independently of their realization, what Durkheim referred to as a *sui generis* existence of "exteriority," that is, objective mind (for the latter, see Freyer 1998 and Popper 1979: 106-90). Nevertheless, for establishing the necessity of distinguishing analytically nationality from religion, this summary suffices.

4. For an evaluation of recent examples of this tradition see A. D. Smith (1998: 97-116). I note in passing a few antecedents to this tradition of analysis: Augustine's discussion in bk. 6 of *The City of God* of Varro's category of "civil theology" and Rousseau's discussion of "civil religion" in chap. 8 of bk. 4 of *On the Social Contract*.

such as the American Thanksgiving or the British coronation function to maintain the structural continuity of the national society (Radcliffe-Brown 1965a) by reaffirming and thereby strengthening the sentiments on which the social order depends (Radcliffe-Brown 1965b), they were indistinguishable from religion; they were, in fact, religion.

Despite the conflation unavoidable in a functional analysis between religion and nationality, expressed most notably in the use of such terms as "religious dimension," Bellah has generally sought to maintain the distinction between religion and nationality by noting that religion claims to derive from an authority that transcends all earthly power. Such a claim is certainly the case with what Bellah calls the historical religions, that is, the axial-age, world religions of the book.

The problem of maintaining this distinction is more complicated with the pre-axial religions, specifically where there exist the seemingly this-worldly "god of the land" and "god of the lineage"; for the worship of such this-worldly deities apparently collapses the distinction between a this-worldly realm and an other-worldly realm, thereby amounting to society worshiping itself. Thus, the strongest case for the category of civil religion or civil theology beyond that of a functional similarity, for example, the fashionable description of several decades ago that Soviet Marxism functioned as a religion for the Soviet Union, would present itself in pre-axial societies; hence, the attractiveness of Durkheim's analysis of Australian totemism. However, the merit of this line of thought is not the forced and misleading one given by Durkheim in the opening pages of *The Elementary Forms of Religious Life* that, by so doing, one discovers what is fundamental in religion. Rather, it indicates the possibility that modern nationality contains of necessity the pre-axial elements of the "god of the land" and "god of the lineage," albeit reformulated in the age of monotheism as patriotism (or, as an indication of Christianity's accommodation to such deities, the national saints of which the Polish saint Stanisław, canonized in 1253, is a good example [N. Davies 1982: 70; Symmons-Symonolewicz 1983: 13]). More will have to be said about this problem. In any event many analyses of "civil religion" brush aside the distinction between the "city of god" and the "city of man" and the ubiquitous tensions within the nation that the distinction conveys by taking as their point of departure an understanding of civil religion as a national collective self-consciousness formed from a fusion of religion and politics, where, as a consequence, there exist only shadings between religion, civil religion, nationalism, and religious nationalism (Hammond 1980: 43; Juergensmeyer 1993: 11–41).

The second concern, contributing to blurring the distinction between religion and nationality, is the analysis of the modern ideology of nationalism of which the most notable example is the work of Elie Kedourie (1993; 1971). A number of years ago, the eminent historian of ancient Greek religion Martin Nilsson wrote a thoughtful essay, "Religion as man's protest against the meaninglessness of events" (1960: 391–464). However, the point of departure for Kedourie is that religion can no longer provide such a protest because modern life has swept religion aside. Yet, the need for meaning around which life can be organized persists; thus, so it is argued, nationalism today fulfils this need by maintaining the organic solidarity of *Gesellschaft*. It is this version of functionalism, where nationalism serves as the religion of "modernity," which has given us the category "political religion": the nation has become god.

The important factor emphasized by Kedourie was that the modern doctrine of nationalism was ideological, that is, millenarian and Manichaean. The element of millennialism had been introduced by the world religions of the axial age because they had posited the existence of an other-worldly ideal realm that would be made manifest on earth at the end of time (or at the end of the millennium). Nationalism incorporated and perverted this millennial tradition by seeking the realization of this other-worldly realm in this world at this time. The vehicle for this realization was to be the national state. Thus, the "true church" became equated with the nation which, in the case of Bolshevism and fascism, became equated with the leader of the party (Mosse 1973). Anyone who did not agree with the nationalistic program of the party and its Führer was viewed, in Manichaean fashion, as an agent of darkness, an implacable enemy to be destroyed. As an analysis of the totalitarian potential of nationalism, Kedourie's contribution is a lasting one; but it also blurs the distinction between religion and nationality.

The deficiency of these approaches that seek to explain the solidarity of the nation as a modern religion is that they do not account for either the *limit* of the contribution of religion to national solidarity, or the *limit* of the capacity of nationalism to be a religion (or, where undertaken, the nationalization of the existing religion, for example, the attempt of the Nazis to create a German Christian church with its "pastoral nationalism"). In the case of Nazi Germany, the first limit was the call of 22 September 1933 for a confessional church "independent of the state and the pressure of all political power." To be sure, the opposition of German Protestantism and Catholicism to the nationalism and fascism of the Nazis was all too selective and muted; but it was nonetheless an opposition (the martyrdom of the Protestant Bonhoeffer and the Catholic Delp) that theoretically must be taken into account. As to the limit to the nationalization of religion, one can point to the Nazi Martin Borman's confidential memorandum of 1941 that asserted that National Socialism and Christianity were incompatible (Bracher 1970: 379-90).

The salience of such limits, indicating the necessity of distinguishing nationality (and nationalism) from religion, vary historically and by civilization. In Christianity, as exemplified by the opposition of Bonhoeffer and Delp to the Nazis, that which belonged to God served, as such, as a limit to the aspirations of Caesar. In Islam the divine law, the *Shari'a*, and the universality of the *Ummah* have served as limits to its nationalization. The tension, to be sure significantly less, between these realms may also be found in pre-axial societies, as the example, often referred to, of the Babylonian New Year ceremony (Frankfort 1948: 318-20) and the conflicts between priest and pharaoh during the reign of Akhenaten indicate. Such tensions, whether intense or relaxed, suggest an incommensurable plurality of orientations of the mind.

This incommensurateness has been obscured by the admittedly theoretically suggestive concentration on "transcendence" in the phenomenological analyses of religion, for example, the work of Friedrich Schleiermacher (1994), Rudolf Otto (1978), Geradus Van der Leeuw (1963). The phenomenon of transcendence–the transcendence of the ego beyond immediate, individually centered satisfaction, or, as Rousseau (1987) formulated it in 1762, "sentiments of sociability"–is the underpinning of such categories as "the religious dimension." Let us consider the phenomenon in an effort to clarify the distinction between religion and nationality, thereby laying the groundwork for a framework of their relation.

Schleiermacher (1994: 4) thought that there were two contrasting orientations of the mind: one directed towards the pleasure of the individual self; the second directed away from the self, a longing to be a part of the greater whole that operates on the self and upon which the self is dependent (1994: 45-51). According to Schleiermacher, the human grounding of religiosity was the second orientation of the mind to self-transcendence, the desire to participate in a higher life that is held in common.[5] For Durkheim (1947: 36), the transcendence of the self, "the elan, even the enthusiasm, with which we perform a moral act [that] takes us outside ourselves and above our nature," was also the basis of religion. However,

---

5. For our purposes, we need not consider Schleiermacher's distinction between intuition, feeling, and abstract thought. For the necessity of the social element in religion, see his discussion of Genesis 2 (1994: 71-72).

for Durkheim, unlike Schleiermacher, the object of that transcendence—which exists outside the individual, having absolute power over the individual and upon which the individual has the feeling of perpetual dependence—could only be society.

This focus on transcendence, while appropriate, raises other problems; for nationality also has transcendental elements—the boundary-generating referents of tradition—in its constitution. This has been rightly insisted upon in the so-called ethno-symbolic analysis of nationality, for example, the work of John Armstrong (1982), Anthony Smith (1986), and John Hutchinson (1987). The nation, like the family, is a structure of kinship. Both are structures of social relation, where the members are related to one another through the recognition, affirmed explicitly or implicitly and usually intermittently by each of the members, of the significance of vitality and its transmission. For the family, the objects of attention that unite the individuals as members of the family are the parents and the direct biological ancestors of the parents, who are understood as being the agents responsible for the creation and transmission of each of the lives of those individuals. For the nation, the consensual objects of attention constitutive of the relation of kinship are territorial co-residence and generally birth in that territory (of which the language one speaks is usually taken as a marker). Thus, both the social relation of the family and that of the nation have a definitive cognitive element manifested in the attributed significance (meaning) to the *this-worldly* origin, locus, and transmission of vitality; this orientation of the mind to the significance of vitality is what I, and Shils and Geertz before me, have meant by the term primordial. This attribution of meaning—a product of the mind—is the element of transcendence in the constitution of both the family and the nation; and it is expressed behaviorally when one affirms that significance by acting, at times with passionate devotion, as a member on behalf of the family or, as the case may be, the nation.

This meaningful element in the constitution of the family is relatively unalloyed as it is centered, but rarely exclusively so (for example, the religious requirements of circumcision in Judaism or infant baptism in Christianity), on the recognition of direct biological ancestors. However, social relations beyond that of the family are generally explicitly allowed with other orientations; in the case of that temporally deep, territorially relatively extensive community of descent, the nation, the significance of vitality coexists, with varying degrees of tension, with other orientations of the mind such as relatively rationalized assertions of meaning and civil order, respectively, religion and law. A necessary, religious element within the constitutive self-understanding that every nation has of itself is its place in the order of the universe.

A relatively stable configuration of these different, conceptually intertwined orientations of a primordially centered vitality, a religious meaning that transcends that vitality, and civil order constitutes the symbolic core of the collective self-consciousness of every nation. Nevertheless, while these orientations permeate one another, they should be kept analytically distinct; for tensions exist among them.[6] The tension between a primordially centered vitality and a religious meaning that transcends that vitality seems, at least theoretically, to be minimal in pre-axial societies because the significance attributed to the ethnic and national collectivity as the this-worldly bearers of vitality appears to be the primary focus of the meaning of the formally other-worldly deities. Indicative of this pre-axial convergence of these two orientations are those assertions of the collectivity as the territorial center of the universe and the deity as either the god of the land and/or the ancestor of the collectivity: in antiquity, for example, the so-called Memphite theology of ancient Egypt and the Babylonian *Enuma Elish*; its modern versions are the "familism" of Shinto (Yoshino 1992: 91–92, 24–27) and, with complications, the religious myth of ethnic election (A. D. Smith 1999). However, even in antiquity, the distinction between these two orientations, however muted, still exists; for the household gods (the Lares and the Penates) usually differ from the divine creator of the putative national lineage and the world. Indeed, because even in pre-axial religions the deity of the collectivity was understood to be involved in the creation of the world, the potential existed for a jurisdictional expansiveness beyond that of the initial collectivity, as was manifested in, for example, sanctuaries whose sacredness was acknowledged by different societies or the proclivity to syncretism.

Certainly the world religions of the book exist, at least doctrinally, in tension with the orientation to vitality conveyed by the structure of the family. This can be seen in, for example, the former's hostility to the latter's "household gods" (or as formulated in Matt 8:22, "Let the dead bury their own dead"; see also Matt 12:48–50) and Augustine's tortured discussion of the place of God in impregnation (1984: bk. 12, chap. 26, and bk. 22, chap. 24). This tension is abundantly clear in the prohibition

---

6. The shifting laws of immigration and citizenship, and the conflicts over them, are consequences of the tension within the symbolic core of the nation between the orientation to vitality, which is relatively resistant to rationalization, and a rationalization of the orientation to order.

against sexual relations among members of the Buddhist religious community, the monastic Sangha. And certainly Christianity, at least as understood by Paul, exists in tension with nationality, as can be seen in his proclamations of universal brotherhood (Gal 3:28; Rom 10:12) and his "deterritorialization" of Christianity as expressed by the "new Jerusalem" that is not of this earth but "above" (Gal 4:26) (see W. D. Davies 1974). Nevertheless, these concerns of life—vitality, meaning and order—as such permeate one another, achieving historically varied configurations. No creation of the mind, except that which is most removed from the concerns of life such as mathematics, exists unalloyed. Thus religion, as one such configuration, although its primary focus is the meaning of life, cannot avoid addressing, in varying degrees, vitality and its transmission. The nation, as another such configuration, although its primary force is the territorial organization of vitality, cannot avoid incorporating, in varying degrees, into its symbolic core a meaning of life that transcends that vitality.

If one confines one's analysis to transcendence per se, then any categorial distinction between these different orientations, and between religion and nationality, eventually dissolves, as is implied by such terms as "religiosity," "the religious dimension," "sacrality," and so forth. One is then left to distinguish various forms of transcendence of the self either by degree of intensity; or by degree of the scope of the social dimension ranging, putatively seamlessly, from the family to the nation to the universal true church as was the case in the Christian neo-Platonism of Augustine (1984: bk. 19, chaps. 5–13) and Aquinas (for example, *Summa Theologica*, Questions 90–97), and as occasionally asserted today for Islam (Piscatori 1986: 83–85). One is thus left analytically helpless to account for the historically ubiquitous tensions between religion and nationality. This is not to deny, as Simmel (1997: 156–57) rightly observed, an "analogy between the individual's behavior toward the deity and his behavior toward society" such that there are "strong similarities between the religious and the sociological forms of existence" (see A. D. Smith 1999: 338). Therein lies both the attraction and the danger of confining one's analysis to transcendence per se.

Rather than remaining content with the observation, important as it is, of transcendence as a modality of being necessary for the meaningful orders provided by both religion and nationality, one must distinguish the patterns of transcendence between them and *within each* by differentiating the objects of reference of the transcendence. One must, for example, distinguish the love a child has for his or her parent from the love one has for one's country—patriotism—and both from the love a worshiper has for his or her god.

If the necessity of differentiating various objects of transcendence in order to distinguish respectively various patterns of transcendence is granted, what, then, is distinctive of religion? Religion is a relation of individuals to one another whose object of reference is an other-worldly being or power(s) and/or an existence beyond this world that, in turn, provides meaning to one's existence in this world. To say this may be not to say very much; but it allows us to distinguish the other-worldly object(s) of religious transcendence from the this-worldly objects of the pattern of transcendence constitutive of nationality, namely, various forms of kinship.

This distinction appears to be most justified with the world religions of the axial age that, once again, posit an other-worldly deity and/or an other-worldly existence (for example, heaven or Nirvana) over and against this world insofar as these religions have minimized the incorporation of the this-worldly loci of vitality, lineage, and territory, into their doctrinal configurations. This point was made by Max Weber (1951: 237) when he observed that the great achievement of ethical religions was to shatter the fetters of the sib by establishing the superior community of faith and a common ethical way of life in opposition to the community of blood. However, as I have observed in passing, even the world religions, either doctrinally or more often historically, cannot altogether ignore other concerns of life, specifically the orientation to vitality that is so manifest in nationality. This point was also made by Weber (1978: 1173), at least this is how I view the significance of his observation that concessions of all the great monotheistic religions to polytheism are inevitable. The difficult case is, yet again, the pre-axial religions with their seemingly this-worldly deities of lineage and territory. Yet, even here, as a justification for the necessity of this distinction, I point to the widespread right of asylum in the sanctuaries or at the altars of the deities of these pre-axial religions.[7] The right of asylum appears to presuppose a belief in a dimension and power beyond a particular society; and especially so when the sanctuary was viewed as an international place of refuge.[8] Such

---

7. For recent discussions of asylum in the ancient Near East and Egypt, see Weinfeld (1995: 120–32); and in the Hellenistic world, see Rigsby (1996). For an older discussion, Westermarck remains useful.

8. For the likelihood of Aleppo as one such sanctuary, see Greenfield (1991), Grosby (1995: 348–49 [in this volume, pp. 160–162]). See also Tacitus's (*Annals* III.60) discussion of asylum during the reign of Tiberius.

a right certainly represents a point of tension between the hierocratic and political authority (as was evident in the early European Middle Ages when the right underwent several restrictions [see Goebel 1976: 150–55]), even where that political authority is itself believed to be divine, as in ancient Egypt.

A Sketch of the Relation between Religion and Nationality

These previous considerations provide a framework for differentiating the extent to which religion is a factor in the constitution and continued existence of nationality based on the degree to which the this-worldly objects of reference to vitality, lineage (ethnicity), and territory, are incorporated into a particular religion. Put abstractly, where the this-worldly loci of vitality are elements within the religion, then there exists a convergence between religion and nationality. Where they are absent, then there exists a considerable degree of tension between religion and nationality.

Straightforward examples of convergence are those pre-axial, monolatrous religions where the jurisdiction of the deity is territorially circumscribed: the deity is explicitly conceived to be a god of the land; each nation has its own god; and that god is to be worshiped only within the national territory, its land. Examples of the "god of the land" are Chemosh of Moab, Qaus of Edom, and probably Assur of Assyria (Grosby 1991 [in this volume, pp. 13–51]).[9] It is also possible that in the pre-exilic worship of Yahweh sections of the Israelite population may have understood the jurisdiction of their God to be limited to Israelite land, as 1 Sam 26:19 would suggest, where David faces the prospect of "serving other gods" if he must flee Israel. Often, in these religions, the territory of the nation is portrayed as the home of the god or gods and the center of the world as one finds in both ancient Shinto and its modern revival.

Explicit references to the this-worldly loci of vitality are doctrinally absent in the monotheistic religions. Thus one would expect, at least theoretically, that in the axial-age civilizations there would be resistance to the emergence and continued existence of nations. The exception to this conceptual state of affairs is Judaism with its explicit recognition of the this-worldly loci of vitality of lineage and territory coexisting with universal monotheism. The explicit presence of these primordial objects of reference in the Old Testament accounts for the salience, but not the

---

9. So Machinist (1993: 81): "the Assyrian convention to write the names of Assyria, the city of Assur, and the national god Assur all as Assur which clearly marks the native understanding of the land as the extension of the city and god."

uniqueness, of the myth of ethnic election in the Occident (A. D. Smith 1999), hence serving as a significant contributing factor for a greater tendency to the formation of nations in Judaeo-Christian civilization (Hastings 1997; 1999).

The resistance of the axial-age civilizations to nationality is clearest in the case of Islam, for the tension between the orientation to vitality and the universal standards of the other world are settled in favor of the latter. Islam, as a religion of "emissary" prophecy (Weber 1946b: 291-92) enjoins an other-worldly transformation of this world through actions in this world, the consequence of which is, at least in principle, the ascendancy of the worldwide *Ummah*, the community of the faithful, with its *Shari'a* law applicable throughout *Dâr al-Islâm* at the expense of ethnic and national traditions (Hodgson 1974a: 185; 1975b: 108, 337, 349). Of course, events took a course more complicated than this characterization would imply, for example, the post-'Abbasid distinction between Caliph as head of the Muslim community and Sultan as political ruler of a particular dominion, or, later, between *'ulama* and Sultan—the sultanate often the vehicle for local traditions (Lapidus 1988: 142-48, 184-86, 353-58). Nevertheless, apparently indicative of this resistance to the continued existence of relatively extensive structures of kinship, the historians of Islamic civilization seem to be in general agreement that the emergence of nations within this civilization took place during the nineteenth century, and then as a result of European influence (Haim 1976; Kedourie 1971; Hodgson 1974c; Lapidus 1988; Lewis 1991; 1994).

While Islam has undermined the salience of attachments to such extensive structures of vitality as nationality, the relation between this world and the other world has been settled differently in Christianity and Buddhism. Because Christianity, in contrast to Islam, has doctrinally recognized the legitimacy of Caesar's realm and confined Paul's universalism to the church and the other world (for example, Augustine's distinction between two cities that was codified into the doctrine of the two swords by Pope Gelasisus I), a considerable degree of latitude remained open for the emergence and consolidation of territorial attachments. Apparently indicative of the continued existence of such territorial traditions within Christendom, many historians have dealt with the various ways Christianity has accommodated itself to them throughout its history (Mews 1982; Kantorowicz 1957). Buddhism has also not directly challenged various territorial structures of kinship. However, their continued existence was not a result of Buddhism's doctrinally legitimating those structures; rather, it was more a consequence of profound indifference to the affairs of this world that is characteristic of a religion of "exemplary" prophecy (Weber 1946b: 285). (Buddhism's lack of a unified church and hierarchy also contributed to the existence of *de facto* national traditions of Buddhism as in Burma and Sri Lanka.)

Such is a brief sketch of a modest framework for analyzing the relation between religion and nationality that turns on the existence, or lack thereof, of referents to this-worldly objects of vitality among the concepts constitute of the religion. The framework provides the broad outlines for comparative analysis; and it is especially helpful in accounting for the millennial elements in various traditions of monotheism that have been incorporated, tragically so, within various nationalistic movements (Armstrong 1997). Nevertheless, the explanatory utility of this framework is limited. This admission is not a result of questioning the validity of Weber's, Jaspers's and Eisenstadt's distinction between pre-axial, primordial religions of locality and lineage that have a high degree of magic, on the one hand, and doctrinal world religions that recognize a chasm between this-worldly and other-worldly realms. Rather, the limited explanatory utility of the framework is a result of so many complications that important qualifications abound. One such qualification arises from the recognition of the persistence and resilience of primordial attachments, specifically but not only nationality, within the axial-age civilizations that calls into question the depth and breadth of that chasm.

For example, even though Islam doctrinally rejects loyalty to those traditions constitutive of territorially extensive structures of nativity as inimical to the unity of the community of the faithful, a degree of "territorial fragmentation" of the *Ummah* occurred long before the twentieth century (Piscatori 1986: 62–69). Evidently, Islam accommodated itself to one such tradition, the Persian, when the Safavids converted Iran to Shi'ism (c. 1501) in opposition to the Ottoman Sunnism on its western border. And is it not the case that an awareness of Egypt as a distinct entity, has persisted, however latently, since the eighth century? Certainly the ethnic designation "Turk" has persisted.[10] The complications involving Buddhism go far beyond its existence as the state religion of the religiously tolerant King Asoka, as may clearly be seen in its historically early contribution to the formation of the ideal of a religiously and ethnically uniform Sinhalese nation, at least so one concludes from the *Mahāvaṃsa* (especially chap. 25) (see B. Smith 1978) and, today, in the worship of the "Four Warrant Gods" as the guardians of that nation

---

10. For a theoretically nuanced analysis of this tension among the Muslims of India and in the formation of Pakistan, see Robinson (1979).

(Gombrich and Obeyesekere 1988). And, despite its rejection of the "thirsts" of life as the cause of suffering, Buddhism has accommodated itself to the familial transmission of vitality, the household gods, as may be seen in the recognition, in Burma, of the protective spirit, the *nal*, of each household (Weber 1958: 261), and, in Sri Lanka, of the personal deity, the *iṣṭa dēvatā* (Gombrich and Obeyesekere 1988: 32–33, 39).

Christianity, as stated, doctrinally recognizes a conceptual opening that allows for the continuation of territorial attachments; however, the historical ubiquity of the relation between Christianity and territorial structures of nativity highlights how theoretically abstract even the category of world religion is from actual events. As the examples of this relation are well known, I mention only in passing a few of them: in the early history of Christendom, Armenian Christianity (Grosby 1996a [in this volume, pp. 120–149]); the portrayal of the Franks as the chosen people (Strayer 1971; Armstrong 1982: 152–58; Nelson 1988: 214–19); early doctrinal schisms that often fell along territorial and ethnic lines (Grosby 1996b [in this volume, pp. 166–190]); and, later, Anglicanism and the national churches of Eastern Orthodoxy; including the condemnation of the Bulgarian church for "phyletism" (Atiya 1968); the emergence of national saints such as Louis for French Catholicism and Sava for Serbian Orthodoxy; explicit concessions, as Rome's recognition of Gallican liberties; and the "territorialization" of Protestantism through the principle of *cuius regio, eius religio* of the Augsburg treaty of 1555.

The persistence of such primordial ties in ethnicity and nationality is one qualification to the above framework. A second qualification arises from the possibility that, rather than a contrast between the community of faith of the monotheistic world religions and the primordial religions of location and lineage, as presented by Weber, those world religions were often factors in the constitution of a territorially more expansive nation, as may be seen by contrasting ancient Greece with ancient Israel. On the one hand, in ancient Greece, the continued loyalty to the *polis* frustrated further developments of those adumbrations of nationality such as one finds in the trans-*polis* military alliance against Persia; Delphi as a common religious center; and references to the trans-*polis* designation *Hellenes* in the work of Hesiod, Herodotus, Aeschylus, Plato, and Isocrates (Walbank 1985). On the other hand, the conception of ancient Israel as a trans-tribal nation achieved stability. Many factors contributed to this difference: the marked geographical heterogeneity of Greece in contrast to Israel; the military success of David; and the establishment of Jerusalem as all-Israel's center which, even if historically limited to the reigns of David and Solomon, remained conceptually so in Deuterono-mistic history. However, it also seems probable that the conceptual con-solidation of Israel as a nation "from Dan to Beersheba" was also influenced by the rationalizing element of Israel's religion that was ab-sent in that of Greece. Within Christendom, the various conversions, willing or forced, during the early Middle Ages, to respectively various configurations of Christianity also contributed to the consolidation of na-tions, for example, the crusade against the Albigenses, a consequence of which was the incorporation of Toulouse into France.

A third qualification to the framework is, as previously stated, that within the conceptual center of each nation there is a religious element. The tradition of the analysis of civil religion is an acknowledgment of this element. Nationalism occurs when the primordial elements within that center achieve a contested ascendancy over the other orientations, often drawing upon and transforming the traditions of millennialism of the world religions. At times the potential for intolerance and the millen-nialism of the world religions achieve a contested ascendancy and con-verge with the primordial traditions, each and together at the expense of civil order, for example, in militant Hinduism. Nevertheless, there re-main varying degrees of tension between these heterogeneous orienta-tions of the mind, even when they permeate one another as elements within the national center—tension made all the more likely because each orientation is usually internally heterogeneous.

These qualifications indicate a misplaced emphasis in Weber's obser-vation of the inevitability of the monotheistic religions to make conces-sions to polytheism. Rather, they indicate that every society addresses in its own way the perennial concerns of life: vitality and its transmission, meaning that in varying degrees transcends that of vitality, and civil or-der. While the extent to which this analysis has clarified the theoretical muddle surrounding considerations of the relation between religion and nationality is limited, a more precise analysis will be more likely insofar as some of the problems of this relation have been brought to the surface.

References

Armstrong, John. 1982. *Nations before Nationalism*. Chapel Hill: University of North Carolina Press.

_____. 1997. "Religious nationalism and collective violence," *Nations and Nation-alism* 3(4):597–606.

Atiya, A. S. 1968. *A History of Eastern Christianity*. London: Metheun.

Augustine. 1984 [413–25]. *The City of God*. Harmondsworth: Penguin.

Bellah, Robert N. 1957. *Tokugawa Religion: The Values of Pre-Industrial Japan.* New York: Free Press.

_____. 1970 [1967]. "Civil religion in America," in *Beyond Belief: Essays on Religion in a Post-traditional World.* New York: Harper and Row.

Bellah, Robert N., and Hammond, Philip E. 1980. *Varieties of Civil Religion.* San Francisco: Harper and Row.

Blacker, Carmen. 1971. "The religions of Japan," in *Historia Religionum, vol. 2: Religions of the Present,* ed. C. Jouco Bleeker and Geo Widengren. Leiden: Brill.

Bracher, Karl Dietrich. 1970. *The German Dictatorship: The Origins, Structure and Effects of National Socialism.* New York: Praeger.

Cody, Aelred. 1964. "When is the Chosen People called a goy?" *Vetus Testamentum* 14:1–6.

Davies, Norman. 1982. *God's Playground: A History of Poland.* New York: Columbia University Press.

Davies, W. D. 1974. *The Gospel and the Land: Early Christianity and Jewish Territorial Doctrine.* Berkeley: University of California Press.

Durkheim Emile. 1974 [1906]. "The Determination of Moral Facts," in *Sociology and Philosophy.* New York: Free Press.

_____. 1947 [1912]. *The Elementary Forms of Religious Life.* New York: Free Press.

Eisenstadt, S. N. 1986. *The Origins and Diversity of Axial Age Civilizations.* Albany: State University of New York Press.

Eliade, Mircea. 1987 [1957]. *The Sacred and the Profane.* New York: Harcourt Brace.

Evans-Pritchard, E. E. 1965. *Theories of Primitive Religion.* Oxford: Oxford University Press.

Frankfort, Henri. 1948. *Kingship and the Gods.* Chicago: University of Chicago Press.

Freyer, Hans. 1998 [1928]. *Theory of Objective Mind: An Introduction to the Philosophy of Culture,* trans. Steven Grosby. Athens: Ohio University Press.

Goebel, Julius. 1976 [1937]. *Felony and Misdemeanor: A Study in the History of Criminal Law.* Philadelphia: University of Pennsylvania Press.

Goldenweiser, Alexander A. 1922. *Early Civilization: An Introduction to Anthropology.* New York: Alfred A. Knopf.

Gombrich, Richard, and Obeyesekere, Gananath. 1988. *Buddhism Transformed: Religious Change in Sri Lanka.* Princeton, NJ: Princeton University Press.

Greenfield, J. 1991. "Asylum at Aleppo: a note on Sfire III, 4–7," in *Ah, Assyria . . . Studies in Assyrian History and Ancient Near Eastern Historiography Presented to Hayim Tadmor,* ed. M. Cogan and I. Eph'al. Jerusalem: Scripta Hierosolymitana.

Grosby, Steven. 1991. "Religion and nationality in antiquity," *Archives Européennes de Sociologie* 32(2):229–65.

_____. 1995. "'RM KLH and the worship of Hadad: a nation of Aram?" *ARAM* 7:337–52.

_____. 1996a. "Borders, Territory, and Nationality in the Ancient Near East and Armenia," *Journal of the Economic and Social History of the Orient* 39(4):1–29.

_____. 1996b. "The category of the primordial in the study of early Christianity and second-century Judaism," *History of Religions* 36(2):140-63.

_____. 1999. "The Chosen People of ancient Israel and the Occident: why does nationality exist and survive?" *Nations and Nationalism* 5(3):357-80.

Hammond, Philip E. 1980. "The conditions of civil religion: a comparison of the United States and Mexico," in Bellah and Hammond (1980).

Haim, Sylvia. 1976 [1962]. *Arab Nationalism: An Anthology.* Berkeley: University of California Press.

Hastings, Adrian. 1997. *The Construction of Nationhood: Ethnicity, Religion and Nationalism.* Cambridge: Cambridge University Press.

Hastings, Adrian. 1999. "Special Peoples," *Nations and Nationalism* 5(3):381-96.

Hodgson, Marshall G. S. 1974a. *The Venture of Islam, vol. 1. The Classical Age of Islam.* Chicago: University of Chicago Press.

_____. 1974b. *The Venture of Islam, vol. 2. The Emergence of Islam in the Middle Periods.* Chicago: University of Chicago Press.

_____. 1974c. *The Venture of Islam, vol. 3. The Gunpowder Empires and Modern Times.* Chicago: University of Chicago Press.

Holtom, D. C. 1974. *Modern Japan and Shinto Nationalism.* Chicago: University of Chicago Press.

Hutchinson, John. 1987. *The Dynamics of Cultural Nationalism: The Gaelic Revival and the Creation of the Irish Nation State.* London: Allen & Unwin.

Jaspers, Karl. 1953. *The Origins and Goal of History.* New Haven: Yale University Press.

Juergensmeyer, Mark. 1993. *The New Cold War? Religious Nationalism Confronts the Secular State.* Berkeley: University of California Press.

Kantorowicz, Ernst H. 1957 [1951]. "Pro patria mori," in *The King's Two Bodies: A Study in Medieval Political Theology.* Princeton, NJ: Princeton University Press.

Kedourie, Elie. 1993 [1960]. *Nationalism.* Oxford: Basil Blackwell.

_____, ed. 1971. *Nationalism in Asia and Africa.* London: Weidenfeld and Nicolson.

Lapidus, Ira. 1988. *A History of Islamic Societies.* Cambridge: Cambridge University Press.

Lewis, Bernard. 1991. "Watan," in *The Impact of Western Nationalisms,* ed. J. Reinharz and G. L. Mosse. New York: Sage.

_____. 1994. "Patriotism and nationalism," in *The Shaping of the Modern Middle East.* New York: Oxford University Press.

Lewy, Guenter. 1974. *Religion and Revolution.* New York: Oxford University Press.

Machinist, Peter. 1993. "Assyrians on Assyria in the first millennium B.C.," in *Anfänge politischen Denkens in der Antike: Die nahöstlichen Kulturen und die Griechen,* ed. Kurt Raaflaub. Munich: R. Oldenbourg.

Mews, Stuart, ed. 1982. *Religion and National Identity.* Oxford: Basil Blackwell.

Mosse, George. 1973. "Mass politics and the political liturgy of nationalism," in *Nationalism: the Nature and Evolution of an Idea,* ed. Eugene Kamenka. Canberra: Australian National University Press.

Nelson, Janet. 1988. "Kingship and empire," in *The Cambridge History of Medieval Political Thought c. 350-c. 1450*, J. H. Burns. Cambridge: Cambridge University Press.

Nilsson, Martin. 1960. "Religion as man's protest against the meaninglessness of events," in *Opuscula Selecta*, vol. 3. Lund: CWK Gleerup.

Otto, Rudolph. 1978 [1917]. *The Idea of the Holy*. London: Oxford University Press.

Piscatori, James P. 1986. *Islam in a World of Nation-States*. Cambridge: Cambridge University Press.

Pollock, Sheldon. 1993. "Ramayana and political imagination in India," *Journal of Asian Studies* 52(2):261-97.

Popper, K. R. 1972. *Objective Knowledge*. Oxford: Oxford University Press.

Radcliffe-Brown, A. R. 1965a [1935]. "On the concept of function in social science," in *Structure and Function in Primitive Society*. New York: Free Press.

_____. 1965b [1945]. "Religion and society," in *Structure and Function in Primitive Society*. New York: Free Press.

Rigsby, Kent J. 1996. *Asylia: Territorial Inviolability in the Hellenistic World*. Berkeley: University of California Press.

Robinson, Francis. 1979. "Islam and Muslim separatism," in *Political Identity in South Asia*, David Taylor and Malcolm Yapp. London: Curzon.

Rousseau, Jean-Jacques. 1987 [1762]. *On the Social Contract*, in *The Basic Political Writings*, trans. and ed. Donald A. Cress. Indianapolis: Hackett Publishing.

Schleiermacher, Friedrich. 1994 [1799]. *On Religion: Speeches to its Cultured Despisers*. Louisville, Ky.: Westminster/John Knox.

Schwartz Benjamin I. 1975. "Transcendence in ancient China," *Daedalus*, spring, 57-69.

Shils, Edward A., and Young, Michael. 1975 [1956]. "The meaning of the coronation," in *Center and Periphery: Essays in Macrosociology*, Edward Shils. Chicago: University of Chicago Press.

Simmel, Georg. 1997 [1906]. "Religion," in *Essays on Religion*, ed. and trans. Horst Jürgen Helle. New Haven: Yale University Press.

Sivan, Emmanuel. 1997. "Arab nationalism in the age of Islamic resurgence," in *Rethinking Nationalism in the Arab Middle East*, ed. James Jankowski and Israel Gershoni. New York: Columbia University Press.

Smith, Anthony D. 1986. *The Ethnic Origin of Nations*. Oxford: Basil Blackwell.

_____. 1998. *Nationalism and Modernism*. London: Routledge.

_____. 1999. "Ethnic election and national destiny: some religious origins of nationalist ideals," *Nations and Nationalism*, 5(3):331-55.

Smith, Bardwell L., ed. 1978. *Religion and Legitimation of Power in Sri Lanka*. Chambersburg, Pa.: Anima.

Speiser, E. A. 1960. "People and nation of Israel," *Journal of Biblical Literature* 79:157-63.

Strayer, Joseph. 1971. "France: the Holy Land, the Chosen People, and the Most Christian King," in *Medieval Statecraft and the Perspectives of History*, ed. John F. Benton and Thomas N. Bisson. Princeton, NJ: Princeton University Press.

Symmons-Symonolewicz, Konstantin. 1983. *National Consciousness in Poland: Origin and Evolution.* Meadville, Pa.: Maplewood.

Tocqueville, Alexis de. 1969 [1848]. *Democracy in America.* New York: Harper and Row.

van der Leeuw, Geradus. 1963 [1933]. *Religion in Essence and Manifestation.* New York: Harper and Row.

van der Veer, Peter. 1999. "Hindus: a superior race," *Nations and Nationalism* 5(3):419–30.

Walbank, Frank. 1985 [1951]. "The problem of Greek nationality," in *Selected Papers.* Cambridge: Cambridge University Press.

Weber, Max. 1946a [1915]. "Religious rejections of the world and their directions," in *From Max Weber,* ed. H. H. Gerth and C. Wright Mills. New York: Oxford University Press.

_____. 1946b [1915]. "The social psychology of the world religions," in *From Max Weber,* ed. H. H. Gerth and C. Wright Mills. New York: Oxford University Press.

_____. 1951 [1920]. *The Religion of India.* Glencoe, Ill.: Free Press.

_____. 1978 [1925]. *Economy and Society.* Berkeley: University of California Press.

Weinfeld, Moshe. 1995. *Social Justice in Ancient Israel and in the Ancient Near East.* Minneapolis: Fortress.

Westermarch, Edward. n.d. "Asylum," in *Encyclopaedia of Religion and Ethics,* ed. James Hastings. New York: Charles Scribner's Sons.

Wilson, Charles Regan. 1980. *Baptized in Blood: The Religion of the Lost Cause 1865-1920.* Athens: University of Georgia Press.

Yoshino, Kosaku. 1992. *Cultural Nationalism in Contemporary Japan.* London: Routledge.

Indexes

Index of Authors

Index of Scripture

Old Testament/Hebrew Bible

Genesis
1-11   101, 104
1-2:3   99
1:28   101
2   243
5   101
6:9   104
9:1   101
10:2-3   102
10:3   142
10:5   202
10:19-20   202
10:30-31   202
11   101
12   101
12:1-3   98, 102-
    103
12:2   101
12:6   73
12:7   102
13:14-17   103
15   103
15:15   101
15:17-18   98
16:14   60
17   103
17:1   103
17:6   101
17:7   5, 98, 104
17:9-14   93
17:19   98, 104
18:19   103
18:25   4
21:33   60
22:1-2   103

Genesis (cont.)
22:3   74
22:9   74
22:16-18   103
24:10   153
26:3-5   103-104
26:5   104
28:11   74
28:15   5
28:16   74
28:17   74
28:19   74
31:33   60
31:49   74
32:23-33   74
32:28   152
33:20   41
34:14-16   93
35:1   74
35:7   60
35:10   152
35:18   19
36:11   41
36:15   41
49:2-27   97

Exodus
3:5   74, 104
6:2-8   98
6:3   104
10:2   108
12:14   108
12:17   108
12:19   4, 86
12:26-27   108
12:43-49   93

Exodus (cont.)
12:48   4, 64
13:7   86
13:8   108
13:14   108
18:21   97
19:6   9, 81, 104
20-24   98
20:2   103
20:8-11   93
20:24   96
21:2   63
21:16   63
22:24   63
24:3-4   108
32   9
32:12-13   105
32:4   93
32:9-10   238
34:10-28   98

Leviticus
11:45   81
18:25-28   24
18:27-28   79
19:2   81
20:2   86
22:18   86
25:23   76
26:11-13   25
26:27-42   27
26:44-45   98

Numbers
5:16-22   97
20:16   124
20:17   28

263

New Testament/Christian Scriptures

Deuterocanonical Literature

Index of Other Sources